DAISY TURNER'S KIN

The Folklore Studies in a Multicultural World series is a collaborative venture of the University of Illinois Press, the University Press of Mississippi, the University of Wisconsin Press, and the American Folklore Society, made possible by a generous grant from the Andrew W. Mellon Foundation. The series emphasizes the interdisciplinary and international nature of current folklore scholarship, documenting connections between communities and their cultural production. Series volumes highlight aspects of folklore studies such as world folk cultures, folk art and music, foodways, dance, African American and ethnic studies, gender and queer studies, and popular culture.

Daisy Turner's Kin

An African American Family Saga

JANE C. BECK

UNIVERSITY OF ILLINOIS PRESS
URBANA, CHICAGO, AND SPRINGFIELD

Manufactured in the United States of America
1 2 3 4 5 C P 5 4 3 2 1
∞ This book is printed on acid-free paper.

Publication of this book is supported by a grant from the Andrew W. Mellon Foundation.

Library of Congress Control Number: 2015939180
ISBN 978-0-252-03923-2 (hardcover)
ISBN 978-0-252-08079-1 (paperback)
ISBN 978-0-252-09728-7 (e-book)

For Sarah Alden Derby Gannett

To "gypsy fires," "lonely inns," and just a "dusty road."

From John Masefield's poem "Vagabond."

CONTENTS

ILLUSTRATIONS

DAISY TURNER'S KIN

INTRODUCTION

The Turner Narrative and Memory

> Nobody but me in my heart knows this wonderful story.
> —Daisy Turner, interview with author, September 16, 1985

Alexander "Alec" Turner (1845–1923), born a slave on the Jack Gouldin plantation alongside the Rappahannock River near Port Royal, Virginia, wanted his family to know its roots. Every night after dinner, he told them stories of their heritage. These became the Turner family narrative, a prized legacy. Daisy (1883–1988), Alec's daughter, drank in these anecdotes and learned many word for word. In 1983, I was fortunate enough to meet Daisy and spend the next three years recording her stories.

Alexander Turner, ca. 1915, Journey's End. Courtesy of the Grafton Historical Society, Grafton, Vermont.

The Turner saga is compelling. It envelops a period in American history that has shaped our culture and helps us come to terms with our slave past. No one alive today has firsthand memories of that era. The Turner family story brings those times alive, along with a strong sense of who the Turners were as individuals, where they came from, and how they negotiated the society of a free world after enslavement. Memory infuses warmth and meaning into dry documents, creating a human story. The Turner narrative portrays some large personalities and bequeaths a distinctive family voice that resonates and conveys understanding about the journey of one American family.

While memory can be unreliable, it is always meaningful.[1] Understanding how it is meaningful offers another way of framing historic material and thereby gaining additional insight. Sometimes this takes extensive digging and examining the circumstances of the narrative from a variety of perspectives. Memory is selective and filtered through an individual's personal recollections. Such recollections reflect emotions and feelings held at the time something becomes a memory. Those emotions and feelings in turn shape the recounting of an experience. Sharing that experience with others allows further reshaping as the audience reacts to the telling. The farther back in time a memory was laid down, the greater the opportunity for misunderstanding and, hence, distortion. Thus, memory is subtly shifting, affected by personal needs and social situations. As such, it is constructed rather than reproduced.[2] Used effectively, memory can illuminate and infuse history with authenticity. Memory can be selective, just as history can be written from a particular perspective.

Oral cultures have always placed a premium on narrative as a way of preserving history and have developed techniques such as stylized language to preserve a large body of memory.[3] Equally important is the orator or performer who narrates this material. In West Africa, the individual invested with the responsibility of maintaining a community's history and genealogy was the griot—master of the spoken word and guardian of knowledge. Schooled by elders, he performed his narratives, conscious of gestures, facial expression, tone, and dramatic use of rhythm and pause to increase the emotion of the moment. Daisy's grandfather came from this tradition, which she learned at her father's feet. As a master storyteller, she performed her family narrative, adding verse and song, enabling her audience to feel the immediacy of her story and visualize a particular incident. Through her mastery of her family's oral tradition, she preserved her family heritage.

Personal reminiscences seldom endure beyond three generations or about 120 years. That expanse of time transforms them into oral tradition.[4] Daisy's longevity extended this time span—from her grandfather's birth around 1810 to her death in 1988—a remarkable 178 years. As a result, the Turners left us an astonishingly complex African American oral epic that underscores the significance and validity of oral tradition.

The overarching Turner narrative is embedded in family memory, grounded in experience, shaped by family perceptions and socialized over two centuries. It is rooted in identity and expresses personal dignity. While the narrative is based in real events, these events are told from a subjective point of view by all the narrators.

A family narrative, or lifestory, incorporates different voices down the generations, and its purpose is to maintain the family's distinctive identity, unity, and continuity.[5] Between generations, there is loss and compression of material through forgetting and misunderstanding, often causing distortion. Different ways of living and changing norms also foster confusion. What remains is the central core: Alec's father was the biracial son of an English woman and an African man. When I asked if Daisy remembered his ethnic group, she could not at first, but when I named some possibilities, she volunteered Yoruba, saying "*Yarraba*." Later, genetic testing of Alec's great-great-grandson David Rogers concluded: "The Y chromosome DNA that we determined from your sample shares ancestry with the Yoruba people in Nigeria today."[6]

A major shift in life experience occurred between Alec and his father, Robert—the name given Daisy's grandfather Alessi when he was enslaved: Robert was born the grandson of a Yoruba chief in Africa; Alec was born a slave on a Virginia plantation. These two very different environments caused both the loss and the reshaping of a number of cultural elements.[7] Alec was a boy of not more than five or six years old at his father's death, but he preserved a core of Robert's story. The lack of detail is not surprising. What is astounding is how much he retained, and Daisy herself acknowledged that she had forgotten many of the details her father had related about Africa. What remains is an emphasis on identity. Alec's father was a man who would not submit to the dehumanization of slavery, a man who maintained his power and humanity by successfully boxing and fighting gamecocks.

The central thread of the family narrative is Alec's own story, rooted in his experiences and shaped by his retelling over a lifetime. It appears he was a reliable chronicler of the events he experienced, with the caveat that he relates them from his unique perspective. He was known as a fine storyteller, both in the family and in the community. Like many storytellers, he sometimes exaggerated numbers, but he was also specific in details, taking care, for example, to give his exact address in Boston. There were key stories he told repeatedly, and his family noticed any deviation from his usual text.

This is also Daisy's story. She absorbed her father's narrative over forty years and added her own touches and experiences. Meaningful stories were told more frequently, while some details were forgotten or garbled. These narrations naturally changed over time, but always there was Daisy's admiration of her father as well as her tendency to aggrandize elements of the story involving the status of family members or sums of money. This is a part of the narrative process, and while rooted in experience, that experience is subjectively formed. Daisy's own stories are more difficult to assess, but where there is documentation, she has proven to be a reliable chronicler. Again, the meaning of the particular incident should be viewed as significant.

There are other family voices, particularly those of Alec's older grandsons, who loved and admired him. I visited with George Hall twice at his home in West Medford, Massachusetts, when he was seventy-six years old. He had been very close to his grandfather. "*I used to listen to him talk. He used to talk to me as a child and I used to be around him all the time. He used to tell me the things he used to do when he was a teenager and when he was a child working as a slave.*" His recollections were different from Daisy's as he identified more closely with his grandfather's feats of strength and athleticism. "*When he was a teenager, it seemed that the only athletic events that they used to do was running and jumping and fighting. And there was nobody on that plantation that could take him in any of those things.*"[8] Likewise John Bruce Turner, who lived with his grandparents as a boy, retained what his grandfather told him about life on the plantation. He, too, was awed by Alec's strength and stature as a man. Of all the grandchildren, Bruce was the most interested in documenting his grandfather's history, particularly his role in the Civil War. Like Daisy, he wanted his grandfather to be awarded his justly earned pension. While the grandsons and Daisy heard many of the same stories, George and Bruce best remembered and related to the tales of his boyhood. Sadly, both men died early in the interview process. Chester Lanier, another grandson, was equally taken with his grandfather: his athletic prowess, his conversational abilities, his home remedies, and his mind. Godfrey Hall, George's younger brother and another good athlete, collected a large assortment of family photographs. A number of granddaughters, Sally Turner Neale, Faith Turner Hawkins, Freda Karlson Knight, Yohanna Karlson McDermott, and Veronica Lanier, remembered more about their grandmother—how she ran the household and how she was known as a delicious cook.

While all these relatives enriched the Turner story, adding details and texture, it is Daisy who maintained the more comprehensive scope of the family saga. Because Daisy was the last to relate the entire family narrative, it was important to know what others, both within and beyond the family, thought about the factuality of her account. One person I had the opportunity to interview was John Leavitt, a logging contractor Daisy wanted to employ to cut lumber.[9] He spent time with both Daisy and her sister Zebbe: "At first I thought, well, a couple old ladies, you know, rambling a little bit, maybe fantasizing . . . but then she started hauling out documents, newspaper clippings, letters, photographs, and then I thought, oh, this is for real . . . I was really fascinated.[10]

Most of her family remembered Daisy as having a way with words. Bruce Turner said:

> *I remember her as a very articulate person who was never lost as to how to express something. She could think when she was talking way ahead of what she was going to say. Her memory was such that she was able to remember dates, names, voice inflections. She could repeat a conversation with voice inflections just the same as if she were on the stage directing players. She had a way with putting things together and putting them across and making them interesting at the same time. She did more talking than any other sisters. There was no trembling, no hesitation, it was just out and at you.*[11]

Sally Turner Neale, Bruce's sister, believed Daisy was the one most concerned with family heritage: "*She could doctor it up to make it sound good. That's why we say, 'well it really wasn't like that.' We can't remember it just exactly like that, but she made it sound good.*"[12]

Daisy tended to increase a sum of money by a factor of ten and to elevate the status of an ancestor. For example, she spoke about an English merchant relative alternately as a lord or an earl. His daughter, Daisy's great-grandmother, was a "*Lady,*" saved by her great-grandfather, the son of an African chief. She referred to her Cherokee grandmother as "Princess Silverbells." She insisted her mother's father, Henry Early, was Civil War general Jubal Early. I spent a great deal of time researching this, as Sally, Daisy's mother, had been born in Fredericksburg, Virginia, and Jubal Early did not appear to be in the vicinity when her grandmother, Rachel, had her five children. Later, I discovered Sally's death certificate on which her daughter Zelma, or "Zebbe," gave Henry Early as her mother's father.

At the same time, I could not automatically dismiss all claims. Her African great-grandfather could well have been a chief's son. There usually was a kernel of truth to her stories. Daisy once told of President Theodore Roosevelt's daughter and granddaughter coming to tea one afternoon. This was fact. Mother and daughter used to meet and go for walks together. One summer's day they met in Grafton, Vermont, and hiked up the Turner Hill road. They came across Daisy, who invited them in for tea.[13]

Daisy did not always heighten dramatic events. She described being attacked one night as she returned to Lexington, Massachusetts, after serving at an evening dinner party: "*He cut me on the neck . . . my throat . . .*

Daisy with her deer, Turner Hill, Grafton, Vermont, ca. 1940. This photograph gives visual credence to an announcement in the *Vermont Phoenix* (Brattleboro), November 2, 1906, that Daisy Turner had shot a 250-pound deer. Courtesy of the Vermont Folklife Center, Middlebury, Vermont.

my face and my hand; tore the clothes off me."[14] The headline in the local newspaper read "Grafton Girl Nearly Murdered," and the article described how she was assaulted and "horribly cut." She received a six-inch gash "on the right side of the neck, narrowly missing the jugular vein," and another cut that "extended from the nose to the neck."[15]

It was Daisy who named the homestead on Turner Hill "Journey's End." She claimed that her father had called it that *"because he never wanted to go any farther."* It is true that he never intended to settle anywhere else, but she was the one who christened the homestead, infusing it with a larger and more dramatic meaning. During Alec's lifetime, his homestead was known as 50 Highland Avenue, an address that suited him. One has to smile at the use of "Avenue" when one thinks of the original narrow track up the hillside.

The core of Daisy's narrative was consistent. While I am sure she always made her stories "sound good," I don't believe she made things up out of whole cloth. I think she genuinely tried to tell her father's stories in the way that he did. Where it appears she has added or omitted details, I have commented, but she tried to maintain his text, which was told from her father's point of view and naturally has that bias. For example, he only talked of his war experiences with the First New Jersey Cavalry and Dr. Ferdinand Dayton, with nothing about his time at City Point, where his pension application stated he went after being left behind while on furlough.[16] This must have been a particular low point for him. Did he choose not to talk about it, or were his children more interested in the battles he described?

Dates, particularly the year, are also notoriously unreliable. Alec said he was fourteen or fifteen when he ran away from the Gouldin plantation, but he was sixteen in April 1862, when the First New Jersey Cavalry were camped alongside the Rappahannock River and the raid was made on the Gouldin plantation.[17] Daisy believed her father was only at the slate quarry in Williamsburg, Maine, for about three years, but it was closer to five years.[18] Daisy always claimed he came to Vermont on November 2, 1872, but research indicates it was November 1873.[19] Snow is always an element in the story of the Turner arrival in Vermont, and in 1873, the first snowfall did not occur until November 12.[20] Likewise, Daisy always said her mother moved up to the shanty on the hill on June 21, 1873, but it was probably June 21, 1874. Details also seemed to change, for example, the family's street address in Boston. I suspect Alec was very specific as to where they lived, but this was well before Daisy was born, and she would have had no recollection of the place. The address would have held little significance for Daisy, but as did her father before her, she was careful to give an exact location. All these details however, are minor and do not detract from the larger whole.

Alec's own story is a personal history of his experience with slavery, his escape, the symbolic and very real act of killing the overseer, his participation in the Civil War, and his struggle to define his freedom, his dignity, and his place within society. Slavery is the central shaping force in the Turner narrative, but this story is also about a steadfast ascent toward self-sufficiency, property ownership, and a home, and with that, dignity, respect, and a better life for Alec Turner, his family, and generations to come. It is a saga that, as did Frederick Douglass's *Narrative*,[21] evokes the bestiality of slavery, the brutality of the overseer, the abiding understanding that something was wrong, and the early determination to be free. It was the ongoing rape of enslaved women that led to Alec's belief that his daughters should not marry white men. Alec grasped the importance of literacy and negotiated his world with the strategies of the trickster and the strong man.[22] During the early years of the war, he experienced life as a fugitive and had to change his name. Through his daughter's words, we experience Alec's spirit, his humanity, and the measure of the man himself.

While enslaved and, indeed, throughout his life, Alec experienced the paradox that lay at the heart of slavery: the system was evil, but not all the people within its sway were malevolent. Alec detested slavery, but like Frederick Douglass, he did not run away from his owner as much as he ran away from bondage.[23] There was a difference between that monstrous institution and some of the relationships forged beneath it. Alec admired Jack Gouldin for acquiring a large plantation and becoming wealthy. Further, he regarded Gouldin as a benevolent master, and he felt real gratitude to Gouldin's granddaughter, Zephie, who taught him to read and offered to help him escape. In remembrance of her kindness, he named his first child born in his new house after her. Once he was a free man, he took genuine pleasure in welcoming Gouldin's grandson, Jack, with whom he had grown up, into his home.

A folklorist is a cultural interpreter. As such, my focus is on individuals and the community in which they exist. I am interested in what the Turner narrative communicates about the cultural history and everyday life of a family living through two centuries that encompassed issues that continue to haunt us. It is a human story, representing a major strand in the story of America itself, revealing one family's survival through bondage and its climb to citizenship, land ownership, and respectability. It is a journey that can help us understand attitudes and values. The subjective, the personal, the emotional must not be overlooked in a human story.

We learn so much about Alec's attitudes as he helps Daisy struggle with her dilemma of whether to accept the role an insensitive teacher has laid out for her. Likewise, with her father's philosophy of "understanding and contentment," we can discern a great deal about how Alec successfully negotiated life. Daisy emphasized the importance her father placed on fully exploring a situation to achieve understanding, which would purge negativity and allow a quiet calm to replace agitation.

Years of interviewing taught me to look for "touchstone" stories. Most individuals have one or two narratives that they will tell several times throughout an extended interview process. These frequently told tales reflect a pivotal moment in a person's life—an instant of decision, change, or crisis charged with emotion. These touchstone stories make up the backbone of the Turner narrative and allow us insight into events they held as most meaningful and significant. We feel the tenderness as well as the strong symbolism of the shipwrecked English mother giving her son her gold locket and wedding ring, all that she had from her former life, and that son, powerfully athletic, arrogant, and unbending, undone when he killed his opponent in a boxing match.

Alec's life is marked by four such stories: The first was his father's funeral, where he believed he witnessed the power of prayer. The second indicated his growing understanding of what it meant to be enslaved—Mistress Gouldin threw his treasured moccasins in the fire. The third showed his increasing determination to gain his freedom—his young "missus" surreptitiously taught him to read, which led to a lashing by her grandmother. The fourth, and the story he told most frequently, demonstrated his triumph over slavery—he returned to the plantation with a small band of the First New Jersey Cavalry and killed the overseer. Daisy's touchstone stories are equally revealing. In the first, she made a stand against racism when she realized she was considered different from her white schoolmates. In the second, she confronted a wrong committed against her family. In the third, she sensed her father needed her when she was far away, demonstrating their deep connection.

In addition to gaining insight into a narrator's inner feelings, if we can verify the historical record and critically assess the narrative, oral tradition can greatly enrich our understanding of the past. Often memory will record an incident that is otherwise unknown or provide hidden aspects of a documented event.[24] An example of this would be Alec's killing of the overseer on the well-documented First New Jersey Cavalry's raid to the Gouldin plantation.[25] Of all the events that Alec relates, this is the most important to him. While the killing of the overseer is not documented, it most assuredly occurred. For those who were enslaved, such verification of facts is often impossible.

While illuminating many subjective cues, the oral narrative also serves as a road map for the discovery of archival sources, pointing in unforeseen directions and suggesting meanings behind the record. For example, the will of Jack Gouldin, owner of both Alec and his father Robert, mentions "the fork of a ditch north of Rose's house one prong of which goes to Skinker's Pines and the other to the old Quarter Spring,"[26] thus giving the location of Alec's mother's cabin, something Alec described, along with its garden, to his children. It was the closest slave cabin to the big house, and as his mother, Rose, was the seamstress, there was considerable traffic between the two. Property and land taxes also indicate a steady rise in Gouldin's income and land over the period of Robert's boxing career, perhaps verifying income won through bets. By going back through the land records and wills, it is clear that the Gouldin family came from a background of yeoman farmers. While not all of this narrative can be validated, key stories within it encompass important emotional flags as well as experiences.

Perhaps one of the most meaningful outcomes from using the research and narrative in conjunction with one another is an understanding of how much Alec observed during the years he was enslaved and how creatively he employed that learning. Many of the techniques he used were unknown in Grafton, Vermont, such as building his blind stone ditches to drain swampland and constructing his new house over a spring. We know that his interior design of the house, with its thirteen rooms and three staircases, was modeled after Gouldin's dwelling. Further, when I first visited the Gouldin plantation, two balm of Gilead trees remained out front, reminiscent of the two that stood before the cellar hole at Journey's End. John Leavitt noted that these trees, a species of poplar, were common in the South but not native to the Grafton area.[27] Daisy had told Leavitt, as she had me as well, that her father had brought them from Virginia as seedlings.[28] Without the oral narrative, these connections would not have been made.

The Turner family saga is an extraordinary narrative, carefully preserved across four generations. It is told by a master narrator with the ability to draw the listener into her account, evoking vivid and lasting images. It embodies one family's journey from Africa into enslavement—a family who successfully maintained a sense of self and dignity through all the abject degradation of an institution that frequently robbed people of a past; a family who seized freedom and struggled successfully to create a family homestead.

Daisy's stories set me on an exploratory journey that inspired and captivated me for thirty years. Her story must be preserved. Too many other family narratives have been lost. Daisy knew what she was doing and succeeded through her mastery of the spoken word. She remains a raconteur for the ages.

CHAPTER 1

Meeting Daisy

> This thing is in me. If I just had read it, it would be a different story. But I've lived it!
> —Daisy Turner, interview with author, March 15, 1984

The phone rang and rang and rang. I knew that the person I wanted to speak with was one hundred years old and that it might take her awhile to get to the phone. I pictured her reaching for the receiver and willed her to answer. I held on, waiting for the moment to present my case, hope eroding. Resignedly, I put down the phone, swallowing my disappointment.

Margaret MacArther, a well-known folk singer and song collector from Marlboro, Vermont, had sent me a clipping in the summer of 1983 about

Daisy Turner, Grafton, 1984. Courtesy of the Vermont Folklife Center, Middlebury, Vermont, photograph by Jane Beck.

Daisy Turner, a daughter of former slaves who was born in Grafton, Vermont, in 1883.[1] The article traced her heritage back to England, Africa, and Virginia. I was intrigued. I wanted to meet her, but at a hundred years of age, was she healthy and mentally alert?

I was serving as folklorist for Vermont's State Arts Council, and my job was to bring traditional arts to the public through a variety of media. What better way than to present an African American storyteller who had grown up in Vermont, the whitest state in the Union? She might make a wonderful subject for a film to be shown in the schools. I called Dot Nadeau, the author of the article, who explained that although Daisy had a fascinating story, she was distrustful and seemed a bit paranoid. As I searched for an introduction to Daisy, I discovered that she had a reputation for being both feisty and suspicious. Apparently she owned a gun that she was not afraid to use. I decided to write her a letter, explaining why I wanted to meet her, and then to follow up with a phone call. I struggled over the missive, mailed it, and then passed the week impatiently, allowing her time to receive, read, and digest it. Finally, I made the call, but there was no answer.

Whenever I called someone to request an interview, I worried that my entreaty might be turned down. The more important an interview was to me, the more I agonized over it. And I felt it was crucial that I meet Daisy Turner. I let one more day pass and tried again, once more with anticipation rising. This time someone responded with a ringing "Hello." The voice sounded rich, vigorous—not what I was expecting. I asked if this was Miss Turner; it was. I explained why I was calling. She listened for a bit and then suddenly cut right to what she believed was the crux of the matter, booming: *"Are you a prejudiced woman?"* Caught off guard, I stammered that I didn't think so. Her voice became warm and welcoming: *"Well, come anytime."*

I drove to Grafton on a bright, warm September day, and after a wrong turn or two, I found Daisy Turner's weathered white frame house just outside the village on Hinkley Brook Road. A figure sitting on the steps, dressed in a dark headscarf and printed skirt, was in animated conversation with a man standing a short distance away. He appeared to be out of patience. It seemed he had bought land from her to put his trailer on and had spent three times the cost of the land in legal fees. He was not happy.

As I was wondering if I should leave, another car pulled up, and a man, maybe seventy years old, climbed out. He took in the scene and called to Daisy that he would come back later. He questioned me as to who I was and, almost as if to whet my appetite, offered that in the past he had worked for Daisy and had played the saxophone and fiddle at her dances on the hill. Dances seemed a long way from the evolving situation. Voices were rising behind us. Daisy was railing at the government for not paying her father's Civil War pension, and in the next breath she was claiming that the Windham Foundation was trying to divest her of her property—first two hundred acres, then five hundred acres.[2] Somebody was running drugs on Turner Hill. Planes and helicopters would fly over, and then one to two hundred cars would drive down the road. The man was trying to focus Daisy on settling the land dispute. Exasperated, he finally stalked off, shouting unpleasantries, and slammed his car door before driving away.

What an inopportune time to introduce myself. I took a deep breath and explained that I had written her and spoken with her over the phone. Yes, she had read my letter and remembered our conversation. In the letter, I mentioned that I was interested in making a film, and she told me someone else had already made a film of her.[3] She was bitter about that, as she had never signed anything allowing it, nor had she liked the film itself. Things were going from bad to worse for me. She said she wanted me to write about her court cases and the people who were trying to kill her. Someone had broken her pipes and caused a flood in her house. Someone else had damaged her garage and tried to both murder and kidnap her.

I sidestepped these complaints and explained that I was not a writer, but rather an interviewer who recorded Vermonters' stories that might otherwise not be heard. The recorded interviews were then preserved in an archive and used in public programming. I had read Dot Nadeau's piece in the *Brattleboro Reformer* and believed her stories were particularly significant and should be recorded. Would she tell me a little about her life? I was surprised after her tirade that she needed no more encouragement to launch into storytelling mode. Suddenly she was in Africa, New Orleans, and Virginia.

As Daisy began to spin out the story of the Turner family, her demeanor changed—her rage dissipated, and she began weaving a credible and astonishing narrative, a multigenerational saga that spanned two centuries and played out over three continents. Her face did not betray her century of years—high cheekbones, wide-set eyes, smooth skin. She must have been a striking beauty in her youth. It was only later that I realized how petite she was—little more than five feet tall, but she seemed larger due to her power with words and the rich timbre of her voice. She was first and foremost a storyteller—vibrant and alive, her voice rising and falling, stories tumbling out one after another. One moment she was quiet, the next electric—performing, her arms pantomiming a reaction, her cane mimicking a task. She knew how to build a story to its climax, using repetition, suspense, and surprise. I forgot her age, forgot the time, and was mesmerized by the power of her voice and the scope of her story. Like the venerable griot, schooled by elders to serve as genealogist, historian, storyteller, and singer for the community, Daisy personified this role.

For two hours, sitting with her on the steps, she held me spellbound, frantically scribbling notes, as she would not allow me to record her. Story after story spilled out, punctuated by a song or recitation, seamlessly integrated. I asked if I could come back, and we made a date for the following Friday. Before I left, she insisted that we must have some ginger ale. Further, she wanted me to sign her guest book and to see the card she had received from President and Mrs. Reagan on her hundredth birthday. She went into the house, and I heard her rummaging around. Her eyesight was poor, and she called me to help her. I opened the screen door and was appalled at what I saw. The room had a small woodstove, two couches, several tables, a large cupboard for dishes, and a radio and television that had both seen better days. But the furniture was overwhelmed by paper bags, newspapers, and assorted items, which appeared to have been randomly strewn about. She knew where the guest book was and pointed me to a basket. Next, she directed me to another basket for the ginger ale, Styrofoam cups, and a box of vanilla cookies. She perched on a stool in front of the stove and waved me toward a chair, telling me to put the cloth bags that covered it on the floor. She had me pour the ginger ale, and as we settled in, she commented on the fact that I was wearing a dress, telling me it was "ladylike" and that she approved. Next, she asked me about my religion. As I am not particularly religious, I tried to avoid the discussion by saying I was Christian, but that answer was not satisfactory—she wanted to know what kind of Christian. I replied that I had been brought up in the Episcopal church, and for the moment that subject was behind us. Over the next few years, I came to realize what a central role religious faith played within the Turner family and how much it shaped Daisy's life. When I was taking my leave, Daisy bid me farewell by way of a long, extemporaneous prayer. I marveled at how the words, liquid and meaningful, flowed off her tongue. There was no question; she had a way with words. She was certainly in the tradition of the griot, a repository of a wealth of oral tradition: stories, songs, and poems, all of which were to be heard, experienced, and remembered.

Because Daisy's life spanned a century, her narrative was a bridge to a much earlier time, one to which we seldom have direct access. She remembered events that took place over ninety years ago—only one generation removed from slavery. She had heard firsthand accounts. Her family story had been preserved across four generations; I knew of no comparable narrative. It allowed insights into the slave trade, two generations of enslavement, escape, the aftermath of the Civil War, and the pursuit of the American dream, all from an African American perspective. The Turner saga was how the Turner family maintained its identity and made sense of its past. I was struck by the unexpectedness of hearing this narrative in Vermont and felt privileged to have access to this historical treasure.

I was unprepared for the immediacy of the narrative. *"This was only a little over a hundred years ago,"* she told me. To Daisy, a century ago was yesterday, and she made me feel it. She emphatically told me (with energetic pantomime to drive home the reality of it) that her father had *"heard the hooves of Booth's horse as he rode away after shooting Lincoln."* For Daisy, this placed her father, Alec Turner, at the scene and underscored the importance of Lincoln to the Turners. John Wilkes Booth was shot and captured just five miles from the Gouldin plantation where Daisy's grandfather and father were enslaved. My own great-great-grandfather had written a letter to his oldest granddaughter describing what it was like on the day that Lincoln was shot. I treasured this as an intimate personal insight into the emotions of the day, but the energy and immediacy of Daisy's words brought me right into the action.

While her stories were arresting, what of her paranoia? Was it some kind of age-related dementia? Once she began talking of the past, she seemed to move into a different realm. Once involved in her narration, she became coherent, taking on her role of storyteller, once more a captivating presence. But could I keep her away from those all-consuming subjects of land and pension? How long would it be before I would be seen as against her? I suspected it was inevitable but was convinced that her story was so significant that it outweighed the risk. The inside of her house was partially the result of her deteriorating eyesight. She had no filing system and apparently no one to help her. No wonder she thought people were stealing her papers. I understood this was a lurking danger to avoid, but I was determined to visit her as frequently as possible.

I began to see her once a week and spend five or six hours with her. Half of that time, I helped Daisy go through papers, collected her mail, and ran errands for her; the other half, I asked about her past and recorded her. Before she would allow any recording, she wanted to know exactly for whom I worked and what I did. I explained that I was a folklorist,[4] employed by the Vermont Arts Council in Montpelier and that my job was to focus on the traditional arts, discover them through interviewing, and then bring them to the public through exhibitions, films, radio, and school programming. I had never used my state employee identification card before, but it was evidence for Daisy that I was telling the truth. She wanted to know something of my background. I told her that I had been born in New York City during World War II, grew up on Long Island, and spent summers at my great-grandmother's farm in New Hampshire. I went to Middlebury College and then to graduate school at the University of Pennsylvania, married a Middlebury College professor, and lived in Ripton with our two children, thirty sheep, and various poultry.

As time went on, our relationship became warm and familiar. We genuinely enjoyed each other's company, and I hoped she was beginning to trust me. She asked me to call her "Aunt Daisy." As we continued to sort her papers, I could find no order to them. All jumbled together were page one and page four of a slave census of Caroline County, Virginia; her father's deed for the Turner Hill property; a card from her sister Violet Hall; letters from the 1970s; old electricity and phone bills; court briefs; and advertisements. I read everything aloud and tried to put things in order, but the next week nothing would be in the same place, and another search would begin. I dutifully took down letters that she dictated extemporaneously, read them back for corrections, and then made copies and mailed them for her. She also had me make phone calls for her to lawyers or to her nephews. She would rattle off their numbers without looking them up. Seldom did we get anywhere; only her nephews would take her calls, and they were seldom at home during the day.

Her recall amazed me as songs, recitations, and events rich in detail spilled out. When she talked about the past, she was in the moment: laughing at something amusing her siblings had done, marveling at her father's ingenuity or her mother's patience. She had a litany of her father's stories that she told over and over. When I asked her for further details, she sometimes became confused, which I attributed to her age. On her bad days, she would mix up generations, but when she was clear, she added new details that I had never heard.

While she still ranted about her father's Civil War pension, her property, the Windham Foundation, and people who were causing her trouble, I learned to interrupt her, sometimes midsentence. Could she tell me what her family used to do at Christmas time or what kind of food her mother prepared? I would ask her if she wanted some ginger ale, and usually she said yes, admitting that her heart was pounding. After one of these episodes, she often was more confused than usual.

Daisy's father was at the center of her world. From her earliest years, Daisy remembered him telling stories of the past. Every night after dinner, she and her siblings would gather and listen to their father. It was important that these stories be preserved. He wanted his children to know where they came from. "*See, we didn't come from nowhere,*" she told me. "*We have a background. And that background can be traced right down to the roots!*"[5]

It was an oral narrative—a well-polished artifact, an heirloom carefully preserved through four generations. It was unique in its extensiveness, its power, and the pride with which it was told. With the end of the Civil War, it was more common for the emancipated to look forward, rather than back.[6] In Caroline County, Virginia, where Alec was born, I was told by local historian Cleo Coleman, the great-granddaughter of a freed man, that little about plantation life remained in oral tradition among African Americans, as few of those enslaved wanted to remember that time.[7]

Alec Turner was an exception. He acknowledged his past while he strode optimistically into the future, determined to succeed. Indeed, the fact that his family narrative encompassed two generations of slavery is unusual. The oral narrative harked back to the importance of oral tradition in Africa and the significance that storytelling held for those who could not write. While Alec was literate, he grew up in a community where oral traditions were carefully preserved, where the role of a griot was deeply respected.

Daisy described her father as tall, slender, graceful, and a born gentleman. He was *"a handsome man, a peculiar man, an odd man, but a gentleman. You wouldn't just pass him by, but you would look at him and wonder what he was—a writer, a thinker, a musician? He had strange features and seemed to be looking beyond you. He had a very deep interior. His words were never light. Everything he said had meaning."*[8]

Alec was born in 1845, a slave on a plantation in Virginia, and died in 1923, a freeman and landowner in Grafton, Vermont. More than anything, Daisy wanted his life to be remembered, honored, and celebrated. She felt it was her obligation to tell the family story: *"This thing is in me. If I just had read it, it would be a different story. But I've lived it and seen it."*[9] She also believed, *"You can't tell a thing unless you tell the good and the bad as they is."*[10]

One day, early in the process, she called me at home. She wanted to make sure I would be there that week because John Daniels was coming. I learned later that the Danielses were an old Grafton family who, among other things, had given land for the Grafton cemetery behind Daisy's house. Her father had helped set out the spruces that now tower over it. Daniels's grandfather, also named John Daniels, and great-uncle Francis Daniels had been instrumental in helping Daisy's father design his house. That Wednesday I was already at Daisy's when John Daniels and his wife arrived. They lived in Sharon Springs, New York, and were over for a brief visit. Daniels had contacted Senator Robert Stafford to help Daisy with her father's pension claims. I realized that she wanted me to meet people who knew her family, were familiar with what her family had accomplished, and were sympathetic to any injustices done to Daisy as a member of this family.

After leaving that day, I visited the Grafton Historical Society to see what photographs they might have. The Danielses happened to be there and introduced me to the society's president, explaining that I was interviewing Daisy. I was taken aback by her negative reaction: she said I was wasting my time, that everything Daisy said was suspect, and that I should find someone more reliable to interview. I was aware that I needed to address the reliability of Daisy's stories, but suspected this was blatant racism. Daniels heard her comments and took me aside to suggest I speak with his cousin,

Harriet Gelfan, for another point of view. She knew Daisy well and lived in Grafton.

Harriet Gelfan cautioned that Daisy had the ability to exaggerate, but she believed there was a great deal to Daisy's story. Her father had been an exceptional man, both respected and beloved by the town, as were most of his family, particularly his daughter Zebbe and her husband John Grant. Harriet explained that Daisy was considered much more irascible and controversial, but this was related to her temperament. She believed that Daisy's family story was an important one that should be documented. She had recently suggested to her young friend Steve Goodman that he work on it for a college project. He interviewed Daisy twice and did a good deal of research in 1976, which he graciously shared with me.

Others had interviewed Daisy as well. Cultural historian, exhibition curator, and writer Allon Schoener recorded both audio- and videotapes of Daisy and her sister Zebbe in the early 1970s and generously made them available to me. He recognized, as did Harriet Gelfan and Steve Goodman, that the Turner story was a significant one.

I began to do some research to document her narrative. As I was on a panel for the National Endowment for the Arts, I had the opportunity to go to Washington, DC, and took the occasion to work at the National Archives. I also went to Fredericksburg, Virginia, to look for the plantation and any members of the Gouldin family who might have family stories, diaries, or photographs.

Sometimes Daisy suggested other avenues of research to verify her story. She told me about novelist Mildred Walker Schemm, who wrote about the Turners in her book *The Quarry* and encouraged me to meet Louise Tanner, who made a film about Daisy.[11] Tanner grew up in Vermont but lived in New York City, and by the time I went to visit her, Daisy had decided she was not to be trusted. In fact, she felt Tanner had been bought off by the Windham Foundation, her favorite antagonist. Stupidly, I decided it was best not to tell Daisy about my trip. Of course, she found out about it and was upset. I explained that I made the appointment on her recommendation before she became angry at Tanner, and I was afraid she would be angry at me, too. To my amazement, she threw back her head and laughed heartily at my discomfort. I was fortunate this was the closest I came to falling out of favor.

From time to time, I asked Daisy about the possibility of videotaping her, and she would say: "*I have to ask my lawyers. I have to ask my nephews.*" I knew Daisy did not have to ask anyone anything, so one day I said I was coming back on Monday with a videographer. After that visit, I decided to go up to the family homestead on Turner Hill to see what scenes I needed to shoot. As I drove up the steep, narrow track, I met a game warden coming down. He said he was looking for Arthur Buckman and asked if I knew him; he told me to let him know if I saw him. According to Daisy, Buckman was connected to her by marriage, and she had let him live on the hill in Birch Dale Camp. In return, he supplied her with wood, did chores for her, and kept an eye on the property.

Two days later the phone rang, and much to my surprise, it was Daisy, who immediately asked if I was coming with "that man" on Monday and blurted out: "*There's been a murder on Turner Hill! Arthur has been murdered! . . . They think by the boy!*" The boy was Steve, who Daisy had led me to believe was Arthur's son. I had seen them several times when they were delivering wood. I went straight out for a newspaper and learned that Steve Kuchta had been charged with beating and shooting Arthur Buckman at Birch Dale Camp, supposedly after Buckman had made sexual advances toward him.[12]

Monday, I met Wes Graff (head of the videography department at the University of Vermont) at the Grafton post office. He had agreed to help me with the project, and we went to see Daisy, who immediately made it clear that she wanted us to go up to Journey's End.[13] She did not want to be videotaped. When we returned to Daisy's, I went in again to see if she would meet Graff and perform for the camera. I knew this was the moment of reckoning and made my case once more. Finally, she agreed, and slowly made her way down the steps. I guided her into one of the outdoor chairs and introduced her to Graff. Daisy allowed him to position her. I decided she would be most at ease if she started with her favorite story about the teacher and the black doll.[14]

With the camera and Graff, Daisy had a new audience. Suddenly she was alive with movement, performing every part of her narrative. She was the teacher, she was the audience, but most of all she was Daisy, defiantly extemporizing her own piece in place of the teacher's, rocking with laughter at her audacity, presenting the confusion of the audience, and then the triumph of winning the first prize. This was just the beginning of the video project, but I knew she would be a marvelous, engaging subject and would take pleasure in it.

I continued to visit Daisy and record her on my own. As time went on, research into her narrative began to bear fruit, and as I found pieces of information in various archives, I brought back copies of documents to Daisy. She became excited: "*My heart is pounding. You see what I told you is true!*" This was when she first began to urge me to write a book. I tried to explain that it was the power of her spoken words that gave her family narrative such force and authority. I told her she was the finest storyteller I had ever heard and that others needed to experience the richness of her family story as related by her. But she was convinced that only the written word would bring legitimacy to the Turner saga and the possibility for her narrative to endure. That was all-important to her.

> *I'll tell you, I've tried to tell you, that nobody but me in my heart knows this wonderful story, this wonderful life, this wonderful something in me. And all through the night, I was thinking how all of these things ought not to be lost. And I wanted to get you to write—I would dictate where you wrote, memories of the slave boy from the South, so that it wouldn't be lost.*[15]

She was not convinced that I would follow through. She wanted immediate action. The narrative had to be in print. She had a point. In today's world, the written word exemplifies authority while oral narrative is dismissed as hearsay. I was convinced her family history had legitimacy and promised her that I would one day write a book using her stories. Meanwhile, I thought it was important for Vermont schoolchildren to hear her relating her experiences. I asked how she felt about radio, and she was interested, but she believed a book to be most important. I again gave her my word that one day I would focus exclusively on it, but I could not accomplish such a task at that time. We left it there.

I came to know Freda Knight, the niece who took care of Daisy, and others who were part of her social network: Alice Cobb, from the welfare office, and neighbors Harriet Gelfan and Norman Wright, who checked on her periodically. I also met other family members, including several nephews who lived outside of Vermont.

We shot the last of the video in August 1985. In mid-September, Daisy had a "bad spell." She was adamant that she wanted to remain in her house and would not hear of going to live with Freda. Her will remained strong, but she was now 102, and her legs were failing her. The family decided that it would be best for her to go into the hospital and from there directly to the Springfield Convalescent Center.

I visited her there and found her propped up on the bed, eyes closed. She seemed a tiny figure on the bed. I took her hands, and immediately she was alert, her voice still strong. She was not happy she was there, but she seemed resigned. "*Freda thinks I'm better off here,*" she told me, "*and I could no longer walk. I fell down.*" That was the first of a number of visits. I remember walking down the institutional corridor several times and hearing Daisy's voice regaling an attendant with stories. They were as spellbound as I had been. But the dynamic had changed. My visits became shorter. She was always glad to see me, but she grew tired as we talked, and I seldom bothered with the recorder. She no longer opened her eyes. I told her we were working on editing the video and that I would bring it to show her as soon as we finished. I was worried because she had responded negatively to Louise Tanner's film, *Homestead: The Puzzle of Daisy Turner and Turner Hill*. It was important to me that she both sanctioned and felt positive about this one. I told her the title was to be *On My Own* because in the story of the black doll, she had commented *"I was saying what I wanted to say on my own."* She laughed delightedly.

I called Freda when we had a final version and arranged to show Daisy. To my relief, she was drawn in right away, singing along with her songs, laughing at her stories, nodding for emphasis at her passages about the Civil War. She told me I could show it to anyone I chose. Inwardly, I heaved a sigh of relief.

Daisy lived two years after that, and to my delight, her story was heard by many Vermonters. It was while she was in Springfield that she was filmed by Ken Burns reciting poetry for his Civil War masterpiece.[16] Sadly, she never saw it.

Before she died, we talked about the possibility of doing a radio program or series, as I wanted to share the larger story of the Turner family. Once she was gone, I did not think this would be possible, as my recordings were not radio quality. I went through them with Ev Grimes, an independent radio producer, and discovered there were some we could use. I began to think about interviewing other members of her family to frame her story. There were a number of Alec Turner's grandchildren still around, and I began to interview them. In doing so, I came to know them better and developed warm relationships with several of them.

While Daisy was central to telling her family story, we needed a narrator to bridge gaps in time and give necessary background material. I wanted someone well known, with whom Daisy would be proud to share her stage, and believed the narrator should be a woman. Sylvia Robison had recently come on my board of directors,[17] and she suggested Barbara Jordan, congresswoman, civil rights advocate, and, like Daisy, known for her eloquence and fine oratory skills. I was thrilled when Jordan, who at that time was teaching at the Lyndon B. Johnson School of Public Affairs at the University of Texas, signed on to the project.

Journey's End: Memories and Traditions of Daisy Turner and Her Family aired during Black History Month in 1990. Much to the delight of all of us who worked on the series, it won a George Foster Peabody Award. Daisy's family was equally pleased. We all knew the award was actually Daisy's; the series served to underscore the power of her voice and the vibrant canvas of her story. Her voice touched all who heard it.

I then worked on a variety of projects at the Vermont Folklife Center, but Daisy was never far from my mind. I remained in touch with several Turner family members and was distressed as their ranks began to thin. I continued to visit them, recorded additional interviews, collected family photographs, and even joined them for occasions on Turner Hill. When I retired in July 2007, at last I had the time needed to do the necessary research to write the book. I worried if I were the right person to do this—I am not a writer and not African American. I asked African American friends and colleagues for their thoughts, and they all pointed out that Daisy had selected me to write her story.

It is important to distinguish Daisy's narration from mine. While Daisy's is the main voice in this story, several other family members contribute insights and supplementary information. To distinguish them, an italic font is used in the text for all quotes from the Turner family. The spoken word does not always translate smoothly to the written page; we can no longer hear the inflections or rhythms. I have kept the words as they were but have removed false starts and repetitions, often unnoticeable in speech, and noted these omissions with ellipses.

I have tried to be consistent in the spelling of names, although some do change over time in documents, diaries, and letters: Alec appears as Alex, Aleck, and Eleck (which probably indicates his pronunciation); Berkeley has a number of spellings, including Berkley, Burekly, and Burkly; and Lindsay appears as Lindsey, Linzee, Linsey, and Linesy. In Maine, Sally Turner's brother, William Armstead Early, went by Armstead Early; in Vermont, he became William Early. Daisy and her sisters go by different names as well: Evelyn is often referred to as Mabel; Daisy was called Jessie during her school years; Florida was called Flossie and Florence; Wilhemenia was known as Susie and Bill; and Violet was sometimes called Cora. For simplicity, I have used a single name for each sister and have noted other names when necessary. Daisy and her sisters appear to have called their parents "Papu" and "Mamu." Daisy claimed this came from her father and was *"African."* I hoped this would direct me to a particular ethnic group or dialect, but it seems to be a general term and did not lead to any discoveries.

What follows is the oral account of four generations of a family as preserved by master raconteur Daisy Turner, supplemented with reminiscences of other family members, and placed on a larger canvas of social, cultural, and historical events.

CHAPTER 2

African Roots

We have a background. And that background can be traced right down to the roots.
—Daisy Turner, interview with author, May 10, 1984

The origins of the Turner legacy remain cloaked in the opaqueness of time, and the exact location of the wrecked vessel that brought Daisy's English great-grandmother into the world of her African great-grandfather cannot be pinpointed. However, based on Daisy's stories and my research, as well as my own maritime experiences, I formed a vivid image of the incident. One does not spend thirty years pondering a narrative without being drawn into it.

The vessel was sailing easily along an endless expanse of sand on the West African coast known as the Bight of Benin. The midday sun shone strong and hot, and only the breeze made the day tolerable. An occasional village nestled under the shade of coconut trees, but mostly it was a world of tawny sand and olive green water. Suddenly, the vessel was engulfed in a *tornado*—a violent squall specific to the African coast, which precedes the rainy season and which can quickly overwhelm a ship if captain and crew do not react instantly. Dark foreboding clouds appeared from nowhere; then a deluge of water descended on the ship. A dramatic wind shift hit and wrapped the vessel in furious violence. All hands were on deck, battered by the elements, attempting to take in sail. The vessel shuddered and strained, the masts and rigging groaned, and the noise was deafening as the ship crashed again and again between towering mountains of water. The young English wife reached for her husband's hand to steady herself, clinging to whatever she could find to maintain her balance. Thunder exploded directly overhead, and she heard a loud splintering and cracking as the mainmast, with sails, shrouds, and crosstrees intertwined, fell into the water. A huge sea slammed down from over their heads, washing them across the deck. She heard shouts, and then all was blackness. Her struggling ceased as she gave way to the inevitable. She was aware of her lungs close to bursting within her chest as the roiling sea spat her out on to the surface. She began to sink again, but weakly struggled to the surface. She grabbed a large piece of the splintered mast and fought

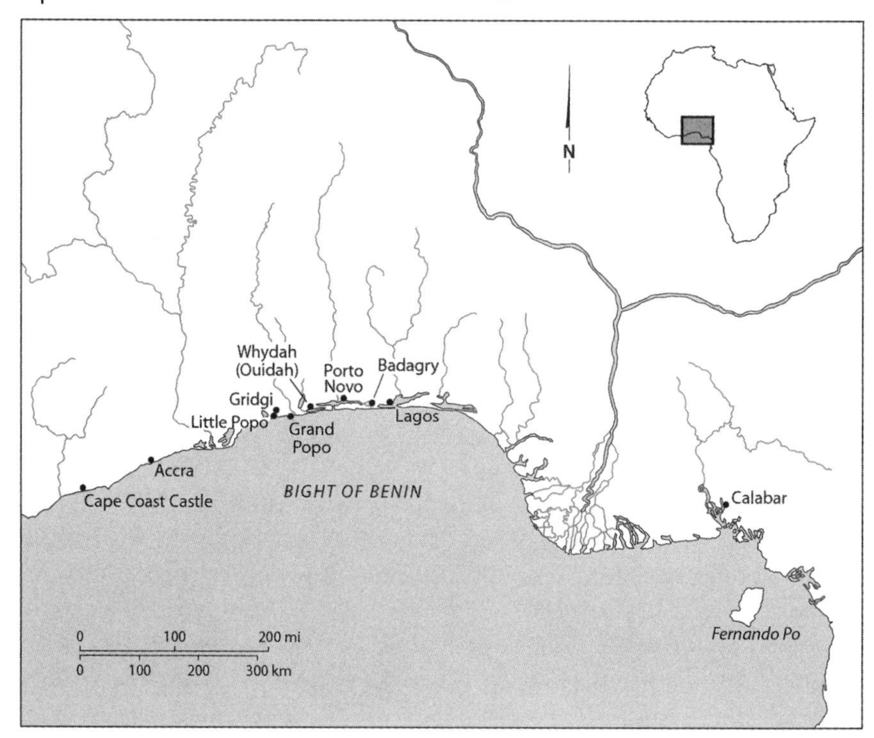

Bight of Benin, Gulf of Guinea, West Africa.

> to drape her body over it. She had no idea how long she clung to it. The sea calmed, the sun came out, but the ship was gone, and she was alone. She could see the shore and hear the surf pounding the beach, but she did not have the strength to reach it. She was not sure she cared. Then she heard a shout, a splash. A black face appeared, and strong arms began pulling her to shore. She made no struggle as he put one arm around her and dragged her through the water toward the shore. Her rescuer lifted her out of the sea and set her down gently on the beach. A giant of a man, and powerfully built, he stood glistening with seawater; then he was gone, back into the sea searching for other survivors. A mass of black faces peered down at her. Several women tended to her, wrapping her in a white sheet of woven cotton cloth. She felt the warm sand under her as she shook with cold and exhaustion.[1]

Daisy always began the story of her family heritage with her English great-grandmother, the second daughter of a London merchant who conducted a lively trade on the coast of Africa during the first decade of the nineteenth century. It was common for a merchant house to take on young men, often relatives, to learn the trade. They started as clerks and then became overseas representatives before becoming partners within the firm.[2] Daisy indicated that this was how the young bride first met her future husband.[3] Her father had his new son-in-law oversee trading operations along the West African coast, and the young couple started their life together aboard ship. Few women undertook such a trip during the early years of the 1800s. It suggests something about the bride; she was young, in love, adventurous, and ready for new experiences.

The usual trading voyage to Africa's west coast was about three months in duration: a month out, a month trading, and a month to return home. The storm is a consistent part of the narrative, and in that area of the world would have been a tornado, sometimes referred to as a hurricane,[4] which precedes the Bight of Benin's rainy season near the end of April. Daisy related, *"this terrible storm came up, and the ship was lost or sunk, went to pieces on the coast of Africa"* or on another occasion *"the boat capsized,"* all consistent with what could occur in a violent tornedo.[5] She put the date in *"the early 1800s."*

In some of the recordings of Daisy in the 1970s, she mentions that the vessel was going to Cape Town, a port where the trader always stopped. One immediately thinks of Cape Town, South Africa, which is unlikely if her great-grandfather was Yoruba, as DNA testing has indicated.[6] Another possibility is Cape Coast Castle, the major British fort and slaving port on the Gold Coast in what is today Ghana. The town behind the fort was known as Cape Town.[7] It is doubtful that Daisy's great-grandmother's ship was a slaver; this would have entailed a much longer trip, and it is unlikely that a father would have allowed his daughter to sail on board such a vessel. Further, Daisy was quite explicit that the merchant vessel was seeking African goods and in turn carried cloth and tobacco for trade.

The shipwreck occurred either after the British abolition of the slave trade in 1807 or earlier, and the vessel was not a slaver. There were traders who were known as "legitimate" traders who were not involved in slaving.[8] Even if the English merchant was not engaged in the slave trade before 1807, Cape Coast Castle, the principal British settlement, would have been a likely port. As the major British fort along the Gold Coast, it was well supplied with local goods and always in need of English products. From later events, the most likely date of the shipwreck would have been about 1810, but it could have been as early as 1802 or as late as 1812.

The vessel would have traded down the Windward Coast, taking advantage of the prevailing winds and currents, to the Gold Coast and Cape Coast Castle. From there it was an easy sail down the coast to a number of ports, including Accra, Little Popo, Gridgi, and Whydah (now Ouidah, Benin), where ivory and palm oil, in addition to slaves, were traded for silks, Manchester cottons, guns, and powder.[9] Little Popo, known as a major source of provisions, was almost certainly a stop, particularly as there were both English merchants and English-speaking African traders there.[10] There were also trading ports further east: Porto Novo, Badagry, and Lagos. Before reaching the Bight of Benin, a trading vessel would need to purchase one or two local canoes and hire canoe men, most likely at Cape Coast Castle, to enable those on board to communicate with those on shore; the merchants on shore would not venture out through the surf to the ship.[11] Heavy surf, strong easterly currents, and sand bars made any landing on the Bight of Benin treacherous.[12] But a lagoon system, extending from the River Volta and fed by lagoons and rivers for over four hundred miles, allowed for a safe and vibrant commerce.[13]

Daisy did not remember where the shipwreck occurred, the town where the vessel was going, the name of the village where her great-grandmother was taken, or where her great-grandfather lived. "*He came not too far from Ghana. They used to go into Accra. And they were a different type and a different breed altogether.*"[14] She may have been referring to her grandfather being Yoruba, while the Ashanti were the major ethnic group in Accra. The fact that he was traveling to Accra certainly suggests that her grandfather was involved in trading.

By the early 1800s, the Yoruba had established themselves along the coast, as far west as Porto Novo in modern-day Benin.[15] The Yoruba maintained close trading connections with the inland kingdom of Oyo, which held a dominant position among the Yoruba at that time.[16] It is possible that the sinking of the vessel may have occurred in the vicinity of Porto Novo somewhere between 1802 and 1812. Porto Novo is over two hundred miles from Accra, a considerable distance, but well within the range of the travel of traders.

Along with the storm and the loss of the ship, a consistent part of Daisy's narrative is the young wife's rescue by the African chief's son, who was a strong swimmer. "*On the coast of Africa where the ship went down there was a son of the African chief who was noted for his powerful swimming. . . . He saved I don't know how many, but among them the bride that was on the ship.*"[17] Just as canoes were not used on the sea by locals, it was not common to swim in the dangerous surf and currents that assailed the shoreline of the Bight of Benin. Trips through the surf were hazardous, and the canoes were frequently capsized, losing both cargo and passengers to drowning or man-eating sharks.[18] Captain John Adams mentioned that some of the paddlers of these canoes were "almost amphibious" and went on to relate that when his canoe was overturned, "an old man, apparently seventy years of [age] swam alongside of me to secure me from the danger of being drowned; and as soon as he had seen me safe in the boat, immediately returned to the shore."[19] How Daisy's great-grandfather learned to swim in the surf we will never know. Perhaps he had spent time on the Gold Coast. But his reputation as a powerful swimmer, and the fact this was unusual, have been maintained and highlighted in the family story.

Those who helped revive the shipwrecked victim took her back to their village. Waterlogged, miserable, and feeling terribly alone, the young wife must have appreciated their ministrations and their attempts to console her and make her comfortable. *"They treated her with royalty, the best they could."*[20] Despite all their solicitations, the bride would have experienced extreme culture shock. Her husband would have had access to the latest trading knowledge available in London concerning African ports and would have been familiar with traditional practices to conduct business: a chief he must contact, appropriate gifts, and elaborate trading customs that had to be followed. But his wife would have had limited exposure to African life. Her own domain on board the ship would have remained very much a European world. She undoubtedly would have absorbed the prevalent British belief that Africans were racially inferior savages. While Europeans knew little of everyday existence within the African villages, they often dwelt on those elements of African culture they considered both savage and exotic: human sacrifice, extravagant rituals and ceremonies, and polygamy. Undoubtedly, such feelings would have informed the young English woman's thinking.[21]

She would have been overwhelmed by grief at the loss of her husband and fear for her immediate circumstances. Anna Maria Falconbridge, who went to Africa with her husband in 1791, wrote to a friend in May of that year: "Everything I see is entirely new to me. . . . To be frank, if I had a little agreeable society, a few comforts, and could ensure the same good health I have hitherto enjoyed, I should not be against spending some years of my life in Africa, but wanting those sweetners of life, I certainly wish to return to where they may be had."[22] Despite the women's kindness, which likely extended throughout the village, the young bride remained alone with her grief, anxiety, and almost certainly depression. Daisy indicated this: *"She was all broke up that she never went back to her English home."*[23]

The village was probably small, perhaps a few extended families or those related by kinship to the chief, and the villagers would have thought of themselves as one family.[24] As chief, her rescuer's father would have had multiple wives, and one of these women probably took the unfortunate young widow under her wing.[25] Among the Yoruba, every woman must have a male protector, and it is likely that her rescuer served in this role.[26] The village itself would have been a typical Yoruba town, with a cluster of mud huts enclosing an open courtyard.[27] Her living quarters were undoubtedly low and dark, with no windows and one doorway. A thatched roof of grass or agidi leaves harbored all kinds of insects and creatures that must have been the cause of extensive discomfort as well as terror: spiders as big as the palm of one's hand, the occasional venomous snake, and a variety of vermin, rustling through the thatch.[28] Mosquitoes abounded, as did a wide variety of voracious ants. Falconbridge described ants coming in such numbers one night as to drive "twelve to fourteen families from their houses." Alec told his children stories of these African ants. The only means to destroy them was through the use of fire and boiling water.[29]

While Europeans experienced a high mortality rate on the coast of Africa, they had little understanding as to the source. The most frequent cause of death was from fevers, both malaria and yellow fever, attributed to "noxious gases" rather than the real culprit, the mosquito, as well as dysentery that resulted from parasites, particularly amoebic dysentery, known as "the bloody flux."[30] Parasites were present in both food and water. Indeed, the Bight of Benin was notoriously hard on white men, hence the saying

> Beware and take care of the Bight of Benin
> There's one comes out for forty go in.

Statistics relate that half of all Europeans who journeyed to West Africa during the eighteenth century died within a year.[31] The rainy season from April to October was considered the unhealthiest season.[32] While aware of the high mortality rate, Europeans failed to understand the causes and blamed illness on "the moist and hot atmosphere."[33] Females were believed to fare even worse than males. John Field, principal of the Women's Institute in Lagos later in the century, wrote: "European ladies cannot live here. One out of ten perhaps may do so for a short time, but no sooner has she thoroughly got into the work than her health obliges her to give way to another."[34] Because of the high death rate of Europeans, it is also quite possible that the young bride did not survive long on the coast.

A stranger who comes to live and participate in a Yoruba community is welcomed, and the young castaway would have soon felt the strong ties of kinship as she was integrated into her protector's family.[35] Did she become the wife of her rescuer? Daisy was not definitive as to their relationship:

> *She lived with them in the African little town and camps . . . . And it wasn't too long of her being there—she stayed right there; she didn't get back to England, and stayed there with the Africans until . . . . her child was born, a son from the African chief's son. And she named him from Alexander the Great, but they spelt it differently and pronounced it differently: Alessi . . . but it was from Alexander. And he grew up there with them and with her and he got to be very clever and smart and learning English from her.*[36]

That she was responsible for naming her son is another consistent part of the family story. As the shipwrecked victim was integrated into village society, she would have realized that life was regulated by elaborate rituals, a strong, coherent belief system, and a variety of artistic practices, particularly of drumming and dance. She would have personally begun to participate in these traditions. Giving birth was a joyous event among the Yoruba. She would have been accepted into her rescuer's family, and women experienced in childbirth would have cared for her, delivered the newborn, and then served as nurses to both mother and baby.[37]

Naming a child is significant among the Yoruba, and ritual ceremonies accompanied the event.[38] Apparently, the English woman had become familiar enough with Yoruba culture to realize the importance of this tradition, and she chose a name that would instill her son with strength, courage, and manliness, all-important virtues among the Yoruba. According to Daisy, her great-grandmother was interested in history and knew that Alexander the Great had never been defeated in battle. During the seventeenth and eighteenth centuries, Oyo was a dominant kingdom among the Yoruba peoples. The *Alafin*, the ruler of Oyo, had colonized an area separated from the adjacent kingdom, which provided access to the sea.[39] There was always the threat of raids by their Dahomean adversaries who were in competition for the slave trade. Such raids became more frequent after 1803, and there was a series of raids for the next several years that disrupted trade.[40] The death of the Alafin around 1810 plunged the Yoruba into twenty years of wars and confusion, as the Alafin was followed by a series of weak successors.[41] The choice of the name Alexander suggests such circumstances were occurring at the time of the boy's birth. Being a good warrior was a necessity; being unvanquished was the ultimate. As the boy matured, the name and its characteristics would have became an important part of his identity, an identity he bestowed many years later on his own son.

Later events lead to the conclusion that Alessi must have been born between 1805 and 1812. Daisy and her sisters speculated that he was between eighteen and twenty-two years old when he left Africa. That, as described later, was probably in 1830. Alessi would have been brought up as any other Yoruba child, helping with other boys to keep public spaces clean and, as they grew older, serving as warriors. He would have undergone all the traditional rituals and ceremonies of circumcision, scarification, and the rites of puberty. Great care was taken to involve children in lineage affairs and rituals.[42] Alessi learned fishing, trading, and warring and was schooled in his family's history and significance within the village. Alessi would have gathered with other children in the evening social time, listening to stories of historic events or folktales with songs and refrains, an educational experience rich in artistic expression.[43]

From what we know of his later life, Alessi exhibited the powerful athletic build of his father—a build that was passed down to his own son, and one that facilitated his ability to live up to his name. He assuredly practiced the traditional belief in spirits, known among the Yoruba as *orisha*. The orisha have specific functions and must be honored through rituals and ceremonies. Following the significance of the boy's name, he would have been destined to become a hunter and a warrior, and to fulfill this role successfully, he would have looked to the spirit of iron, the powerful orisha Ogun, to control his life. Explicit characteristics of an individual are believed to characterize members of certain cults.[44] Both arrogance and impatience are associated with Ogun, and interestingly the characteristic most often mentioned in association with Alessi was arrogance. Also in association with Ogun was the art of boxing.[45] Those who boxed were strong men and underwent a ceremony after the age of seven, where ritual boxing took place, to prove that they were men.[46] It is very likely that Alessi took part in such a ceremony.

Alessi also would have received additional instruction from his mother. We do not know how long she lived, but according to the family story, she schooled her son and made sure that he understood and spoke English. Before she died, she gave him her two most treasured possessions, the only things she had from her former life: a gold locket and her wedding ring. According to Daisy, the locket and the wedding ring were heirlooms passed down in the Turner family and were lost when the homestead burned in 1962.[47]

Alessi grew to manhood during a time of continued unrest and must have honed his fighting skills in raids and skirmishes with the enemy. His exceptional athletic ability would have brought him honor and acclaim. He would have gained expertise in handling a canoe along with fishing skills. If he were enterprising, as Daisy indicated, he would have been involved in trading. He would have viewed trade as a route to wealth and power, and most certainly he knew of successful traders who wielded political influence.[48] He was probably involved in legitimate trade. Cloth, fish, salt, and gum made for a thriving indigenous commerce, and as the Dahomeans made raids on Porto Novo, they drove the slave trade onto the lagoon where the Dahomeans had no expertise in canoe warfare.[49] Was it during one of these raids that Alessi captured prisoners he later sold as slaves, or was he acting as a middleman in the slave trade?

By the late 1820s, he must have been dealing most frequently with the Spanish and the Portuguese; however, he may have had contact with English legitimate traders as well as Americans engaged in illegal slave trading. His ability to speak English was a likely advantage. We know that African traders who became successful frequently sent their sons abroad to be educated.[50] Daisy was always dismissive of her grandfather's role as a merchant. She depicted him as unscrupulous, "*selling a piece of red cloth . . . for $10, when it was worth 10 cents.*"[51] She spoke of him as "*a smarty with his parentage and his education.*"[52] She pointed out that the slaves had been caught unnaturally and had been fooled.[53] She could not forgive her grandfather for selling his own people. She lamented: *"nothing was done about it in Africa. He [Alessi] had a power there."*[54] I suspect this may also reflect Daisy's father's attitude toward his father.[55] This may well be a later reshaping of an unapologetic story.

It is doubtful that Alessi sold his own blood. Yoruba tradition held that there was a "universal law" that prohibited the enslavement of those sharing the same facial scarification of *abaja*—three or four horizontal or vertical parallel lines.[56] Once the civil wars of the Oyo kingdom began in the 1820s, various Yoruba warring groups took many Yoruba captives, but these were considered hostile opponents.

Despite the abolition of the slave trade by the English in 1807 and by the Americans in 1808, it continued until well into midcentury. The captives gained through warfare nourished the slave trade, and ships continued to carry cargos, particularly to Brazil and Cuba. Lagos replaced Ouidah as the largest exporter of slaves, and the trade took on an even more sinister cast as captains and crews filled holds beyond capacity and threw slaves overboard when chased by British cruisers.[57] However Alessi acquired his slaves, according to the family story he was involved in selling them directly to the ships:

> *He was very smart, too smart, because he got interested in the African slave ships that seemed to have come to that section about every three months and they were gathering Africans as slaves to take back. . . . We figured this all out . . . he was between eighteen and twenty-two, when this particular incident happened, that he was getting different slaves together there for the ships . . . And at this time they took him on the slave ship as a slave . . . which he wasn't expecting . . . because he was trading and doing business with the Africans and with the United States*[58] *slave buyers.*[59]

About 1829, Lagos was the leading port for exporting slaves on the Bight of Benin.[60] African merchants maintained control of the trade, and it is probable that Alessi took captives to Lagos for sale. If he was still living near Porto Novo, this would have entailed a journey by canoe across the lagoon, which was a battleground as well as a highway. Another way to gain slaves was through "waterborn raiding parties of sometimes eight to ten canoes."[61] Perhaps this was how Alessi gained his slaves. Such war parties might return with thirty or forty slaves at a time.[62] If Alessi served as an intermediary between one of the slave factories on the lagoon and slave ships, this also would have involved a canoe trip across the lagoon, although nowhere near as great a distance.[63]

There is no way of confirming what captain or vessel Alessi was dealing with at the time of his capture; however, from the family narrative, as well as by later events that help date Alessi's arrival, all indications point to the Spanish schooner *Fenix* (also referred to in documents as *Phoenix* and *Feniz*) out of Havana. At first glance, this vessel does not mesh smoothly with the oral narrative, but once elements of the story are analyzed, it is possible to understand the distortions.

> *When they got all of his business done . . . then they caught him and brought him on the boat. That's why they wasn't able to do nothing with him. They couldn't make him work or do anything, when they finally got him. And, of course, he was so arrogant and everything that he sold cheap. Nobody wanted him. He could talk good English, and he knew what they were doing. He knew that he was a prisoner in his own nest. He was going to be a big shot there in Africa, but they brought him here.*[64]

One constant in the family narrative was that Daisy's grandfather was brought to New Orleans and sold cheap because he was a troublemaker and so arrogant that no one could do anything with him. From events discussed in the next chapter, I suspected that Alessi might have arrived in New Orleans sometime between 1830 and 1832. I searched *The Trans-Atlantic Slave Trade Database* and discovered that there was only one slave ship in that period that came into New Orleans: the *Fenix*.[65] The database indicates that little is known about this ship, except that it was a Spanish schooner, had taken on ninety-one slaves, and reached New Orleans with seventy-four slaves. My first thought was that Daisy's description of the Middle Passage was reflective of the loss of seventeen slaves: "*It seemed to have been one of the worst . . . trips that the slave owners had made in their work of getting slaves from Africa. The slaves died . . . and different diseases cropped out, and so many died that they had to bury them at sea.*"[66]

Searching for more information on the *Fenix*, I discovered a reference to the "capture of the slaver *Phoenix* by the *Grampus*." This eventually led to a number of documents at the National Archives and to a local historian, Gail Swanson, who had done a great deal of research on the Fenix. I became convinced that this most likely was the ship on which Alessi was transported to New Orleans.

In April 1829, the *Fenix* sailed for Puerto Rico and waited there for insurance documents before leaving for Africa in late May or early June. Despite both Britain's and America's abolition of the trade, Cuba's slave trade was flourishing as the sugar plantation economy thrived. In the decade between 1821 and 1831, it is estimated that three hundred vessels landed sixty thousand slaves on the island.[67] While Spain had signed a treaty in 1817 to prohibit the slave trade, the Spanish authorities in Cuba ignored it due to self-interest.[68]

The American-built *Fenix* was a topsail schooner, a small, 90.5-ton vessel that relied on speed to outrun its foes. It appears to have been a pirate, preying on other vessels, as well as a slaver, something that went hand in hand with the illicit trade.[69] A number of Spanish slaving vessels were involved in plundering slaves, as well as goods, from similar nefarious traders and merchant ships. The Cuban slaver *Guerrero*, considerably larger than the *Fenix* with several times the gun power, committed such piratical acts. This was considered a general practice of Spanish slavers.[70] These vessels were held in low regard by Governor Colonel Edward Nicholls of Fernando Po, a strategic island off the Niger delta, which was owned by Spain but leased to the British, who used it as a base to suppress the slave trade. He described the lot as outlaws and murderers:

> The individuals engaged in this traffic are persons of the most infamous and unprincipled descriptions; they come in their ships to the mouths of the different unexplored rivers, where they land a quantity of trade goods of the worst kind, and, leaving their supercargoes to exchange them with the chiefs for slaves, return to the sea whilst their cargoes are collecting, where, as pirates, they rob our merchant ships, murder their crews and when glutted with plunder, return to the coast to ship their victims for whom they pay about 7 or 8 pounds apiece, and sell them for 70, 80, or 100 pounds each.[71]

The Spanish captain and crew, twenty in number and mostly in their twenties, well suited Nicholl's description.[72] The *Fenix* was armed with a long gun mounted amidships, eighteen muskets, eleven Spanish knives (long knives), eleven boarding pikes, kegs of powder, and canisters of round shot.[73]

While in Puerto Rico, the captain of the *Fenix*, Francisco de la Torre, received a letter from Joaquin Roig, friend of *Fenix* owner José Givert, who wrote that the English were blockading the coast and suggested going to the north of the island of Fernando Po. He directed de la Torre to a river in Calabar, just as Nicholls had described, where he would find an individual "who will give you whatever you need." He elaborated: "Large vessels can come in there with a pilot but this does not seem necessary for the *Fenix*, nevertheless you will take all possible precautions to avoid stranding and its consequences."[74] The bar was not a single bar, but rather a number of sand banks across the mouth of the river, with navigable channels between them. These were dangerous to navigate; it was not uncommon to go aground and be left stranded as the tide went out. When stranded, a vessel was at the mercy of locals, who could carry off everything on board.

The *Fenix* arrived in Calabar in July, after successfully skirting any blockading English ships and avoiding the hazardous bar, and found the agent of whom Roig had written—Don Juan Menesdez, most likely a Cuban or Spanish resident who had developed a network that linked African traders with the slavers.[75] As the crew of the *Fenix* would have arrived in the rainy season, they most likely remained in Calabar until the rains let up in October, making the necessary overtures to African slave suppliers, negotiating price, and giving the necessary gifts. The wet season not only made it difficult to get around on shore but also increased the likelihood of illness from deadly tropical diseases and parasites; and, of course, the longer the stay, the greater the mortality on board. It was a slow process acquiring a full cargo of slaves; they were usually purchased piecemeal with captains sailing along the coast to complete the quota of slaves for a full cargo.[76]

There is no way to know where the *Fenix* came across Alessi. It could have been anywhere along the coast, but it was most probably in Lagos. Here the slave centers were located on the lagoon that Alessi undoubtedly knew well. It was from the long beach in front of the lagoon where the captives most frequently were taken by canoe through the perilous surf.[77] With the necessity to evade capture by the British, slave traders devised places where they could embark clandestinely.[78] It must have been just such a place where Alessi embarked in a canoe, with canoe men and a complement of naked slaves—men, women, and children—to the waiting *Fenix*. Once his captives were delivered, he would have unsuspectingly turned to climb back down the rope ladder to his canoe. But he had not foreseen the extent to which these men would go to gain one more large, strong slave. Alessi was placed in chains and shackles and shoved below into airless stench and darkness with the other captives.

Alessi could have been held five or six months aboard ship, below deck where temperatures reached 130 degrees in the dry season, before leaving the coast of Africa.[79] Or perhaps he was more fortunate by being in one of the last groups to be placed on board, before the *Fenix* returned to Calabar. He must have been furious and looking for any opportunity to escape. While his treatment was certainly inhumane, he would not allow himself to be humbled. He held his head high, with a defiant demeanor. This is the Alessi who comes through vividly in the Turner narrative. Daisy described him: *"he thought he could win the world, like Hitler."*[80] This underscored her disapproval of him.

The *Fenix* likely returned to Calabar toward the end of February to take on its major cargo of slaves.[81] The crew would also be making ready for their passage back to Cuba, a trip of seven to nine weeks and one that was providential to complete before the advent of the hurricane season in August.[82] The *Fenix* would have taken on supplies for the crew including water, rice, African beans, white beans, barrels of beef and pork, and bags of bread. There was a high death rate on board Spanish vessels that could be linked to inadequate water and food supplies.[83] The enslaved were only fed a diet of rice.[84]

The *Fenix* left Calibar around May 11, 1830, successfully avoiding interception by the British.[85] The ninety-one human hostages aboard the ship were miserable. The vessel was small, and conditions were crowded.[86] The hold was most likely divided into three sections: one for men, one for boys, and one for women and young children. The men were shackled together in twos, lying on their sides; there was no room to stretch out, let alone stand up. As the sails filled and the *Fenix* left Fernando Po well astern, many of the captives, not familiar with the relentless pitching, swaying, and hobbling of a vessel, retched as they lay in the airless, stinking hold.

The *Fenix* was off the coast of northwestern Santa Domingo within twenty-four days—an exceptionally fast passage. It was then something happened that gave credence to the ship's piratical role. As dawn broke, the *Fenix* spied the *Kremlin*, an American brig returning from Antwerp and on the way to Havana.[87] Christopher Hall, the captain of the *Kremlin*, watched the *Fenix* follow for twenty-four hours and then shorten sail in order to stay close. With alarm, he noted crew stationed at the long gun. The *Fenix* was within speaking distance and still had not shown its colors.[88] Captain Hall called all hands to clear away their three guns for action and distributed small arms among the crew. De la Torre, the captain of the *Fenix*, "peremptorily ordered" Hall to send his boat on board the *Fenix*, to which Hall replied that his boat was leaky. De la Torre stated he would send his boat aboard the *Kremlin*, but Hall refused to shorten sail. Hall believed his show of force prevented the *Fenix* from attacking. Instead, the *Fenix* raised its Spanish colors, crossed the *Kremlin*'s bow, "and luffed off until 1 o'clock p.m., when he jibed and stood again towards me." Just as things were looking dark, Hall spied a sail in the distance that proved to be the U.S. schooner *Grampus*, whose captain, Isaac Mayo, claimed that at one o'clock he saw "a long low foretopsail schooner" standing for the *Kremlin*.[89] When the schooner saw the *Grampus* coming up, it immediately jibed and headed north.

By two o'clock, the *Grampus* was alongside the *Kremlin*. On hearing what had occurred, the *Grampus* took after the *Fenix*, which was no match for the largest of five U.S. cruisers built in the 1820s to help suppress piracy and protect merchant vessels. By three o'clock, the *Grampus* was "within musket shot of her." When the *Fenix* did not show colors, the *Grampus* fired, and the *Fenix* complied and hoisted its Spanish colors, but it continued to maneuver to try to escape. Captain Mayo ordered the schooner to lower its sails, threatening to fire into the ship if it did not obey. When it failed to lower its jib, Mayo "fired a shot close under her counter, which threw the water on board of her."[90] Finally, it lowered the jib and mainsail, and Lt.

James T. Wilson boarded the *Fenix* with an armed crew. He found eighty-two slaves below decks and learned that the *Fenix* had sailed fourteen months previously from Havana to Africa and had spent the intervening time on the African coast. Mayo questioned this statement as he thought perhaps the *Fenix* had been preying on other vessels in the Caribbean. "We know that most piracies recently committed, have been by vessels engaged in this traffic."[91]

In his report, Wilson added that de la Torre told Mayo, when questioned why he "molested" the *Kremlin*, that "he was in want of provisions." Mayo requested an inventory of the provisions aboard the *Fenix* and concluded that the crew was not in need of supplies or water but definitely had piratical designs on the *Kremlin*. Apparently the rice on board lasted another ten days before having to be replenished. If the passage had taken the usual seven weeks, the enslaved would have been out of rations four days before they arrived in Havana.

The passage of the *Fenix* continued another six weeks, which proved devastating for the captives. On June 7, the *Grampus* took the *Fenix* in tow as they headed toward Key West and transferred ten days of provisions. On June 19, they discovered land, and the *Grampus* parted company with the *Fenix*.[92] During the two weeks it took to reach Key West, two more Africans died. By June 25, the *Fenix* was on the way to Pensacola, this time with the revenue cutter *Pulaski*. By the time they arrived on July 8, another three were dead. The deplorable conditions were recognized by Jesse Elliott, commander of the U.S. squadron at Pensacola: "The small size of this vessel, and her crowded state, make it necessary she should arrive at New Orleans as early as possible."[93] The *Fenix* took on additional provisions but was not allowed to land; it was to proceed to New Orleans.

In recounting the horrors of the Middle Passage, I think Alessi told about the misery that was magnified as the journey continued and as they stopped at Key West and Pensacola. As Daisy told the story, I suspect some major changes occurred due to misunderstanding. Daisy always claimed the ship put in to Boston, because it had been a terrible crossing and people were dying. The ship was not allowed to land because slaving had been outlawed, and the ship had to push on to New Orleans, where the owners and crew could be prosecuted. Daisy had most likely confused Pensacola and Boston. There was also a good chance Alessi had not known the name of the port. Further, no vessel coming from West Africa to New Orleans would be on a course to go into Boston. I believe that Daisy confused another incident that she associated with Boston, and this became a part of her narrative; the two were always linked whenever she spoke about the vessel carrying her grandfather to New Orleans. This is an example of the kind of distortion that can occur as a component of memory.[94]

The Captain and the crew decided that if they could get in Boston, that would help to save the situation. And we had part of that history firsthand from a Mr. Goodridge, whose people had landed from the early settlements, sixteen and something down in Plymouth, that one of the head officials there who was white had married a free slave man, a relative, it seems as if it was his aunt. . . . They also were head officials in Boston. So, when they wanted to have a slave market in Boston, they said no . . . that they wouldn't start slavery up in Massachusetts. So they refused to allow this slave ship to stop or stay in Boston.[95]

The voyage had been one of the worst they ever had. People had died, and all these slaves that they were bringing over had a disease and died, and no food down in the hold, and no way of good living. It was going to be one of the biggest gains but . . . instead of making money with nigger slaves . . . they lost because they took this disease. The women died, went crazy; they throwed them overboard; women had babies. They said it was something terrible. It was one of the worst sights that any human being had ever seen—that slave ship. So to help themselves out, they decided to stop quickly at Boston. Well, then when they wouldn't let them stop in Boston, more died, and then they kept on down to New Orleans.[96]

The significant part of the story to the Turner family is the death and utter misery experienced by the enslaved. That is what has been encapsulated in this memory, along with the vessel being unable to land, and I believe it gives credence to her grandfather actually having been aboard the *Fenix*.

By the time the *Fenix* reached New Orleans on July 19, another four had died, and only seventy-four captives remained. This deadly decline set in motion by the unspeakable conditions and overcrowding continued after they were removed from the *Fenix*, and by September 21, only sixty-one remained.[97] There was an attempt to get medical help for the most seriously ill, and a number were diagnosed with the yaws, a contagious bacterial infection affecting skin, bones, and joints.[98] It is possible that the drop in numbers during these two months may not have been totally due to death. There is a strong possibility that some were sold illegally, and that Alessi, with his reputation for troublemaking, was among them. Records for New Orleans at the National Archives indicate this possibility. In February 1832, a member of the Colonization Society in Washington complained that of the 240 Africans entitled to go to Liberia, about 100 had been illegally sold.[99]

On September 21, the remaining Africans were turned over to the U.S. marshal. A series of hearings, under Judge Samuel Harper, determined that there was not enough evidence that the Spanish schooner had committed a piratical act, but affirmed that the Africans should be placed under the care of the marshal. Two lawyers appealed to Judge Harper on behalf of the Africans to have them declared free and under the protection of the government, but the judge's opinion stated that if he made the Africans free, they would be seized under Louisiana state law and that other free people of color would be endangered as well. In January, President Andrew Jackson recommended "that suitable legislative provision be made for the maintenance of the unfortunate captives, pending the legislation which has grown out of the case."[100] On May 27, 1831, Harper accepted a $500 bond from Joshua Lewis, a superior court justice, to hire out the Africans; they would work his fields in return for his caring for them. The Lewis estate returned thirty-seven Africans on July 17, 1835, to the marshal.[101] Five years after seventy-four Africans disembarked the *Fenix*, only thirty-seven remained to be sent to Liberia by the American Colonization Society. If some of them were sold illegally, and in poor condition, it is logical that they would have been sold *"cheap."*[102]

As long as Judge Lewis was on the scene, it is doubtful that any illegal sale would have taken place, but his health began to deteriorate, offering the possibility for some underhanded dealing. Lewis died in 1833, and it is possible that an overseer may have taken advantage of an opportunity to be rid of the arrogant Alessi, who was disinclined to work, if indeed he was not already with Jack Gouldin. While this is possible, 1833 seems late for Alessi to be sold to Gouldin. It was during this period that Gouldin was considering buying a large property, in which case he would need to purchase a number of new slaves.[103] Daisy said that her grandfather was incarcerated for a short period in New Orleans to be fattened up before he was sold, another indication for the earlier sale.

Whatever happened remains a mystery, but if Alessi was on the *Fenix*, he was sold illegally. And the *Fenix* seems to be the prime candidate for the vessel that brought Daisy's grandfather to New Orleans. Daisy always claimed that her grandfather was sold to Jack Gouldin of Port Royal, Virginia, on the auction block in New Orleans. I suspect the auction block in New Orleans became an iconic image for Daisy, something she learned about in later life. It was more likely that Alessi was first sold in New Orleans to a slave trader, who then took him north by mule team, through the Deep South to Virginia, and once there, sold him to Jack Gouldin, probably in Fredericksburg or Port Royal. *He didn't know what they were going to do with him. Nobody wanted him, and carried him with ropes and chains all through the south by mule team.*[104] Unfortunately, there is no bill of sale to confirm this. Indeed, no records survive from the Gouldin plantation. I wondered whether it was the slave trader or Jack Gouldin who bought Alessi cheap. Daisy always said it was Gouldin, but there is no mention of a slave trader in the story, probably because Gouldin, as master to both father and son, is the significant person to the Turners. Being bought cheap was an insult to Alessi. He was a warrior, a man of athletic prowess, and in the prime of his life. He held himself above his fellow slaves and was resolute in his refusal to work.

> *He got Grandfather on the plantation and of course, he was looking around at the other slaves. He didn't figure he was in their class. And of course, they resented him, and he resented everything and everybody. He didn't intend to be no slave. He didn't know exactly what the slave thing was over here. It was all new. . . . So, he was very arrogant. But the old master saw he had culture from his English mother and being smart. He was very arrogant. So, the master commenced using him a little different.*[105]

In other versions of the narrative, Daisy said it was the overseer who came to Gouldin, because her grandfather refused to work. Gouldin was known as a sporting man—someone who liked foxhunting, horse racing, cockfighting, boxing matches, and betting. He promoted matches among the enslaved: those best at wrestling, cockfighting, and fistfighting.[106] William Steward, born enslaved to a Captain Helms of Prince William County in 1794, described Helms in similar terms as a sportsman: "He generally kept one or two race horses, and a pack of hounds for fox-hunting, which at that time, was a very common and fashionable diversion in that section of the country. He was not only a sportsman, but a gamester and was in the habit of playing cards, and sometimes betting very high and losing accordingly."[107] Perhaps Gouldin purchased Alessi because he thought he might prove to be a good fighter. This was not unheard of; slave traders sometimes auctioned off a youth, emphasizing his prize fighting capabilities as a selling point.[108]

Daisy explained that many of the enslaved used to compete in wrestling and boxing matches, foot races, and jumping contests for sport among themselves. Through these events, Gouldin was well aware who were the best athletes; he removed them from working in the fields and gave them special training. He would then challenge another planter to hold a competition between the two best fighters on their respective plantations. "*They would make matches like they would play tennis.*"[109] This role was much more to Alessi's liking and much more familiar. He knew about bare-knuckle fighting. Through these matches, he could exhibit his superiority. This was reconcilable with his self-image.

No story remains as to how he acquired the name Robert rather than being called Alessi. It is surprising, as Alessi must have regarded this as one more indignity. He rectified this slight by bestowing the name Alexander on his son, thus honoring his mother's memory. Alessi gave himself the surname Berkeley, although we do not know how this occurred. According to Jack Gouldin's will, most male slaves on the Gouldin plantation had both a first and last name.[110] However, women and children were noted simply by their first names. Alec's half brother and sister were referred to as Lindsey and Judy, children of Rose; Rose is given no last name. Daisy believed that her grandfather had witnessed a successful duel fought by a man called Berkeley and that her grandfather had taken that name because he admired the man's triumph. She also said that the Berkeleys were wealthy slave owners in the area. This seems to be in keeping with a name Robert would have chosen for himself.

Within the confines of enslavement and through his success as plantation champion, Robert was able to live life on terms that were acceptable to him or, more precisely, on negotiated terms that were somewhat better than those around him. Most important for Robert, he could maintain his dignity.

CHAPTER 3

Jack Gouldin and Robert Berkeley

The master couldn't make him work like a slave, so he put him to prizefighting.
—Daisy Turner, interview with author, March 1, 1984

Jack Gouldin was in his mid-forties when he first encountered Robert. Who was this man who became such a dominant figure in the lives of Robert and his son Alec? Both father and son spoke of Gouldin as wealthy, keeping *"high-tone slavery"* (meaning he did not like to whip his bondsmen), being *"soft spoken"* and a passionate *"sporting man"* who loved cockfighting, boxing, horse racing, and foxhunting.

Without the Turner narrative, we would know very little about Jack Gouldin. He left no collection of letters or plantation records, and there were no family stories that came down through the generations, other than the belief that he had once been a prosperous plantation owner who had lost everything during the Civil War.[1]

From the tax records, it is evident that Gouldin became very wealthy. Through land records, plats, the inventory at his death, his will, and court records, we can see how extensive his plantation was and what a prime location it occupied along the Rappahannock River in eastern Virginia. The records indicate Gouldin was using the most modern agricultural methods and the most innovative farming equipment, including a "wheat machine," or combine harvester,[2] and that his household goods included sets of china, crystal goblets, silverware, and fine furniture. Presumably, he could be considered one of the elite planters of Caroline County. Where did his money come from? The only description of Gouldin does not seem to indicate that he came from an aristocratic or moneyed family. Rather, it described him as "a man of unusually strong though uncultivated intellect. By industry, economy, and wise management, he accumulated a large property. For many years he was a solid, reliable and useful member of a Baptist Church."[3]

His roots were in Essex County, and he came from a long line of yeoman farmers. His great-great-grandfather, John Goulding, who came from Dunston, Lincolnshire, England, in 1657, had three sons, the second being

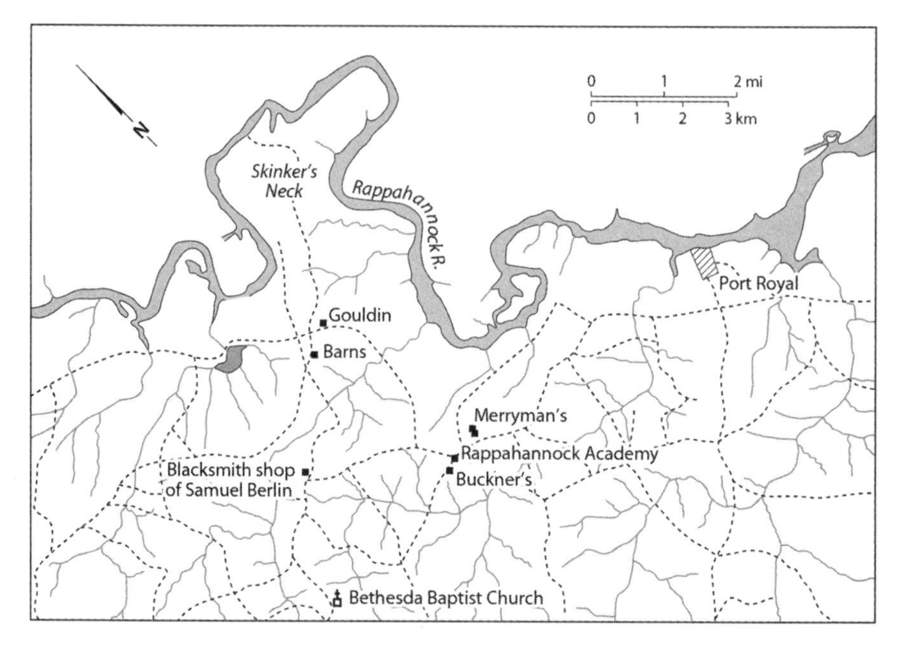

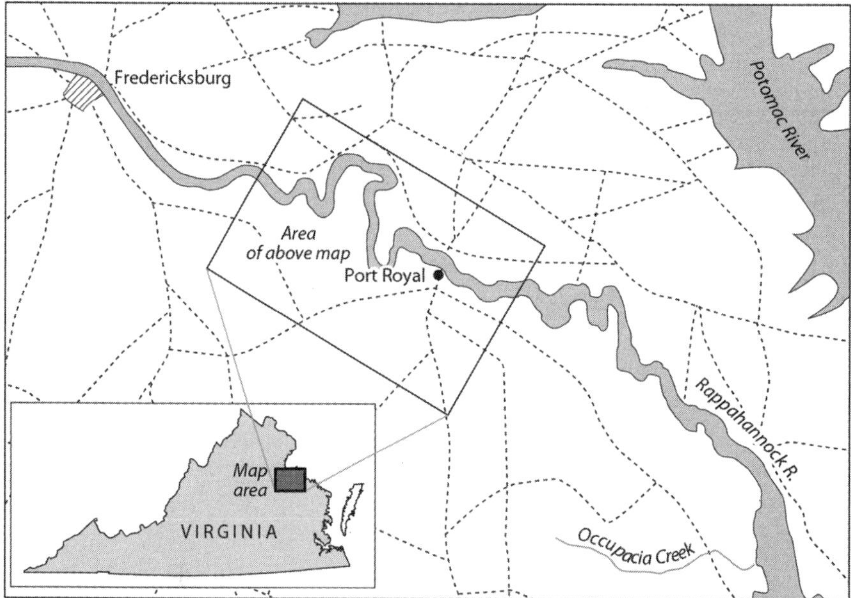

Virginia, with insert of Skinker's Neck.

William, Jack's great-grandfather.[4] William was born in 1675, and in 1705 or 1706 he purchased 300 acres on Occupation [Occupacia] Creek and added another 150 acres to his holdings twelve years later.[5] Although "overrun with briers, thorns and wild beasts," this was considered good land because it was near the Rappahannock River and on Occupacia Creek.[6]

In the early 1700s, the average plantation was about 527 acres, and the major crop was tobacco—premium "sweet scented" tobacco for overseas markets.[7] Tobacco was also used as currency, and land was acquired for the consideration of so many pounds of tobacco.[8] William died in 1747, requesting in his will "that my body be buried in a decent manner" and leaving his four children the bulk of his estate.[9] As his oldest son, Simon, Jack's grandfather, received 250 acres of land. When Simon died in 1789, he had five living children, among whom his land was equally divided.

Simon's oldest son, Simon Jr., remained on the property, while his two younger brothers, John (Jack's father) and Jesse moved to Caroline County, not far from Port Royal. Caroline County had been established in 1728, and the brothers, their name now spelled Gouldin, moved to land that was formerly part of Essex County, roughly fifty miles from where they had grown up. The two living sisters, Sarah (Sally) and Tabytha, also remained on the family land. When Simon Jr. died in 1795, his will indicated he had been a successful farmer.[10] He had a riding horse, a gun, twenty-three head of cattle, a pair of oxen, ten sheep, eighteen hogs, and ten additional fat hogs. He raised both cotton and wheat, and he made brandy. There is no mention of slaves in his will. In 1790, Essex County census figures show 5,400 slaves in the county, outnumbering the white population of 3,500.[11] This lack of slaves would have differentiated the Gouldins from wealthy planters. Education also reflected a distinction between the common planters and the gentry.[12] While the aristocracy was predominantly literate, yeoman farmers seldom were. None of the Gouldins could read or write. They all signed their wills with an X.

Essex County was known for its "keen sportsmen."[13] Hunting was a favorite sport for men during colonial times. Parties of hunters went after deer, birds, and waterfowl. Hunting provided sport as well as variety for the table. There was also foxhunting, horse racing, and cockfighting, all of which brought men together socially and for competition. These latter events were rife with excessive drinking and heavy betting, and it was said that "over indulgence in sport ruined many men."[14] Still, these contests proved irresistible. While foxhunting and horse racing were more for the gentry, cockfighting was popular throughout all ranks of society. Cockfights were often conducted for valuable purses. One in Essex County in 1752 offered a prize of sixty pistoles, a valuable gold coin worth about an English pound.[15] Such a generous prize would have attracted men from all over the area. Birds were trained and fought to the death, wearing steel spurs on their claws. Undoubtedly, Simon's gun was used for hunting. The Gouldin property bordered the Beverleys—one of the major aristocratic, landholding families—and one wonders if perhaps some of the Gouldins first sampled foxhunting there. The two older brothers, Simon and John, probably gained a taste for the sporting life that was all around them in

Essex County, attending some of the frequent cockfights and horse races held in their area of the county.

John Gouldin, Simon's second son and Jack's father, moved to the Port Royal area of Caroline County in 1788, when he bought 111 acres of land.[16] By this time, he was married and had two young sons, Philip and Jack. John bought a small farm that is now part of Fort A. P. Hill,[17] on land well suited for farming, but several miles back from the Rappahannock River where major plantation owners like Corbin, Taliaferro, Buckner, and Skinker settled. He sold all the land he inherited in Essex to his two sisters after their brother Simon died.

When John died in 1816, without a will, he had a four-hundred-acre farm on which he grew tobacco, corn, and wheat and raised sixteen head of cattle, eight sheep, and fourteen hogs. He worked his fields with three yokes of oxen and owned three horses and two guns. He had fourteen slaves, among them Presley, who may well be the individual who became Alec's nemesis and who more than any other individual, as cruel overseer, symbolized the horrific institution of slavery for Alec.[18] These slaves accounted for the major assessment of his estate, valued at $5,100, while the remainder of his property was appraised at $1,835. John was apparently literate, as he owned a "parcel of books" listed in the inventory of his estate and almost certainly, like his brother Jesse, made sure his sons were educated.[19] He made brandy, as did his older brother, Simon, back in Essex. His wife Jane was a spinner and wove cloth for family use as well as to sell.[20] It is surprising that John Gouldin did not leave a will, but there was little to be divided among his seven children. Jack, the second oldest, took the lead as his father's executor, having served in the same capacity for his uncle Jesse in 1813. He kept the estate together in the form of a trust as two of his siblings, Betsy and Henry, were young children, and saw that his mother received the house and 175 acres of land.[21]

Jack Gouldin was born in 1787 and grew up in a large family of scrappy "uncultivated" yeoman farmers. He was literate, owned a bookcase full of books, an atlas, spectacles, and a looking glass, and was recognized as having "a strong intellect."[22] We also know from the Turner family narrative that he had a passion for hunting, horse racing, fighting gamecocks, and boxing. Daisy always referred to him as a *"sporting man."*

As a youth, Jack must have attended cockfights, horse races, and boxing matches. A number of court cases about horse racing in Caroline County, as well as elsewhere in Virginia, attest to its popularity.[23] With such sporting events, there arose the strong likelihood that participants would be involved in heavy drinking and wagering. Informal matches among the enslaved often took place on a Sunday or a holiday. They included foot races, wrestling, fighting, jumping, feats of strength, cockfights, and dances. Athletic accomplishments and physical prowess were viewed with great pride.[24] But it was also common for planters to back one individual slave against another in wrestling or boxing matches. These often took place during the harvest season at cornhuskings and other communal gatherings.[25]

One of the best known boxers was Tom Molineaux, who is indicative of this tradition. He was born in 1784 into enslavement on a plantation in Virginia or Maryland.[26] According to Nat Fleischer, the founder and publisher of *Ring Magazine*, Tom Molineaux was descended from a family of bare-knuckle fighters. His father, Zachery Thompson Molineaux, fought in the Revolutionary War but remained enslaved rather than being freed by his service.[27] Zachery, one of five brothers Fleischer points to as "the first bare knuckles fighting men in our country," had four sons, one of these being Tom.[28]

A frequent story told about Tom Molineaux is that he gained his freedom when his master promised to manumit him if he won a particular boxing match. When Molineaux succeeded, he won substantial money for his master and was awarded his freedom. Elliott Gorn, a scholar who has researched bare-knuckle fighting, insists there is no evidence for "this charming story."[29] Whatever the origin of his manumission, Molineaux did fight as a free man outside London in 1810 and 1811 against English champion Joe Crib. Gorn also casts doubt on plantation masters pitting their slaves against one another in such matches, pointing to it as "a motif in Afro-American and white southern folklore."[30] Except for the Tom Molineaux incident, the understory of enslaved boxing matches orchestrated by white plantation owners has remained only in African American traditions and a number of the Works Progress Administration (WPA) slave narratives.[31]

In 2010, Sergio Lussana combed the WPA slave narratives and autobiographies of former slaves, focusing on the period between 1830 and the outbreak of the Civil War—the same time in which Robert was fighting. He referenced a number of these matches spread widely throughout the southern states.[32] This indicates the popularity of fighting and certainly its existence. This fighting was depicted as a rowdy affair, controlled by whites, and including drinking, heavy betting, and violence. News of a contest was passed by word of mouth; these gatherings were never mentioned in newspapers. It was said, "More money was won on wagers on fights than on horses."[33]

In 1808, at twenty-one years of age, Jack married Elizabeth Jones Broaddus, two years his junior and also from Caroline County. Their first child, Silas B. Gouldin, was born in 1809. According to Daisy, he was known as Si, and as the oldest son, he may well have accompanied Jack to cockfights and boxing matches. Daisy always indicated that Jack's brothers were involved with him, but here she seems to be confusing generations as she mentions the names of his sons, rather than his brothers. Perhaps it was through events such as these that Si first experienced a taste for alcohol. He died suddenly before his fiftieth birthday from erysipelas, a skin disease frequently associated with alcoholism.

It appears that Jack remained on his father's farm, helping to run it as he began to raise his own family. When his father, John, died in 1816, Jack became the farm manager, living in a separate household.[34] He continued in this role until 1826, when he moved to Essex County, where he again probably served as a farm manager. He did not own land until he was forty-seven years of age, in 1834.

In 1830 Jack lost his pocket book on his way from Port Royal to Port Tobago, a couple of miles south of Port Royal. It contained two fifty-dollar notes and "Bonds and due bills" for six thousand dollars, a substantial amount of money. He offered a hundred-dollar reward for its return.[35] Could this have been associated with Jack's interest in sporting matches? Unfortunately, we only know of Jack Gouldin's love of sporting events through the Turner narrative.

That the tradition of inter-plantation boxing matches has been maintained so widely in African American tradition underscores its significance to the black participants. Such matches validated the competitors' honor in a society that degraded them. There was nothing about these competitions that was relevant in this way to white society. If anything, they were considered distasteful by the aristocratic planter class.

Robert's identity is closely linked to this tradition, and it is through his success that these matches hold a major place in the Turner story. His connection to these events is both personal and emotional. This was how he maintained his dignity, his respect, and his identity under the crush of slavery. His superior athleticism, key to his identity in his homeland, continued to play a paramount role in this new order. Fighting shaped his life and defined who he was. It also gave Robert the influence to negotiate a solution to his enslaved existence. As long as Jack provided a platform for Robert to show off his prowess and gain standing in the eyes of those who witnessed his mastery, as long as Jack gave him the accoutrements of that stature (a mule to ride on, fine clothing to wear), and as long as Jack showed him special treatment, Robert would allow Jack to make money on him through his wagers. This was Robert's power over Jack Gouldin. He wanted his family to understand this and remember. While Robert's ability to win shaped his own life, we have strong indications that it played a defining role in Jack Gouldin's life as well.

It is through the Turner family narrative that Jack Gouldin takes on a personality. Although this is from the Turner point of view, it provides a sense of the man, with all his complexities. Nothing in the documents draw him out of the shadows. Perhaps we gain an inkling that he was considered to have a head for jurisprudence by his family, that he was innovative in his agricultural practices, that he seems to have been engaged in some kind of business, but we have no understanding of his passion for sporting events, nor his attitude toward those he enslaved. Through his will, it is possible to determine that his choice was to keep enslaved families together, but it is through Alec and Daisy that we hear: *"He was soft-spoken and didn't believe in whipping his slaves unlike some slave owners, because he said it spoiled them and hurt them—like a good cow. So he would try and punish them in other ways. He was nice with his slaves."*[36] He was paternalistic but believed he treated his slaves fairly and with their best interests at heart. In other words, he equated paternalism with benevolence.[37] *"He kept high tone slavery . . . he was nice with his slaves and they all got along. They were all friendly. He treated them just the same as some men abuse an automobile while another man takes good care of it."*[38] This treatment was indicated in a note Gouldin sent to his neighbor, Robert Holloway. In it Gouldin worried about one of his slaves called Moses, who was ailing and whom Jack had treated. Gouldin sent him home to his wife (who was enslaved by Holloway) not so much out of kindness, but because he believed Moses had contracted the sickness from his wife, and was concerned that Moses might infect Gouldin's "other hands." Gouldin asked his neighbor to allow Moses to stay with his wife and, as Holloway was also a doctor, to treat him medicinally if necessary.[39]

Daisy's constant reference to Gouldin as a sporting man also gives us insight into some of his other dealings, such as his purchase of Corbin's "race track lot" and his ownership of a black colt, almost certainly his "race horse," that was sold for five hundred dollars after he died.

When Gouldin bought Robert, he would have been living in Essex County in the Occupacia Swamp area where his forebears had lived. Once Gouldin realized he had a potential winner, Robert's life transformed dramatically. From uncontrollable pariah and chronic reprobate, constantly met with implacable force and punishment, he suddenly found himself in a role more to his liking—he was recognized and validated as a man; indeed he had a platform on which to affirm his superiority. He was relieved from working in the fields, something that he believed was beneath him, and he could concentrate on a challenge worthy of his attention. While he had probably never fought gamecocks, he learned quickly about training and handling birds from older handlers.[40] Boxing was almost certainly part of his African upbringing as it served as a powerful Yoruba masculinity ritual. When asked how her grandfather learned to box, Daisy said: *"They used to do it in Africa."*[41] With his commanding size and catlike reflexes, he was a natural, and boxing in Africa had marked his status as a man of iron.[42] Here was a way he could survive living under conditions he could not control. It was a transformational opportunity, and he seized it. A life based on physical prowess as a competitive athlete suited him very well indeed.

Having been born in Africa, Robert would have been viewed as different; at this time most of the enslaved population in Virginia had been born in America.[43] Speaking English with his mother's accent would have further set him apart. His steadfast resistance to carrying out the duties of a slave must have won him secret admiration, despite his arrogance and standoffishness. That he was selected by Gouldin to fight in the ring would have further singled him out, engendering him with both respect and envy, and perhaps a hesitant caution as his relationship with Gouldin grew.[44] Robert must have enjoyed other privileges as well. Daisy noted that he had *"different and better food"* than her father and his mother and that *"he dressed more or less like the white men"* and *"had a mule of his own."*[45] He also may have lived in close proximity to the gamecocks, rather than in the slave quarters. Gamecocks were carefully watched over, conditioned, trimmed, fed a rigid diet, and provided just the right number of sparring matches before a fight.[46] Robert's ability to win at both fighting gamecocks and boxing enhanced his reputation.

All this was unfolding somewhere between 1830 and 1833, depending on when Gouldin first acquired Robert. In February 1832, Charles C. Taliaferro died, leaving his estate in Caroline County to two nephews. He had 1,390 acres along the Rappahannock River, prime land for anyone with

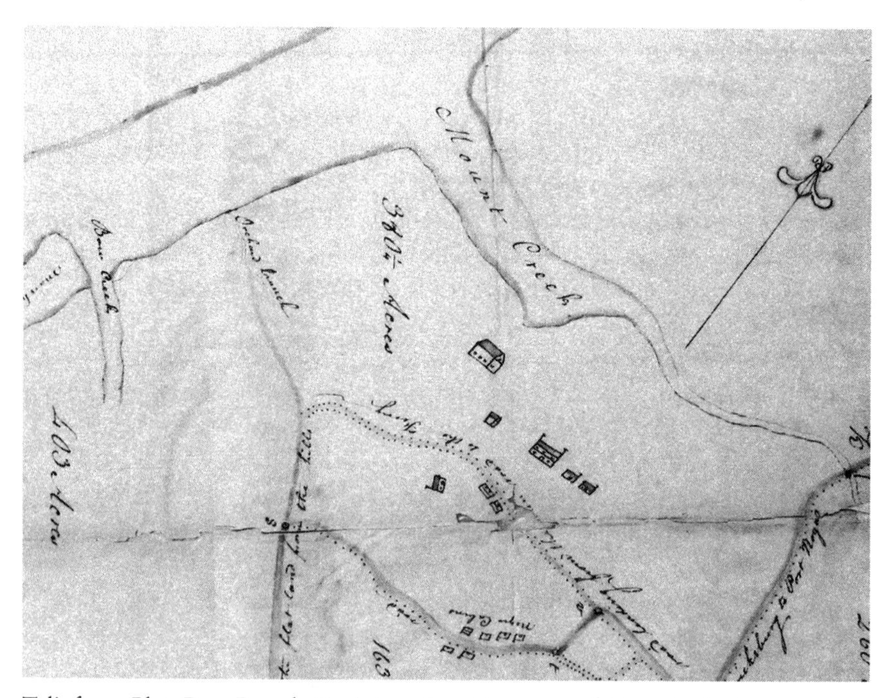

Taliaferro Plat, Port Royal, Virginia, 1832. Courtesy of Historical Court Records, Circuit Superior Court of Law and Chancery of Spotsylvania County, Fredericksburg, Virginia.

the money to buy it and a goodly number of slaves to work it. In 1834, Jack bought 720.5 acres of this land for the substantial sum of $17,009.[47]

Where did Gouldin find the resources for this purchase? It is possible, and even likely, that he won some good size wagers on Robert. Gouldin recognized Robert's prowess and saw that he received training. "*They had four or five men that used to fight and spar and teach the other men how they done it, how they won.*"[48] Likewise with the roosters: "*These cocks, they didn't start them right off . . . they trained them up.*"[49] Gouldin probably bred and raised his own gamecocks. He would have followed Robert's progress and, when he believed Robert was ready, set up matches with other plantation owners or taken Robert to events where slaveholders pitted their slaves against those of other plantations. Before the competitions began, contestants were often given whiskey.[50] Some slaveholders raised young fighters, training them and scheduling matches throughout the year at different plantations for money.[51] Daisy spoke of her grandfather being away from home a great deal, both boxing and fighting gamecocks.

A particularly good description of a boxing match is given by Henry Bibb, who was born into slavery in 1815 in Kentucky, the son of a slave mother and a state senator. After several unsuccessful attempts, he finally escaped and became an ardent abolitionist, telling his story in antislavery lectures. These became the source for his autobiography, *Narratives of the Life and Adventures of Henry Bibb, an American Slave.* Matches between bondsmen on one plantation were very different from those where the enslaved fought for different owners. Here drinking and gambling became prime ingredients:

> Those who make no profession of religion, resort to the woods in large numbers on that day to gamble, fight, get drunk, and break the Sabbath. This is often encouraged by the slaveholders. When they wish to have a little sport of that kind they go among the slaves and give them whiskey, to see them dance, "pat juber," sing and play the banjo. Then get them to wrestling, fighting, running foot races and butting each other like sheep. This is urged on by giving them whiskey, making bets on them; laying chips on one slave's head, and daring another to tip it off with his hand; and if he tipped it off, it would be called an insult, and cause a fight. Before fighting, the parties choose their seconds to stand by them while fighting; a ring or a circle is formed to fight in, and no one is allowed to enter the ring while they are fighting, but their seconds and the white gentlemen. They are not allowed to fight a duel, nor to use weapons of any kind. The blows are made by kicking, knocking and butting with their heads; they grab each other by their ears, and jam their heads together like sheep. If they are likely to hurt each other very bad, their masters would rap them with their walking canes, and make them stop. After fighting, they make friends, shake hands, and take a dram together, and there is no more of it.[52]

As indicated by Bibb's description, this is not a boxing match as we know it today. The "kicking," "knocking," and "butting heads" suggest African techniques, techniques Robert would have perfected and utilized. These techniques were different from those used by poor whites in bare-knuckle matches. It was the slaveholders' role to determine the rules of the fight. When big money was at stake, the fighting was especially vicious; even biting was allowed.[53]

Drinking always cast a shadow across such events. Josiah Henson, another former slave, described these competitions in his autobiography. Planters came together on Saturdays and Sundays to "gamble, run horses, or fight gamecocks and drink whiskey and brandy and water, all day long. . . . Of course quarrels and brawls of the most violent description were frequent consequences of these meetings."[54] Excessive drinking at such events was a way of life and fed by the availability of brandy and homemade brew, such as that made by Jack's father and probably continued by Jack. With large amounts of money at stake and extensive drinking, such matches were recipes for a waiting conflagration.

Robert was successful in cockfighting, winning a pair of silver spurs as a prize for Gouldin. We know this because his son, Alec, made a point of entering Gouldin's office, where he displayed his trophies (*"he had a room full of trophies"*)[55] and pocketing his father's silver spurs before escaping from the plantation. Daisy spoke frequently of her grandfather traveling *"everywhere"* winning *"medals and money"* for Gouldin, *"a big noted sportsman."*[56] Most likely, it was his wise management of the money gained through these bets that helped Gouldin acquire a large number of slaves and a considerable amount of land.

Daisy always claimed that Gouldin and her grandfather traveled *"to where Georgia and the Carolinas meet"* for a series of different competitions,[57] and it was at one of these matches where Robert fell in love with a Cherokee woman, known as Rose Silverbells, and brought her back to the plantation by ox cart. This was the significant part of the story. However, subsequent research indicated that other elements of the story had become distorted. Daisy said: *"My grandfather had been fighting, oh, certainly a year before he went to Georgia and Carolina to fight."*[58] Robert may well have gone as far as North Carolina to participate in various competitions. Daisy explained: *"They planned these meets."*[59] North Carolina, particularly in the northern and eastern regions, was an extension of the Virginia plantation culture, and there was an element of the population that reveled in such contests. "The North Carolinians have been accused of leading an idle and dissipated life; of being addicted to spirituous liquors, gambling, horseracing, cockfighting, boxing and gouging," wrote D. B. Warden in his discussion of North Carolinian manners and character.[60]

This was a period of constant conflict and unrest between the white settlers and their native neighbors, particularly in the southwestern parts of North Carolina and into Georgia. The white settlers' fear of the Cherokee, their lack of understanding of the Native American way of life and culture, and their insatiable desire for Cherokee land made coexistence untenable. When gold was found on Cherokee land in northern Georgia, removal became even more imperative.[61] In May 1830, Congress passed the Indian Removal Act, and it was clear that President Andrew Jackson's commitment to that course was unqualified. Cherokee in North Carolina lived a more isolated, traditional lifestyle than Cherokee in Georgia, Tennessee, and Alabama, and they were strongly opposed to removal.[62] The treatment of the Cherokee and the resulting Trail of Tears, the forced exodus of the Cherokee from their homeland by the U.S. government in 1838, is a shocking story.

The region where Georgia and the Carolinas join is mountainous land, in the foothills of the Great Smoky Mountains, and there are no plantations in the region. While there were both cockfights and bare-knuckle boxing matches in the area, it is doubtful Gouldin would have traveled that distance over difficult terrain for one competition or, for that matter, for a series of competitions. This country seems well out of Gouldin's element. It is much more likely that this is a part of Rose's story, which has been forgotten and compressed over the years. Daisy acknowledged that the Cherokee were having difficulty with the white settlers living in their midst: "*You know the white people had been fighting very hard and desperately to get the Indians under control. But the Indians had been fighting back and had put the terror in the white people.*"[63] She told this story about her grandmother:

> *She was born down between Georgia and Carolina. That is where the tribe lived of purebred Cherokee Indians. They called [her father or uncle]*[64] *White Cloud. That's where she was born in this Indian camp. And my grandfather was down there fighting for old Gouldin, when he came on this Indian camp . . . and he fell in love with her at once, and she with him. And, of course, old Gouldin, being a sport and a factor and a livewire everywhere, he arranged it so that the Indian girl, he took her back to Virginia to be on his plantation. But he didn't want to make them slaves like the other slaves, and they couldn't ever be, cause they was different anyway, but that is why he put her to sewing, and let them have a different camp on the white people's ground. They didn't live in the slave quarters. They had this little cabin . . . on the white people's ground, and the place was all laid off.*[65]

This story is a consistent part of the Turner narrative and is one of the more problematic stories of the saga: not whether it happened, but how it happened and over what length of time. Often Daisy referred to her grandmother as "Princess Silverbells," a doubtful moniker, and certainly added by Daisy and her sisters at a later date, when the Indian princess motif became popular at the turn of the century. Rose was also known as Rosa or Rosabel, the latter a contraction of Rose Silverbells. In some cases, the Cherokee were known to fasten bells to their clothing or moccasins,[66] and her name may be indicative of this. When asked about the name "Silverbells," Daisy said: *"The Indians named her that."*[67] In other words, this was the English version of her Indian name.

From the family story, there is absolute certainty that Rose was Cherokee, and it is difficult to believe that Alec would be mistaken about this. Still, the question arises, when did she come to Virginia? Daisy said that Jack Gouldin brought Rose home to his plantation from her birthplace. This would have meant she was going voluntarily from freedom into slavery. Daisy related that Rose *"didn't understand slavery."*[68] Even so, it is doubtful that she would choose to be enslaved. She appears to have been dark skinned as in all the records she is described as a Negro or noted by *N*. She is never described as Cherokee or Native American. What happened that caused her to leave her home and how she was enslaved remains lost to us. A traumatic event must have occurred. Kinship ties were enduring and all-important to the Cherokee;[69] to part with one's family forever was almost unthinkable. It is doubtful that Rose voluntarily turned her back on her family. It is more likely that some misfortune befell her or she was stolen away and sold into slavery.

I discovered that she was already a slave by the time Robert met her, through a court case in which Jack Gouldin's ownership of Rose was dis-

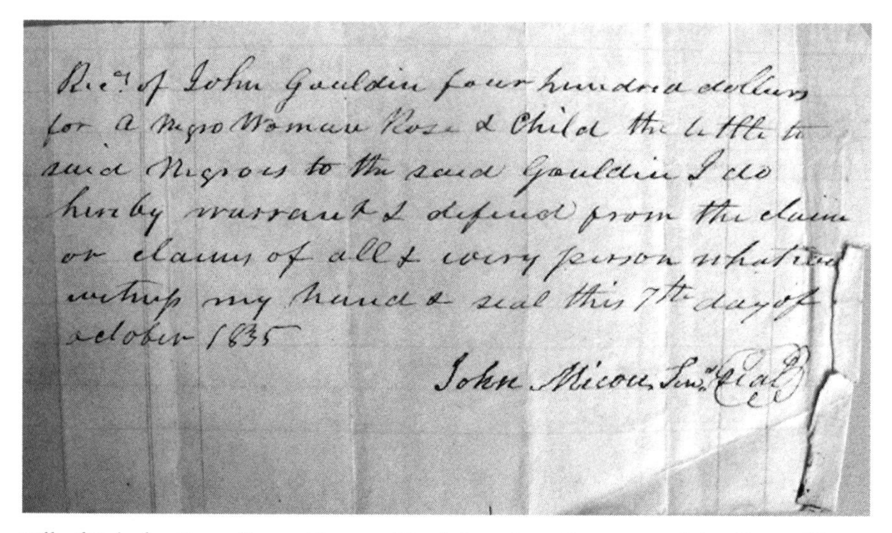

Rec.d of John Gouldin four hundred dollars for a Negro Woman Rose & Child the title to said Negroes to the said Gouldin I do hereby warrant & defend from the claim or claims of all & every person whatever witness my hand & seal this 7th day of October 1835

John Micou Jun.r {Seal}

Bill of Sale for Rose, Essex County, Virginia, 1849. Courtesy of the Central Rappahannock Heritage Center, Fredericksburg, Virginia.

puted by the children of her former owner. The documents describe Rose as a "Negro woman." She belonged to John Micou of Essex County and probably first met Robert between 1831 and 1833, when he was competing at cockfights and boxing matches. She had her first child, George, by Robert in late 1834 or early 1835, as he was described as "little above an infant" when Gouldin bought both George and twenty-five-year-old Rose on October 7, 1835 for four hundred dollars.[70] Micou was moving from Essex County to Mississippi when Gouldin offered to buy her and her child because he "owned her husband." Micou needed the money to prepare for his trip, and as Rose was lame in her hip, she would have been unable to walk the distance.

This court case indicates something else. Robert had been fighting in Essex County, probably before 1834 when Jack bought the Taliaferro property. Robert considered Rose his wife and George his son, and Alec regarded George as his full brother. In 1849, Gouldin stated that Rose and her children, George, Susan, and Alec, were in his possession. Alec would have been four. Unfortunately, there is no mention of Robert to suggest whether he was still living in 1849.

Such a court case indicates the distortion that has taken place in the narrative. The crux of the story, its emotional core immortalized in the Turner narrative, is that Jack Gouldin bought Rose for Robert: "*the Master trying to please my grandfather in every way he could allowed him to marry her . . . and then she was allowed to go with my grandfather.*"[71] He carried her back by ox cart (because she was lame) to Hays Mount in Caroline County. Daisy's narrative also gives further insight into Robert, offering a description that indicated that he got on well with people if he did not feel belittled. "*My grandfather was the type that . . . was friendly and tried to get on, and was learning with each and everybody.*"[72]

Jack Gouldin lived in Essex County from 1826 until 1834, and it was probably during this period that he gained the money to return to Caroline County to buy Hays Mount, as the Taliaferro parcel was known, in 1834.[73] He bought this land for its assessed value of $17,009, more than $500,000 in today's money. He also acquired thirty-seven slaves, a major increase from the five he owned the year before.[74] He most likely gained the bulk of these with the land he bought. It is difficult to comprehend how Gouldin acquired such wealth. There is nothing that signals this change in his economic status. The next year Jack added only one slave, probably Rose.[75] Rose joined Robert at Hays Mount in October 1835. According to Daisy, Gouldin's wife admired Rose's beaded dress and moccasins, and so Rose became seamstress for the plantation: "*and when she found that she could sew and mend . . . they knew how valuable she would be.*"[76]

We only know that Rose was Cherokee from the Turner family story. Daisy's older sisters knew Rose well, and Daisy remembered her: "*Oh, yes! Indian! Talked it, and lived it, and used it.*"[77] Apparently, Alec learned Cherokee from his mother and spoke it with her. Cherokee women had a strong hold on the social and economic welfare of their families. Membership in one of the seven clans was determined through one's mother; thus families living in clusters were related maternally. Women were the agriculturalists, as well as the owners and managers of the home and selectors of their marriage and sexual partners.[78] They were very much equals with their husbands. Certainly, Rose was the dominant parent in Alec's life.

Rose's first son, George, was born around 1835.[79] We do not know if George was as interested in family heritage as was his younger brother Alec. Alexander "Alec" Burekly was born August 10, 1845, probably two years after his older sister Susan.[80] Often Robert was away a week at a time,[81] and Alec was too young to remember a great deal about his father. He told his children that he was "*gone most of the time.*" But he did recall that Jack Gouldin treated Robert differently than he did the other slaves:

> *He always seemed to have awful good food—used to give him little bits and pieces. But he had much better and a different food than he and his mother had all the time. . . . His father seemed to have a sort of authority like that . . . most of the Negro slaves didn't seem to have. He was nice with all the slaves. Everybody liked him. But he had a different way, and he was with the white folks a lot. But that was because his master used to like to show him off. He used to go with his master to these places. . . . he had a mule of his own. . . . of course, the master kept him dressed right up. Because he didn't get no money, only just a little to spend. And father told how every once in a while on holidays or when they had won a big fight, that the master would give him a box of these peculiar cigars.*[82]

We hear little of Rose's role as seamstress, except that she became a favorite of the Gouldins and an indispensable person on the plantation. She was in charge of making slave clothing as well as finer wear for those in the big house. Apparently, there were a number of women who made slave clothing in, as Daisy put it, a series of apartments. These women did not work in the fields; producing clothing for the other slaves was a full-time occupation. One of Rose's specialties was making "*those red coats for the white men to wear when they went horseback riding,*"[83] which were indicative of the hunt, one of Jack's favorite sporting activities and a pastime of the gentry. The red coats symbolized that Jack was part of an elite club, or so I thought until two suggestive indicators made me reexamine my assumption.

The first of these was the commonplace book kept by William R. Bernard from 1847 until 1850.[84] He lived just a few miles from Jack Gouldin at Gaymont and kept track of Gaymont's visitors. Bernard had frequent dinner parties, and one of his slaves is said to have commented: "Dey wuz mouty frien'ly wid all de qual'ty folks, 'speshully dose on de nex' plantation an' in ole Po't Royal. Dey had plenty money an' de bes' ob ebything to eat an' drink, an' parties wuz gwine on mos'eby week."[85] Although the book was filled with names of "quality folk" from neighboring plantations, the name Gouldin was significantly absent.

The omission of the Gouldins made me wonder if Jack Gouldin and his family were shunned by the elite of Caroline County plantation society. I came back to the Broaddus genealogy and the use of "uncultivated." Was this indicative of class? Was his participation in inter-plantation competitions looked down upon by the more refined gentry? We know that all classes engaged in cockfighting, but by the 1830s, the gentry tended more to gracious living than to participation in events of violence. The aristocratic slaveholders took pride in their well-bred family heritage, a curious intellect, an emphasis on a wide-ranging education, and a cosmopolitan lifestyle. They were society's leaders, socially, culturally, economically, and entrepreneurially. They gained and maintained their wealth through inheritance, mercantile interests, shrewd investments, constant diligence, and marriages with suitable and wealthy mates. They did not gain their prosperity through wagering and sporting competitions.[86]

The second indicator that the Gouldins may not have been held in high regard came from a diary of Kate Buckner, the twenty-two-year-old daughter of William Buckner, who lived on the plantation next to Jack Gouldin. The diary is from March 1857 until late October the same year. Although the Liberty Baptist Church was her congregation, Kate often attended Bethesda, the Gouldin's church, where she felt the preaching of Andrew Broaddus was superior. Much of her time was taken up with her family, sewing, and chores such as painting the summerhouse. She mentioned a number of neighbors with whom she visited, picked berries, and walked, but Jack Gouldin's daughter Bettie, near Kate in age, was never mentioned. In addition to Jack's household, three of his married offspring and their children lived nearby. Proximity should ensure at least a reference to one of the Gouldins, and indeed, two other neighbors, Mrs. Dunn and Catherine Merryman, are mentioned frequently. One July evening, Kate attended a local picnic that did not meet her expectations: "T. R. Thornton here this morning and promised to come by for us to go to the picnic in the evening. We went early, staid only a short time. No nice people there."[87] Is this an oblique reference to the Gouldins? We cannot know, but the lack of mention of any Gouldin by name is another indication that the Gouldins do not appear to have been an intimate part of the community.

While the prime land and major estates were along the Rappahannock, agriculture was the focus of Caroline County. The community was class conscious, with wealthy landowners in the top echelon, and yeoman farmers and tradesmen below them. Further down were poor whites and freed blacks, and at the very bottom were the enslaved. In advertisements of land sales, the neighborhood was described as "well settled and a cultivated and excellent society equal to any in Virginia," and in another, "the society is unsurpassed."[88] This rosy view of the neighborhood was countered by bitter local disputes waged in the courts. One case that flared about the same time as these land sales was an altercation between John W. Holloway and Joseph M. Richerson that began with Holloway teasing Richerson about a childhood event. According to Holloway, Richerson "snagged" his testicles on a fence. Richerson denied this, tempers flared, and they came to fisticuffs. Then Holloway shot Richerson, for which he was fined $250 and sent to jail for six months.[89]

New evangelistic movements at this time were pressuring all elements of society to forego such devilish pursuits as drinking and gambling. Still, many were irresistibly drawn to such events. Elliott Gorn documented only white boxing matches, asserting that they were carried on by lower-class whites, generally living in the backwoods.[90] Through slave narratives, we know that enslaved bondsmen participated in boxing matches both on individual plantations and between plantations, and that when these occurred between plantations, it was the owners who initiated them. It is likely that these owners were not considered plantation gentry, but rather the owners of smaller farms with just a few enslaved workers. Because there is such a paucity of written records, we can assume that these events were either held without the knowledge of the public or were dismissed as not worthy of notice.

How Jack Gouldin was perceived in taking part in these matches, and apparently winning consistently, is difficult to assess 150 years after his death. His family remembers he was wealthy, not how his wealth was attained. Turner testimony suggests another possibility. The term *uncultivated* adds credence to this testimony. As long as Robert was fighting, he continued to win money for Gouldin, at least for another ten or twelve years. Jack continued to buy land and by 1846 had bought all of Taliaferro's original estate and more. He acquired seventy-one slaves, as well as nineteen horses and mules and a four-wheel carriage. He was doing very well for himself.

It is difficult to reconcile Jack Gouldin's soft-spoken manner as described by Daisy with the violence he was a part of at these fights. Henry Bibb noted it, and William Faulkner left no doubt in his rendering of a match in *Absalom, Absalom!*: "in the center two of his wild Negroes fighting, naked, fighting not like white men fight, with rules or weapons, but like Negroes fight to hurt one another quick and bad."[91] Supposedly, the owners, who both staged and supervised the event, would step in to keep a fight from becoming dangerous, but with money riding on the outcome, sometimes they waited too long. Daisy told of a Fourth of July event, when Robert was pitted against another slave from Kingston, Jamaica. "*When the fight took place, they fought until Grandfather killed this man. He died right there, hands and fists fighting him. After he killed this man fighting, then they couldn't make him fight anymore. Every time they had a match, he wouldn't fight, and they couldn't do much more with him."*[92] She commented another time, "*And the old master was discouraged too.*"[93]

This must have been a brutal fight, two men in their prime, using their heads, butting, kicking, hitting, biting. Robert never recovered from it. "*He got angry with himself and everybody.*"[94] After a fight, the two combatants were supposed to "make friends, shake hands, and take a dram together."[95] It is evident that Robert was his own man, no matter what the circumstances. His actions reveal the inner man, not the arrogant, unfeeling victor Daisy described who cared for nothing "*and thought he could win the world . . . like Hitler.*"[96] He wanted no part of a match that allowed him to kill his opponent. There was no negotiating this. He would no longer compete.

One wonders about the effect of the match on Jack Gouldin. According to Daisy and Alec, Gouldin was "*discouraged.*" We cannot know for sure what this meant, but in 1847 Jack Gouldin did something that seems out of character. He took a leadership role in establishing the Bethesda Baptist Church, helping a group of disgruntled parishioners from the Liberty Baptist Church establish a new church that was based on the prohibition of the manufacture, sale, serving of, or imbibing of intoxicating liquors. Jack Gouldin had been a member of the Liberty Baptist Church since November 23, 1839, and his name was linked with thirteen enslaved members who were listed in the front of the Liberty Baptist Church Minutes, 1830–1851, as black members.[97] Among these was Robert's name, although "dead" was written after his name. All we can be sure of is that his death occurred before 1851, when the book ended.

The Baptist movement swept through both Essex and Caroline Counties in the 1770s, and the Upper Essex Baptist Church was founded in 1772. By 1810, the church had over 210 members.[98] In Caroline County, the Baptists followed a similar trajectory. After the Revolutionary War, there was a rapid expansion of the Baptists. At first, there was a division between the Baptists, who generally lacked wealth or education, and the gentry, who were associated with the Anglican tradition. The Baptist worldview was democratic, incorporating both whites and blacks as essentially equal.[99] Its emphasis on singing held great appeal for the enslaved. Upper Zion was organized as early as 1774, and it was here that Jack Gouldin was first a member.[100] Church records have been lost, but with his sporting lifestyle, it is hard to imagine that the Baptist church was a strong part of his life.

Temperance societies had been part of the Baptist church since 1826, when Abner W. Clopton launched the Virginia Society for the Promotion of Temperance.[101] In 1836, there was an increasing emphasis placed on the evils of alcoholic beverages and the offensiveness of indulgence. In his leadership role at Bethesda, Gouldin hosted meetings and served on the committee to "purchase a lot of land at some convenient point on which to erect a house for the worship of God."[102] By September 1847, that decision had been made, and a brick structure was erected by December of the following year.[103]

We know from tax records that at sixty years of age, Jack Gouldin was one of the wealthiest men in Caroline County. And we can follow his role at Bethesda through church records. The Gouldin family became pillars of the Baptist church, with Jack's sons Tom and Frank taking on their father's role as he aged. During this same period, Gouldin was focused on farming, buying more land, and acquiring business interests such as a warehouse lot on Gassells wharf in Fredericksburg in 1851.[104] Virginia's agricultural economy was revitalized with new scientific practices, and Jack Gouldin was in the forefront, employing the newest methods, including using marl as fertilizer, rotating crops, and employing the most modern equipment.[105]

When Robert refused to fight any more, Gouldin discovered he was skillful with a circular saw and could do carpentry work. Alec could just remember him at this point and described him to his children as *"a sporting man, but he drank heavy, he was heavy, and a fighter, and he didn't care for anything."*[106] Robert's body would have absorbed a great deal of punishment during his years of fighting, and while still a relatively young man of around forty, he must have appeared older than he was, particularly to young Alec.

Alec was close to his mother but did not like his father much. I wondered about this, but Daisy was allusive when questioned about their relationship. She certainly condemned her grandfather for *"selling his own people."*[107] The most direct response Daisy gave me was that *"he didn't seem to care for the boy at all. And Papu was very peculiar—something about him. Standoffish, you know, with anybody or anything he didn't like. And his father wasn't too strong on him."*[108] On another occasion, she answered: *"No, he didn't like his father, but he knew him and remembered him. His father had taught him. And Father was smart . . . because everything that his father had taught him, he remembered to a hairline."*[109] One time she simply replied: *"He was suspicious of everybody."*[110]

It is not surprising that once Robert stopped fighting, and particularly after the death of his opponent, he would turn to drink. He probably acquired the taste for alcohol, and the opportunity to consume it, at his competitions. It is fortunate for his family that despite negative feelings toward his father, Alec listened carefully and retained so much of what his father related, for he could not have been more than five or six years old at this time. *"He remembered his father being out and singing these southern songs and dancing."*[111] He recalled his father's stories, his situation, how he dressed, and that everyone seemed to like him.

Despite his status, Robert was still enslaved. Gouldin's major crop was wheat, and he wanted a larger barn for wheat storage. Robert was engaged in building the barn when part of the structure collapsed, crushing and killing him. Because of Robert's reputation as plantation champion, his death would have been noted within both the enslaved and the white communities. The funeral, rooted in African tradition, was an important event in the slave lifecycle. It could be held as long as a month after the burial. Traditionally, the body was escorted to the burial ground by a torchlit procession, and this would have been the case for a man of Robert's status.[112] He would have been carried to the graveyard of the enslaved, just a short distance below the big house, toward the Rappahannock. In contrast to the burial, the funeral was a celebration of respect for the dead, which included singing, dancing, and, before Gouldin had taken up abstinence, drinking.[113]

As Robert had been a well-known boxer and gamecock fighter, his funeral would have been well attended by both races. A funeral cake was prepared for the celebration, and it seems that young Alec took a proprietary interest in it: "*Father said at funerals they always had a special funeral cake, just like a wedding cake. . . . It was cut in little pieces and . . . all the mourners took a piece . . . just like a pound cake or fruit cake, a very rich cake.*"[114] The cake was placed on top of a cabinet, and Alec marshaled his friends to help him reach it:

> *He was the ringleader. . . . He told us many times how he had climbed on chairs and the table and reached up to the top of a cupboard where the cake had been set and cut or scratched with his hand, pieces out of this cake. . . .*[115]
>
> *Instead of just taking one little piece, he had been back two or three times cutting slices out of this cake. Until he fell and that was what broke the thing up. Then they found out it was him that had been at this cake. And so you see he was steadily being bad.*[116]

Alec's memory of the funeral became a significant one for the Turner family, and Daisy recounted it a number of times. She also remarked that for Alec these two events around her grandfather's funeral were "*the beginning of his really plainly remembering different occasions. He knew that he wasn't quite five.*"[117]

> *My father told us about this very special half-breed colored man—mulatto, tall and thin, one of the slaves that was a preacher. He was educated . . . and he was known all over. . . .*[118]
>
> *They say he could preach, oh, from way back. Why he just called the angels out.*[119]
>
> *The white masters had given the preacher special clothes to wear, and Father remembered the long coat and the necktie that he wore always at these funerals.*[120]
>
> *They'd start the funeral anywhere around nine o'clock and it would be three or four before they got the person buried.*[121]

> *There were these singers that could sing . . . spirituals . . . and they played the music. . . . The minister had just commenced preaching the sermon when this storm came up, and he said it wasn't an ordinary storm. It was a storm that just rocked everything [a hurricane] . . . the rain and the hail were coming down and all of those people out in the open with no . . . shelter. This was in the summertime, warm weather. . . . Father says that this minister took off his coat, and it was one of those long tailcoats that come almost down to his ankles. . . . He was in this shirt thing that he had on. And Father said he threw up his hands, just like that [Daisy demonstrated by throwing up her own hands to heaven] and he prayed a prayer. And he said the storm stopped. The wind stopped blowing, and the hail and the rain stopped, and the rainbow came out. The rainbow came out and shone. . . . He said it cleared right up so that my grandfather's funeral went on.*[122]

Long after the event, the rainbow served as a symbol that Alec used repeatedly, and his daughters used rainbows to represent something both extraordinary and positive. One time, Daisy waved some napkins decorated with rainbows at me, exclaiming that her nephew Godfrey Hall had sent them to her for her birthday, "*because he remembered that story that my father told.*"[123] The rainbow might also have held significance for Robert. Had he ever spoken of this to his son? If so, this might bestow greater meaning for Alec. The rainbow serpent is a significant spirit for the Yoruba, known as Ananyidohoe, and those who held it sacred had rituals they must perform and taboos they must keep. As long as the individual maintained these strictures, the rainbow serpent would bestow abundance and happiness.[124] Whether or not the rainbow had further connotations, Alec was touched by what he witnessed. On another occasion, Daisy stated that her father was converted when he saw the manifestation of the power of the preacher's prayer, "*he prayed for the wind and the storm to cease. And everything stopped. Just like magic. The sun came out, and a rainbow, so that they was able to continue with the funeral.*"[125]

According to Daisy, many people attended Robert's funeral, including both white planters and slaves. After the Nat Turner uprising in 1831, slave gatherings were banned. As late as February 8, 1864, a case was brought in Caroline County against Dr. Wesley Wright for holding such a funeral, and itinerant preachers were banned;[126] however, some plantation owners maintained a blind eye to this prohibition. Funerals were an important rite to the slave community.[127] As a benevolent master and a strong Baptist, Jack Gouldin may well have believed that such a funeral was closely associated with the moral and religious instruction of his slaves and that it was a tradition worth honoring for such a special slave. Daisy always claimed an itinerant preacher presided: "*He was known all over the south, going to different officials and prominent men's funerals.*"[128] The slave preacher was known for his oratory skills and his prodigious memory to recall biblical passages.[129] Not only could he *"call the angels out,"* but his delivery was dramatic.[130] The power that an individual could stop the rain was a common folk belief, and Daisy told of her father, in later life, praying for most of a day to stop a three-day downpour.[131] That he was successful was seen as a testament to his faith and the power of prayer.

Those who considered themselves enlightened masters often viewed preaching as a boon to the morality and spiritual needs of their slaves. On some plantations, the preacher, though enslaved, was exempt from manual labor. White observers described such an individual as "conscious of his own importance," and going about "all dressed up in frock coat and store bought shoes."[132] An itinerant preacher would have been the only religious leader those enslaved on the Gouldin plantation had, for they attended Bethesda Baptist Church, which had just a white minister until the appointment of John Pendleton Jr., a former Gouldin slave, after the Civil War.[133]

Daisy said, *"everything changed in a way,"* after Robert's funeral.[134] It was an ending for young Alec, and his witnessing of the power of prayer forged the strong religious underpinnings that sustained him throughout his life. Robert left a strong legacy. He maintained his identity and honor despite living under the weight of slavery. In return for being exploited by Jack Gouldin, Robert maintained an identity that embodied respect and honor. This had been important in his homeland, and it was important in Virginia. He accepted his agency in the slave trade. He had been both warrior and trader. He had endured the terrifying Middle Passage into an unknown world, which he faced with the unbending defiance suitable of a Yoruba warrior. And he had negotiated his profession based on athleticism and techniques forged in his homeland. He never lost his identity. Under enslavement, there was a shift in orientation. His name changed, his clothing was transformed, but he still walked tall and proudly, until he believed that he had crossed a line—his line and no one else's—after which he could not be swayed. He was still Alessi.

If he had lived longer, or if Alec had been older when his father died, we might have more details of his life in both Africa and Virginia, but Robert remains the progenitor of the Turner family in America. The essence of his life has been maintained and carried on in memory, as well as through physical inheritance—all of his great-grandsons were outstanding athletes. Robert bequeathed a strong sense of identity and rootedness to his family. This does not mean that his enslavement had no lasting consequences, nor that he escaped unscathed, only that he was able to maintain his identity through sheer force of will and through the fortuitous circumstance that Jack Gouldin was a *"sporting man."*

CHAPTER 4

Plantation Life

> Old Gouldin, he owned twelve square miles on the Rappahannock River.
> —Daisy Turner, interview with author, January 4, 1984

By the time Alec Turner was born in 1845, Jack Gouldin was fifty-eight years old and had become one of the richest landowners in Caroline County, if not a member of the aristocracy. Gouldin seemed old to Alec,[1] and indeed Alec's view of the plantation was from youthful eyes; nevertheless, he clearly absorbed the full import of his lot as an enslaved individual and gradually determined to take action to free himself.

Daisy told me repeatedly that Jack Gouldin owned twelve square miles on the Rappahannock River, and perhaps this is what Gouldin himself said. It certainly makes the statement that his landholdings were extensive,

Hays Mount, Port Royal, Virginia, 1985. Courtesy of the Vermont Folklife Center, Middlebury, Vermont, photograph by Jane Beck.

and while he owned over two thousand acres at the end of his life, this is closer to three square miles. Interestingly, he referred to his land as a farm, rather than a plantation.[2] The latter was defined as a large farming operation with twenty or more slaves.[3] The average farm of the day was about two hundred acres—a tenth of the size of Gouldin's holdings.[4]

Most of the twenty slave cabins on Gouldin's lands were at a distance and out of view of the big house.[5] Alec's mother's cabin was an exception, as it was at the edge of the manor yard with easy access to the Gouldin residence.[6] This was most likely a practical consideration due to Rose's role as plantation seamstress. Rose's dwelling, lathed and plastered with a dirt floor, was small but clean, with a stone chimney at one end and a loft for sleeping above. The cracks were chinked with clay, and the whitewashed walls were scrubbed to keep ahead of the black residue from countless fires. Outside she kept a well-tended garden with peppers, collards, potatoes, turnips, peas, and watermelons, as well as a small flock of hens. It was from his mother that Alec gained his knowledge of planting by the moon. He learned to distinguish the different kinds of growing moons—for example, vegetables with vines were planted on a new moon. The garden produce, eggs, and the occasional chicken, possum, raccoon, or muskrat supplemented the staple diet of salt pork and cornmeal. One of Alec's favorite foods was hoecakes made from a mixture of cornmeal, water, lard, and salt pork or slab bacon and cooked over the open fire on a skillet, or if a skillet were not available, on a hoe—hence the name. Even as a grown man he enjoyed hoecakes.[7] In season there were berries for the picking—wild blackberries could be had easily, but Jack Gouldin probably also had beds of strawberries and raspberries, and an orchard with cherries and peaches. Later in life, Alec made sure his family enjoyed similar fruits from his own orchard of apples, plums, and peaches.

When Alec was a boy, his household included George, Susan, and later, after his father died, two half siblings, Lindsey and Judy Coleman.[8] Alec remained close to his siblings, at least George and Lindsey. This attested to a deep-seated sense of the importance of family developed in early life.[9] Although there was friction between Alec and his father, Rose was a major figure in his life.[10] From her he felt a warm encompassing love despite the interferences demanded by enslavement, and from her he retained many tenets of Cherokee culture, including the Cherokee language and an extensive knowledge of plants and herbal remedies. Rose believed in watching the moon for growing herbs in her garden and referred to the best time to plant these as on the healing moon. She taught him to recognize herbs, taking him with her as she gathered them along the creeks, on the edge of fields, and in the woods on a Sunday. She taught him how to dry them or steep them in a kettle over the fire for a variety of tonics, baths, salves, ointments, and remedies for deadly diseases such as diphtheria. He learned the value of ginseng, red oak bark, wormwood, catnip, and thoroughwort, as well as how to boil a poisonous snake with a number of different herbs to provide a mixture to control weeds and how to make a liniment out of skunk's oil.

He remembered his mother constantly at work on her treadle sewing machine, another instance of Gouldin's attention to innovation and something he provided especially for her to make red foxhunting coats for the men, fashionable gowns for the ladies, and coarse homespun clothing for the slaves.[11] As the plantation seamstress, her cabin contained bolts of cloth, especially linen, linsey-woolsey, and cotton for the bulk of her work.

> *My father was a little boy with this Indian mother, and she used to sew for the missus up at the big white house. She had a cabin right over near the big house. . . . She did all the sewing for the ladies at the big white house, and she made those funny garments that they had for the slaves. They was a kind of brown material and very coarse. She made pants, suits, skirts, and dresses—all the same kind of material. So, she was sewing and doing everything that was agreeable, and so she was treated a little bit better.*[12]

Her position as seamstress, along with her sewing machine, gave Rose status within the hierarchy of the enslaved.[13] Likewise, the fact that her cabin was the one closest to the big house added to this perception. Rose was allowed to keep her young children with her, while those women who worked in the fields had to leave their young ones behind with an elderly slave woman too old for labor.[14]

As a small boy, Alec experienced a certain freedom to his movements. This was common on plantations with children of six and younger.[15] He played around his mother's cabin and interacted with the white children around the big house. He also spent time with his cohorts from the slave quarters, where the play was in some instances more violent than we would find acceptable today. Young ones would butt heads—getting down on their hands and knees and then coming together much as two rams would. Alec also remembered pulling sticks, an activity that required the two competitors to sit facing each other, with the soles of their feet against each other and their hands holding a common stick. The winner was the one who succeeded in pulling his opponent from the sitting position.[16] Wrestling, another popular entertainment, often consisted of kicking, biting, scratching, even hair pulling. If the fighting grew too intense, youngsters would be made to take part in "cutting jackets." A member of the older generation would strip off their clothing and make them cut switches. Then they would whip each other until they had enough fighting. The result was that such occasions did not come up again so frequently.[17]

Even at a young age, athletic prowess was a great source of pride for these enslaved children. Alec's grandson George Hall told me proudly that "*my grandfather used to tell me . . . that the only athletic events that they used to do was running, jumping, and fighting. And there was nobody on that plantation that could take him in any of those things.*"[18] This, of course, would gain Alec the admiration of his peers and undoubtedly a leadership role. It certainly would not escape the notice of Jack Gouldin.

The Gouldin house, one that Daisy frequently referred to as a mansion, still stands today. The oldest part of the dwelling, thought to date from the late 1700s, is a one-and-a-half-story structure that sits over the kitchen, which was built over a spring. The larger, two-story addition was thought to have been added by Charles Taliaferro, but this may well have been Jack's doing as in 1838 his taxes increased by $150, indicative of a substantial addition, with the notation "to new house add $150 fee."[19] The structure contains fourteen rooms with three chimneys—two at either end of the dwelling, and one that separates the newer addition from the original house.

Hays Mount, as the Gouldin house was called, sits on one of several terraces about one mile from, and over 150 feet above, the Rappahannock River.[20] Its height was desirable as a healthy location. During the hot summer months, those who could afford it moved to higher ground to escape the malaria of the lowlands.[21] Today there is no longer a view of the river, but during Alec's time there, it was probably open to the waterway that winds its way in a large arc below.

While the house faces west toward the river, to the east it overlooks the cultivated fields. In Alec's day, there were outbuildings, which gave the appearance of a small village with structures including barns, stables, a carriage house, a granary, a carpenter's shop, a corncrib, a root cellar, a meat house, a springhouse, a milk house, and an icehouse.[22] While a number of farmers in Caroline County raised tobacco (as had his father and his second son, Tom) Jack Gouldin grew mainly wheat, corn, and oats.[23]

The large plantation owners and the wealthiest families held the most fertile land along the valley of the Rappahannock, while the smaller farmers settled on the upland tracts of the backland, where Jack Gouldin's father and his uncle Jesse had owned property. Of his two thousand acres, Gouldin owned eleven hundred acres of fields and pastures, which stretched out over flats of sandy clay loam from the Rappahannock to the low hills extending a few miles west of the river. The river land was known for its fertility.[24] In the lowland, there was a large marsh, drained by a canal or manmade ditch leading to the river. On higher ground, the fields were vast, broad, and flat, the perfect landscape for Jack's foxhunting.

Gouldin's household and extensive acreage ran smoothly on the backs of his enslaved labor force. During Alec's youth in the 1850s, there were anywhere from seventy to ninety-two "servants" who worked the fields with teams of mules, horses, and oxen.[25] They cleared land, repaired fences, built structures, drained the wet land with ditches, broadcast seed, hoed corn, cut oats and hay, and cradled wheat.[26] Many slave work songs and spirituals came from this work experience. Heavy and monotonous labor was eased by song. Alec remembered listening to the men singing as they cradled the wheat—the typical call and response in which the lead worker sings out a phrase and the rest respond with a variation or refrain. He loved to hear the cadence and blending of their voices drifting up from the fields and the rhythmic sweep of the cradles.

> Well, come along Moses and don't get lost,
> Sitting in the golden altar.
> Well, stretch your rod and come along cross,
> Sitting in the golden altar.
> Well, John saw the number, John saw the number,
> John saw the holy number, Sitting in the golden altar.
>
> "JOHN SAW THE HOLY NUMBER"

From an early age, Alec absorbed the harmonies, the beat, and the improvisation that nourished his soul and grew within him. His love of these spirituals sustained him throughout his life. He made sure that his children knew and cherished these songs, singing them with fervor as his powerful tenor filled a room.

Other workers were engaged in home manufacture such as weaving baskets, coopering, carpentry, and the tanning of hides. Many took great pride in the mastery of these crafts. They butchered hogs and the occasional beef, they churned butter, made cheese, extracted honey from beehives;[27] during the spring, they operated the fishery, pulling seine and salting away the catch in barrels of brine, mostly for plantation consumption but some for local sale or barter.

They carried out all the domestic chores as well: preparing food, rendering lard, making soap and candles, salting pork and fish, housekeeping, looking after children, and the endless chore of spinning and sewing all matter of clothing. The plantation was a self-sufficient unit overseen by the owner and a manager. Alec always told his children that the field hands, both men and women, were the darkest in skin color and lived the farthest away from the big house, while the house servants were usually lighter in complexion and lived nearer, or in, the big house. He described how different the enslaved were from one another, coming from a variety of regions and backgrounds, and explained how the institution of slavery affected each one uniquely and in a host of negative ways.

> *Some of them you could break their spirit easy. While others, you could never break their spirit. They were always doing something mean to the master—like bad boys. If the master was selling . . . bags of wheat, they would either whip it inside or do something so that when the master got*

the sale of it, he wouldn't get back a full return of money. They would be hurting him like that. While another Negro slave would put all the very best he could in for the master, and do it up and sew it right. So when the bag was sewed, he would feel proud to sew his master's thing. And that is the way they felt. Like Papu said, you could trust some of them, and others you couldn't trust.[28]

Resistance took many forms: apparent compliance with the situation, playing the trickster and gaining an advantage, or perhaps pilfering.[29] Jack Gouldin experienced his share of the latter. In some cases he could identify the culprit, but more often than not, he must have considered it the cost of running such a large operation.[30] Almost certainly, he deemed himself a kind master with the best paternalistic intentions toward his servants.

To the north and west, just out of view from Hays Mount, were most of the slave cabins, or the quarters, which would have been a haunt of Alec's. There was a well-worn path from his own cabin leading to where he went for the latest news, for camaraderie, and for sociability. Here, often with the smell of pungent black smoke cloying to the nostrils as a rag fire smoldered to keep away the persistent mosquitoes, he listened to stories from Aunt Suki.[31] In the winter, they huddled close around her crackling fire. In the summer, she held forth on the steps of her cabin. She was a woman of ancient years, and from listening to her, he stored up knowledge and understanding of plantation life.[32] Here, too, he learned of the atrocities of slavery, such as the man so badly beaten that he could no longer walk. He heard of parties held when the master was away, and of the trickster who rode his master's horse to death but was able to ward off punishment by stealthily pushing the horse's body on a cart and returning the dead carcass to its stall, where it was discovered by its owner.[33] He also absorbed the value of silence and active resistance.

Both the masters' and the slaves' young children were often watched by an enslaved woman who served as the white children's nurse.[34] Early bonds were forged in these formative years. Daisy always said the Gouldin family numbered twenty-three. This number would have included grandchildren, for by the time Alec was a boy, most of Jack's children had moved out of the household. Jack's two oldest sons, Silas and Tom, had growing families of their own. Jack, Si's oldest son, lived in his grandfather's household, and Alec knew him well.[35] Perhaps Jack was training his oldest grandson to learn the complexities of plantation life to take some kind of managerial role. Si lived in Essex and Westmoreland Counties before moving back to Caroline County in the last year of his life. When he died "in his fiftieth year" in 1859, he left, according to the *Fredericksburg News*, nine "interesting" children and a "devoted" wife.[36] Gouldin's second son, Tom, a doctor, lived on a farm known as Chestnut Grove, bordering his father's land, and had eleven children. Family gatherings would have been large, with a number of children close to Alec's age.

Alec had his slave family, including his mother, siblings, and those he considered his extended family—the community of the slave quarters. He also had his white family, to whom he was tied through bondage. While he despised being no more than a valuable piece of property—such as a prized horse or gun—the situation led him to identify with the wealthy status, rather than the social rank of the Gouldin family.[37] He was proud of Jack Gouldin's standing in the community, at least in terms of wealth, and that his master was one of the most successful and innovative farmers around.[38] Likewise, he developed an attachment to the members of the Gouldin family who treated him kindly.

While the enslaved had a distrust of those who held them in bondage, it was through Alec's relationships with the younger Gouldins that he learned how to interact with whites and how to relate to them to his best advantage. As a boy, despite his "lapses" in behavior, the "badness" Daisy refers to, he obviously was likable, and he used this characteristic to his benefit, improving his position.[39] Throughout his life, Alec was able to forge warm and meaningful relationships with whites who in turn helped him in a variety of constructive ways. This was a major asset in establishing himself as a citizen and a landholder.

Alec first came to know Zephie, Gouldin's young granddaughter who lived in his household, when he was about five years old.[40] This is also when he began to sense that he was different from his white playmates. It was a realization that grew slowly and led to an understanding of his wretched state. He asked his mother why he was dressed differently from his white playmates and why he did not have shoes.[41]

> *He was always barefoot. He never had any shoes, or little stockings with rings turning around them, or little short pants, or little white blouses and colored blouses that had little ruffles at the neck and ruffles around the sleeves. . . . All he wore was this one little piece belted in, and sometimes little pants underneath with no shoes ever. . . . He was just their size, and they played together, and he wondered why he didn't look like they looked or have the same kind of little clothes on.*[42]

Rose attempted to console her son by making him some red moccasins from left over scraps of material she used for the red hunting coats, beading the toes in a traditional Cherokee pattern. For Alec, these were better than any shoes. He was proud of his moccasins and loved to "*strut*" around in them. This may have been when he received one of his nicknames, "Pompey," which Daisy explained indicated that he was pompous and liked to show off. Perhaps it was simply a cry for personal dignity that was stripped from him at every turn. Throughout his life, to be treated with dignity continued to be all-important to him.

Alec quickly became conscious that his mother was careful to hide the moccasins whenever "the missus" approached their cabin or when any other white person might see them. Thus, his distrust of white people and secretive behavior was instilled in some of his earliest memories.[43] Elizabeth "Bettie" Gouldin, *"the missus"* to Alec, often came to Rose's cabin to oversee the sewing or to give Rose particular instructions. While Alec always described Jack Gouldin as being *"nice with his slaves,"* Mistress Gouldin was much harsher in her treatment of them, at least in her handling of Alec. Possibly her relationship with enslaved servants stemmed from an incident that had occurred within her family. Her father's brother, Ned Broaddus, had been murdered by two of his slaves in 1802, when Bettie was a young girl.[44] This could well be the foundation of her deep-seated fear and mistrust of servants. Her deep and pervasive anxiety was not an isolated case and fed many whites' fear that the enslaved were dangerous, insubordinate, and malicious.[45] Bettie was from a yeoman farm family and lacked both training to manage a large household and experience caring for the enslaved. Possibly, she was overwhelmed by her position, causing her to be harsh. This reaction and the power of her status created a recipe for maltreatment of those who did not please her.

Daisy commented that her father was a great favorite with everyone, *"excepting the missus who couldn't bear Papu for some unknown reason. I think it was because Father was kind of brazen—maybe stuck his tongue out at her."*[46] Even at this early age, Alec apparently had a winning personality, but also a growing seed of resistance. There was not much Alec liked about this woman who was his nemesis, and he communicated this to his children in a number of stories. He described in detail her odd way of walking as she held her dress up so that it would not touch the floor of the slave cabin. *"She had a very peculiar habit. Her dress was more or less ruffles and silk, and whenever she came down she always held her dress up from behind—kind of lifted it off the ground so that it didn't touch, and walked a peculiar walk."*[47]

Alec first experienced her inexplicably cruel behavior when she discovered the young boy wearing his favorite red moccasins and threw them in the fire. Unfortunately, his mother had neglected to remove them when the missus appeared. She and her granddaughter, Zephie, came to Rose's cabin because Zephie was having a dress made for her upcoming eighth birthday party. The destruction of his moccasins inflicted a permanent scar and a deep internal wound; Alec never forgave her.

> *What did she do, but grab those little moccasins from his feet and throw them in the fire! He just made a rush for her and grabbed her and tore*

her dress and skirts and ruffles off. He bit her legs and he bit her hands. Oh, he fought with her terrible. And finally, she fainted dead away. Of course, he said he never forgot as long as he lived that awful, awful look in his mother's eyes. It looked like her eyes were going to pop out, and water begin running right out of them. She started hollering, and he said these two very tall light men who were house servants came and lifted the white missus up and took her up to the big house. And he said his mother couldn't sew any more that day. She just trembled all over because she knew that they would take her little boy and sell him away. That's the way they used to do. That's why she so went to pieces.[48]

This behavior was new to Alec, and his outrage was instant and explosive. As far as he was concerned, the missus received her due, but he was racked by the look in his mother's eyes. This was his first real lesson in what it meant to be owned by somebody, and he knew without question that he despised it. With that pivotal incident came a flash of comprehension and a hardening of every fiber within him against slavery.

Slave mothers were careful to teach their children early in life how to behave toward their white masters and mistresses so that their actions would not invite disastrous punishment.[49] Feared above all other punishments was being sold away from the plantation and from the family group.[50] It became more common for the enslaved to be sold and sent further south, where their labor was increasingly necessary to keep pace with the growing of cotton made "king" by the advent of the cotton gin.[51] Rose's abject terror that this most devastating punishment was about to befall her shook her to the core of her being. To her relief, nothing terrible was done to her young son.

Zephie, who always displayed kindness and compassion toward Alec, looms large in Alec's life saga. While Daisy portrayed "the little missus" as the daughter of Jack Gouldin, in fact she was his granddaughter. This does not make much difference in the overall story; however, it does indicate that details on which Alec may well have been clear, or that perhaps were not important in his mind, were overlooked in Daisy's retelling. Certainly, the Gouldins were bringing up Zephie as their daughter. She was part of their household, and possibly Alec was not aware of their exact relationship, although that would be surprising.[52] Born in 1842, she was three years older than Alec, a detail that was clear in Daisy's story. She became a major influence in his life and was apparently close to all of Rose's family. Her grandfather left Alec's younger half siblings, Lindsey and Judy Coleman, to her as "servants."[53] It was common to leave to family members servants of whom they were fond. As Daisy said: *"My father had this awful grudge against the white people. It is the little missus that held it down, because of her kindness to him."*[54]

On the day of Zephie's birthday, Rose took the finished piece of clothing to the young girl, bringing Alec with her. They went up the big wide steps, into the large central hall, and passed by tables spread with decorative cloths and covered with sweetmeats, cookies, and a variety of delicious dishes for the party. Alec eagerly drank in the display. For any young boy, the sight of those delicacies would be more than inviting, but for one who seldom had such things, the vision and aroma were overpowering. As they climbed the enclosed staircase, leading from the great hall to the upstairs, Alec feasted on the cookies in his mind's eye. Rose made sure the dress was perfect on Zephie, then turned to her son, but he was already dashing down the stairs.

> *And what did he do, but run to one of these big dishes of soldier cookies! He remembered that they were ginger cookies made in the shape of soldiers. He ran to the dish and grabbed handfuls of those soldiers and began biting off their heads. . . . Well, of course, his mother rushed and grabbed him back, but it was too late. He had tipped them over and ate a lot and spoiled the whole dish. Well, Father said he never could forget that day!*
>
> *They didn't know . . . what they were going to do with him. Finally, they decided to put him in the field, and he was then five. They had large pails of water, and then they had the smaller dish to dip the water out of the pail. He would go up and down these long rows, and he said some of the rows were almost a half a mile long. Up and down . . . all day long in the hot sun, carrying water to the slaves that were working in the fields. . . . So, it was a pretty hard life.*[55]

We do not know how long his punishment continued, but it was enforced and carried out under the watchful eye of the overseer Alec came to detest, Presley, or as he pronounced it, "Pusley."[56] As overseer, Pusley was under the farm manager with whom Gouldin would have had a contract.[57] It was common in those days to put in writing that the manager should

> be humane to the Negroes and not use any unlawful weapons to chastise them with; Negro women with child are not to be put to improper work. They are to be allowed time to suckle their children. Negro men and women are not to be driven when sick and every possible attention is to be paid to them when they are sick. The Negro women are to spin during the winter and in all bad weather. The Negro women are to be allowed to attend their children when sick.[58]

However, there were those under the manager who pushed the limits. Pusley was such a man and earned Alec's hatred at an early age. He was also in charge of the whipping post.[59] While Gouldin differed with Pusley over this, Pusley sometimes took matters into his own hands. Daisy went on to explain that on occasion the enslaved would pay the driver not to whip them too much. Over the years, Alec and this overseer had frequent run-ins, and Alec's hatred smoldered.

According to Daisy, Pusley was a mulatto, and a slave himself, perhaps originally enslaved on Jack Gouldin's father's farm.[60] There is a slave named Presley listed for five hundred dollars in 1817 in the inventory of John Gouldin's estate.[61] The most valuable slave was appraised at six hundred dollars, and this may indicate that Presley was a youth at the time of his master's death. A young boy had the potential of having real value upon maturing. If this is the same individual, it would indicate that Presley had won Jack Gouldin's trust, while at the same time antagonizing his fellow workers. The master's trust allowed him to flex his power over the powerless, another gross injustice in the system of slavery. He was no friend to his fellow workers. He was known for cobbing slaves who committed an infraction—boring holes in a board, then beating a slave's bare back with the board until the holes cut into the skin. He also swabbed the wounds with brine to increase the pain. To Alec, Pusley symbolized all the evils of slavery, and he came to hate him even more than he did Mistress Gouldin.

Once Alec's punishment was over, he was given the daily task of driving sheep and cattle to pasture and bringing them home at night with other boys of his age.[62] They were also responsible for mucking out the stables. The responsibility of tending the livestock was a typical charge for young slave boys. *"He used to have his line [an allotted number of livestock] to tend to the cows and . . . the sheep, to drive these cows to the pasture. All the boys of his age worked under this one overseer [Pusley], taking care of the cows and bringing them in at night to the barns. And then cleaning out the stables. Then the other men had the dump cart that they carried all the rubbish away to the land down to the fields."*[63]

Gouldin had about twenty-five horses and mules, thirty-five cows and oxen, fifty-five sheep, kept mostly for their wool, and fifty hogs.[64] It was during this period that Alec must have learned the different calls he used: one to call sheep, another for cattle, and a third to call horses. His children remember him using the distinct cries to call his own animals. Throughout his life, Alec enjoyed animals and gained a reputation of being good with them. He also had opportunities to learn the skill of a teamster, for Gouldin had a number of teams of oxen and several ox carts. In later life, Alec proved to be a fine teamster himself, using oxen to work in the Vermont woods.

Religion played a central role in the lives of all the enslaved, allowing them a positive identity, creative expression, and defiance in the face of white society.[65] Religion and belief were not only the heart and sustenance of the slave community, but their recreation, their social strength, their creativity, and their resistance. Alec's early memory of his father's funeral and the preacher who stopped the coming storm was his first manifestation of the power of prayer, and it was an enduring memory. Indeed, it helped shape his deep religious conviction and his lifelong belief in God. Prayer and hymns were his direct communication with the Lord, and they were both intimate and constant. In his early years, his ardent belief in the power of prayer became an important tenet throughout his life, one that was confirmed repeatedly and that nourished his determination. As Daisy said: "*They didn't have anything to go upon, only their prayers.*"[66]

Alec's faith brought him both hope and joy. He joined in the spirituals at weekly prayer meetings in the quarters. He sang during strenuous work, to help with the rhythm as when pulling in a seine net. For the enslaved, spirituals communicated on more than one level of meaning, and they could sing about veiled hopes and dreams. As he grew older, Alec developed a strong tenor voice and a real enjoyment of singing. When he had children of his own, he ensured they knew all his songs and under what circumstances he sang them.

On Sunday, many of Jack Gouldin's enslaved men, women, and children walked three miles to Bethesda Baptist Church, the small brick building Gouldin had been instrumental in erecting, and climbed up into the balcony that surrounded and overlooked the white congregation. From there, they could participate in the service and listen to the sermon. It is said that slave owners in Virginia tended to be Baptists "because the Baptists were not as opposed to slavery as the Methodists."[67] Baptist services also appealed to many of the enslaved. Indeed, they outnumbered the whites by as many as three to one.[68] Andrew Broaddus, known for his speaking abilities, and whom Gouldin's young neighbor Kate Buckner described one Sunday in 1858 in her diary as preaching "well as always," was someone Alec would have heard.[69]

Before going to church on Sunday, Alec told his grandson, mothers were encouraged to rub their children's lips with fat meat (traditionally done to prevent lips from drying and cracking), so that by the time they reached their destination, their mouths would be covered with dust, and people would think they had just finished a meal.[70] In other words, the perception would be that Gouldin's slaves were well fed, which would increase his reputation as a benevolent master. The enslaved ate what they were provided, supplementing it when they could with fish and game, but frequently there was not enough.

The Baptist church was a further means for owners to exert social control over the enslaved. A basic tenet of Baptist belief was that the church was the presence of God on earth, and as such it could not continue if it contained evil.[71] It followed that all members were required to attend regular monthly meetings where the main order of business was focused on the social behavior of its members. From the minutes of the Bethesda Baptist Church meetings, it is clear that the church fathers "attended to matters of discipline among the colored members." For example, in February 1856, "Silas, a servant of John Gouldin dealt with for theft and upon professing repentance was released in the fellowship of the church." And in June 1856, "the committee appointed to decide the case of Jim and Susan [one wonders if this might be Alec's sister Susan] servants of brother John Gouldin reported upon the recommendation of which Jim was retained in the fellowship of the church and Susan excluded for the sin of fornication."[72] This is just one example among many.[73]

Both whites and blacks were baptized, usually in August, in the Rappahannock River. There is mention in the Bethesda records of five "persons of color received for baptism" and then again in November: "On Lord's day evening five persons of color were baptized."[74] Alec would not have undergone baptism before he left the plantation, because the Baptists did not believe in baptizing an individual until that person was mature enough to profess faith.

An experience that often became transformative for many of the enslaved was conversion. This encompassed both a rebirth and a rededication to one's faith. Conversion took a variety of forms. Most commonly, the spirit descended at formal services. Frequently, the individual fainted or spoke in tongues. While conversion was a personal experience, it was viewed as a distinctive event that also led to greater self-esteem within the black community, both during enslavement and after emancipation.[75] Daisy claimed that Alec had experienced two conversions: once after his father's funeral, and once as he went into his first battle in the Civil War.[76] Conversion also played a role among a number of Alec's family, and all who experienced it had an individual story held to be extraordinarily significant. "My father has been converted" was a line from one of Alec's favorite spirituals.

While the power of religion nourished an enslaved person's soul, the physical work was never ending. As he grew, Alec was given other tasks on the plantation. At age ten, he was employed in the milk house, filling bottles of milk for slaves and for the poor whites who came to purchase it. There the milk sat in shallow pans, to allow the cream to rise to the surface. Eventually he worked his way up to head boy. It was during this period that Zephie began to teach Alec how to read. This was a momentous event in Alec's life. He knew he needed to better himself through education, and he thirsted after literacy, something denied to all slaves. It was forbidden in Virginia to teach the enslaved how to read or write.[77] Zephie schooled Alec in his letters and helped him put them together to read words. By the time Alec left the plantation in April 1862, he had the rudiments of reading and writing, something he determinedly pursued. His grandchildren remember him avidly reading three or four different newspapers daily.

It was Zephie who first encouraged Alec to run away from the plantation, and according to Daisy, she told him he should go to Vermont, where "*slavery was outlawed and he could be free.*"[78] She earned his lifelong devotion by offering to help him accomplish this. We cannot know the depth of her feelings about abolition, whether she believed that all slaves should be freed, but we do know that she communicated to Alec that he needed to escape and that she stood ready to help him. Perhaps this was a generational difference with her grandparents, or perhaps she simply was drawn to Alec's humanity. Alec treasured the bond between them and honored it by naming one of his daughters after her.[79]

> *The little missus had somehow obtained a primer. . . . She was teaching my father A B C, and rat, and things like that. And she told him (because my father wanted to get away) . . . that up north in Vermont . . . the white people would let him be free . . . and she would help him run to this Vermont. . . . The [grand]mother came down behind the milk house, because somehow the [grand]daughter had made it obvious that she planned to be down there at certain times. [The missus] had this big bullwhip that they use to whip the [slaves] with. . . . When she found her little [grand] daughter was teaching Father, and Father had the primer, she undertook to take the primer from Father, . . . and sent the little [grand]daughter to the house. When Father held on and started to fight her to keep the little primer in his own hands, she struck with the whip across his cheek and cut Father's face, which ordinarily would need at least fifty stitches to sew it up. . . . He bled on the primer . . . but Father kept it. The place on Father's cheek healed so it hardly showed. It was like a thread running through his face. It was a peculiar oil that his mother put on.*[80]

The incident with Mistress Gouldin and the primer was a defining moment for Alec. He resolved he would be free and began to act on that determination. Such an instant has been noted by scholars and is frequently seen as "the beginning of a change in the slave's character."[81] Alec began stealing money every time he had the opportunity—penny by penny. He was planning to save enough to buy his freedom. To ensure its safety, he wrapped his money in sheepskin and placed it in a tin that he buried in his mother's garden, planting watermelon seeds over it. He would save the watermelons by burying them under a pile of hay, and then bring them out for Christmas, when watermelon season was long past.[82] The spiritual "Bury Me in the Garden" had a special meaning for him and illustrates what Frederick Douglass meant by "words which to many would seem unmeaning jargon, but which, nevertheless, were full of meaning to themselves."[83] This was common among many spirituals sung by the enslaved.

While Sundays were a day of rest from labor for the master—an opportunity to go to church, work in one's garden patch, or attend to a more pleasurable chore—it was the week between Christmas and New Year's that was the major holiday for the enslaved. All looked forward to it with eager anticipation. There was music, dancing, singing, visiting between plantations, and competitions such as wrestling matches or running races. Alec would have had the opportunity to hunt possum or raccoon, probably going with an older member of the slave quarters who might have a dog, or perhaps to trap muskrat along the creeks. Because Gouldin was closely involved with the temperance movement, he would not have passed out Christmas libation after 1847, but he did provide his most loyal servants with a variety of gifts, such as a tin plate, a set of dishes, or a pair of underwear. And for those musically inclined, an instrument, which would be used in entertaining the master and his family and friends. The master would allow greater rations of food, and there would be plum puddings and Christmas cakes as well as fresh pork and beef. It was a festive time for all, and it remained Alec's favorite holiday.

On January 1, slaves were often hired out for the year.[84] Gouldin seldom did this, except as a favor to one of his sons, but Alec spoke about working for a kind woman called Turner. He was probably hired out as a boy, for a day at a time, to help her bring in wood, sweep the yard, or perform other chores around the house. Mrs. Turner was likely Mary Turner, wife of Gouldin's neighbor John Turner. Obviously, Alec found her warm and hospitable, as his grandson Bruce Turner said: "*She was a lady who had been very kind to him*."[85] When he ran away from the plantation, it was her last name that he made his own.

By the time he was twelve in the summer of 1857, Alec was maturing into a large, well-proportioned youth reminiscent of his father, full of strength and vigor. This was not lost on his nemesis, Pusley. A slave trader noticed him and offered to purchase him as a breeder.[86] According to Alec, Pusley thought Gouldin would be receptive to the prospect and went to his master with the proposal, but Gouldin would have none of it. He reiterated to Pusley that Alec was not to be beaten. Like a prize horse, he was too valuable and undoubtedly a favorite. Daisy always claimed Gouldin was offered $10,000 for Alec, but $1,500 is more probable.[87]

Alec acquired both knowledge and skills that he would put to good use in later life. From the clearing of pastureland, he recognized the value of removing the bark from the hemlocks and sending it to the tannery down the road.[88] The woods were replete with game, and the river and creeks abounded with fish and wild fowl. He learned to snare and trap in the woods, swamps, and streams, and how to catch fish, supplementing the family larder not only with fish and wild fowl, but also with possum, muskrat, raccoon, squirrel, and the occasional rabbit. Alec found that he could add money to his tin by selling muskrat pelts to some of his young masters. Most certainly one of these was Jack, Gouldin's eldest grandson.

He also went along with members of the Gouldin family who hunted with dogs on foot as well as on horseback. Hounds were a central element to the foxhunt, and judging from Alec's later ownership and training of hounds, it is likely that he was engaged in caring for, handling, and even training these hounds. Some foxhunting dogs were fed a special diet known as ash-pone meal (cornbread baked in ashes) and were bedded down among fine leaves strewn with a few leaves of tobacco. They were carefully watched for signs of mange, fleas, and other diseases, for which there were special remedies. For example, a hound with mange was given three spoonsful of sulfur in milk for three successive mornings.[89] Alec learned quickly and carefully absorbed this knowledge.

The hunt was a major social event in the fall of the year, and while Rose spent many hours sewing the red coats for this fashionable sport, the household servants were engaged in cleaning, polishing, and preparing numerous dishes of food for the participants. Friends and family members from any distance would spend the night to be ready for hard riding at five o'clock the next morning, after a festive and sociable evening.[90] Alec must have looked forward to these events. The guests arrived with their own grooms and dog handlers, who brought news and fresh conversation. The stables would have been alive with activity, bedding down both dogs and horses. Alec received good training from these visitors, who would have been glad to have a boy's help in caring for their charges and delighted to talk about it, as they took pride in their care. Alec's experience with animals, and his love for and care of them, developed an essential expertise he practiced during the war years and later in Vermont where he cared for his own livestock and often helped his neighbors with theirs.

Alec learned most of his skills by doing. He helped build fences. He helped drain terraces and fields by digging ditches and lining them with flat stones, on both the top and the bottom so that the soil covering them would be firm and the water could run off easily. He also helped to pull the seine net at the fishery, a valuable operation for those who lived along the Rappahannock. In early April, herring, shad, rockfish, and perch were caught as they spawned. Some would be sold, but most were salted down for an additional food source for the plantation. This was such an important industry that Gouldin went to his fellow parishioners in 1858 for permission "to give to his men engaged in seine hauling spirits to be used in moderation," an interesting request coming from a leader in the prohibition of alcoholic drink.[91] It suggests that this was a tradition and that those who pulled in the seine may have languished in their efforts without it. Seining, or hauling in a fish-filled net, was monotonous and grueling work. The men used spirituals to both lighten the load and help with the rhythm of pulling together. Alec taught his family many of these spirituals, and Daisy could sing a great number of them. She remembered one he used to sing while seining was "Been a'Listening All the Night Long."[92]

Alec's strength and athleticism must have reminded Jack Gouldin of Robert. He was aware that Alec could best his contemporaries at running, jumping, and wrestling. Like his father, Alec gained genuine respect for his prowess on the plantation. He was conscious of his father's reputation as the bare-knuckles champion, and although Gouldin was no longer as actively involved in boxing matches between plantations, when another planter with a slave whom he felt could best Alec challenged Gouldin to let the two have a match, Gouldin agreed. George Hall, Alec's grandson, remembered with pride his grandfather telling him *"that he was never beaten in his life."* When they had some free time, his cohorts would gather to wrestle and fight. *"Nobody could ever put his back down on the ground."*[93] But for such a challenge, Alec wanted to make certain he remained unbeaten. There would be betting on the outcome, and Alec was determined not to lose. He modeled himself after the African trickster, a figure like Br'er Rabbit or the spider Anansi, who triumphed over the more powerful by cleverness and trickery, another defensive dimension of resistance.[94] Bruce Turner remembered his grandfather telling him about it.

> *The overseers, the family members, and the slaves would all appear at a predetermined site on a given day. My grandfather was determined to win this fight. So, he went to his mother's garden and picked hot peppers, took the seeds out, dried them in front of the fireplace. After they had dried amply, he ground them and put them in a little bag to save them for this particular day of the fight. On the day of the fight, they had these two young men come together, and they went at one another hell-bent for leather with everything they had. My grandfather had taken the pepper out of the bag and put it in his pocket, and he maneuvered himself so he got behind the person, put his legs around him, and got up on his back. He reached in his pocket, and he brought this pepper and rubbed it in his eyes. The other boy had to give up because he was hurting and couldn't see. So that was one of his favorite tales of victory that he would tell.*[95]

As he matured, Alec was acutely aware of the situation around him. Not only did he despise slavery with all its dehumanizing characteristics, but he began to understand what was happening to enslaved women, and he was repulsed by white men forcing themselves on those powerless to resist.[96] This was brought home to him personally when he was fourteen and began to have warm feelings toward a young enslaved girl.

> *Father said such a terrible situation was existing that no one could imagine it at all. He told about the first little slave girl that he kind of liked. He didn't know why he liked her, but he did, and they used to talk some*

together. He said some of the white men started after her, and she didn't know what to do. She ran and jumped in the Rappahannock River and was drowned. He said that was the year he was fourteen—going on fifteen. He said she was drowned, and he began realizing more and more that he must get away for this freedom.[97]

In some versions of this horrifying incident, Daisy claims the young girl was chased by some of Gouldin's sons or grandsons. The point remains that Alec was appalled by this treatment of enslaved women and had witnessed it firsthand. He communicated his abhorrence of such situations to his children, and it influenced his own attitude toward intermarriage between the races.

By 1860, there was talk of war in the slave quarters, in the master's house, and everywhere. White southerners and their black servants had very different viewpoints. Differing views also existed among Northerners—a minority were hard-core abolitionists, while the majority believed that the war was necessary to preserve the Union. News spread like wildfire among both the slave quarters and the planters, each wondering if and when such a conflagration would begin. Each group began to feel that war was inevitable. Most of those in Caroline County believed that the Confederates would win their independence from the Union.[98]

The first shots were fired at Fort Sumter on April 12, 1861, and no one foresaw the destruction of life and devastation that would ensue. The general attitude was that it would only continue for a few months. As Daisy said many times: "*No one dreamed it would run four long years—one of the bloodiest wars ever fought in history with brother fighting brother and father fighting son.*"[99] This was a common theme running throughout our conversations, and Daisy repeatedly told me that the Gouldin family itself found members on opposite sides of the conflict, although I found no evidence of this. When I asked Gouldin family members, they were adamant that all their relatives fought with the Confederacy, and the war records of family members who were enlisted indicate they all fought for the South. What is more likely is that Alec mentioned examples of father and son fighting on different sides and reportedly witnessed such a scene that was seared into his memory during the war.

On April 17, five days after those first shots at Fort Sumter, Virginia seceded from the Union. In June, Richmond became the government seat of the Confederate States of America. Caroline County, midway between Richmond and Washington, DC, was strategically positioned for the two opposing armies. As fighting erupted, the area began to feel the pressure of the ordeal and the debilitation of war. After the First Battle of Bull Run, on July 21, 1861, two Union officers escaped from their Confederate captors and found their way alongside the Rappahannock. Alec and his mother eagerly befriended them, helping them to ward off capture by hiding them until the Army of the Potomac came down beside the Rappahannock. Alec wrote about it in his application for his Civil War pension: *At the first Battle of Bull Run, two officers escaped from the rebels, and my mother and I kept them hid in a dug out four months, feeding them. At the end of that time, the Yankee Army got down beside the Rappahannock River in King George County, and we got them back to the Yankee Army again.*[100]

While Confederate soldiers patrolled the area, Union soldiers made occasional forays into their territory. One afternoon as John G. Gouldin (Jack, his grandfather's namesake and eldest grandson, now a member of the Ninth Virginia Cavalry, Company H, and someone Alec knew well) came to visit his grandfather, he spotted a group of five Union soldiers drinking buttermilk under a tree.[101] Fast thinking and immediate action allowed Gouldin's young grandson to capture them at gunpoint and carry them to Colonel W. F. "Rooney" Lee, Robert E. Lee's son, who was just a short distance away at Rappahannock Academy.[102]

By late November 1861, the Confederates had taken up headquarters at Rappahannock Academy, and the elder Jack Gouldin, never one to miss a business opportunity, began to do a healthy trade with them. On November 25, 1861, he hired out a wagon and four mules for thirteen days at four dollars per day. After this, he did a steady business—selling wheat, corn, hay, fodder, straw, bacon, and beef cattle—and earned well over four thousand dollars.[103] This was during Alec's last winter at the plantation in 1862, a winter during which Confederate soldiers camped on Gouldin's property. During this time, someone from the house, undoubtedly Gouldin's son Frank, who was serving as farm manager, itemized what the soldiers "borrowed" from the house, scrawling the date and the items on a closet wall; this is still visible today.[104] "Father's blanket," among other things, giving away the identity of the scribe, is penciled in firm hand, tethering us to those events playing out 150 years ago.

By 1862, Jack Gouldin was seventy-five years old. His youngest son, Frank, had moved into the house along with his wife and infant son, relieving his father of the responsibilities of running the business of the farm. Jack continued to buy land, acquiring 737 acres from the Corbin estate in 1860, including the "Race Field Tract"—indicating that Gouldin was ever the sportsman. The major portion of the land bordered the river and included a wharf, a fishery, and additional barns.[105] He also added 99 acres from the Catherine Merryman estate in 1861, including a house, barn, stable, and outbuildings.[106] But his health was deteriorating. By 1862, he was noticeably absent from church meetings, and the participation of his sons Tom and Frank increased. His wife, Bettie, Alec's nemesis, was also unwell; when Gouldin wrote his will the next year, he referred to his "afflicted" wife. Daisy confirmed that she was bedridden in her later years and thought the affliction was the consequence of a fall from a horse. Both Jack and his wife died in 1863.

While Gouldin owned a great deal of land, maintained top-quality, up-to-date farm equipment, and had a houseful of fine furniture, the bulk of his wealth was in slaves. He must have been uneasy, for all over Caroline County slaves began to disappear. A requisition went out from the governor for four hundred slaves between the ages of eighteen and fifty-five, which required each slaveholder to allot one out of every three of his slaves to the state. These men would be taken to Richmond and put to work on the railroad for which Gouldin's executors were eventually paid $207.[107] This requisition was unsettling to both the enslaved and their owners and was a stimulus for many to contemplate a run to freedom.

The tense atmosphere that accompanied two opposing forces within shooting distance of each other also had an unsettling effect on the slaves and encouraged many to take "unprecedented risks."[108] Although plantation owners considered flight as treason, the enslaved grew in confidence that escape was possible. Sometime after April 21, 1862, when the First New Jersey Cavalry was camped down along the Rappahannock in King George County, Assistant Surgeon Ferdinand Dayton crossed the river in a boat and came upon Alec and a few companions. This proved to be a significant meeting for Alec, as Dayton would become a pivotal figure in his life. Dayton came from a strong abolitionist family, and with the zeal of a reformer, he offered Alec a means to escape. Alec was ready, looking for an opening, thirsty for the opportunity, as he yearned for freedom. This underlying hope gave him the courage to talk with this white stranger. Alec told his children later that he did not know what made him so bold. Apparently, Dayton questioned Alec about *"where the food was and where the meat house was, and the milk house."*[109] Before they parted, Alec had arranged an appointed time for their escape. Certainly, this contact was an important impetus in Alec's successful flight. He was given an opportunity, and he seized it. He knew the road ahead of him was a dangerous one, but anything was better than living under the bondage of slavery.

Later when Gouldin and his sons Tom and Frank filed a list and statement of lost slaves with the Confederacy, they complained that the enemy occupied the Rappahannock with their gunboats and "frequently landed on the farms adjacent and had constant intercourse with the slaves of farmers bordering on said River."[110] Winter Coghill, the manager of Silas Gouldin's farm, signed an affidavit for his estate "that gun boats frequently anchored off from the farm of said S.B. Gouldin dec'd and their crews came ashore and had every means of talking to and persuading off the slaves."[111] They

Ferdinand Dayton, 1863. Courtesy of John W. Kuhl Collection, U.S. Army Military History Institute, Carlisle, Pennsylvania.

believed fervently that their slaves had been "abducted" and "induced" away. Silas also lost two boats that "were seized and carried away" by the enemy. It is likely that one of these carried Alec across the river when he made his dash for freedom.

Observing from the King George side of the river, First New Jersey chaplain Henry Pyne described the steady exodus of slaves across the Rappahannock that April: "Night after night, in canoes, on rafts, by swimming, the slaves beyond the river made their way to us from their thralldom. No difficulty nor danger seemed sufficient to deter them from the path to freedom; and escaping every man, they brought in to us many valuable pieces of intelligence."[112] Slaves of the neighborhood were also being gathered at Thomas Gouldin's farm in preparation for being sent to Richmond to work for the Confederate military on the railroad. Humphrey, a fellow bondsman of Alec who fled at this same period, mentioned this as an impetus for his flight, and it may well have been another incentive for Alec as well.[113]

Before he left, Alec managed to steal into Gouldin's office, just off the great hall in the big house, and abscond with the silver spurs his father had won cock fighting for his master. He brought these with him, along with the blood-stained primer Zephie had given him and that he had refused to relinquish to Mistress Gouldin, despite her whip. He also dug up his tin of money, which contained about twenty-five dollars, and with a few bits of clothing he was ready. With both anticipation and trepidation, he said good bye to his mother and siblings, wondering if he would ever see them again.

Excitement, anticipation, and adrenalin must have been pumping wildly as he snuck down to the river after dark to meet the others who planned to go. Later he told his family that there were to be many more, but that only a small group appeared—an indication of what a frightening decision it was. *"Some were afraid to defect because they didn't know what the consequences would be."*[114] The risk was great, and all those fleeing faced an uncertain and precarious future. When the youths were ready, they were to wave sheets on sticks to signal two cavalrymen to come with boats to carry them across the river.

All went as planned, and Alec was relieved to climb into the skiff. It was banged up and leaky, but as far as he was concerned, it was his chariot to freedom. He had left the plantation and was determined never to return as a slave. One of his first acts was to change his name so that anyone who recognized him could not claim that he was the property of Jack Gouldin and return him to his master. He was no longer a slave or chattel, he was a free man. His life was before him. Alec Berkeley became Alexander Turner.[115]

CHAPTER 5

Civil War

> The second night after joining the Yankee Cavalry, I took 40 men and led them five miles after crossing River to a rebel picket post and took eight rebels.
>
> —Alexander Turner, letter to Bureau of Pensions, June 16, 1916

This foray across the Rappahannock River to a rebel picket post proved to be what Alec considered the most significant experience of his life: not only was it his first exploit as a free man, but it also represented his triumph over slavery.[1] No wonder he told the story many times to family and friends. It is natural that such an important event would take on larger than life dimensions over time for Alec, but the story is still recognizable when related by a Union cavalry chaplain. Transformed from a sixteen-year-old

Thomas Gouldin, son of Jack Gouldin, ca. 1860. Courtesy of the Vermont Folklife Center, Middlebury, Vermont.

Chestnut Grove Estate, owned by Tom Gouldin and the site of the First New Jersey Cavalry Raid, ca. 1860. Courtesy of the Vermont Folklife Center, Middlebury, Vermont.

slave boy to a free man, literally by crossing the river, Alec had traveled a short physical distance, but a new world had opened to him. He was ready to do anything he could to maintain and protect this new world that allowed his freedom. He was invigorated. For the moment racial inequality and class difference were subtleties that paled beside this inalienable right.

In later life, Alec took full credit for leading the raid. Indeed, this incident incorporates Alec's triumph over slavery, and the event remains at the core of his coming of age as both a man and a citizen. In written accounts, circumstances are described somewhat differently from the version Alec related to his children. According to First New Jersey Chaplain Henry Pyne, an escaped slave called Humphrey first alluded to a small number of Confederate cavalry stationed at Dr. Tom Gouldin's plantation.[2]

Humphrey, also enslaved by Jack Gouldin, escaped about the same time as Alec, although he had a more terrifying experience. He left from the marsh below the Gouldin homestead with two cousins in a dugout canoe. Their canoe was swamped, and Humphrey's cousins drowned. Humphrey was pulled from the river just in time by members of the First New Jersey Cavalry's Company K.[3] According to Pyne, Captain Virgil Broderick, the thirty-four-year-old commander of Company K, overheard Humphrey talking about this Confederate outpost and questioned him. Humphrey probably had been in conversation with Alec and other Gouldin bondsmen. From his queries, Broderick learned that these Confederate couriers and vedettes were about ten miles away from the river at Tom Gouldin's Chestnut Grove farm without any backup. Their mission was to oversee this outpost serving as the drop-off point for slaves to be transported to Richmond to work on the railroad for the military.[4] With this information, Broderick conceived a daring escapade to capture the rebel couriers. He gained permission from his superior, Colonel Wyndham, gathered several eager volunteers for his raid, and made preparation to go the following night.

In most written accounts, Humphrey served as guide. In Broderick's letter to his father about the raid, he wrote that he was "guided by a Negro two shades lighter than the night itself,"[5] but he does not refer to Humphrey by name. Donald E. Kester in *Cavalry Men in Blue* leaves out names as well, but refers to the raid as "guided by local runaway slaves."[6] Most certainly, Alec was one of the local fugitives who participated.[7] Humphrey was ten years older than Alec, and it is natural that he would defer to Humphrey in front of the white strangers. Although Alec was younger, Gouldin placed the higher value of $1,500 on Alec, while he ranked Humphrey's worth at $1,200, probably indicative of such qualities as intelligence, initiative, and trustworthiness.[8] At any rate, both Humphrey and Alec were on the raid, although Humphrey appears to have served as the chief guide.

A band of twenty crept away from camp in a deluge of rain, crossed the river, two at a time, in a leaky dugout—likely one of Silas Gouldin's missing boats—and began their escapade as the last note of taps drifted across the water. The blackness was intense, the night air cold and raw. It was a long slog through newly ploughed fields, sometimes knee-deep in mud from a month of heavy spring rain, and through woods strewn with blowdowns, along winding tracts and byways, and eventually across the main road that led from Fredericksburg to Port Royal. Even in the dark, Humphrey and Alec knew the country intimately from many stealthy, late-night sojourns and led the men toward their quarry. Dressed in their light-colored homespun cloth, sewn by Alec's mother, Alec and Humphrey were visible in the darkness. The soldiers followed them closely, without their usual spurs and swords, but equipped with carbines and pistols. Alec had a colt revolver given to him by Dr. Dayton before he left on the raid; he carried it throughout the war and treasured it until the day he died. Well after midnight, Humphrey halted and pointed out the main house and the smaller building in which the soldiers were quartered.

The Confederate outpost proved to house young men of the neighborhood, including Eugene Broadus, Dr. Tom Gouldin's nephew.[9] All had volunteered for service and had found a decidedly pleasant situation in the Gouldin household. The doctor had a number of young daughters (Edmonia, Lucy, Virginia, Sally, Mollie, and Anne) who, with several friends, were staying in the house. One of the daughters had a fondness for the sergeant of the squad, and under such congenial circumstances, the men neglected to take prescribed precautions.[10]

Broderick and his men attacked the unsuspecting outpost, mortally wounding Eugene Broaddus and breaking another man's arm with a pistol shot.[11] This was the first action the men had seen, as well as the first killing that they had been a part of, and they found it both sobering and disturbing. Dr. Gouldin could do nothing to save his nephew, who writhed in agony until death ended his misery.

The shots had woken the household, and there were "shrieks" from the ladies and a chorus of "yells" from the Negro women.[12] It must have been during this time of confusion that Alec set off on his own mission to find Pusley, Jack Gouldin's overseer, whose house was only half a mile from Chestnut Grove.[13] From Daisy's account, the purpose of the raid in capturing the outpost is overlooked, and the emphasis is placed on taking food and other items and, for Alec, on extracting vengeance on his hated abuser Pusley. For his children, other details were irrelevant.

> *After [he] got in the army, the white Yankee soldiers went back to burn the plantation*[14] *and to get food and . . . everything they could—horses . . . all their harnesses . . . carriages and things. . . . Father said old Pusley had been left . . . overseeing his master's plantation. . . . He was the main one that wanted to be beating him from the time that he'd been a little boy. From those red shoes, this Pusley had been working on him. Everything that Father done, he was ready to abuse. . . . He just seemed to hate him. Old Pusley was upstairs, and he came to the window and wanted to know what they wanted. He said, "Who is there?" And Father says, "This is me. This is Alec . . . I'm going to shoot you." And he said he shot him right through the stomach, like in his chest. . . . [My father] was part way up on a ladder. The house wasn't too high. It was two-story I think he said. Anyway, Father shot him and . . . when he fell he hollered for water—give him some cold water, cold water. But he died right there. . . . He said that was the first shooting that he done . . . I've heard him tell that many and many a time.*[15]

Few escaping slaves found such ready complicity by the Union Army in helping to right offensive wrongs. Some stole a mule or a wagon from their master, but few had the satisfaction of such explicit revenge. Alec held Pusley accountable for his greatest misery, and not only did the killing settle a score, but it both demonstrated and symbolized Alec's triumph over slavery and the reclaiming of his dignity, individuality, power, and manhood. With this act he successfully turned his back on slavery and made a decisive declaration of freedom, forever shedding his bonds. This was the story that became a touchstone for Alec. It is no wonder he told it more often than any other.

Alec said that while he willingly showed the men where to find food in the smoke house, the springhouse, and the milk house, he pleaded with them not to set fire to any of the buildings. Later, the troops did burn a number of plantations, but Alec hated to see that. "*Papu said it was something terrible to see those big plantations go down. The white people's houses was just like big hotels.*"[16] Once free, Alec did not hate everything he left behind. His roots were still in Virginia, and he had been shaped by all he had learned on the plantation, but he was going to use it for his own benefit and live according to his own terms.

The raiders returned with their captives, their horses, and "with their own mementoes"—whatever they could carry in the way of food and other items.[17] According to Tom Gouldin's report filed with the Confederacy, this included one of his horses valued at $200 and several wines from his house.[18] As they reached the river, the men heard the first strains of reveille and crossed in triumph, the horses swimming alongside.

The contrabands, as the escaped slaves were known, were eager to earn wages and looked for jobs among the Union soldiers.[19] Since May of 1861, when three slaves escaped to General Benjamin Butler's lines at Fortress Monroe, Virginia, and were hired by him, these refugees had been sheltered. Their former owners came for them under a flag of truce, claiming them under the fugitive slave law. Butler refused to release them, pointing out that Virginia had withdrawn from the Union, and therefore the fugitive slave law did not apply; thus the slaves were "contraband of war." Because Lincoln felt the need to keep border states in the Union, he did not acknowledge the contrabands' right to freedom. Instead, the policy was that if slaves had been employed by the Confederate Armed Services, only then should they be considered contrabands.[20] By March 1862, Congress had passed an act prohibiting Union soldiers from returning fugitive slaves to their masters.[21] This only increased the number of contrabands looking for protection.

Many northern regiments, such as the First New Jersey Cavalry, followed the lead of Congress, giving the contrabands refuge and refusing to yield them to their former owners. When the Gouldins filed complaints of lost slaves, one witness, Samuel Berlin, who ran a blacksmith shop next to Jack Gouldin's farm and knew many of his slaves well, told of being captured twice by the Yankees and being held for several months.[22] During that time he saw one of Frank Gouldin's slaves, John, a twenty-five-year-old valued at $1,450 who almost certainly escaped with Alec as he was reported missing in April. I suspect Alec escaped on April 27 and was involved in the raid on the Tom Gouldin house on April 28.

In their application for reimbursement in the Confederate Citizens Files, the Gouldins, particularly Jack, are loose with their dates. Jack stated that all his slaves left June 15.[23] It is probably more accurate that they left at different times, beginning in April, when Union soldiers appeared across the river from Gouldin's property, and continuing into June. For Alec to have gone on the documented raid to Tom Gouldin's, he would have to have left after April 21 when the First New Jersey Calvary first arrived. It is impossible for Broderick's raid to have taken place on April 18, as Tom Gouldin states. From Pyne's and Jack Gouldin's statements, as well as from Alec's story, it is evident that Humphrey and Alec escaped about the same time. They are both listed as "abducted" from Jack Gouldin and "harbored by the enemy."[24] The First New Jersey Calvary returned to John Seddon's farm near Falmouth by May 1.[25] It is most likely that John, Frank Gouldin's slave whom he claimed was abducted from his residence (Frank was living with his father), was also among those who left at the same time as Alec. Berlin reported seeing John in King George County in the presence of the enemy, probably the First New Jersey Cavalry, and later seeing him in September at Fortress Monroe—known by fugitives, because of General Butler's policies, as "Freedom Fort"[26]—where a large contraband camp had grown up. Berlin reported: "I saw many slaves that I knew and talked with them. A good many were anxious to return to their owners but the U.S. authorities would not permit it."[27]

It seems important to the Gouldins to believe their slaves had been abducted. Accepting that Alec stole away of his own volition would have forced Jack and his sons to confront the reality that those enslaved by them only appeared subservient and loyal because of the power held over them. It would have been difficult for Jack Gouldin to understand why Alec would leave of his own will. He was well looked after and kindly treated. He was a trusted slave: the son of Robert, his premier boxer, and Rose, his plantation seamstress, who was almost a member of the family.[28] From the complaint Gouldin filed, it is evident that he and his sons continued to believe, as Samuel Berlin stated, that the Federal authorities were preventing his slaves from coming back. It is doubtful that it would have occurred to him that Alec had no intention of returning and took steps to prevent this from happening by changing his name.[29]

Alec first found work as an assistant cook and helped forage for local livestock. "*They ate and killed the cows and dried the meat in the sun because it made them sick to eat the raw meat. They would make a fire, cut up the meat, and put it on the stones and let it dry off.*"[30] Eventually, as the regiment's ranks swelled with contrabands, only fugitives who were retained by officers were allowed to remain in camp. At this time, they would not have been permitted to enlist. Both Humphrey and Alec stayed, rewarded for their service in the raid. Colonel Wyndham, Broderick's superior, kept Humphrey as a scout and a guide.[31] Alec was detailed as an orderly in the Hospital Department for Assistant Surgeon Ferdinand Dayton, the man who had facilitated his escape, and as such received wages from the federal government. An officer was permitted to keep a personal servant for whom the government would pay.[32] By July 1862, Congress had recognized the military's dependence on black labor and passed the Second Confiscation Act and the Militia Act, which authorized wages for those of African descent "to suppress the rebellion and granting freedom to slaves so employed and to their immediate families."[33] This also was the Union's acknowledgment of the significance of black labor in its war efforts.

While Alec never served as a soldier officially, there is no question that he was there, carrying out Dayton's orders and giving his all in his personal fight to maintain his freedom. Later, the absence of official papers and the rejection of Alec's service claim caused both him and his family a deep hurt. As did most of the contrabands who served as servants for Union officers, Alec took up arms in his own defense and fought bravely when necessary. He even had certificates of bravery to show for his efforts (described later in this chapter). While Alec considered himself an orderly for Dayton, he also thought of himself as a member of the First New Jersey Cavalry, doing whatever any other soldier was doing to win the war.

One of Alec's main tasks was picking up the dead and wounded on the battlefield, which put him at risk from enemy snipers. The War Department's distinction as to how he enlisted, or did not enlist, was not significant to Alec at the time. As far as he was concerned, he was there and serving to the best of his ability. Later, the Bureau of Pensions declared that there was no evidence of his name on the roles of the regiment.[34] His family always hoped to right this wrong.

In most regiments, officers employed contrabands as personal servants.[35] They fought bravely "using knives, bludgeons, & fire arms with telling effect," wrote Ninth Illinois Cavalry assistant surgeon Charles Brackett in a letter to his wife.[36] He explained: "You are to understand that they were Officers servants. Each Officer is allowed one or more servants, & they are most generally negroes who are employed. . . . The servants of course are armed & the negroes take especial delight to be well armed."[37] This was clearly Alec's position in the First New Jersey Cavalry and the means by which he received his pay. But he was also fighting the enemy at every opportunity, as indicated by the two papers he received for bravery. The role of her father as servant to Dayton is one that Daisy could never accept. To her it was an unjust distinction.

Alec served with Dayton faithfully until he was given a furlough in November 1863. New orders came unexpectedly to the regiment while Alec was still on furlough, causing him to miss the train that took the regiment to Cincinnati and then by boat to Tennessee. He connected with the doctor after the war, and despite Dayton's premature death on November 1, 1866,[38] the surgeon played an important role in Alec's life both during and after the war. Alec only knew Dayton for five years, but in those years, he was a larger-than-life figure, indicating what an important relationship this was for Alec. I was stunned to discover what a short time they had been in each other's presence. As Daisy said: *"Dr. Dayton treated him just like a younger brother. That's the way he loved and treated my father. He was a colonel and a lieutenant and oh, a very fine man, a very fine person. You know he was a wonderful man. He kept my father going."*[39]

While the majority of Union soldiers believed in abolition, this did not mean that they considered the freed slaves as equals, and many viewed them as inferior. Often, the contrabands were the first black people the Northerners had met, and men such as Alec must have favorably impressed them in their day-to-day contact. As the Yankees grew to know Alec, he became a distinct individual, a real human being, rather than an abstract figure. Such associations were critical in changing attitudes within the Union ranks.[40]

Dayton was not without his own class prejudices that showed themselves in a letter he wrote to his mother in which he referred to the white people living in Mississippi: "The people [are] the same as [those in] Tenn. Probably a little more refined but still ignorant and bigotted [*sic*] as all the persons here are."[41] While we know he was an abolitionist, and that he enabled Alec to escape, we know little of his relationships. But Alec's warm attitude toward Dayton speaks volumes. Alec was likable,[42] eager to learn, intelligent, and honest. Living in close association, the two men came to know each other well and under many different and difficult circumstances. The intensity of daily life during the war bred a closeness and deep respect between the two. For Dayton, an ardent abolitionist, Alec made his cause real and personal.

When Alec first met Dayton in 1862, Ferd, as he was known, was twenty-eight years old, the eldest son of William L. Dayton, a prominent New Jersey lawyer, judge, senator, and diplomat. In 1861, Lincoln appointed the elder Dayton as his minister to France, where he was described as "honorable, generous, affable and urbane," all qualities his son acquired along with his father's ardent abolitionist views.[43] Ferd graduated from the College of New Jersey (now Princeton) in 1854 and went on to the University of Pennsylvania for a medical degree, which he received in 1857. He traveled to Paris to study, France being viewed as the leader in the practice of modern medicine,[44] and returned to practice in New Jersey and New York until he volunteered for the First New Jersey Cavalry. He joined in September of 1861 as an assistant surgeon.[45] Surgeons and assistant surgeons were not supposed to take part in military action except as it related to medical obligations.[46]

After serving with Dayton for nine months, Dr. William Phillips, surgeon of the regiment, wrote his associate's father that he could "without hesitation bear testimony to the correctness of his deportment, and to his devotion to his duties" and that he had been "an excellent assistant."[47] Dayton took his duties seriously, was meticulous in the practice of his craft, and was unflagging in dispensing care no matter what the conditions. Major Myron Beaumont portrayed Dayton as "a good Surgeon, thoroughly educated, gentlemanly in manners and a 'bon vivant' and was well liked by all. . . . A jollier companion never lived."[48] Dayton was sociable, liked people, and enjoyed a good time. While he was known for a wild streak and exuberant spirits, he had "sufficient steadiness" to anchor him. Beaumont went on to comment about Phillips and Dayton: "Never was a regiment better supplied with medical talent or surgical skill."[49]

Dayton was an accomplished surgeon, even under conditions he described as "the most disadvantageous and trying situations a surgeon could be placed in."[50] He also had ambition and resented not having his worth as a surgeon fully acknowledged by the military. In a December 1862 letter to his mother, Dayton wrote: "Dr. Phillips makes sure that he is Surgeon in Chief of Bayard's Cavalry although he still had to hold his position in the Regiment so I will in fact be Surgeon in all but rank and pay."[51] This rankled. And then again from near Ripley, Mississippi, in June 1864, he wrote his mother: "I did expect to be appointed Med[ical] Inspector for the District of West Tenn. But starting off on this expedition has postponed it for a short time. It is with Genl Washburn. The higher I get the higher I want to go and it is only human nature."[52]

Shortly after the raid on the Gouldin plantation, the First New Jersey Cavalry moved back to Falmouth and encamped four miles below it on a farm owned by John Seddon, brother of Secretary of War James A. Seddon. According to Sergeant Joseph E. Layton, an enlisted man who later wrote reminiscences of the First New Jersey Cavalry, this piece of land was known as the Hop Yard.[53] Here in early May, the regiment joined with the First Pennsylvania Cavalry to form a brigade under General Bayard.[54] It was during this time that Dr. Phillips wrote to Dayton's father. He described how he and Dayton found themselves under heavy fire while attempting to remove two wounded men from a vessel on the river. Both were pleased to discover they had acted well under these circumstances "with entire self possession throughout, notwithstanding the close proximity of some of the flying balls to us."[55] Sergeant Layton, who had taken possession of a boat and seine net while in King George County, was fishing with his companions out on the Rappahannock, when the Louisiana Tigers, on picket on the south side of the river, opened fire on them. The men dropped into the river and escaped by swimming alongside the boat and pulling the net until they reached a ditch. The Confederates opened fire on the camp, "killing two or three horses and wounding others."[56] Their fire continued on and off, with the result that holes were dug for pickets to stand on guard day and night.[57]

Contrabands were still appearing in great numbers; many were mounted on horses taken from their masters. And daily those who had lost their slaves and horses came to Colonel Wyndham to try to recover their property—one reason Alec changed his name from Berkeley to Turner. Wyndham, however, ignored all their requests and instead used the horses that the contrabands brought to replace some of the mounts his men had lost. This attitude was reflected in statements concerning the enemy "harboring" slaves at Fredericksburg.[58] The Gouldins advertised widely and offered a reward for their servants who had been abducted by the enemy.[59] Early the following year of 1863, when the First New Jersey Calvary returned to Fredericksburg after a sojourn in the Shenandoah Valley, Humphrey was so unnerved by Tom Gouldin's reward notices that he moved north to Newark, where friends of Colonel Wyndham provided for him.[60] Alec never wavered in his determination to fight for his freedom. He remained.

In addition to the serious issues that contrabands brought to the Union military camps, they also helped break the endless monotony of camp life for the Union soldiers, few of whom had ever witnessed the fluid grace and rhythm of their dances or the melodious harmonies of their spirituals. They found both exotic and arresting.[61] Even more exciting was the arrival of a contraband couple with a wagonload of milk for sale. The fresh milk brought to mind the possibility of eggnog, and instantly the entire quantity of milk was bought, much to the delight of the suppliers. The daily humdrum was replaced by a swirl of activity. The most enterprising participants (Dayton and Alec probably among them) left to locate whiskey and returned at dusk with six dozen bottles. They procured a washtub to mix the ingredients, and by eight o'clock all was merriment. Dayton and Phillips took active part in this gathering, suggesting that Alec was witness to it all as well. Over the course of the war, this incident would be replayed in a variety of scenarios as a means of counteracting the pressures of wartime life.

The regiment received orders to join General McDowell at Fredericksburg, and by the end of May 1862, they started for Richmond. On the evening of the second day, as Joseph Layton wrote: "Just as we captured a Confederate picket post and the Confederate drums began to sound an alarm," orders came to turn back.[62] General Stonewall Jackson was threatening Washington by way of the Shenandoah Valley. Once again, the men passed through Fredericksburg, crossing the Rappahannock on pontoon bridges, and from there toward the Blue Ridge Mountains.

Later, describing the Blue Ridge Mountains and Manassas Gap, Alec told his children about *"washing [my] hands in the clouds."*[63] The heavy clouds, which hung low as they rolled across the ridge, cloaked Alec in dense moisture. He found he could cleanse himself of some of the dirt and grime that encased him by rubbing his hands together, fostering this image. Water was in short supply, and he relished this unexpected opportunity. As the men and horses climbed upward, the accompanying wagon trains carrying all their supplies were halted by obstructions placed by the enemy and by the natural hazards of the terrain. Thereafter, the men and their mounts were forced to survive without provisions or water and scavenged from the land. During this period, John Lucas wrote to his brother that "the horses have been on the march for two days and have had four ears of corn."[64]

The troops continued down into the Shenandoah Valley and into Front Royal. The men heard distant artillery thundering as they pushed on toward Strasburg. The Shenandoah Valley was where the First New Jersey Calvary had its initial skirmish with the enemy. As Alec steeled himself for his first engagement, he experienced a vision of both his Lord and Pusley. This was another critical moment in Alec's life. His symbolic act of overcoming the bonds of slavery by dispatching Pusley was sanctioned by his Savior. From then on, he could fight for a universal end to slavery. *He had this manifestation, and Pusley showed himself, and Alec fell on his knees. The Angel of the Lord appeared, and he didn't know what to do, but the Angel led him. Papu said then that he knew the Lord forgave him. And from that time on he tried to help the soldiers. And he was there fighting. He had the revolver.*[65]

Alec was fearless as he threw himself into the fray of battle, retrieving the wounded. *"My father was daring. He didn't stop at nothing."* Daisy cited the *"two papers for bravery"* as evidence.[66] After his decision to help the soldiers, it did not take him long to show his mettle. The first paper for bravery was for an action that Alec performed somewhere in the Shenandoah Valley as the First New Jersey Calvary attempted to prevent General Jackson from marching on Washington. *"He crawled on his belly along a stone wall so as to warn the Union Army of Stonewall Jackson who was one of the cleverest generals of the war."*[67] This action would have impressed the Union soldiers and been a step toward humanizing the former slave.[68]

While Alec was steeling himself for battle, the troops arrived in Strasburg just in time to see the Confederate rear guard leaving. Following in hot pursuit, they captured prisoners and had ongoing skirmishes until the enemy passed Mount Jackson and crossed the Shenandoah River, burning the bridge after them.[69] The river was so high that the Union soldiers had difficulty setting out a pontoon bridge because the anchors would not hold.

The fast-paced march was grueling—two hundred miles in scorching sun, blinding dust, sweltering heat, pelting rain, and crashing thunder and lightning. The caravan of horses and men, now without supply wagons, made their way as fast as they could toward Strasburg, Woodstock, and then south to Harrisonburg, desperately attempting to stop Jackson. Neither the men nor the horses had enough food. This was only the beginning of the trials of endurance that became so much a part of the war.

Once the Confederates crossed the river, they made a bold stand to cover their exodus and opened with twelve-pound cannons on the First New Jersey Calvary's advanced guard.[70] While the explosions were disquieting, they inflicted minimum damage, with "a few men being slightly wounded, and one or two horses killed."[71] Among the injured were two women who had come to watch their hero "Stonewall Jackson defeat the Yankees."[72] Instead, a shell from their own Confederate cannon seriously injured them, tearing the leg from one woman. Drs. Dayton and Phillips tended to them, amputating the ruined leg and dressing their wounds. Alec must have been witness to this as well.

The skirmish near Harrisonburg the next day, June 6, was a discouraging one for the Union. As Chaplain Pyne declared: "If a cavalry charge is glorious, a cavalry rout is dreadful."[73] Dayton penciled home a dispirited letter telling his family:

> Last night when we called the role there were 36 men missing: the Col. [Wyndham], Capt Shelmire, Co. A, Capt. Clark and Co G Tom Haines. The last two we know were wounded and Tom H I have no doubt was killed as he was seen to fall from his horse and when our Regiment fell back, it was each man for himself. A perfect rout. The enemy occupied its ground. We have been unable to look up the killed and wounded.
>
> . . . [We] went into the woods and were opened on by about 2 or 3 regiments. And were cut all to pieces. Col. Kane wounded and taken prisoner and about 50 of them wounded and missing. Gen. Bayard's Brigade that is ours in fact. Our Regiment of Bucktails[74] has done all the fighting and suffered all the hits. But of our Regiment there is about 140 fit for duty today. The horses have all given out as well as men. Any Cavalry Officer can tell how a Regiment falls off on a march of over 200 miles with no rations, water for men or horses except what can be picked up. . . . We are all used up. We lost our Regimental colors to sum up our misfortune it being shot out of the hands of the standard-bearer when the enemy were not three jumps off of him.[75]

Neither Dayton nor Phillips had followed the charge, "thinking the men would be back in a short time." Although not on the front lines, they experienced shot and musket balls raining down in close quarters. "Yesterday when I was trying to get up to the wounded a round shot just missed me and hit in the ground in front of my horse." Dayton ended his letter: "Our Regiment is now pretty well cut up. I don't know what will become of us." There is no mention of Alec, but he was there, living these same experiences, horrified by the carnage, skirting burning ambulances, dead bodies, and fallen horses as he carried the injured from the field on stretchers. While Dayton practiced his skills to save his patients—filthy from the grime of battle, groaning with pain, misery, and thirst—Alec was transporting the wounded and dying to the ambulances and then to local buildings that were turned into makeshift hospitals.[76]

As the days of June lengthened, the regiment returned down the valley beaten, disheartened, and weary. They once again crossed the Shenandoah and pitched camp "in a large field of sweet smelling clover" near the village of Mount Jackson, where the men used a millpond to wash off the battle grime and to rejuvenate body and spirit.[77] War was an awful business, and there was a desperate need to recoup, even if it were just to fight another day. The commissaries turned to slaughtering beef cattle and removing choice cuts for roasting. Some of the officers armed themselves with axes to split open the skulls and extract the cattle brains. Bread was scavenged.

> *The women made this bread—they would put it in the ashes and cover it over and bake it. Then they would make great baskets and bags of it and carry it to the lines to the soldiers. Why those soldiers had nothing to eat for two and three days sometimes. And beans. They could put them in these crock containers so they wouldn't spoil. They didn't care if they did spoil—just so long as they could get them to eat. And baked pans of corn bread. They made these meal sacks that they could put the corn bread in—no papers to wrap them.*[78]

A feast was proposed to some of the officers, among them Ferd Dayton, who set himself the task of finding the wine. He rode off, probably with Alec, and after a number of "adventures," including losing his pocket case of instruments in the enemy's camp, returned with four bottles of Rhenish wine.[79] A merry feast followed with song and high spirits, counteracting battle fatigue and loss. Over the next several days, the regiment took its ease. Their supply wagons finally caught up. Horses were shod, clothes washed, letters written. Then they moved on to Manassas and Warrenton Junction, where the troops rested in the cool of the woods and enjoyed the abundance of blackberries and cherries. Never still for long, they continued to Culpeper Court House before preparing for skirmishes on the Rapidan River.

The Battle of Cedar Mountain began on the afternoon of August 9. There was no protection against the advancing enemy, and the hospital stewards, including Alec, were bringing up the wounded to the ambulances and then to Dayton. Sergeant Joseph Layton was wounded in the left leg with a piece of shell and lay against a haycock until he could be carried off the field. Alanson Austin was critically injured when his right thigh was almost severed from his body, "the crushed and torn muscles showed among them the broken bone, and the blood dropped slowly to the ground, mingling with the dust."[80] He was "almost a child in look and a sort of a pet among officers and men."[81] He was placed on a stretcher, carefully loaded into an ambulance, and taken back to the makeshift hospital, which had "the ghastly apparatus of military surgery."[82] Gently he was brought to Dayton for amputation. "Oh Chaplain, if I could only pray!"[83] he apparently murmured to Pyne, and as the chaplain recited the Lord's Prayer, Austin's lips moved. He was placed on the table, a sponge of chloroform applied to his nose to help dull the pain, and Dayton removed his leg while "the shells of the enemy struck the fence behind which the surgeons plied the knife."[84] Only a few moments could Austin be left to lie still before he was once more loaded into an ambulance and moved back to a house in the rear. Under the influence of the chloroform, his mind wandered. He feebly waved his arm and gave orders as if still on the field of battle. "Then, with a half-articulate cry of 'the Star Spangled Banner,' his voice was hushed in death."[85]

While only eleven were lost from the regiment, the slaughter of Federal forces was great, and Alec was on the field hour after hour, carrying the wounded on stretchers to the ambulances. Dayton labored into the night, working by candlelight. Earlier that day he had been suffering from the effects of chronic diarrhea, but he was there when he was needed. Surgeon Phillips was on sick leave in Washington, and Dayton was the surgeon in charge. He continued working until eleven o'clock at night, when he sank down in complete exhaustion next to the man he was attending.[86] He was up again when the enemy opened a cannonade, and he took charge of a train of ambulances filled with fifty wounded men, leading them to Culpeper, where he found a church he could use for a hospital. Then he proceeded to set it up—no easy task with the need to assemble beds, medical supplies, instruments, food, and crockery, all of which he accomplished with Alec's help. The next day he received thirty more patients. Because the Battle of Cedar Mountain had been unexpected, there were limited medical supplies, fewer nurses, and no preparations had been made for the wounded. The injured were packed into stuffy, unventilated buildings heated by the August sun and stifling weather that only encouraged infection, and as a result, there were a number of deaths from the wounded.

Nevertheless, Chaplain Pyne pointed to the hospital under Dayton, aided by Alec and others, as a model. With more than a hundred wounded, there was only one death from a critical mortal injury. Rather than using amputation—the most common form of surgery in the Civil War—Dayton treated his injured, except Austin, without amputation. He provided his patients with dry, clean beds of hay or straw, adequate portions of well-cooked food, and reasonable ventilation, all of which encouraged recovery. His attention to these details indicates not only his genuine concern for his patients but also his up-to-date medical practices. The belief that agents of infection were airborne, which led to an emphasis on the value of ventilation, was still in its infancy.[87] Dayton was vigilant and exacting in his care, and when men were moved from Culpeper to Washington, each was given "a draught of sound light wine . . . to strengthen him for the journey."[88]

> So marked was the difference between these men and the patients from other hospitals, that the surgeons in Washington inquired under whose treatment they had been, remarking approvingly the superiority of their condition and the intelligence of this fact had great effect in rallying Dayton from the depression of his own illness. Anyone who has seen the difficulties to be encountered in field hospitals, even where every appliance is procurable will acknowledge that the result obtained in this instance was a reasonable cause for self-gratulation.[89]

The morning after the hard-fought battle, a good breakfast was prepared, and talk turned to the necessity of a drop to drink. Ferd Dayton's name immediately came forth with a chorus of voices to see if he could provide some sustenance. Poor Dayton was still at the field hospital, operating on the wounded, and had to refuse the request for his presence at breakfast, but he did send a little whiskey to be administered "medicinally."[90]

Cedar Mountain was followed by three weeks of exhausting marches and skirmishes, and it was perhaps in one of these, or as Daisy indicated, in the aftermath of the Second Battle of Bull Run, that Alec had an astonishing experience: he met two of his ex-master's grandsons on the battlefield. Alec was picking up the dead and wounded when he discovered two sons of Silas Gouldin, Jack's oldest son, one of them wounded. They were young Jack (John G. Gouldin), whom Alec knew so well, and his younger brother, Wilton, both serving in the Ninth Virginia Cavalry.[91] Alec genuinely embraced these men fighting against him. He knew them intimately and had deep feelings for them. Daisy exclaimed: *"They hugged each other. They were so glad to see my father. And my father was so glad to see them."*[92] For that moment, the horror and cruelty of the conflict were put aside, and they reveled in each other's company. With the chains of bondage removed, the situation had changed. This occurrence was important to Alec and was a story he related over and over to his children, suggesting its emotional impact.

August concluded with the Second Battle of Bull Run. The fields were littered with dead and wounded, overwhelming those whose job it was to pick them up. As the fields changed hands, Alec told his children: *"They'd [The rebels would] stick their bayonets in them [Union] soldiers that lay on the ground dying."*[93] The dead were everywhere, and the wounded lay among them, covered with dirt, blackened by powder. Alec must have listened for their groans as he searched for the living. As the hours turned into days, this chore became worse as the dead turned into bloated, maggot-covered corpses, with protruding bowels, vacant eyes, and open mouths, all cloaked in the terrible cloying stench of death, which also clung to the living who were tending them. Death and suffering had become daily fare.

After the First Battle of Bull Run, only dilapidated vestiges of buildings remained standing; they were destitute of comfort and barely afforded shelter. There were no bandages, no stores, no food, and no water to quench the wounded's agonizing thirst, as the wells had been wantonly destroyed. The ambulances returned again and again from the field, bringing men to the surgeons who operated nonstop. Medical Inspector Richard Coolidge arrived with a staff of surgeons from Washington, along with supplies and assistants, and order began to emerge from the chaos of disaster.[94]

Dayton continued to experience chronic diarrhea and finally, in October, was given a leave of absence and sent home, where he ended up in the hospital. Alec may well have gone with him as Daisy told me that her father went home with the doctor at least once. *"He took my father right home to Trenton, New Jersey, into his house and home with him."*[95] On December 9, 1862, Dayton wrote his mother, who was in Paris with his father, that he had come from the hospital the day before.[96] "I am quite well again and hope I will not be troubled with the diarrhea at least until the end of the war." He planned to leave for Washington that night and then go to Acquia Creek, expecting to find his regiment between there and Falmouth. "Everything looks like a severe fight soon between Burnside and Lee at or near Fredericksburg." He had heard the previous night that "General Bayard had ordered to have 12 days rations on hand which looked as if it was intended to serve for a long scout. I hope I shall catch them before they go. The Gen. will not move if he can help it as he wants to be married on the 18th."[97]

Dayton must have made it back just in time to learn the disheartening news that Bayard had received a mortal wound at the Battle of Fredericksburg (Marye's Heights) on December 13. Federal casualties totaled thirteen thousand killed or wounded, while the Confederates lost less than half that number. Rather than being in the thick of battle, Bayard had been knocked down by a shell that "shattered his right thigh just below the hip" as he waited by General Franklin's field headquarters to see if the division commander had a more useful position for his brigade.[98] He refused an amputation and "lingered till two o'clock the following afternoon, writing letters to his fiancée, his parents, and close friends."[99] His body was escorted home by his father, and he was buried on December 18, the day set for his wedding. Bayard was beloved by his men, and his loss was deeply felt. The eulogy for him captured his spirit: "Quick to act, brave to a fault, careful of his men, and dearly beloved by his whole command."[100]

The First New Jersey Calvary moved back across the Rappahannock to their former camp at Seddon's Farm. They were demoralized by recent events, had lost any faith in General Burnside, and were made miserable by the constant cold. Daniel Holt, assistant surgeon in the 121st New York Infantry Regiment, wrote his wife about the "quiet way" he and Josh, his Negro servant, lived: "[Josh] is maid of all work. On him devolves the duty of rising in the morning, making fires, sweeping out the tent, making bed, and feeding Fannie [his horse]. That done, he proceeds to get breakfast, and here carries our kit and stock in trade, which consists in all told of two dishes . . . in which we cook our potatoes, fry our meat and after cooking use them as our dishes."[101] It is more than likely that Alec served in this role as well as performing his duties in the field.

Bad weather and constant picket duty took a toll on both men and horses. There was too little forage for the horses and the necessity of leaving them saddled for hours at a time, sometimes extending into days. There was also a lack of veterinarians, and Alec found his own talents with herbal medicine, vigilantly acquired from his mother, called into practice. He carefully tended Dayton's horses and helped others in preventing the loss of their mounts. *"In the army, they didn't kill the horses. They kept them as long as they could."*[102] Horses were crucial for the cavalry, and officers looked to escaping slaves to help tend to them. Captain John Lucas also had a contraband caring for his horses, and when he sent two home to his brother to be turned out and allowed to recover, he wrote: "I have sent my servant with them. He is a very good darkey. You can let him help you awhile if you want any help and he even takes care of them . . . he is a good hand for it. I know they have got a little scarred up."[103] Alec did his share of "doctoring," but the First New Jersey Calvary still lost numerous horses to malnutrition and diseases such as "grease heel" and hoof rot.[104] If left untreated, both led to lameness. The constant mud and lack of sanitary conditions made these problems inevitable and rampant.

The war was not going well for the Union, and Lincoln replaced Burnside with General "Joe" Hooker, who restored morale and transformed the men "into a well-disciplined, contented, enthusiastic body of soldiers."[105] He introduced reforms, including furloughs to deserving men, more and better rations, and new arms and equipment.[106] Aggressive and inspiring in battle, despite his reputation for drink, he was in stark contrast to the indecisive Burnside.

By June 8, the night before First New Jersey Calvary's engagement at Brandy Station, Alec had been serving for more than a year and must have adjusted to cavalry life, with its intense periods of vigorous action, the grueling marches, and the boredom and hardship of military camp life. It was in this battle that a rifle ball wounded Alec's hip, and he received a second certificate of bravery.

> *We children used to like to hear him tell those different battles of fighting that took place. The last three years he said it was hell. He never expected to come out alive. Never! Never! Something terrible. It was just a dog fight. Why fight to the death. What an awful battle it was. The men on horseback, and at that time the generals*[107] *was right in front, they didn't stay back with seeing glasses and all of that. They were right in front, leading the army to fight. They didn't care whether they'd be shot down or anything at all.*[108]

His children listened attentively as he described battle scenes but also reveled in such intimate details as how the men might curse the enemy, calling out the name of the opposing officer: "*We call in thy name: Three drops of blood we draw from thee. The first from your wicked heart, the second from your liver, the third from your vigorous life. By this we take all your strength and you lose the fight!*"[109]

Brandy Station was the largest cavalry battle of the war. It was bloody and brutal, with fierce hand-to-hand fighting, but it was inconclusive. One participant described "the awful noise" and the scene of devastation: "dead and wounded men lay as thick as clover. . . . riderless horses were galloping madly about the field and six of them attached to a caisson were going on a dead run."[110] It may well be a scene from this battle that Daisy remembers her father telling about the "*horses that were just like people. A master had got thrown in battle, and this horse was around smelling the dead men, looking for his master.*"[111]

Broderick's horse fell dead beneath him twice during the fight, and both times he escaped and was provided with a new mount, but the third time his luck ran out. He fell mortally wounded and was found with a saber through his body; at his side, lay his adversary, pinned in death by Broderick's sword.[112] Virgil Broderick was in the prime of life at thirty-five. Alec must have felt his loss as keenly as any of his men, for it was Broderick who gave him the first opportunity to assert his independence and with it the chance to avenge himself against the institution of slavery through his dispatching of Pusley.

Alec experienced his own hell in the battle and was given an accommodation for rescuing a Confederate officer "*whose legs had been shot off in battle, but his body was caught up in the stirrups. And father with his colt revolver in hand, he jumped at the horse and got this rebel colonel off. Father said he had a small voice, like a lady's, and he swore terrible 'You sons of bitches! Take me! Take me!' That was to the Union Army [officers] after Father had saved him from the battle."*[113]

The toll of this engagement was severe on the Federal troops. Of 280 officers and men in the First New Jersey Calvary, six officers and over fifty men were killed, wounded, or missing, and of thirty-nine horses, twenty-seven were left behind on the field.[114] Despite tremendous losses, the Union cavalry had matched their Confederate counterparts' skill on the battlefield, and this provided much-needed confidence to the New Jersey Cavalry.

We have no idea as to the length of Alec's recovery from his hip injury, but according to Daisy, the shell was not removed until much later.[115] Dayton probably probed the wound and realized it was safer to leave the fragment there. Alec was young, strong, and healthy, and he must have made a quick recovery, for he was fit for the Battle of Gettysburg, or the Battle of Little Round Top as he referred to it. Little Round Top is the smaller of two rocky hills south of Gettysburg and was the scene of a major turning point in the battle when Federal forces successfully repulsed a Confederate assault.[116]

It was also during this battle that Daisy told of Alec seeing a father and son on opposing sides, the son doing the unthinkable and shooting his father down. The horror of this scene left its mark on Alec, and he told the story many times, commenting, "That was slavery and the Civil War!"[117] Sometimes Daisy confused the participants in this incident with members of the Gouldin family, but this is doubtful.

Ferdinand Dayton was promoted to surgeon in the Second New Jersey Cavalry on July 2, 1863, and took up his new commission on July 28. This became effective on August 10, Alec's eighteenth birthday, and the regiment left Trenton for Washington on October 5. In his pension letter to the War Department, Alec wrote:

> *The first Cavalry Company I time was out in 1864. They formed a new Cavalry Second Regiment at Trenton New Jersey under Gov. Parker. The first was discharged at Washington, D.C. I went as orderly again for Dr. Dayton. Ferdinand Dayton. While with him from '61 to '64 I done big service for the government carrying wounded from Battle fields and waiting on them in hospital.*[118]

I assumed Alec had gone to the western front for the last years of the war, but could not understand why there was no mention of Tennessee or Mississippi in his stories. One day as I was going through his pension file, I found a scrawled note tucked in after the January 27, 1906, form, which reiterated that he had escaped from his master and had served as an orderly for Ferdinand Dayton, and that when the Second New Jersey

Cavalry Regiment was instituted he continued with Dr. Dayton. *"My work there was to wait on the wounded soldiers and take care of the Doctor's horses."* Then I saw a significant sentence that I had previously overlooked: *"I then had a ten days furlow and went to Wash. and while I was away they had an order and went to Tenn."*[119] The regiment had started for the West on November 9, going by rail to Cincinnati, and then by steamer to Eastport, Mississippi. By December, they were in Union City, Tennessee, "employed in Garrison duty and scouting," the severe winter taking its toll on both the troops and the horses.[120] In a cryptic sentence, Alec wrote: *"I was then miss of them by going to City Point, Va."* I interpreted this as "I was then missing from them, and went to City Point."

Alec had to have been devastated when he returned from Washington to discover everyone gone. What an awful, empty feeling must have clutched him—one he does not seem to have talked about, not even to his children. Everything I heard from Daisy indicated that he had spent the entire war in Dayton's company. That was what he spoke of. But there were no stories of the western front. Instead, Daisy told of the destruction of Richmond, the "March to the Sea," and the Morgan horses that had been valued for their endurance and hardiness. I had not been able to reconcile those stories with where I thought Alec was. While I was startled by this turn of events, it made much more sense.

I suspect Alec was embarrassed, perhaps to the point of feeling ashamed, that he had been left behind. Even though he could not control the situation, he probably felt that he had let Dayton down. As a camp servant, the army would have had little interest in him, and he would have been on his own. However, he did say he went (was sent?) to City Point, which was neutral ground serving as a place for prisoner of war exchange. Thousands of soldiers were sent there to be exchanged. Both sides had field hospitals there, and as Alec had cared for the wounded under Dayton, it is likely that he was sent there.[121] It must have been a very low time—one of which he apparently never spoke. Despite this devastating setback, eighteen-year-old Alec was resourceful and determined to make his own way.

City Point became a major supply and communications hub for the Union troops under Ulysses S. Grant. Grant understood the necessity of establishing a logistical support center that could supply his men and repair their equipment, as well as setting up hospital facilities, with the extensive Depot Field Hospital to attend to the wounded. City Point served as Grant's headquarters and nerve center during his siege of Petersburg, June 1864–April 1865. By June of 1864, Grant changed his strategic objective from capturing the Confederate capital to destroying the Confederate forces. If he could take Petersburg with its critical transportation networks, Richmond would fall through starvation and lack of supplies.

City Point was strategically located at the junction of the Appomattox and the James Rivers, fifteen miles south of Richmond and ten miles northeast of Petersburg. The building of the infrastructure to efficiently support Grant's army in such a short amount of time was a tremendous feat overseen by Major General Rufus Ingalls. Wharves, built from locally cut and milled lumber, supported 150 to 180 vessels daily. Warehouses were put up to hold six hundred tons of grain and hay per day—twenty days forage or thirty days of subsistence—as well as clothing, military equipment, and hospital stores.[122] A railroad network was constructed and post facilities established. Tons of supplies arrived daily by both ship and rail. A bakery was erected that could supply 123,000 rations of bread daily.[123] There was a constant need for laborers, and the majority of these were contrabands, or undocumented Negro laborers as they were called. Alec may have worked in the hospital or perhaps turned to manual labor. He would have been familiar with the hardscrabble life in a refugee settlement. He may not have been much better off with the First New Jersey Calvary, but he always had Dayton to help him. Now he was on his own—one contraband among thousands. However, there were social comforts. A New York soldier recalled: "often, in the evening when it was quiet, we could hear the colored people, near City Point, who used to hold religious meetings in the open air, sing their quaint but soulful melodies with such volume and earnestness, as to effect listeners even at such a distance."[124] Alec would have taken part in those prayer meetings. They would have served to raise his spirits and nourish his peace of mind during the days of continuous labor, uncertainty, and miserable living conditions. The contrast of the black laborer's subsistence in the midst of apparent abundance must have been striking.

As a gateway to the war, Alec's stay at City Point makes some of his other references to the war understandable in terms of his experience. Alec had access to war news: of the wounded, the captured, the prisons, the terrible living conditions, and the lack of goods. Alec painted a grim landscape for his children:

> *It was such a holocaust. It looked like the end of the world. It had got to be just like a nightmare. The men were dying and hungry, and no food and fires and no home. They were in prisons, and I heard my father tell more than once how the Yankees ate the beans out of the stool of the Rebels at the prison. Father said it was just a dogfight that last year of the Civil War. The people were hungry, the men had got to where they didn't care, and it was just a mad bulldog fight.*[125]

Alec must have been at City Point when an ammunitions barge exploded on August 9, one day before his nineteenth birthday. The explosion was considered an accident and attributed to carelessness, but it was espionage.[126] According to *Harper's Weekly:* "Upward of 50 were killed, 32 of whom were colored laborers."[127] The latter would have been unregistered and "had simply ceased to exist."[128] Alec must have been working away from the center of the explosion.

Lincoln's arrival at City Point on March 24, for what became a two-week stay of waiting as the war wore down, must have been exhilarating for Alec. Possibly Daisy was referring to this when she explained: *Lincoln was doing the best he could to keep calm and straighten out the tangle with all those refugees, slaves—with nothing to eat, nowhere to go, and no clothes. It was something terrible.*[129] By the time Lincoln left, Alec would have been aware of the devastation of Richmond and Lee's surrender at Appomattox on Palm Sunday, April 9, 1865.[130] *As soon as the war ended and Lee gave up the flag, the fighting was done. Well, they couldn't fight. They didn't have any more bullets. They didn't have guns. Their arms was off, and their legs was off. And they didn't have no hospital and nothing to eat. It was such a relief. Why he said it looked like the end of the world. That's all . . . the end of everything.*[131]

According to his grandson, Bruce Turner, Alec headed north toward Washington after the war.[132] He would have been in the company of others like himself, perhaps tagging alongside a regiment going to Washington to be mustered out. He stopped in Richmond, where he was shocked by the devastation but exhilarated by the jubilation of the Union soldiers and his fellow bondsmen, whom he undoubtedly joined as they crowded the streets dancing and singing:

> Slavery chain done broke at last
> Slavery chain done broke at last;
> Slavery chain done broke at last
> I'se goin' praise God till I die.[133]

One of Daisy's favorite stories places Alec on the edge of Washington on April 14, the day Lincoln was shot. She claimed that Alec was with Dayton waiting to be mustered out. Dayton was not mustered out until October 1865, but Alec may have been with the doctor as he was given a sixty-day leave in March and April 1865.[134] Perhaps this is when Alec and Dayton reconnected, underscoring a joyousness that may well have infused his later memory. By Alec's own account, on his pension request, he wrote: "*I was not discharged.*"[135] I doubt he mentioned either this or that he was not with Dayton throughout the war to his family. The period with Dayton and the First New Jersey Cavalry furnished Alec's stories of his war years, and naturally Daisy thought he was with Dayton and the regiment throughout the war.

Alec always maintained that he had heard the hoof beats of John Wilkes Booth's horse as he fled the scene of his assassination of President Lincoln. Alec was on the outskirts of Washington, waiting with a number of former contrabands to be issued freedom papers, when they heard the hoof beats of a rider racing by. A short time later, one of the sentries on guard duty told them that Lincoln had been shot and that the man who had gone by on horseback was Booth, the man who had killed him. We can only guess whether Alec heard Booth's horse, but his conviction that he bore witness to a part of this national tragedy is striking. This story became an important part of his personal saga, something he told repeatedly. It is a vivid expression of emotion, of loss, and of being in the moment. He viewed Lincoln as responsible for his social and political freedom, and he experienced the reality of Lincoln's death through his own senses—hearing those pounding hooves as Booth headed for Alec's former home as a slave, Port Royal, Virginia. Those hoof beats were emblazoned in his psyche and remained a vivid connection to the loss of a man whom he believed restored his freedom and his dignity as a human being. Lincoln always held a special place in Alec's heart. Alec admired and identified with him, believing in his natural shrewdness. "*Lincoln had the strategy brain, and he held on for a long while. He didn't have the education at all, book learning, to work with strategy . . . but he had horse sense.*"[136] For Alec, the Emancipation Proclamation of January 1, 1863, was intensely personal. *That is when Lincoln signed those papers for each and every slave in 1863, after he had given Jeff Davis, the southern rebel leader, the ninety days to come back into the Union, and all go on together again and to give up slavery. And he said that if he didn't come back in the Union, then the war would go on and they was going to fight to the death, to the last man. That was the ultimatum.*[137]

The Emancipation Proclamation was his Declaration of Independence, making him a full citizen. Instead of a piece of property, he was a man with rights. Alec viewed "*this velvety piece of paper-like cloth,*" signed by Lincoln, with great reverence. "*We always called it a Freedom Paper,*" Daisy recounted. "*That made the slaves free. Otherwise I'd be a slave as I talk to you!*"[138] Alec brought out this "Freedom Paper" frequently, instilling in his children the same reverence with which he regarded it. It was a tangible reality, and another personal connection to Lincoln. Daisy commented often how similar her father's signature was to that on the document. Throughout the years of family life, Lincoln was always a subject of reverence. Sally Turner, Alec's beloved wife and steadfast partner, shared his deep feelings for Lincoln. One of her few stories of slavery was that she sat on Lincoln's knee when she was a small girl in Fredericksburg. It is true that Lincoln was in Fredericksburg on May 23, 1862, when Sally would have been seven, but whether Sally actually sat on his knee is not possible to verify.[139] What is significant is the awe with which Lincoln was viewed in the Turner household.

Alec's personal connection to this monumental event infuses his story with dramatic power: "*And then on top of it all, in the very midst of a terrible situation, Lincoln was shot. Shot dead. Well, then Father said, as he, with his group, was getting ready to be mustered out—they heard, my father told it again and again—he heard the hooves of Booth's horse as he rode running away from shooting Lincoln. They was on the edge of Washington ready to be mustered out. And so Father said, 'What a time!'*"[140]

CHAPTER 6

Postwar

> I was now my own master. There was no work too hard.
> —Frederick Douglass, *Narrative of the Life*

Once in Washington, Alec would have found refuge in one of the Freedman's Bureau camps. The city was filled with over sixteen thousand refugees, who, like Alec, were full of optimism but facing a sobering reality and a deep uncertainty as to what the future held.[1] Black refugees flocked to the city, inundating the facilities set up for them at Freedman's Village in Arlington. These camps intensified the separatism and cultural marginality that came with emancipation.

Alec Turner (with hands on hips) and other freedmen working at Merrill's Quarry, Brownville, Maine, ca. 1871. Courtesy of the Maine Historic Preservation Commission, Augusta, Maine.

Alec was resourceful, but the conditions were miserable, including subsistence living, overcrowding, inadequate sanitation, and rampant disease.[2] Most freedmen were destitute and desperately in need of food and clothing. It was assumed that the great demand for labor would lead to refugees being in the camps only temporarily, but instead, numbers of refugees never envisioned overwhelmed the camps. Rations of food, clothing, and wood for cooking and washing were issued. Alec may have been sent directly to Mason's Island, a camp that was also a depot from which contrabands were hired.[3] But the steady press of refugees—the old and infirm, women and children, as well as able-bodied men—overburdened the island. Seven buildings, used as barracks for the "colored" troops during the war, were filled to capacity. An inadequate supply of water came from two wells. A pass was needed to leave the island. An early description of the conditions depicted men and women "tumbled" together into the badly crowded barracks and sleeping on the floor "promiscuously."[4]

At some point Alec returned to Caroline County to find out how his mother and the rest of his family and friends had survived the war. Daisy indicated that he did so more than once. She said that Alec's brother George had been sold down South, and that Alec had to go in search of him. This seemed unlikely; I did not think Gouldin would sell him, particularly as he was married with two young children.[5] Court documents provided the answer. Tom Gouldin explained that because some of the servants had run off, his brother-in-law, William White, begged Jack to carry his servants south to safety. Shortly before he died, Jack Gouldin finally agreed, and William White and Frank Gouldin took almost all the remaining servants to Pittsylvania County to hire them out.[6] Alec did go south to find his brother, perhaps his mother as well, and helped them back to Caroline County.

Alec returned no longer a slave boy of sixteen, but a man of nineteen who had experienced the extremes of war: survival and death, destruction and victory, suffering and comradship. Since he left three years earlier in April 1862, Jack Gouldin had died, the enslaved were freed, and the lush landscape was scarred by the ravages of war. The warring armies left a swath of destruction in their wake: They burned plantation houses. They threw up earthworks. They ravaged crops and land wantonly. They laid trees to waste for firewood.

Whereas Jack and his wife had died, many of the younger Gouldins remained. Frank was managing the remainder of the estate, although a sale of the bulk of Gouldin's personal property had taken place in September 1864.[7] Zephie, who was now twenty-two, probably still lived in her grandfather's household, as she remained unmarried until 1870.[8] She bought a bed (most likely the one in which she slept) and a looking glass from her grandfather's estate. Alec would have made a point to see her. He also must have seen Gouldin's oldest grandson Jack, who had bought land next to his uncle's former home, Chestnut Grove.[9] The original plantation was greatly diminished in size, and by his father's will, Tom was required to turn the title of his farm (where the raid had taken place and near where Alec had killed Pusley) over to his father's estate in exchange for land that fronted the Rappahannock.[10] Tom's farm was then sold by the estate to his sister and brother-in-law, Martha and William Broaddus.[11]

Life had changed dramatically for the Gouldins. Not only had Jack Gouldin lost his slaves, a substantial part of his wealth, but his $36,000 investment in Confederate bonds was a significant loss. Without slave labor, the Gouldins were no longer able to cultivate their lands and turned to paid labor or tenant farmers. In May 1865, Tom Gouldin wrote President Johnson for amnesty and claimed that at fifty-four he had "a large and dependent family of children, most of whom are females," and that the property that remained would "barely suffice with my own exertions to enable me to maintain them."[12] Alec told his children about the young "misses," probably Bettie Gouldin Conway, Gouldin's youngest daughter, who once dressed in silks and satins while a slave shooed the flies off her, but who now was *"bare-foot with just one piece of a sack bag thing tied around"* her and hungry and poor.[13] Daisy explained that when her father described the Gouldins' *"terrible situation,"* he felt real sympathy for them, *"the tears rolling down his cheeks."*[14] Alec did not hate them, nor did he want to extract retribution; he simply *"wanted a different life and freedom to do what he wanted to do."*[15]

Once back in Caroline County, George worked as a farm laborer as he weighed his options for the future. He must have listened avidly to Alec's war experiences, but also to his stories of refugee camps and hard labor. There was a gulf of difference between him and his younger brother, who did not have the responsibilities of a family.

Alec knew that Caroline County was no longer where he wanted to remain. He was set on moving north as quickly as he could, determined to forge a new life for himself.[16] He was young and strong, unafraid of hard labor, particularly when he was working for himself, and unwavering in his belief that he would succeed. Alec returned to Washington, which was full of people like himself. But as Daisy said, *"like Martin Luther King, he had a dream,"*[17] and I would add the determination and the will to make it a reality.

If Alec did not connect with Ferdinand Dayton during his sixty-day leave in March and April of 1865, they certainly met after Dayton was mustered out in late October. It would have been a reunion full of deep feeling and considerable joy. We can only wonder how they found each other, how difficult it was, and how long it took. Daisy said: *"This doctor found him through Washington,"* meaning through the Freedman's Bureau.[18] Dayton's efforts in finding Alec speak volumes about their relationship. Mustered out of his regiment at the end of October 1865, in Vicksburg, Mississippi, Dayton probably returned to Washington by train from Cincinnati. Once in the capital, he must have made an effort to locate Alec.

> *He took my father right home to Trenton, New Jersey, with him and immediately got my father into a school. My father studied engineering and graduated with top honors in two years. Dr. Dayton had got him in the college going to night school and got him the job to work in Cameron and Osborn's Grocery Store delivering groceries in the daytime. Everyone for some reason liked my father. He was a favorite everywhere he went. And so the teachers and the professors and everybody helped him all they could. He was unusually smart.*[19]

Dayton had received little news from his family, but by 1866, after his father's death, his mother, sister, and younger brothers had returned from Paris. Ferd, as eldest son, took on a new role as head of the family. He certainly would have traveled to Camden to visit his grandmother and his uncle, and brought Alec along.

It was probably in Camden where Dayton found Alec a job at Cameron and Osborne, a local grocery store. Alec delivered goods to customers during the day and attended school in the evening.[20] There was a considerable black community in South Camden, and a schoolhouse had been erected in 1860 for their children to attend school separate from white children. Many of the adults wished to gain an education as well, and the Philadelphia Friends set up a night school for colored adults in the schoolhouse. The Philadelphia Friends, and then the New Jersey Friends, supported this school until 1865.[21] Who financed it, or if it was financed after that, is not clear, but because of the dates that Alec had to have been there, I suspect this is where he attended night school for two years. Fred Reiss, in his book on public education, notes that public night school was held in 1867–68, but was not considered successful and was closed down.[22] In 1872, "adults in the colored ward, beseeched board members to establish night school in the Ferry Road School House," so there was a steady and strong desire for education.[23] The curriculum, rather than a college course as Daisy suggested, was much more basic, consisting of "spelling, reading, writing, and the rudiments of arithmetic."[24] Alec thirsted for learning; school provided a chance to better himself, and he made the most of it. Throughout his life, he remained grateful to Dayton for this opportunity. It was in New Jersey that he first began to read the newspaper. He became an avid reader, although he never trusted his writing skills. Later in life, if he had an important letter to write, he would turn to one of his daughters.

The family story that is most well known from this era is Alec Turner's exuberance on St. Patrick's Day, which, according to his grandson, Bruce, did not end well for him.

> *In Trenton,*[25] *New Jersey, on one St. Patrick's Day he came out of a saloon and shouted when he got out on the street, "Hooray for St. Patrick or any other SOB." And he was immediately arrested by an Irish policeman and thrown in jail, and he stayed in there all night until they let him out the next day. So that cured him about expressing himself about someone else's Saint. He used to tell that over and over again because that was sort of a low point on his life story.*[26]

One day as I was going through papers for Daisy, which she frequently asked me to do, I came across a card sent to her on St. Patrick's Day from her sister Violet, with a dollar enclosed. Daisy explained that she and her sisters had celebrated St. Patrick's Day for over eighty years because of her father's story of this event.[27]

Dayton returned to Natchez, Mississippi, where he had leased a cotton plantation. He died there suddenly on November 1, 1866, of "congestion of the brain."[28] Alec would have been devastated. Dayton had survived the war only to succumb to some sort of bacterial disease, probably brought on by a mosquito bite. Daisy believed Dayton was a friend of A. H. Merrill, the owner of a slate quarry in Williamsburg, Maine, and that Dayton had helped Alec procure a job in the quarry. Perhaps Dayton knew Merrill and recommended Alec, but there is no way of confirming this. Dayton died almost two years before Alec got this job, and it seems doubtful that Dayton was involved. It is more likely that Daisy confused Dayton and Merrill, two white men she never met, but who played significant roles in Alec's life. For example, in different versions of her story of her parents' marriage, Daisy interchanges Dayton and Merrill as the provider of their wedding clothes. Due to the date of their marriage, Merrill would have been their benefactor.

When Alec finished school, probably in late 1867 or early 1868, he returned to Washington, found lodging in the refugee camp on Mason's Island, and lived there until he was able to secure the job with A. H. Merrill.[29] *"There was still this awful dilemma in Washington,"* Daisy recounted. *"The situation was terrible."* Alec found employment cleaning out latrines. The work was done at night, and the waste was hauled to farms outside the city. He explained with delight to his grandson George Hall that because he worked at night, he was able to present himself dressed up in his best during the day. *"The young boys and young women around there that he was acquainted with didn't know how he made his living, and he never would tell them."*[30] This is perhaps another indication of the characteristic that led to his nickname of "Pompey" on the plantation: his love of fashionable dress.

We know little about Alec's social life at this time. However, he told another grandson, Bruce Turner, about a girl he courted in New Jersey. He decided to ask her to marry him, but he must not have been too sure of himself as he waited until the last minute before leaving to catch his train back to Washington to ask her. Probably sensing Alec's uncertainty, the young lady rejected his proposal. Bruce recounted his Grandfather's response: *"I ran so fast for the train that one could have played marbles on my coat tail."*[31]

The Bureau of Refugees, Freedmen, and Abandoned Lands was created by an act of Congress in March 1865 to help the thousands of newly freed and displaced refugees. President Andrew Johnson appointed Oliver Otis Howard as commissioner of the bureau in June 1865. Howard, known as "the Christian General," had gained prominence through his actions in the Civil War.[32] He had been in the thick of battle, lost his right arm, suffered defeat, and risen to be a co-leader in the March to the Sea. Howard was a native of Leeds, Maine, and visited Adams Merrill to arrange for "a small colony of Negroes" to be sent to work in the quarry.[33] Merrill's granddaughter, Susan Merrill Lewis, made note of his visit and recounted that some of the children "slept on the shelves in the bathroom so he might have their room."[34] She believed that her grandfather brought the freedmen to the quarry because he supposed he had found an unlimited supply of cheap labor, but also because he wished to help them.[35] The second statement is upheld by Merrill himself. Prior to the group of workers arriving, he brought home a young refugee, named George Washington, whom he introduced into his household and educated with his children. Merrill made a trip to Washington during the Civil War to investigate hiring quarry workers,[36] and it is likely that he returned with the boy, who remained with the Merrills until he was fifteen in 1871. Like so many of the quarry workers, he was vulnerable to the harsh winter, which later proved to be the death knell for Merrill's experiment with refugee workers. Through the years, George Washington retained a fondness for the Merrills and remained in touch with them. His last letter came forty years later in 1911. He reported that he was a lawyer in New York City and had established a home with his mother and sister from whom he had been separated during his childhood in slavery.[37]

Adams Hewes Merrill, born in 1806 in Belfast, Maine, was of Welsh extraction and first came to Williamsburg, Maine, in the late 1820s. In 1839, Merrill married Percis Greenleaf, the daughter of Ebeneezer Greenleaf, who, with his brother Moses, founded Williamsburg in 1810. The area between Brownville and Williamsburg contained a number of slate quarries that began to be developed in 1840. Others from northern Wales, the center of the Welsh quarrying industry, joined the effort. They were well schooled in slate production from their earliest apprenticeships; they learned to run errands, absorbing the necessary signals that pertained to the work, then they learned the art of drilling, hanging by ropes, blasting, and, finally, the skill of splitting slabs of slate into shingles.

Merrill bought his quarry in 1849 and made a successful business of it. By his death in 1888, he owned two slate quarries, 2,369 acres of timberland, nine houses, mules, machinery, and the company store.[38] He needed a workforce of eighty men to operate the quarry and the mill where the roofing slate was produced. During Alec's tenure, a six-mule team was necessary to haul the roofing slate to Bangor where it could then be loaded and shipped out to Boston.[39] Later in the 1870s, Merrill was successful in lobbying for tracks to be laid and the advent of rail service.

Up until 1868, Merrill's workers had been mostly Welshmen. They came with their families and traditions, but it was difficult to keep a full crew—they were in demand in Vermont and New York slate quarries as well. After a generation or so, finding the working conditions too crude and dangerous, they began to move to larger towns and factories. The prospect of finding a new source of ready labor was a matter of utmost concern to Merrill. In a letter dated July 12, 1868, to the Freedman's Bureau, Merrill requested twenty men, stating his wages as $1.25 to $1.50 per day, and then shortly after, he made a second request, increasing the number of workers to forty.[40] On July 29, a group of thirty-eight refugees was sent, among them one family of four, two married couples, and the rest single men ranging in age from fifteen to forty-three. Twenty-three-year-old Alec was one of the youngest. While it is unclear exactly how Alec obtained the job, and despite being one of the youngest of the refugee workers, he lost no time in making the most of the opportunity by establishing a leadership role.

When the freedmen first arrived at the quarry, they must have felt they had traveled to the end of the earth. They went by train from Washington to Boston, then another two hundred miles by boat, first from Boston to Portland, and then on to Bangor. From Bangor, they traveled fifty miles inland in a quarry wagon pulled by a team of mules. When they reached Williamsburg, they found a few scattered houses, a church, a school, and a vast open pit surrounded by mounds of stone rubble and wooden sheds. The refugees' first task was to build three or four small, uninsulated houses at the quarry, and then that many more on the road between Williamsburg and Brownville.[41] These were painted red and described by Daisy as the size of "*hen house[s]*." Still, after the conditions they left behind in Washington, such quarters must have been a relief—that is, until winter set in. *At least they had a place to go and a home. Then Merrill had another friend that run a factory. Merrill would take them all over to this factory and fit them up with clothing. They paid twenty-five cents a week down on clothes—shoes, dresses, and things—because they were about naked.*[42]

Alec remained in Maine almost five years and impressed Merrill with his intelligence and work ethic. From the beginning, he consistently worked the longest hours and received the highest monthly pay of those earning the standard wage of $1.50 per day. (The superintendent of the quarry and master quarryman, Meshach Jones, a Welshman, drew the highest wage of $3.50 per day.)[43] The pay records of the quarry give evidence of Alec's determination to succeed, his astonishing capacity for hard labor, and his strong constitution. His strength of purpose is both striking and reminiscent of Frederick Douglass's statement that once he was working for himself, "I went in with a glad heart and a willing hand. I was now my own master. There was no work too hard."[44]

The process of extracting slate was arduous. Work was six days a week and twelve hours a day—although in the dark winter months, the workday was shortened to eight hours. While the freedmen were used to long hours and hard labor, the circumstances in the quarry were very different from what they had ever experienced. The fear of heights and vertigo were a reality. The deepest pit at Merrill's quarry was three hundred feet.[45] The men were either lowered into the pit—by placing a foot in a hook, grabbing a rope, and being lowered—or they climbed down long, narrow ladders. Once in the pit, the first task was to expose the slate by clearing away waste stone. They drilled by hand and blasted with black powder to cause cleavages in the slate. Then they used pry bars along the cleavages to break off slabs of slate from the quarry wall. Once the slate was extracted, it was hauled up in buckets and finished off in the mill. Skilled workers split the slate, and then it was trimmed to the correct size before being loaded into a freight wagon and carried to Bangor to be shipped to urban centers.

Not only was this work backbreaking, but it was also hazardous. The smaller the quarry, the more danger, with little opportunity for escape if something dropped from above or let go. The worst accident at Merrill's quarry occurred when the dumping mechanism on a bucket bringing up a crew from the pit malfunctioned. The men were catapulted into the pit, and two were killed.[46] This work was difficult in good conditions, but horrible in the winter months when the thermometer hovered near zero. The men from Virginia had never known such cold. They knew little of frostbite, and they found it difficult to keep their extremities warm. Their drafty, uninsulated shacks tended to encourage sickness and pneumonia during the extended Maine winter. A great many fell ill, and a number died. As the winter wore on, many became anxious to return to a warmer climate.

None of this fazed Alec. His constitution was strong, and he remained healthy throughout his time in Maine.

Merrill was disappointed that more of the men did not bring families, as had the Welsh before them.[47] After the long winter, he was aware that many of the refugees wished to leave, and he wanted to find other freedmen who might come with their families. He discussed this with Alec, who already had proven his leadership qualities. Alec told him that he knew a number of good workers who would be willing to come north if he went to Virginia to find them. He was thinking particularly of his brothers George and Lindsey. This idea appealed to Merrill, and he arranged for Alec to take back the freedmen who wished to return to Washington, and then recruit a new group of workers.

At the end of May, Alec left the quarry with the trust of Merrill, substantial responsibility, and a project he was certain he could accomplish. He traveled first to Washington and looked for recruits before continuing to Fredericksburg and on to Port Royal. Lindsey Coleman was nineteen years old and single. Alec had no trouble convincing him to come north. His older brother George was interested, but not quite ready to travel that distance with his family. Rose, still living with George, listened to all of Alec's stories. His appearance, enthusiasm, and obvious success in comparison to their situation as sharecroppers made an impression on all of them. After Alec left, both George and Lindsey submitted letters of dismissal from Bethesda Baptist Church and prepared to leave.[48]

This trip is especially notable to the Turner family because it was when Alec first met Sally Early, his future wife. He was gathering those who had come from Caroline County to Washington to make the journey. Sally, a girl of just fourteen, was with a group of refugees from Fredericksburg. She felt lost, alone, and vulnerable, having been separated from her mother and younger sister Rebecca and torn away from all she had known. She had no education and little knowledge of the world. Alec's heart went out to her. Daisy described that time and brought it to life:

> *So, my father was carrying them to Maine when the last shipment that they were going to take out for some months was the Early slaves in Washington, DC.*[49] *And among them was my mother. There they were in Washington, and they were stranded, not knowing what they were going to do or where they were going, only that they were going with this man to Maine. And Father says he fell in love with my mother. He says she stood there with the Early slaves, pitiful-looking, and not knowing anything either. She was fourteen in February, and this was June, when she stood there to go in the crowd. Father said they couldn't get this group ready to go in this shipment. He talked with her and told her that he would be back for another shipment, that his boss would have ready for them in*

September. So, Father says she eased up a little. Father said he had a gold watch with a fob that Dayton had given him, and he took the fob off from his watch chain and gave it to Mamu. He said, "I will write you a letter." So Father said they both left, and he came to Maine with the group, but every minute of his time was most on her.[50]

Alec appeared as a savior, reassuring and kind, a protector, and a man who knew his way around. Sally was at once forlorn and appealing, and under the warmth of his attention, she became radiant and alive. She was beautiful, and Alec was smitten. He would be twenty-four on August 10 and was ready for a wife.

Daisy always claimed that Sally was the daughter of Civil War General Jubal Early and a slave mistress, Rachel. Daisy pointed out that Jubal Early had never been married, but that he had five children with Rachel, three of whom survived into adulthood: Sally, a younger brother, William Armstead Early, and a younger sister, Rebecca. While Alec made sure his family knew his history, something most uncommon at that period, the same cannot be said of Sally. There is certainly confusion about her past. Daisy always claimed that Rachel was a household slave on the Early plantation. This is probably the case, although the plantation did not belong to Jubal Early; it belonged to Henry Early. According to Daisy, Sally's master was Tom Slaughter, but not much seems to be remembered about him. Sally told her grandchildren that she lived in the big house and had been treated kindly. However, when the Union troops were in Fredericksburg, they would come by the house begging for food. At night, Sally's mother would hide corn bread and biscuits in her bosom and take them to the Union soldiers.[51]

Alec went back to Maine in late July with some of the workers and returned to Washington in late August to bring back the remaining families and to marry Sally Early. This time, another of the freedmen, Dick King, known to be a hard worker, came with Alec. King, too, returned with a bride.[52] Daisy's narrative continues, with details that bring her family story into vivid, sometimes poignant, reality:

When it got to be the last of August, and he went back for this last shipment, he had told his boss his story. Hardly without Papu knowing, Mr. Merrill bought a dress, got the minister, and got everything arranged just as if my mother was his own little daughter, and had the wedding all prepared and ready with the Reverend Lee in Washington. These wedding clothes all bought with the suit and shoes and silk underwear for my father. My father said he stood up—the stuff that was on him was worth a thousand dollars, paid for by Mr. Merrill. And my mother's wedding dress, there must have been six or eight little moons all joined together, like half hearts and three ruffles. And that was what my mother was married in—this beautiful white dress, along with a pocketbook, a ring, and all

> *the things that a bride would want. My mother and father was married on the second day of September 1869. Along with it, the minister had the wedding certificate. All around the edge of it were little pink and white rosebuds, and then the reading on it that this day, Sally Early, the daughter of Jubal*[53] *Early, was wedded to Alexander, ex-slave. And my father and mother carried that. It was wonderful at that time because slaves weren't allowed to marry, and they didn't have weddings with ministers.*[54]

A proper wedding was important to Alec and Sally, and they remained grateful to Merrill for the role he played. A photograph of Alec in his wedding clothes—a waistcoat and tails, with a gold watch chain draped down his vest—was a treasured possession for Daisy. Shortly after Alec and Sally's marriage, the group of new quarry workers and their families traveled north to Boston, and then by boat from Boston to Bangor. This proved to be the newly married couple's first adventure together.

Alec Turner's wedding photograph, Washington, DC, September 2, 1869. Courtesy of the Vermont Folklife Center, Middlebury, Vermont.

When they got out in the ocean to a certain place where they said there was a whirlpool and they always had bad going . . . a storm came up and when they got to this place, the boat struck a leak. Father told, oh, I've heard him tell it so many times, how the water came in. They put in mattresses and they pumped the water. They done everything that could humanly be possible, until they saw there was no hope. . . . Then the captain came and said there was no hope. The boat was going to sink. The women and children first, to take the little lifeboats they had. . . . Father said that from the storm and everything, there wasn't going to be any hope for anybody, as far as he could see. He never could tell anyone—only describe the situation and his feelings. He said he prayed as much as he could and tucked Mamu in his arms. . . . But he said this woman . . . her name was Liza, she could pass for white, and she was kind of short—a slave, but she was older, like in her forties with kind of reddish hair, and she had blue eyes and peculiar features.[55] *She didn't seem to be educated. Father said she came up from where they were on the deck and rushed out in the open. She raised both her hands. And Father said she started praying to "Jesus Christ that was born in the manger to the Virgin Mary and died on the Cross of Calvary and who had walked upon the sea." Father said she was praying like that, and almost instantly the wind and the boat stopped rocking—gradually, easily, and the water stopped coming in. He said he don't know what was taking place. But the captain who had been so brave and bold, kind of succumbed, and the tears were running down. . . . The calm came, and they patted her on the back and says, "Pray Liza, Pray Liza, Pray on Liza." And Papu said that woman prayed—he don't know for how long, a few minutes, a half an hour. But he said everything calmed, the boat stopped [rocking], and they made [their destination] all right.*[56]

This terrifying event occurred on Wednesday, September 8, 1869, just six days after Alec and Sally were married, and was known as "The Great Gale," a violent hurricane that struck New England, causing extensive destruction from Providence to Bangor. Those traveling from Gloucester to Boston aboard the steamer *Escort* described the wind rising "to a furious height" with a "tremendous" sea.[57] Pounding rain and dense blackness obscured everything beyond the steamer. "The waves ran mountain high, dashing over the steamer, oftentimes breaking and causing her to strain, roll and pitch fearfully."[58] Numerous vessels went to pieces in the gale, while others were wrecked or driven ashore, with considerable loss of life. For those traveling in Maine waters, the storm struck at night, which must have made it that much more frightening. The passengers and officers of the steamer *Cambridge*, headed for Bangor, reported a "fearful night."[59] The *Cambridge* experienced the full force of the gale a little after 7:30 p.m. The vessel proved unmanageable, its sails shredded by the heavy gusts, and it lay disabled. The ship "rolled and pitched fearfully, and it was hardly expected by any one on board that she would survive the storm. Their preservation is regarded as entirely providential."[60] The gale is reminiscent of the storm that befell Alec's grandmother's vessel off the coast of Africa, and the story has elements of the storm the preacher dissipated by prayer at Alec's father's funeral. Certainly, the occurrence substantiated Alec's strong belief in the power of prayer and strengthened his young bride's trust in the power of her husband's arms to protect her and keep her safe.

After their travels, Alec and Sally would have been relieved to reach their destination where they were to begin their life together in one of the little red cabins on the road to Brownville. Sally must have felt she had been brought to the edge of a vast wilderness as she gazed out across the deep gaping, quarry pit to strange-looking equipment, piles of rock rubble, and the scattered houses of the village. She would have been reassured when greeted by Mary Scott, Louise Williams, Annie Taylor, and Susan Walker, wives of freedmen John Scott, Wesley Williams, Henry Taylor, and Harry Walker. Here were women who had survived a year in this distant land and were as excited to meet the newcomers as Sally Turner, Liza King, Lucy Carter, and Caroline Howard were relieved to receive their warm introduction. They provided a great deal of companionship, comfort, and solace for each other, particularly during the long days their husbands spent in the quarry or later when tragedy struck, as it did when Susan Walker's husband died. It would have been the women who helped Sally adjust to her new life. All these changes had to have seemed overwhelming to the fourteen-year-old wife. She had come to trust and idolize her husband, a trust and devotion that would only deepen over a lifetime together. While she knew nothing of the world, she had helped in the big house with cooking, sewing, and innumerable domestic chores. She was ready to care for a husband.

Alec was back at work in the quarry early on the morning of Friday, September 10, just two days after their harrowing experience. It was reassuring to have both Alec's brother Lindsey and Sally's brother Armstead Early as part of their group. All the freedmen, though only thirty-five in number, became a close-knit community. (Alec's older brother George decided to remain in Washington with his family and Rose.) Armstead Early was only thirteen years old but kept pace with the older men. The new workers would have been given the unskilled jobs while they grew more familiar with quarry work, but unlike the first refugees, they had nine men who had been there a year to help them overcome anxieties about the newness, strangeness, and difficulty of it all. A slate quarry has 80 percent waste material; thus there is a great deal of backbreaking work: shoveling, clearing away, hauling, loading. Alec continued to be at the top of the list in days worked and pay received. His brother Lindsey, while capable of hard work, never attained Alec's level of success.

As winter came on, the newcomers found they were not prepared for the harsh weather. The cold permeated their cabins, and living conditions must have been unbearable for them. Their health suffered, and again, several contracted pneumonia and died. There were longer absences from work as the winter dragged on and the men's health failed. The workers, careful to keep the slate from freezing overnight, covered it each afternoon before leaving the quarry. Alec was working overtime, probably indicating that during the winter he tended the steam pump. This was a twenty-four-hour responsibility and at times meant going down into the quarry at night by the light of a lantern, not a task for the fainthearted.

Whether in winter or summer, living in a small, isolated New England village brought very different social conditions as well. The children of the freedmen attended school and played with the local children. Alec, with two years of schooling under his belt, volunteered to teach his fellow workers to read, write, and do arithmetic. They, too, thirsted after the rudiments of education. Alec told his grandson Bruce about the process, and Bruce described how *"the persons learning would go to work with their pencils behind their ears as a badge of some kind of education that they had. They were very proud of their ability to put their ideas on paper."*[61]

As they had in the contraband camps, the freedmen held prayer meetings. The Protestant New Englanders were surprised by the obvious feeling displayed at these gatherings. Susan Merrill Lewis, Merrill's granddaughter, remembered: "They joined hands and circled round the room, singing and cracking their knuckles at intervals and shouting fervent exhortations and prayers. In singing they improvised parts sometimes carrying eight parts at once, all in harmony."[62] These meetings were an important part of Sally and Alec's lives. Both had deep religious underpinnings. They loved to sing the old hymns, Alec with his rich tenor and Sally with her true soprano. This, too, was a lifelong enjoyment they shared. *"My mother could sing soprano just like a mockingbird,"* Daisy reported proudly.[63]

Daisy remembered her Uncle Early (known as Armstead at the quarry) as a great singer and dancer. He and another young quarry worker, Bob Williams, made visits throughout the neighborhood to sing, particularly to the Merrills. The New Englanders were probably familiar with some of the songs, including "Barbara Allen," but others must have been new to them, such as "Hail Brethren Hail." Singing in the neighborhood was the freedmen's way of honoring someone or participating in community life. Bob Williams knew how to yodel and taught many of the boys. The younger generation moved most easily across racial boundaries; it is doubtful that the older generation had more than a passing acquaintance with the black quarrymen. The locals remained standoffish and held themselves apart. Still, they were kind to the workers, and when Sally had twins and became ill, they helped care for her.

The quarry records tell us nothing about the wives and children of the workers. Only through the 1870 census do we know that any women and children were there. Early in 1870, still before her fifteenth birthday, Sally would have known she was pregnant, though she would not have realized that she was having twins. From Daisy's account, she was in no way emotionally prepared for this. The other freedmen's wives helped and encouraged her through her pregnancy, and Alec and some of the wives treated her with teas and herbal remedies, but otherwise she had no prenatal care. As is common for young mothers having twins, Sally gave birth early. On September 26, 1870, Rachel and Rose were born, in that order, and named after their two grandmothers. Alec was absent from work September 26 and 27 to help care for his wife and newborns.

Sally was petite, and carrying twins had been difficult. *"From the early birth, and my mother's no care for maternity or understanding or anything, [my mother] was very ill and went into quick consumption."*[64] Sally did not recover her strength from this event while in Maine. The other wives rallied around her, as did some of the white women in the community. Not only did Sally need care, but so did the twins, and Sally's mother Rachel was sent for. Sally's spirits must have soared at the sight of her mother.

In June 1870, two months before his twins were born and two years after arriving in Maine, Alec's pay was raised to $1.75 a day; the standard pay was $1.50. He most likely was made foreman of his shift, reflecting his leadership and strong work ethic.[65] He responded to his new status by immediately earning $45 for a month's work. Finally, he was making real progress; he must have been exhilarated. He continued to earn well above $40 until August 1871.

Meanwhile, the cold winters and difficult work were taking their toll on the freedmen. They were grateful for the work and steady pay, but they felt isolated. After a year, men began to leave. After his second winter in 1871, Lindsey left at the end of April.[66] By August, only nine freedmen were left.[67]

In July of that year, Merrill went to New Sweden, Maine, for replacements for his dwindling supply of freedmen as they died or headed farther south.[68] Twenty-two Swedes arrived in August; Alec was moved to another job, and his pay lowered back to $1.50. This is almost certainly indicative of racial discrimination. The other foreman working at $1.75 per day, Welshman William Perham, maintained his position and pay. Undoubtedly, Alec was angered by this. Later he would tell his children: *"You have to forebear and learn to forgive and overlook circumstances that are out of your control."*[69] This became part of his philosophy of "contentment and understanding," which he carefully imparted to his children.[70] Outwardly, he simply worked that much harder. A year later, despite his pay cut, he brought in $42 for the month, and by December 1872, he managed $51—a testament to his determination and spirit.

In May 1872, Alec finally succeeded in luring his brother, George Burekly to the quarry.[71] He arrived with his family and Alec's mother, Rose, who was still a part of his household.[72] Daisy always claimed that both Rose and Sally's mother Rachel spent time in Maine. It must have been a warm family gathering. Sally had never met Alec's mother or brother. George proved to be a good worker, but not of Alec's caliber.

By December 1872, there were only four freedmen remaining: Dick King, Alec Turner, George Burekly, and Armstead Early. Alec was thriving, but Sally's health was desperately poor, and she was pregnant again. Ellen, better known as Nellie, was born May 24, 1873. Sally was attended by both her mother and mother-in-law, as well as by the local doctor. Alec did not work May 23 and worked only a quarter of May 24. The doctor warned that Sally's health was deteriorating and that she would live only a short time *"on account of the hemorrhages setting in. Mr. Merrill did business in Boston with his slate and all, so he said to my father, 'Alec, I will get Sally up to Boston.'"*[73] True to his word, Merrill contacted a Boston specialist who promised to take the case.

> *Mr. Merrill as quick as he got to Boston, contacted a doctor. . . . The doctor talked to Mr. Merrill and told him to get my mother and father to Boston just as quick as he could, and he would find a place for them to stay and start working on my mother to see what could be done. At any rate, anything and everything that could be done to save her would be done. So, Mr. Merrill immediately got the grandmothers, and they . . . got my mother up to Boston, at 27 Phillips Street.*[74] *The doctor found an apartment for them near the Massachusetts General Hospital where this prominent doctor could work on her.*[75]

The Turners left the quarry near the end of June. Only George Burekly, his son Robert, and Dick King remained at the quarry, but by mid-October 1873, George was ready to return to Washington, leaving only King and his family as the remnants of Merrill's experiment with the freedmen. Dick remained until 1880, when sores broke out on his legs. Merrill was concerned that the climate would hinder his recovery,[76] and frugal businessman that he was, he feared that if King grew worse, he could become dependent. Merrill's son Fred drove King and his family to Bangor and reported that the Kings wept silently all the way.[77] Merrill may have helped King find a job in Washington, but shortly after his arrival, King's former owner, Joseph Ganley, discovered him and offered him work, which King accepted gratefully.[78]

Merrill appears to have felt some responsibility for his workers, particularly those who had been reliable, and he continued to look out for the Turners. At the same time, he did not want them to be a drain on his resources, and he found Alec work at the North Station loading freight on

Adams H. Merrill. Reprinted from Richard Herndon, Philip Willis McIntyre, and William F. Blanding, *Men of Progress: Biographical Sketches and Portraits of Leaders in Business and Professional Life in and of the State of Maine* (Boston: New England Magazine, 1897).

the trains. Alec always spoke warmly about Merrill and remained grateful for his help. In later years, Susan Merrill Lewis, a granddaughter who had grown up at the quarry and became its historian, visited the Turners. After Alec's death, Sally sent a letter to Susan, giving her an account of her family's welfare.[79]

Alec busily read the want ads in the Boston newspapers. There were a number of positions offered for farm work and haying, for colored porters and bell boys, laboring men for general work in coal and wood yards out of town, and for trades like granite cutters, blacksmiths, wheelrights, even boat steerers, coopers, cooks, stewards, and carpenters for whaling voyages. These ads clearly indicate that African Americans remained on the lowest rung of the class system. Their wording included: "wanted: a colored man to take charge of a horse during the summer; also a colored cook and domestic;" and "a colored man to work on a gentleman's place."[80] Alec had no intention of applying for such a job, no matter what the pay. But an ad that ran for two days in early July in the *Boston Herald* caught his eye: "Wanted—Woodchoppers. Apply to Arthur Towne."[81] No mention was made of the job being in Grafton, Vermont.[82]

Charles White ran a sawmill and logging operation in Grafton, Vermont. Short of help, White decided to advertise in the Boston newspaper. Alec and Armstead lost no time in seeing about the job possibility. When Alec found it was in Vermont, he remembered a lifetime ago when Zephie, Gouldin's granddaughter, told him that he should flee to Vermont. He decided to meet with Charles White.

Despite the doctor's best efforts and the attentive care of the two mothers, Sally grew steadily worse. Her voice was gone, and she was spitting up blood when she coughed.[83] *Well, Mother kept a'failing until I think it got down to the last of August when the doctors give her up completely. She was having hemorrhages. Father said that this particular day he had fed her himself before he left. He had put two or three teaspoonfuls of chicken broth between her lips. He forced it between her lips. But it was no use, and they had told him she couldn't live through the day.*[84]

This proved to be a significant turning point in the Turners' lives. Daisy claimed that on this day, not only did Alec meet Charles White and Vestus Wilbur,[85] but Sally underwent a conversion experience. Daisy described her mother, still only six months past her seventeenth birthday, as *"so ignorant and so young and she didn't know what anything was all about. . . . She didn't know what to do, what to say, nor what to think. She was just like a lamb."*[86] Daisy explained that Sally did not understand the power of prayer. *"Her head wasn't able to take it in."* She heard the doctor tell Alec that she could not get well, and not knowing what else to do, she turned to prayer. *She prayed that if heaven was like it was, and she had the little children, for Him to help her and to give her the right way of thinking, her life, her living, so that she could do His will. She had this conversation, and Jesus came into the room. That was the same day that Papu met Vestus Wilbur and Charles White in the depot. . . . And so that was it. The thing begin to work, and the next thing she knew, they were getting her ready [to come to Vermont].*[87]

Daisy's story of Alec meeting Charles White and Vestus Wilbur in the North Station while loading the express for Bellows Falls is poignant. It is doubtful that this occasion was happenstance; it was almost certainly prearranged. This is an occasion where Daisy makes it sound better. After all, it was a significant moment in the Turners' lives. Alec was wiping his eyes with his handkerchief for he had just come from his struggle to feed Sally and from hearing the doctor say that he doubted that she would live through the day.

> *When he looked around, this white man was standing across from him wiping his eyes, too, with a white handkerchief. Father wondered for a minute what was his trouble, that he was so broke up like that to openly betray his feelings. When Mr. Charles White, that had wiped his eyes, came across and spoke to my father. And he said, "You'll pardon me, sir," knowing Father was one of the ex-slaves, "but I wonder, I see you are so strong and sturdy, if you would be interested or would know of some*

other ex-slaves that would like to come up to Grafton, Vermont, to work for me and my partner in the lumbering. We have some expensive lumber that could be utilized and we are about to lose our town.[88] *We're about to go down and out for lack of money, and we came to Boston to borrow some money, and we haven't been able to borrow it. So we're going back to Grafton, Vermont, and everything is lost. Our town is lost, we are losing our town. That is why I am so broken up." In the meantime, he said where Grafton was and what a healthy place it was. Well, Father said, the minute that he said "healthy place" he thought of Mother, and something went through him again—like on the ship and these other experiences he had had. That feeling went through him.*[89]

Alec assured them that he could find a number of men to work and asked why they described Grafton as such a healthy place. They replied that it was cold and snowy, but had invigorating, healthy, fresh air—apparently a common belief of Grafton residents. According to the *Bellows Falls Times:* "Balmy breezes from verdant mountains bring health of body and buoyancy of spirits to its one thousand inhabitants, rendering it rather a hard spot for lawyers, doctors, and undertakers."[90] Alec told them about the condition of his wife *"who was dying of old-fashioned consumption"* and that the doctor did not think she would make it through the day. "*So they said, 'You don't mean it!' They said, 'We'll pray.' That's why I know there's power in prayer. So right there and then, those three men standing there, all broken down with their different troubles, and said a prayer to Jesus Christ. . . . And Father says they prayed right there in the North Station. And he was so faithful and believing, my father, that he said that this warm wave just come over him there and he knew*"[91] that this was the answer to his dilemma.

He asked how much money they needed to borrow to prevent the loss of the town charter, and upon learning it was under five thousand dollars, suggested that Mr. Merrill, who would be down from Maine the next day, could arrange a loan through his bank.[92] The next morning, Alec took White and Wilbur to meet Merrill as he came into the depot at seven o'clock. *Of course, the first talk was on my mother and the doctor, and then these men. Mr. Merrill took them right down to the South Boston Bank that had just started in April 1863—a new bank from the Civil War. And they got the money they needed and wanted.*[93]

Daisy remembered Wilbur telling that story more than once on Turner Hill and at Wyman's store. He would *"wipe his eyes, and go and hug my father and say, 'Alec, you saved this town!'"* She elaborated: "*They took the eleven o'clock train from Boston to Bellows Falls and came up on the stage. They got Baxter Walker, who was driving the stage, and oh, they took off their hats, and they shouted and they hoorayed from Bellows Falls the minute they stepped off the train.*"[94]

After this meeting, Alec and his brother-in-law decided to visit Grafton, Vermont.[95] Along with the necessity of earning a living for his growing family, Alec was concerned that the situation be a healthy one for Sally. He stayed for a couple of weeks to make up his mind.[96] He wanted a spot where he could earn a living, Sally could recover, and they could settle as a family and gain the respect of the community. He visited White's mill east of the village along the Saxtons River, saw that it was a thriving operation, and talked with the men who worked there. He would have gone up the hill to view the timber he would be cutting—his first sight of the area that would become his home for fifty years—and spent time in the woods working to pay for his trip. He almost certainly visited at least one of the two general stores, probably Bill Wyman's in Grafton. Wyman proved an important figure in Alec's early life in Grafton, and his store, a social and economic hub in the community, became one of his hangouts. He certainly encountered disbelief that two colored men from Boston could be successful in Vermont. Lyman Philips, who was driving a team for Wilbur, reputedly said: "By golly, you men from the city will freeze up in this country before winter is over." According to onlookers, they did not say much, but when Turner and Early returned for the winter, they did not suffer from frostbite, but Vermont native Philips managed to freeze his feet.[97]

Alec had no worries about the skeptics. He had confidence in his ability. He liked the rural life. From his boyhood in Virginia, he had learned a number of skills that would be useful in Vermont. Further, he was practical and knew how to dress for the cold. He also overheard locals warning that he would not be able to make enough money to buy salt, considered a luxury, to put in his bread.[98] This only hardened Alec's resolve to prove them wrong. He liked the men he met, and over the years many would prove to be good neighbors and friends. He believed what White and Wilbur originally told him about the invigorating air of Grafton and made a consequential decision, one that turned out to be a turning point for his family. Once satisfied that Grafton was the right place, he contacted a number of men. Among them were his half-brother Lindsey, Morris Gray, and Buck Carter. All had been in Maine. Those who were married had wives who were Sally's close friends.

In early November, Sally, who had managed to cling to life, was carried on a mattress to the train. The first snow of the season had fallen the day before, and Grafton would have appeared wintry indeed. Rachel made the trip to care for her daughter and her three grandchildren. Rose had returned to Washington, DC, to live with George and his family. George had had enough of cold weather and isolation and did not consider coming to Vermont; he would stay in the capital the rest of his life. Rose only visited Vermont, but Rachel came and went in the early years, at times a part of her son's and daughter's households.

Charles White, Vestus Wilbur, and several women—Mrs. Ephraim Wilbur, Mrs. David Wilbur, and Mrs. Zenith Holden, the local midwife—met the Turners as they arrived and brought a feather bed, blankets, and chicken broth for Sally. They helped her into a sleigh driven by Baxter Walker and took her to Mrs. Ephriam Wilbur's house on the Townshend Road. She appeared comatose.

> *But when the white ladies commenced working on her, rubbing her with skunk's oil*[99] *and different oils, and [feeding her] with broth, and warm freestones to her back, she commenced opening her eyes. And they had her laying on a little breezeway between the kitchen and the barn and the water closet. And that is where my mother was with the open air. . . . Then they got her into the bedroom off the kitchen, and they started working on my mother. Well, they said it wasn't over three or four days before my mother was able to kind of sit up, and she stopped having these hemorrhages. And so that is where my mother lived, and they worked on her for weeks, for months, until she got stronger.*[100]

Daisy claimed the women cared for her mother "*just like she was one of their own.*" As Sally grew a little stronger, she told Alec that she thought if she had a little turkey broth, she might be able to drink it. It was said that no wild turkeys had been seen in Grafton for some years, but as if in answer to her request, Alec spotted and killed one while working in the woods. They regarded this as an omen. Sally steadily regained her health and was never again plagued by sickness; indeed, she developed a robust constitution that lasted for the rest of her life in Vermont.

CHAPTER 7

Vermont

> About one week since, a half-dozen Negroes marched into town. So rare a sight alarmed some of our ladies, but the young men passed quietly on and pitched their tent about two miles south of the village, where they are engaged in chopping wood.
>
> —"Local Intelligence, Grafton," *Vermont Phoenix* (Brattleboro), November 21, 1873

In 1873, Grafton, Vermont, was considered a thriving town, despite its declining population of about one thousand.[1] Two branches of the Saxtons River join and wind through the village, at that time providing power for a number of mills in the district known as Mechanicsville. Among them was Charles White's sawmill and millpond. In the spring, when the water was high, the mill ran night and day.[2]

Most of the residents were farmers, working small, subsistence farms, following the rhythm of the seasons. By the time of the Civil War, these small farms began to decline. With the allure of gold and open land, the West was attracting easterners, including men and families from Grafton. Since the 1830s, Vermont farmers had raised merino sheep, but they could not compete with the large sheep ranches of the West. Many Grafton residents still maintained flocks of sheep, a few cows, perhaps a pair of oxen, a horse or two, some poultry, possibly a hive or two of bees, a sugar (maple) and fruit orchard, fields sown to potatoes, corn, and hay or wheat, a wood lot, and, of course, a garden plot to feed the family.

A number of small industries flourished in town, primarily logging. Smaller operations included Sidney Holmes's production of butter churns and the French Carriage Company's production of sleighs—both anticipated a record year in 1873. A fish pole business, a chair-splint factory, and blacksmith shop thrived as well.[3] The Phelps brothers' hotel attracted numerous summer visitors. Much of the business was carried on by barter or by note. There were two, and then three, general stores, each serving a variety of functions: local bank, community center, and dispenser of goods and information. Two churches, the brick Congregational meetinghouse

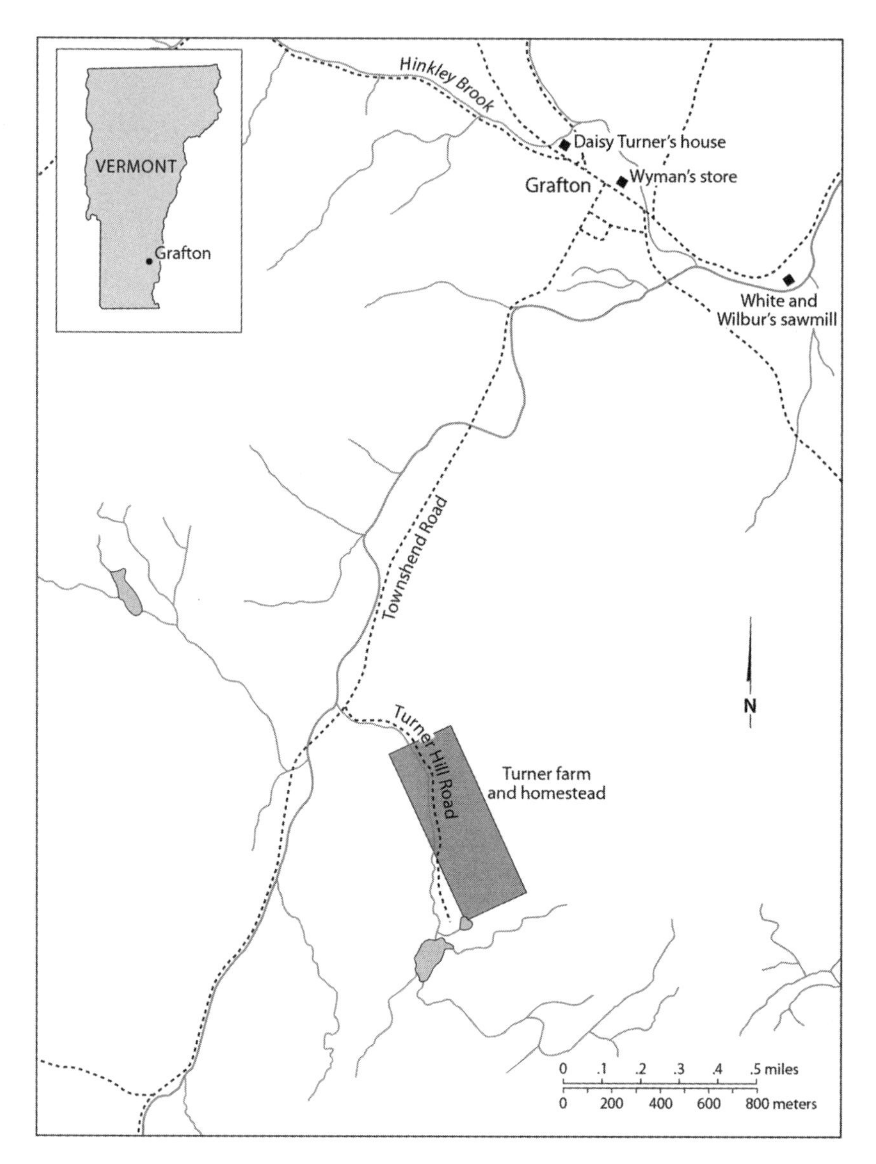

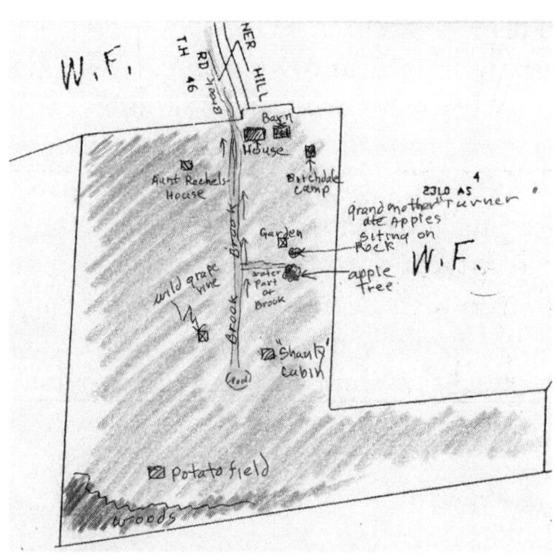

Grafton, Vermont, and Godfrey Hall's sketch of the homestead complex on Turner Hill. "W.F." indicates land owned by the Windham Foundation. Courtesy of the Vermont Folklife Center, Middlebury, Vermont.

and the wooden, white-spired Baptist church, administered to the spiritual needs of the townspeople.

When Alexander Turner arrived in Grafton, he was twenty-eight years old and in the prime of life. He was a massive man; according to his grandson, he stood six foot three, was broad shouldered, and carried about 235 pounds.[4] He was impressive, well-proportioned, and good-looking, with a long face, steady eyes, resolute jaw, and an expressive mouth. *"His lips and eyes could just talk."*[5] Vermonters were known for their admiration of the strong man, and feats of strength were frequently the subject of conversation—the more astounding, the greater the veneration and awe. Standing head and shoulders above most of the townsmen, Alec was ready and able to prove that they had met their match. Having found that most Vermonters wielded a 3.5-pound ax, he had a 4-pound ax specially made and set to work to show them that indeed he would earn enough money to buy salt to put in his bread.

Alec was a sociable man, a good conversationalist, and enjoyed the company of others.[6] He found a congenial society at Bill Wyman's general store. Wyman sold a wide variety of merchandise, including flour, molasses, rum, fertilizer, pickled fish and oysters, cloth and clothing, hardware, and drugs such as castor oil, tincture of rhubarb, and morphine. Alec joined his fellow workers around the wood stove, listening to the stories of the town, snacking on crackers and cheese, unloading merchandise, and always ready to offer help when something needed doing. While most of these men had never seen a man of color, Alec's engaging personality helped to mitigate the fact that he looked so different from the rest of the townsmen.

In many ways, the general store was Alec's best conduit into the town. It was a men's gathering place, a hive of social interaction. Men pitched pennies, played checkers, and traded goods—sometimes horses for maple syrup.[7] Bill Wyman was a likable, well-respected man and shared several of Alec's interests. He was an avid foxhunter, keeping a number of hounds, and he and Alec enjoyed exchanging hunting stories. Wyman was always good to Alec, offering him products he brought to Grafton from Boston at cost. Once Alec set up his farming operation, Wyman carried his maple syrup to Boston to sell and extended him credit until he had cash.[8] When Alec acquired poultry and cows, he sold eggs and butter to Wyman, carrying three pails at once—one in each hand and a third on his head. The men considered this an incredible feat. Likewise, they were amazed at Alec's use of his head as a weapon. They scoffed when he told them he could break a wheel of cheese in half by butting it with his head, and Wyman, always ready for a little fun, challenged him to do so, sweetening the deal with the wheel of cheese if he was successful. Alec performed the feat and went home with the cheese, leaving the men astonished. The story was still told well over a hundred years later.[9] Initially, young boys would follow Alec around, staring at him in amazement—they had never seen the likes of him. One asked him to roll up his sleeves, wanting to know if he was the same color all over.[10] This did not offend Alec. He was ready and willing to make his own way as long as he was given the same chance as everyone else.

While Jack Gouldin's granddaughter Zephie had told Alec he would be free in Vermont, he no longer held the illusions that he had had as an enslaved youth: that once he was free, he would truly be an equal citizen. He quickly learned that racism persisted: There were deeply held negative attitudes toward dark skin color. There was a difference between liberty and equality. People of color were treated as second-class citizens. Alec witnessed this in New Jersey and thought he might outdistance such attitudes farther north, but they existed in Maine, too. An optimist, Alec believed in himself and realized that the white men who came to know him, particularly Dayton and Merrill, gained respect for him. He wanted this opportunity in Vermont and vowed that he would succeed. He believed that in Grafton he would be taken as an individual on his own merits and treated with courtesy.[11]

From 1790 to 1870, the state was only 0.2 or 0.3 percent black, yet Vermont was susceptible to racism.[12] In the 1780s, Bijah and Lucy Prince, free blacks who owned land in Guilford, Vermont, were continually in conflict with a white neighbor, John Noyes, who spent his time trying to drive the Princes from their land.[13] Similarly, Lemuel Haynes, a black preacher in Rutland for thirty years, 1788–1818, eventually resigned his post due to racism rather than be asked to step aside.[14] Two decades later, racism was in evidence as Frederick Douglass traveled to speak at Middlebury College. He climbed aboard a stagecoach when it made a stop after dark. The other passengers did not realize he was African American, and during their conversations, he was treated with all manner of respect. However, after first light it could be seen that Douglass was black, and one passenger whispered to another: "Egad, after all 'tis a nigger." Douglass was treated with dark looks and disrespect for the rest of the trip.[15]

While racism was alive in Vermont, Alec apparently did not experience it in such blatant fashion in Grafton. Prior to the Civil War, Grafton townspeople had provided shelter for escaping slaves. Charles Barrett, a member of one of Grafton's most respected families, held strong abolitionist views and was a leader in this effort.[16] According to Daisy, her father was always treated with courtesy and kindness. The *"white people took them in just as family."*[17] And indeed, Alec's grandchildren reported that they did not experience racism until they left Grafton. George Hall, son of Daisy's younger sister Violet, who in Massachusetts was denied a high school athletic award because he was black, was adamant that he had never experienced discrimination in Vermont. Although skeptical, I came to believe that a number of things sheltered Alec from the latent racism that remained just below the surface. First and foremost was the man himself—the force of his personality, his extraordinary capacity for work, and his willingness to view himself as different. He had been a slave; that was part of who he was. But with the opportunity to make his own way, he was determined to be a productive member of society. The town fathers were willing to help such a man. I suspect that, even before they knew him as an individual, he served as a symbol of all former slaves, and they wanted to offer him an opportunity to succeed. As they came to know Alec, they came to respect him. This was all-important to Alec. The admiration he engendered allowed him and his family to truly become part of the community.

Daisy once asked if I had read Mildred Walker's book, *The Quarry*.[18] I had not, and she explained that Walker had written a book that included information about the Turners. I discovered that Walker was a fine writer and had created an engrossing and well-developed historical novel of Grafton—called Painsville in her story—spanning the years 1857 to 1914. Her main characters were a white farm boy, Lyman, and a black boy, Easy, who had escaped slavery and come north via the Underground Railroad. Their friendship matured into a warm comradeship of equals. I quickly recognized Alec, singing his slave songs, a head taller than anyone else, a masterful driver of oxen, with a slight wife who only came to his shoulder. Further similarities included his love of Lincoln and a story of killing the overseer—although this was attributed to Easy's father. His warmth and easy manner were emphasized. Was this how Alec appeared to others? From positive reactions to him throughout his life, I suspect this was the case. He had a winning personality that drew people to him. Daisy always said: *"Everybody loved my father!"* Walker suggested that Easy served as a symbol to the townspeople of the South's wrongdoing, much as Alec did for the town fathers, and as an "interesting social phenomena" to visitors.[19] Indeed, the villagers were disappointed that Easy did not have stories of beatings and cruel treatment received at the hands of his master.

The author warned her readers: "The characters and situation in these pages are wholly fictional and have lived only in the world of this book." But Walker was a careful and perceptive observer. She was born in 1905 in Philadelphia and lived there, but she spent three months every summer in Grafton. Her daughter Ripley Hugo tells us in her biography of her mother, *Writing for Her Life*, that in *The Quarry*, "both her main characters take their inspiration from villagers whose stories Mother grew up knowing and later telling to us."[20] Asked if Walker had spent time with her family, Daisy responded: *"Oh, she lived up there half the time. She and . . . Phoebe*

Frost. . . . Our hill used to be full of children."[21] Mrs. Walker and Mrs. Frost would drop their children off on Turner Hill when they went to Saxtons River, a few miles away, to do errands or visit. So, Mildred Walker had direct experience with the Turners and heard Alec sing and tell stories.

The Turners also took paying guests as additional income. Many were from the Boston area, and Walker took note of this, pointing out that although the townspeople were so used to Easy that "they hardly remembered he was colored," they were not accustomed to the sight of "the strange Negroes."[22] Here she reveals a subtle difference in attitude and an air of superiority reflected by the Grafton residents toward these visitors. This is probably a good indication of local sentiments. Walker would have listened to stories about the Turners and would have been sensitive to racial discrimination. Indeed, her book detailed patronizing behavior and prejudices such as not wanting to sit next to a black man and the assumption of white privilege. On the other hand, Easy never pushed these situations and, without losing his own self-respect, sidestepped them gracefully, probably a good indication of Alec's own actions. Walker's novel allows us another insight into Grafton, one that sensitizes us to the emotions and feelings of the townspeople.

The Civil War was still an important topic and a close reality as over a hundred townsmen had served in the Union Army.[23] "*Papu and these different white men here in the town used to like to set to talk over this slavery.*"[24] Daisy often made this point and would call out specific names, a litany of the foremost families in Grafton. "*At every one of the turning battles where the victory was won, it was the Vermont and the Grafton boys: the Danielses, the Duncans, and the Barretts, and the Burgessess, and the Halls, even to the Hemenways who went when he was fourteen years old as a drum major to fight this war.*" She said that the "*ground is fertile with the blood of these brave Vermont boys. How could we not help but love them!*"[25] This was a significant shared experience. Alec would have taken comfort in Grafton's sympathy for abolition and the town's role in the Underground Railroad. Indeed, in later life, he told his children that it was a miracle he had found his way from Virginia to Grafton. "*And this was a slave center for runaway slaves. . . . it was God that was leading [me].*"[26]

Alec's strength, his willingness to help, his remarkable voice and wealth of songs, his ability as a storyteller, and his energy and creativity helped him negotiate the social politics of the town. The same qualities that had attracted both Dayton and Merrill to intervene on his behalf had a similar effect on the people he dealt with in Grafton. Mary X. Barrett, Charles Barrett's daughter-in-law, referred to Alec's "fine personality and superior qualities" that so impressed the villagers "that he was given assistance to settle in Grafton and there built a home for himself and reared his family, valuable and respected citizens of Grafton."[27] Today this sounds condescending, but the point is clear: the Turners were accepted as Grafton citizens in the fullest sense.

Alec had confidence in his abilities to prove himself, first in his capacity as a woodchopper and, more importantly, as a citizen and a landholder.[28] This was his goal, and Grafton proved the right location to fulfill it. Alec's dream of ultimate success included land ownership, establishing a family homestead, and security for his family. He lost no time in establishing himself as a citizen and paying the poll tax to vote.[29] When his fellow workers arrived in Grafton, Alec began the task of chopping down trees, sawing logs, loading them behind a team of oxen, and driving them down the hill to the sawmill. Alec was the men's natural leader. From their shared experience at the slate quarry in Maine, they knew about his stamina for work and recognized his ability to manage a situation.

In the years following the Civil War, Vermont's forests experienced their greatest depletion. Logging companies were always looking for greater access to timber and easier ways of processing it.[30] Vermont's land was 80 percent clear, but there was still plenty of timber in the hills above Grafton. "*When Papu and them first come up here, I've heard them tell, there wasn't a place big enough [for] two chairs to set, for the lumber and the trees.*"[31] The best timber was difficult to reach because the extensive wetlands on three plateaus of Bare Hill merged into extensive forest. This problem reminded Alec of the plateaus above the Rappahannock and of how as a boy he had helped build blind stone ditches to carry off the excess water. He proposed draining the land in this manner to reach the trees they wanted to cut. He started with a meadow that was flooded by beaver dams—trapping the beavers, breaking their dams, and then building ditches by placing flat rocks about three feet in depth, smaller stones on the side, and covering it over with flat rocks and then dirt. This allowed the men to reach a large stand of timber previously unavailable. Some of these trees were huge; one measured four feet and five inches across the stump.[32] The men used some of the smaller lumber to build a log shanty as housing. Alec based the design on his mother's cabin on the plantation, with its one room, loft, and dirt floor, increasing the size to about eighteen by twenty-four feet and adding a central chimney.

People noticed the success Alec had with his ditches. George Hall, a wealthy Grafton sheep farmer, hired Alec and his crew to drain the land around the Chester Reservoir. Hall was impressed with their work. I asked Daisy what she knew of the men who were working with Alec, most of whom had died or left Vermont by the time she was small, but she said, "*They were all anxious to learn . . . and made everything count. Every ten cents was laid away just like it was a dollar bill. And they knew how to do things. And they didn't seem to mind. And they were all very quiet and dignified, very gentlemanly.*"[33]

Alec managed to put aside some of his earnings to purchase a team of oxen. Eventually he would own three teams. To buy a yoke of oxen required some cash, which indicated that Alec was able to save at least enough money for the down payment. Alec probably paid thirty dollars in cash with a note for ninety dollars.[34] He used the oxen to snake logs out of the woods and pull them on a sled down to the sawmill. In the off season, he used his team to do road and bridge work, as well as to cultivate his own land.

By spring 1874, Sally was healthy, and Alec prepared to have her join him in the shanty. He divided the room and placed a cloth across the loft for the hired men. *"Mamu and Papu . . . slept in the kitchen with the wood stove. They had a beautiful oak bed. . . . The bed was up high and . . . Father had made a trundle bed with rollers in it that three of the youngest children could sleep in. . . . And you could shove this trundle bed right underneath the big bed."*[35] In the second room, platforms were hinged to the wall, with legs to prop them up. During the day they could be used as tables, and at night, they would be pulled up, and bedding was brought out for sleeping. There was no running water, but Alec dug a spring and had Bill Wyman test the water so that he was sure it was safe for his family to drink.[36]

On June 21, 1874, Sally moved up on what became known as Turner Hill, three miles south of the village off the Townshend Road, with her three children—the twins were three and Nellie was barely more than a year old. Nineteen-year-old Sally had regained her strength and lived on the hill for the better part of the next sixty years, taking an active role

White and Wilbur's sawmill with Bare Hill in background. Alec settled on the south side of Bare Hill, Grafton, Vermont, in 1873. Courtesy of the Grafton Historical Society, Grafton, Vermont.

alongside her husband. They made a good team. Alec set out a garden with a good southern exposure, where the sun's warmth was felt at least an hour earlier than in the valley. The soil was rich, and he was careful to plant his vegetables on the appropriate moon.[37]

Grafton's principal exports the next winter were sleighs and poplar timber.[38] The Grafton correspondent in the *Bellows Falls Times* wrote: "Grafton was never more prosperous. The sale and transportation of hard wood, bark and pulp wood makes business brisk and cash plenty."[39] Alec continued to work in the woods, cutting trees and clearing the land he would later buy. I suspect he was already planning for this. Sally was once again pregnant and on June 29, 1875, gave birth to their first son, Linesy, named after Alec's younger half brother, Lindsey Coleman. The selection of a child's name was always significant for the Turners, and Daisy described Alec keeping a book detailing the birth of each child and after whom each child was named. In the next couple of years, Lindsey Coleman married Mary (according to Daisy, the daughter of one of his fellow quarry workers in Maine) and brought her to live on the hill. When they had their first son in 1879, Lindsey honored Alec by naming his first born for him, an indication of their close relationship. At Linesy's birth, Alec's occupation was given as a laborer. By January 1877, when his daughter Carrie was born, Alec was listed as a farmer, suggesting he was making steady progress toward his dream.[40] Eleven-year-old John Barrett, who was in and out of the Turner shanty, named Carrie after his mother, Caroline "Carrie," the wife of portrait artist and abolitionist Charles Barrett.[41]

Although Alec did not yet own the land, he made strides in acquiring animals and building a small log barn, a hen house, and a pigpen.[42] On a piece of the meadow he had drained, he set out peach trees and grafted some apple trees. He continued to work for White and Wilbur but was enterprising in looking for additional income. He cut cordwood—not only did people need wood for cooking and heating, but the trains out of Bellows Falls ran on wood, so there was always a ready market. Daisy claimed her father could cut four cords a day, a feat that must have added to tales of his legendary strength. During the warmer months, he expanded his farming operations, turned to sugaring in the early spring, and took in hunters from the Boston area in the fall.

Despite their progress, there were setbacks. They had a difficult year in 1875: January was a long, cold month. The next month proved even worse—February 13 brought "the coldest weather ever known in Grafton, 36 degrees below zero."[43] There was still three feet of snow on the ground in April.[44] Weather extremes continued throughout the year. By September 1, one observer noted it was "terrible warm, 92 degrees in the shade," but three weeks later, it was "as cold weather as I ever knew for this time of year."[45] These extremes took a toll on William (previously Armstead) Early's family. He had married a young girl, Emma, in Williamsburg, Maine, who was a close friend of Sally's.[46] They established a household a couple of miles from the Turners and had a son, Henry E. Early, named after William and Sally's father. Emma died of endocarditis, an inflammation of the lining of the heart, in early October, followed two months later by Henry.[47] According to Daisy, two men who had come with Alec to work in the woods also died. A third man found the winters too difficult and left, leaving only Alec, Lindsey, and William.

White's sawmill continued to thrive, and Alec was sent to Canada to bring back French-Canadian workers who were more acclimated to the weather.[48] In the spring of 1878, White installed a machine for sawing shingles. His cider mill brought in additional revenue each fall. In 1881, Vestus Wilbur bought half the company, and two years later, White and Wilbur were making improvements, including the addition of a gristmill.[49]

Another bet with storekeeper Bill Wyman proved to be a defining moment, gaining Alec considerable respect. Alec was helping Wyman unload groceries, including barrels of white flour, each weighing three hundred pounds. White flour was sold at a premium for twenty-five dollars a barrel. Alec told Wyman that he could not afford a whole barrel, but would like to buy ten pounds for Sally. Wyman threw down the gauntlet: *"If you could carry a barrel of flour home, Alec, I'll give it to you!"* One can almost hear the disbelief in Alec's voice when he replied, *"You don't mean it!"* Daisy recounted the conversation:

> *"Yes, I mean it! If you could carry a barrel of flour home, Alec, I'll give it to you."*
>
> *"Well, you have lost, cause I will take it up when I go"*
>
> *At that time, the men all used to congregate around the store and the big stove and talk. So they says, "Alec's going to carry a barrel of flour . . . up to Sally in the shanty." Oscar Rice and all of the different men . . . said, "It can't be done." But they didn't know how strong my father was. . . . So they talked and ate cheese and crackers. . . . Finally, when my father got ready to go, he says, "Which one do you want me to take, Bill?"*
>
> *"Any one of those barrels that you want, Turner."*
>
> *Father finally got ready and he started. . . . He told me many times just how to do it: just right on the parallel of his shoulder. And started from right down here at the post office, where it is now. . . . And when he got to the first bridge . . . he didn't take it off, but he changed it a little—like that, just a little bit further [over.] Cause he said that he knew he had to make the hill and the barrel would have to lay a certain way. So he shifted it, then went on.*

And my father—Glory to his name, Alexander, my father. I'm proud to be your daughter—went on up that road and up that hill and across that long field, because we lived in the shanty. And my father never set that barrel down until he got up in the shanty door. . . . There must have been at that time forty men following him with little jugs of jimmy-john and hard cider. After Father put the barrel of [flour] down, they all was saluting him and congratulating on him. And my father carried that barrel of flour from Grafton Village up on our hilltop for us children to eat, to have bread. Now that's the truth if I never speak a word again.[50]

This event established Alec's reputation as the strongest man in town. The story was repeatedly retold and became a town legend. It was after this that Alec was made a deputy sheriff. Whenever the constable knew that he would be dealing with someone unruly, he took Alec with him. Alec knew how to subdue another man. He referred to it as *"hitting a man between the wind and water."*[51] His technique was to kick a man in the solar plexus, and when he doubled up, kick him under the chin with his left foot.[52] Alec took this role seriously, but despite his ability to dispatch a man, he believed in peace. One time he learned that a group of townspeople was going to tar and feather the minister because he was having an affair with a married woman. According to Daisy: *"Father went right down and talked to the crowd and broke it up."*[53] Using his strength as a deterrent, he warned in graphic detail what he would do to anyone making a step toward the tar and feathers, and then he waited as the grumbling crowd dispersed.

While admiration for Alec as a strong man was unequivocal, he also functioned as any other member of the farm community. He shared work, helped neighbors, and was helped by others. Some of these moments are documented in the diary of Henry Thompson, Alec's good friend and neighbor. Thompson's father was the original owner of the land that Alec eventually bought. Thompson had been deeply touched by the Civil War. Although he enlisted in 1864, he never saw action. He remained vitally interested in Civil War battles, and it was said he could talk about Gettysburg as if he had been present.[54] This topic fueled endless conversations with Alec. Thompson was reputed to have a prodigious memory and knew many anecdotes of local people and the early days of Grafton.[55] As did Alec, he enjoyed trapping, hunting, and fishing, and possessed a depth of knowledge about the weather, seasons, and planting that likely would have led to many discussions between the two men.[56] Thompson would have followed Alec's experiments with peanuts, muskmelons, and peaches with great interest; he also would have been interested in Alec's use of herbal remedies.

They were neighbors, both deliberate and careful in their farming practices.[57] Together they mended fences, drove oxen, plowed and planted, cut and sold cordwood, and worked on the roads. Thompson served as a highway commissioner and put in considerable time repairing roads and bridges. Both were badly damaged by serious flooding in March 1877, and a massive storm in December 1878 brought, according to Thompson, "the highest water I ever saw on December 10th" with "bridges, roads, etc. destroyed."[58] Once more there was road and bridge work to be done. With his oxen, Alec carried stone for bridge foundations and provided stringers up to sixty feet long.[59]

The two men rubbed shoulders every day and treated each other with warmth, compassion, and respect. When Alec's young son died, "*Henry Thompson lugged the casket on his back from off top of that hill down to the main road to the hearse—with my father walking by his side, cause my father didn't want to lug his little son.*"[60] They must have seemed an unlikely pair walking slowly down the hill: one short and slight, bowed under the coffin; the other towering above him, head downcast with the burden of his sorrow. They met the undertaker, Sidney Holmes, at the foot of the hill, to carry the coffin to the cemetery. They recognized each other as equals. Both men had wives ten years younger than themselves, and both had growing families who attended school together. Their children followed suit. When Daisy was ten, she went into the brook after ten-year-old Betsy Thompson, who had fallen in and was having difficulty climbing out.[61]

Daisy spoke frequently about Walter and Louise Thompson, Henry's grandchildren, and urged me to meet them. One morning I visited them in Saxtons River and gained another glimpse into Alec's life in Grafton—one underscoring that Alec was comfortable in Grafton. Walter Thompson remembered Alec visiting his grandfather. They would have hot cider as they discussed town affairs and solved the problems of the day. While Walter did not remember his grandfather singing, he enjoyed listening to Alec's rich tenor filling the room as he sang with fervor and enthusiasm:

> John saw the number, John saw the number
> John saw the holy number sitting in the golden altar.
> The paradise was wide and fair, sitting in the golden altar.[62]

Alec bought his first piece of property from White and Wilbur on October 13, 1881—land sold to them by Henry Thompson in 1872 as a timber lot.[63] The parcel of land consisted of fifty acres in Grafton, which Alec had drained and farmed, and another forty-five acres in Athens, where his sugar orchard was located. He agreed that White and Wilbur could cut the trees that they had selected for a period of five years (beginning in 1878, which may indicate when he first expressed his intent to buy the land), and they continued to pay the taxes on the land until their lumber was removed.

He paid $525 and received a mortgage from Butterfield and Smith for $450.[64] This was a moment of celebration for Alec and Sally. Eight years after coming to Vermont, they were homesteaders, farming and working their own land for the benefit of their own family. And their family was increasing. Since coming to Vermont, they had had five more children, the last a son, Alexander, born in June of 1881. The eighth child, he was nicknamed Enough, the thought being that their family was complete. Sadly, he was the boy carried down the hill by Henry Thompson nine months later when he died of pneumonia. Despite his nickname, Enough was not the last. Sally and Alec were still to have five more girls.

The 1880 agricultural census provides some indication of how Alec was doing in Grafton. Although his purchase of the land was not finalized until 1881, he considered himself the owner and listed himself as such. His operation was valued at $900 with forty acres of cleared land. He had $300 in livestock including two oxen, ten assorted yearlings, calves, and heifers, and two cream-colored Jersey milk cows, which provided a hundred pounds of butter a year. He had ten sheep, which when sheared provided fifty pounds of wool; the ewes had seven lambs, six of which he sold. One hog and a flock of thirty chickens rounded out the barnyard. He estimated the barn and outbuildings were worth $25. His one-acre orchard, won from the beavers, was making progress with twenty-five bearing trees (including apple, plum, and peach) providing 10 bushels of fruit. He produced thirteen tons of hay, 150 bushels of potatoes, and 8 bushels of beans, with three acres in cereal crops (two in Indian corn, and one in rye), yielding 60 and 10 bushels, respectively. He had cut fifty cords of wood, which at $100 brought $2 a cord. He estimated that the value of all he produced was worth $225, and to accomplish this he paid wages of $10 for hired help. Quite an accomplishment considering he began only with his ax, facing a wilderness of trees and water. Daisy gives a little more description:

> *Papu started right off planting some potatoes and things. The soil on the hill was so rich, you could grow anything. We had plum trees and peach trees. Papu had a wonderful apple orchard. The way the sun shone they could raise anything: watermelons, cantaloupes, musk melons, and peanuts. We had a record of having some of the biggest, longest, and peculiarest vegetables. We always used to put them down in the store. And the special ones went up to the fair over in Brattleboro or Rutland. Papu always planted on the moon. He believed in that. He planted on the hillside where the sun shone first, always very early. He would have peas to eat the seventeenth day of June. He planted on a new moon to make lots of vines, and if he wanted his grapes to grow heavy and thick, or his beans to be a particular way, he would plant them on a certain moon.*[65]

Alec was sugaring on the property across the Athens line. He had never tapped maple trees and probably received help from Henry Thompson, who tapped over two hundred trees. Alec built an arch of square stones, to boil the sap, broke out sugar roads with his oxen, and tapped seventy-four trees using eighty buckets. From these he made over 650 pounds of sugar—an excellent yield.[66] Alec's name began to appear in the local paper, either the *Bellows Falls Times* or the *Vermont Phoenix*, which frequently covered Grafton news. Sometimes he was "a colored man," but as time went on he became simply Alexander Turner. "Alexander Turner recently showed us a stalk of herd's grass five feet and two inches in height, and one of rye six feet and eleven inches high."[67]

All farming is dependent on weather, and Vermont with its fickle temperature swings is not always kind at higher elevations. In late August 1884, Alec's crops were hit with a killing frost, which he estimated did $150 worth of damage to his two acres of corn, as well as decimating his pumpkins, squashes, watermelons, and muskmelons[68]—a substantial blow, particularly hard to bear as the lower elevations were spared. Alec watched over his livestock carefully and was proud to show his oxen and horses at local fairs, along with his vegetables, and he was particularly pleased when he brought home a ribbon. His family enjoyed these outings as well, and Daisy talked about the girls making special dresses for these occasions.[69]

Doctors were not plentiful, for either animals or people, and home remedies were important as families used them to tend to their own. Alec, with his rich store of Indian remedies, was always willing to help when people came to him. He made an ointment of different barks steeped with green hemlock boughs to keep black flies off both people and animals.[70] He gathered herbs his mother had taught him to use, such as thoroughwort, wormwood, catnip, ginseng, pennyroyal, and red oak bark, and he had remedies for most common illnesses. Alec also began to get a local reputation for doctoring animals. He partitioned his henhouse so that one side had a stove. "*He had an old bench in there that he could sit on, and a stove and a table. You could go in there and heat milk up . . . so that if any of the animals was sick or got lame we could put them in there . . . and take care of them.*"[71] In a community that valued livestock, he found he was in demand. "*That's how come everyone come to know him at first.*"[72] Daisy went on to illustrate with the story of Bellows Falls banker Mr. Williams, whose prize horse had broken its leg. Several veterinarians decided shooting the horse was the only thing to do.

> *At any rate, Papu was delivering his chickens and milk and butter and things in Bellows Falls, and they all knew of him, of course. So, Williams asked Papu what did he think about the horse, would he look at him.*

So, Father said, yes, he'd go. . . . So, my father went and looked at the horse—beautiful horse. They used to keep them, oh, just shining. . . . So, Father says, "Well, I'll come down and stay two or three days and work on him and if we can do anything, all right. And then if . . . I can get him up on the hill where I can tend to him regular I think I could mend that leg, because we've done worse than that in the war."

So, Father got in his best clothes . . . and he went down there with cans and things to make, and bandages . . . a suitcase full of things. And do you know, he got that horse's leg all right. And the bone knit, and I think the Williams gave him something like $250—that was like a fortune then.[73]

Another story involved horses shipped to the Morgan Horse Farm on boxcars.[74] Something went wrong, and the horses broke loose and ran through the streets of Bellows Falls. All were corralled except one young mare, *"a beautiful mare, smooth as silk and like chocolate"*, who jumped fences, fought with her feet, and terrified anyone who came after her.[75] Two young men who knew of Alec's skill with animals went up the hill to see if he would be willing to help. He was mowing with his scythe, but changed clothes and went with the men, bringing a salt box, some oats, and some lump sugar.

The horse was angry, and onlookers warned him to be careful. Alec had a number of different calls he had learned on the plantation: one for sheep, one for cows, and one for horses. He called to her and shook the box of salt. Slowly, tentatively she took a step toward him, then another, as he continued to call and shake the salt. Alec inched toward her, careful not to frighten her. He put sugar on the edge of his fingers, and she took it. Then he added oats. Onlookers began to cheer. After about an hour, Alec began to rub her face, her neck, and then put his hand under her mane, rubbing her and giving her more sugar and oats. As he moved away, she followed, and eventually he was able to slip a bridle over her head and fasten it. She reared and pawed, but he quieted her down again. With half the town following him, he headed for Grafton, six miles away. It was long after dark when he reached Grafton, and he was exhausted.

And she was tired too . . . and he says she laid down and almost like going to sleep, lay her head right down on the ground. And he sat there on the bench beside her, the two of them. Just set there and rested, he says, till pretty near midnight, he and the horse. And the people all following him.[76]

This only enhanced Alec's reputation. Alec named the horse Maggie and took her up the hill, putting her in a fenced pasture and adding pins on top to deter her from jumping out. He left her there to feed for six weeks, and he alone handled her. Alec kept the horse, although I suspect there was some sort of a financial arrangement between Alec and the horse's owner.

According to Daisy, her mother made up a poem about this event, but sadly, she could no longer recall the words. Three months later, Alec brought a stallion to breed with Maggie, and thereafter the Turners had horses. Topsy, one of Maggie's offspring, had a mind of her own, and when she grew tired of waiting for Alec at the store, she would *"switch her head, slip the rope off the post"* and take off *"with the old buckboard and groceries."* Half-way up Turner Hill, she would open the gate with her nose and come home with the groceries. When the horse would appear in the yard without Alec, Sally, always the mother hen, would worry and immediately dispatch one of the children to see what had transpired. Daisy explained:

> *The men was bound to make [Papu] drink cider and things, but he wasn't a drinking man and never was, and never took to drinking. . . . He was like a woman if he took the least little bit. It would go to his head, you know. But sometimes the men would give him this hard cider or some of the men put in a little homemade ginger . . . and Father would go to pieces. They'd think that would make him sing more down in the store or something. But that happened two or three times.*[77]

Not all of Alec's attempts at calming animals proved as successful. His neighbor, Butterfield, had a wayward heifer that terrorized the neighborhood. This episode was reported in both the *Vermont Phoenix* and the *Bellows Falls Times*. "A colored man of strength and courage voluntarily undertook to capture the animal."[78] As he had done with Maggie, he approached the heifer slowly, but at the last instant, she lowered her head and charged. Alec escaped up a tree, possibly the first time he had ever backed down from anything. "In her own time the heifer was enticed into a shed and was lead peacefully home."[79]

Alec's younger half brother, Lindsey Coleman, was following his lead in establishing himself. He remained on the hill, living in the shanty, working for White and Wilbur, helping Alec as he developed his farm, and cutting cordwood for Henry Thompson to sell in town. Eventually he rented a cider mill on Chester Road.[80] In October 1882, Thompson picked 178.5 bushels of apples, most of which he drew to "Coleman's cider mill." In November, Thompson noted that he spent three days threshing cooperatively with his neighbors Coleman and Conant; it is likely that Lindsey was threshing Alec's crop.

Alec never forgot his religious underpinnings. Daisy made a point of saying that he became a member of the Baptist church almost as soon as he arrived in Grafton. Unfortunately, the church records, which might have given us an understanding of the Turners' interaction with the Baptist community, have been lost. Alec's daughters were married at the church, and a granddaughter, Reverend Veronica Lanier, preached there in the 1970s. The Turner family had three pews. Sally, her brother William Early, and Morris Gray were all baptized in Hemmenway Brook by the minister. Alec and Sally sang slave songs at the town hall or the hotel and donated the proceeds to the church. Alec was always careful to end these concerts before midnight on Sunday, singing as his closing song:

> It's half past eleven o'clock
> Can't you hear the watchman's song
> While weeping and sleeping
> We'll bid you all good night.
> Good night, good night, good night kind friends,
> We'll bid you all good night.[81]

Alec's spiritual beliefs coursed through every part of his family's daily lives. Each day began with a prayer. *Our house . . . was full of prayer. And we were great believers, and we children were brought up as believers. And my father and mother didn't do anything without asking the higher power to sanction it. There was no little piddledy, diddledy lies. There was no crookedness, and there was no underhand work or anything going on. There was no swearing, no loud hard talking.*[82]

Easter was always an important time. On Good Friday:

> *We had prayer in the morning and nobody ate anything until after the Crucifixion and the death that he had died. And then of course he laid in the tomb. My mother always had the food prepared the day before. . . . And then we always had our own wine and broke bread. . . .*
>
> *At Easter . . . when the sun would be coming over the hilltop, then that would be the time we had breakfast outdoors. . . . My mother would always have ham boiled . . . and eggs and sausages. And they would feed the children the most they could eat and there would always be fresh doughnuts. . . . Some would be sprinkled with coconut, others with sugar, others would be plain doughnuts. . . . But Father always . . . said a prayer and a blessing for the family to watch us and to guide us. . . . And we sung different hymns. . . .*
>
> *Well my mother's been true converted*
> *Ain't that good news*
> *I'm going to lay down this world*
> *Shoulder my cross*
> *Carry it home to Jesus,*
> *Ain't that good news.*[83]

Alec was a kind man, tender with his wife and ever solicitous of her. When things seemed bleak, he would comfort her with "*Sal, it's always the darkest before the dawn.*"[84] But his compassion extended beyond the family. "*He used to pray for the people in town. When anybody was sick, he always went to them and helped them and gave them strength. . . . One of the men was sick and needed shaving. He would shave him and give him a bath and help him.*"[85] Daisy thought that "*he got part of his strength and smartness from God, from spiritual life. Cause he was spiritual, and he fell on his knees and he talked with God. He talked with Jesus.*"[86]

> *We always had to say "good night" and "good morning." And if we were angry or anything wasn't just right, before we went to bed we would excuse the other person or end it. And we always said a prayer [beginning] at a certain age up to a certain age at my mother's knee or my father's. And after we were older, we always kneeled in our bedrooms and said a prayer and asked God to keep us through the night and to bless our mother, and father, and the different ones, and love us, and forgive us our trespasses. And we never dared to think of eating without saying a grace.*
>
> *"God is great and God is good, and we thank him for this food.*
> *By His hands must all be fed, give us Lord our daily bread."*
>
> *That was one. And then we would say, "We thank thee blessed Lord for thy love," and this and the other. Or, "We thank thee for the hand that prepared the food," which was our mother. And we thank Him that we had plenty to eat and different things. And pray for the different ones that was sick or in sorrow or got hurt, for their blessings to come on them. And then on . . . Saturdays, we had to do all the work that we needed to do, and Mother done all of the big heavy cooking and everything on Saturday. And Sunday . . . dinner was very light with not much cooking. One of the girls could put it on or serve it. . . . And there was never no quarrels or anger with each other.*[87]

There was no question that Alec was the man of the house. He always had the last word.

> *My father was a strong, strong man—with strong words and strong actions. Doing just like a president. Father, he was firm, and if the children done wrong, Mother would say, "Oh, Alec don't be so hard on him, give him a chance." And he'd say, "No, Sally. Right is right, and they've got to do what's right," and that's the way he was. Firm.*
>
> *He seldom punished us. Very seldom. He gave us that Turner look with his eyes—bout all he ever had to do. And if he was going to punish us, his lips would always tremble. He always punished us in a peculiar way: with food or eating.*[88] *Or doing something more times than usual, or denying us special privileges that we had planned on.*
>
> *My father taught us never to do things wrong—to take time and to be cautious and careful always in everything we done. And truthful. No*

matter how bad a thing was, to tell the truth. He couldn't stand a lie. He didn't tell a lie. We didn't dare to—not any one of us. And he wanted us to decide for ourselves. Almost everyday things keep coming up that you've got to decide on. They may not be big things or important things, but little issues where you got to depend on your own self. I think that's one of the things that made us as we went out in the world to work and to live—we were able to meet issues and be fair, because we had to do it growing up. . . .

He said we had to learn contentment and understanding. He said if we had them two things, we could weather the tide: contentment with what we had and understanding of the situation. . . . That's the way we come up. We were never uneasy or unhappy cause we were satisfied with what we had. And that's what made us easy tempered and how we got along together.[89]

Alec believed that "*you have to forebear and learn to forgive and overlook circumstances that are out of your control.*"[90] When anything came up that was complex or did not seem quite right, he always thought it through from several angles. He was deliberate and careful in his thought process, gaining both understanding and a contented mind.[91] He warned his children to consider what they took on thoughtfully and cautioned, "*Never take any more on your heels than you can kick off your toes.*"[92]

Alec had a number of sayings that his children came to know well. He frequently cautioned them to keep their thoughts and dreams to themselves, pointing out that "*no one can tell how far a frog would jump.*"[93] Daisy concluded, "*So our lives run very easy, like a brook.*"[94] After thinking a moment, she threw her head back and let out a warm laugh as she remembered: "*The worst thing was my brother was going to cut my sister's head off one day with the big ax. My mother hollered, 'Wait, wait until I get there.' And she was running for life and death, and he with my father's four-pound ax. And she said she just got the ax out of his hands and fell to her knees. Another second, another minute, and my sister's head would have been cut off with the ax.*"[95]

This was Willie, attempting to behead his twin sister, Susie. He had watched his mother killing chickens and noticed that they often continued to run around with their heads off. He wondered if the same thing would happen if he decapitated his sister. Willie, it seems, was constantly in trouble. Bruce Turner describes him as "*a flip little guy.*"[96]

One time he told my grandfather, "I'm double-breasted and double-backed." And [Alec] picked him up and bounced him off the ceiling, and let him drop to the floor, and that took care of that very briefly. On another occasion, he insisted on rearing back in the chair on the back legs, and this was forbidden because it wasn't good for the furniture. And time and time again he was reprimanded with no results. So my grandfather sawed about four or five inches off the front legs of the chair and said, "This is your chair. You sit on the back legs any time you sit at the table or anywhere else. And I don't want to see you sitting in any other chairs but this one." And over a period of time this cured him.[97]

With her growing family, Sally's work was never done, but her stamina never seemed to flag. Despite the procession of babies, her figure remained girlish, and she never weighed more than 110 pounds.[98] From the age of fifteen until she was thirty-eight, Sally was either pregnant or lactating. She adored her children and intervened on their behalf if she felt Alec was too severe. Her daughters considered her beautiful with brown hair, light skin, and lovely blue-gray eyes, favoring the Earlys. While Sally was small and appeared vulnerable, she was made of strong fiber. She ran the household efficiently, accomplished a prodigious amount of work, was always protective of her children, had a clear sense of right and wrong, and did not

Sally Early Turner, ca. 1905. Courtesy of the Grafton Historical Society, Grafton, Vermont.

believe a person should back away from anything. "*My grandmother was a very proud person, and if anything came up, and someone did something to her, she might not be able to whip them in a fair fight, but she always said, 'hit at him if he's big as a house and let him know how you feel.' You might lose, but hit at him just the same.*"[99] While Sally had never been to school, she understood people. She learned through observation, and her observation was keen. Daisy always said: "*My parents were great imitators.*" This was how they absorbed many northern ways and manners, which at first seemed so different from those of the South. When there was trouble, Sally's daughters remember her bolstering her resolve by singing:

> *Oh a little talk with Jesus makes it right, all right*
> *A little talk with Jesus makes it right, all right.*
> *In trials of every kind thank God I always find*
> *If I have a little talk with Jesus, then it's right, all right.*[100]

Just cooking for her brood, extended family, and the hired men would have been a full-time job.[101] She made pots of soup with vegetables from their large garden. She canned everything, including fruits and berries. There were fresh eggs, chickens, and wild game: partridge, rabbit, squirrel, raccoon, beaver, venison, and trout from the streams. Daisy claimed the men used to bring her mother partridge and raccoon, which were thought to give strength to those eating them, to maintain her health. Sally steamed most foods, from squash to raccoon. She would steam the latter until it was tender, make dumplings and dressing flavored with sage, and stuff the raccoon, rub it all over with olive oil, and put it in the oven to brown.[102] She was known throughout the neighborhood for this dish, which many visitors could not distinguish from lamb.[103]

Daisy said that her mother fed twenty-five people at most meals. Frequently she made a samp, or mush, from cornmeal, which she would cook overnight with maple syrup, oatmeal, or cream of wheat, so it was ready to eat in the morning. There would be a big platter of doughnuts, a plate of cornbread, and fried fresh pork, fried or boiled eggs, and perhaps a big pan of salt codfish in gravy, which was scooped over potatoes. Always there was a dish of applesauce that the men could have with their bread and butter. Another favorite dish was steamed brown bread cooked with raisins and dried apples. She would steam it from right after breakfast and would have the brown bread with baked beans, meat, potatoes, a vegetable, and either rice pudding, bread pudding, or some kind of pie at noon. She made eight to ten loaves of bread at a time, as well as all kinds of pies, puddings, and gingerbread. In the spring, she picked dandelion blossoms for dandelion wine and daisies for daisy wine, and later in the season, she made blackberry and elderberry wine. She also made sap beer from the last sugar run, or frog run as it was called because as sugaring was ending, the peepers would begin to hum. Sap beer was a rugged drink that Alec liked to give the hired men. "*You could get dead drunk on it,*" Daisy admonished.[104]

Food preparation was just the beginning. There was also washday, usually Monday. Sally had three large round washtubs, made by Alec, which sat on a bench outside. "*All the women at that time boiled their clothes. Everybody had a boiler . . . on the stove. And they had to . . . boil the cold water and then salt it up.*"[105] Sally used a big wash stick with two prongs, fashioned by Alec, to submerge the clothes. She had a washboard to help rub out any stains or dirt, but no wringer. Once the clothes were washed and rinsed, they were hung out to dry. Ironing took another day; irons were heated on the stove, and special care had to be taken to make sure the iron left no telltale marks.

Sally was also an accomplished seamstress and made all her family's clothes, including Alec's overalls. When Daisy, who had rickets as a child, needed dresses that would cover her legs, her mother made her pleated and ruffled skirts. Sally also spent time quilting, embroidering, crocheting, and knitting—all arts she had been taught by her mother. She had learned to spin in Maine, and Alec made her a wheel on which she spun flax and then wove it into linen sheets, pillowcases, and tablecloths. She churned butter and made soft soap and candles. Through all this, she never raised her voice. "*My mother's voice was always low and sweet.*"[106] All nine daughters remained close to her throughout their lives and remembered her with great warmth and tenderness. "*I've often thought how wonderful my mother was. She was a wonderful person. And no arguments and no long talkings on things.*"[107]

Five more children, all girls, followed Enough. The first of these was Daisy, born on June 21, 1883. A number of neighbors attended to Sally (as would be the case in any household at that time), chief among them being Aunt Mary Holden, the local midwife who had helped Sally when she first arrived in Vermont. Another neighbor, Mrs. Belle Rice, named Daisy.[108] "*Mrs. Belle Rice said, 'Oh Sally and Alec, I'm going to name this little girl myself. . . . And I'm going to name her after my mother and me. I'm going to call her little Jessie Daisy Turner.'*" "Daisy" was after the wildflowers that covered the fields Alec had cleared over the years. They carried them into the house in sugar pails, and Alec claimed they had enough to fill his ox cart. Two years later came Cora Violet, and again Aunt Mary Holden was on hand.

> *Every time that she came to our house she always left a baby, don't you know. And, of course, that didn't sit on my brother William at all. He didn't like it. . . . Aunt Mary Holden was coming back and forth up to*

our house because they were expecting a baby. . . . So, when Willie got a chance, he took the bag and put it down in the brook and put stones on it. . . . When she got ready to go she couldn't find that bag. . . . She said, "Sally, I bet that little rascal has hid it or something." So, she got right after Willie. And, of course, he broke down and told that he had hid the bag in the brook. "My gracious, Sally, did you ever!" And so they went right down to the brook and sure enough, there was this bag all wet and everything ruined.[109]

When asked what happened to Willie, Daisy laughed. "*They told my father, and my father said he'd punish him. I don't think he done much. He didn't blame the boy!*"[110]

Family life was close and, despite occasional disagreements, full of affection. Alec set the tone. "*My father was just like a lover to my mother. He was always, 'Sally dear', or 'my Sally.'*"[111] And he was always encouraging to his children: "*Gal, don't give up.*"[112] Daisy commented, "*My father said he wanted his children to enjoy life and to be able to wear shoes or go barefoot. And they done everything they could for us, and they give us a good schooling, and he taught us to [pray]. . . . We were very happy.*"[113]

It was important to Alec that his children know their history, their roots. He did not want to turn his back on the past, even the slave experience. That was a part of his and of his parents' lives. Every night after dinner "*when we all got calmed down. . . . settled around on the floor and on our stools. . . . Father would tell us stories of things that went on.*"[114] As Daisy pointed out, this was before the telephone or radio, and not only did their father want his children to "*know things firsthand*" and to learn his stories, but this was also family entertainment.[115] He taught them both songs and recitations, many of which he had learned on the plantation from one of his young masters.[116] Alec taught his daughters recitations for special occasions. In turn, they began to contribute, making up their own poems about local events and happenings. On such an evening, Sally would have recited her poem of Alec bringing home the Morgan horse, Maggie.

The Turners were fond of music and dancing as well. Someone made up "The Turner Hill Waltz," but Daisy could no longer recall the tune. "*They could dance wonderful!*"[117] Daisy remembered her father "*could take a tin pan and play a tune right on the tin pan—a tin milk pan.*"[118] Neighbors would bring a fiddle, banjo, or homemade harmonica, and the dancing would start. The Turners became known for this and attracted many of their community to participate.

With nine children, the shanty seemed smaller and smaller, and by the fall of 1885, Alec wanted a real home for his family. In 1884, he had bought another 45 acres, a timber lot bordering his land in Athens for eighty-five dollars from Harvey Wheelock, bringing his holdings to 160 acres.[119] Alec worked on plans for a two-and-a-half-story building with thirteen rooms, modeled on the old Gouldin house in Virginia. It was to have three staircases and be built over a spring, as was the Gouldin house. After drawing the plans, one of the Danielses assisted him in working out the details. John Butterfield, who ran the soapstone quarry near Alec, agreed to fund an additional three-hundred dollar mortgage and to front Alec the money for materials and labor.[120]

The previous year, Alec had cut the lumber, which he drew with his oxen to White and Wilbur's sawmill. Once the lumber was cut, he hauled it back up the hill, where Sally and the children helped stack it and cover it with large burlap bags to keep it dry. All was prepared. He signed the mortgage on July 19, 1886, and began building that same week. His neighbors were encouraging and helpful. Some promised to give every Saturday, others a day of work when they could. Henry Thompson noted in his diary on Wednesday, August 25, 1886: "worked for Turner on new house; cloudy warm."[121]

First, he prepared the cellar, digging down eight feet to lay the stones for the foundation. Within the cellar was the spring, which he had previously prepared to the depth of six feet, later putting in a trout to keep the water fresh and free from insects. He placed the spring directly under where he would put the pump next to the kitchen sink. The water never froze, and the spring always remained full. He left an area for overflow in the cellar from the spring to the cellar wall, and then he built one of his blind ditches that led from the wall to the stream.[122] Alec made his own plaster as well, something that was common in Vermont.[123] He curried his oxen and mixed the hair with lime and sand as mortar for the plaster.[124]

> *We had a piazza and went into the kitchen. The kitchen was sixteen by sixteen—a good big kitchen. And then on the right of it was a pantry, the whole length of the kitchen—the length of the house, thirty-two feet or thirty-six feet . . . then a bedroom down off the kitchen [for her parents] . . . then the dining room . . . the parlor, and then a back parlor. We had a Mason and Hamlin organ in there and a little couch. . . . The older guests and people could go in there quiet, if the young people were entertaining. The piano was in the parlor. And a beautiful mirror that was one of the town talks. It . . . rested on a little stool-like, and then you could see your whole figure with this beautiful mirror.*[125]

The kitchen had a big woodstove with a large copper boiler in which to heat water. While there was no indoor plumbing or electricity, there was a bathroom, with a bathtub and white toilet pails, right over the kitchen with a pipe so that it would stay warm. Another small room served as a drying room for wet winter clothes, raincoats, rubber boots, and overshoes. *"Course we had two closets downstairs, and right behind where the stove set in the kitchen . . . where you could put your dishes up top and boots down underneath. With a door on it."*[126] Most of the rooms had eight-by-four closets, and they all had small woodstoves for warmth. In most cases, there were two girls to a room, although in one, there were three small beds. On all the beds were cornhusk mattresses covered with feather beds and pillows. Sally made all the bed linens and quilts, while the wool sheared from their sheep had been sent to Philadelphia and returned in the form of blankets. The privy or backhouse was through the woodshed.

> *When [my father] built his toilet, he built it away from the water, from the milk house and the smoke house . . . like they had down in the South. Then, he made . . . a long wooden box and on it a hook . . . And this box was shoved in [under] and then every day or two Mother would pour ashes in. Once a month, Father would take the oxen and hitch a chain [to the hook] and pull this box out in the field where he had a deep hole dug, and empty this box, and wash it out clean, and then the box was put back in.*[127]

The house was a large undertaking, but Alec was up to the task, and he had many neighbors willing to help. This was to be the family homestead of his dreams. He continued at a steady pace throughout the summer,

Turner house, Turner Hill, Grafton, Vermont, ca. 1920. Courtesy of the Vermont Folklife Center, Middlebury, Vermont.

Turner Hill, Grafton, Vermont, ca. 1920. Courtesy of the Vermont Folklife Center, Middlebury, Vermont.

and by November 5, 1886, thirteen years after he arrived in Grafton, the *Vermont Phoenix* reported: "Alexander Turner's house is completed and his family have moved in."[128] As a final touch, Alec planted two balm of Gilead trees in front of his new home, as Jack Gouldin had done. They served as a statement that this was the family seat of a successful farmer and landowner, an assertion of his independence, and a testimony to his social identity.[129]

CHAPTER 8

Journey's End

The home place was named Journey's End cause Father never wanted to go no further after he got up there on that hilltop.
—Daisy Turner, interview with author, February 1, 1984

Daisy was three years old when the family moved into the new house. She suffered from rickets, caused by a deficiency of vitamin D, resulting in a softening of her bones, which was particularly noticeable in her legs and left her unable to walk.[1] *"I was fast and quick in talking . . . but I wasn't able to pull [myself] up."*[2] Her father, always practical and creative, built a small stool, with two handles on top, that she could push to help her learn

Alec and Sally at Journey's End, ca. 1920. Courtesy of the Vermont Folklife Center, Middlebury, Vermont.

to walk. The kitchen was the nerve center of the new house, and as her mother cooked, Daisy practiced. She remembered how large the sixteen-by-sixteen-foot kitchen seemed as she tried to keep her balance behind her prop. "*It would keep me off from my knees all the time and would let me kind of lift my back and my body a little with my hands pushing this thing. And that is why I kept on gaining strength.*"[3] Eventually able to pull herself up off her knees, she would push the stool a little way and then fall back onto her knees. Daisy continued pushing the stool for another two years. As she grew, her father heightened it, and as she gained strength and balance, she began taking steps aided by braces on her legs.[4] By the time she was five, she could walk behind it. She remembered that year was the first time she walked in public, up the steps of the Baptist church, holding the hand of lifelong friend Amy Davis.

Although Daisy was small and disabled, she was bright and alert. She also had a voice, something she learned to use at an early age to take part in family life. It was her voice, rather than other physical attributes, that Daisy developed over a lifetime. Because she could not get about like her brothers and sisters, her father taught her to count and the basics of reading, writing, and reciting pieces before she went to school. Her facile mind retained these early lessons, and as she practiced the recitations, she absorbed the rudiments of oratory.

Alec continued to expand and improve his farm. He added two turkey houses with long roosts inside. One day, some wild geese flew in, one with a broken wing, and he began to feed them. The other geese stayed with the injured one, and Alec was able to start his own flock. He raised them from eggs and clipped their wings as they transformed from goslings into young geese to keep them from taking flight. He built a gate in the brook for the ducks and had another side brook for his geese. He added a hen house, a new horse barn with a stallion stall, and a hay barn with room to keep the covered carriage and two sleighs.[5] He also fashioned many of his tools, even carving and bending an ox yoke for his team from an ash tree.

The winter of 1888 brought the worst blizzard ever known in Vermont. The snow began on Sunday night, March 11, after a deceptively warm Saturday. By Monday afternoon, the rising wind reached gale force, gusting ferociously—some reports claiming gusts of ninety miles per hour.[6] Roaring, destructive, and unrelenting, the White Hurricane, as it came to be known, continued through the early hours of Wednesday, March 14.[7] Drifts reached fifteen feet in height and twenty feet wide.[8] At the Turners, the two hired men had to stay over until the storm was spent. Forty inches of snow fell, covering the first floor windows. The wind packed the snow in a solid mass so that it was impossible to open the doors. Alec tied a rope around his waist and with a shovel and a bucket of hot ashes and coals, climbed out a second story window to dig out the kitchen door.[9] As he worked, those above lowered down buckets of hot ashes. Eventually, he was able to clear an entrance and, with the help of the hired men, tunnel his way to care for his livestock. Then he used the oxen to break out roads through the snow. They were isolated on Turner Hill, but they had everything they needed and were no worse off than the townspeople of Grafton.

The death rate in Grafton was high that year, and the Turners lost another child.[10] Eleven-year-old Carrie succumbed to typhoid, having taken sick on July 27, 1888.[11] Originally, it was thought green apples caused her stomach pains, an early symptom of typhoid, and her sickness went untreated until too late. Rachel, Nellie, and Alec were under the weather as well when they finally called the doctor. Daisy, who was not yet five, remembered that night—Carrie died at eleven o'clock, and Zebbe was born at two o'clock the next morning on August 17. Daisy recalled that the house was full of people, and she felt frightened by the commotion. Carrie had died, and her mother was giving birth, neither of which she really understood. She crawled under the kitchen table crying. "*Mrs. Townshend, one of the white ladies, came and picked me up.*"[12] She realized her father was upset, adding to her distress. "*Father was so broke up. He went out on the piazza, listening. . . . And when he did, he heard the voices singing, like a band of angels. And they was coming from the Goodridge house this way east, going west over toward Uncle Early's place. He couldn't see, but he could hear the music and these voices singing.*"[13]

Once again, Alec was bolstered by his deep faith, always sustaining in a moment of crisis. The voices of angels seemed to carry away the soul of one child and usher in the birth of another, Zebbe, who was the first child born in the new house. Her father honored his young mistress, Zephie, who had shown him such kindness on the plantation. He named his daughter Zelma Ida May, to be known as Zebbe.[14]

The neighbors had gathered to support the Turners. As always, Aunt Mary Holden had been on hand to aid Sally, and after the burial, they rallied round to assist Alec in putting up his hay crop.[15] Alec and his family were very much a part of the neighborhood.

With the new house, quarters were no longer so cramped, and they were joined by Sally's mother, Rachel Early. She had been living in the village after she left the home of her son, William Armstead Early, "Uncle Early" to the children. He was in Alec's shadow, but the two men had been in close association since Alec's marriage to Sally and the quarry work in Maine. He had proved a reliable worker and was a good craftsman, making baskets and decorative ironwork. After the death of his first wife, Emma, he had married an African American woman, Kate (according to Daisy, the daughter of General Wade and a Jamaican woman), and bought land a few miles from Turner Hill; however, he never had children after he lost his infant son. For a number of years, he worked at Butterfield and Smith's soapstone quarry. In later life, most of his great-nephews considered him mean. When his four-year-old nephew noticed a gray mass in the currant bushes and asked what it was, Uncle Early shoved him into what was a wasp's nest, and the boy was stung all over his body.[16] The nephew recalled: *"He used to set in the chair in the kitchen all the time . . . cross his leg and be like he was talking to the governor of Vermont or talking to himself, shaking his head. We kids would look at him and kind of grin. We thought it was fun, but it wasn't fun. It was mental."*[17] In those days, mental conditions frequently went undiagnosed.

Uncle Early had an unpleasant temper, which is captured by the most significant family story told about him. It was a cold day in October, and his mother, Rachel, had a fire going in the house. Her son came in, said that October was too early to have a wood fire, and threw a bucket of water on the flames, extinguishing them. Rachel cursed him, saying that when he died, *"there would be nobody around to wipe death's dew from his brow because he was such a mean, miserable man."*[18] She went on to say that nobody would ever know how or where he died. According to the story, Rachel then grabbed her shawl and walked to her daughter's house on Turner Hill, about five miles away. The day Sally died, Uncle Early disappeared. He went to the barn to milk the cow and was never seen again, despite an extended search. *"They had Boy Scouts out, they had State Police, they had everybody out. All the townspeople around there looked for that man, and they never found him. . . . No one has ever found any sign of that man. . . . His mother prophesied it."*[19]

Daisy could only dimly remember Rose, her father's mother, suggesting she came for a visit when Daisy was very young. But she had a distinct memory of Rachel, her mother's mother—a memory that reflects her through the eyes of a young, rather mischievous girl. She painted an amusing picture of her:

> *She was really a very beautiful woman, but . . . light-headed. When I say that I mean she didn't have no heavy education. . . . She just thought it was nice to be able to sew well and crochet and always to be very dainty . . . never show her strength or let anybody know she was able to lift a pail of water . . . or wouldn't think of being caught on a bicycle. A very kind of refined [lady] and wouldn't be seen without gloves on. . . . We used to laugh and say we'd like to see how she sat down on the toilet. . . . because she was so immaculate you know in everything. She wouldn't let anybody see her brushing her teeth or combing her hair. Whenever you see her, she was always classy and all prepared. . . . And, of course, she*

had been accustomed to everything nice, and when they got into the new house, she felt like she had just found herself. Everything went good.[20]

Another time, she said that Grandmother Early modeled herself on *"the old aristocratic white people. She thought a still tongue makes a wise head."*[21] Daisy commented that in those days women were supposed to keep their place. Even at a young age, Daisy knew that would not be the case for her. *"And their place was like a child's now. They weren't supposed to do a lot of talking."*[22] They were to defer to their husbands and let them do the talking. Daisy had no intention of letting anyone, particularly a man, do the talking for her.

Rachel Early came to live with the Turners during her last illness.[23] Sally felt she could take better care of her mother if she lived with them, and placed her bed in the dining room so her mother did not have to use the stairs. Sally had ten children at home, but it was important to her to take care of her mother, which she did faithfully for the next four months. Rachel died peacefully in her bed on February 24, 1890. The cause of death was heart disease. Although her grandchildren thought of her as old, she was only fifty-eight.

Alec's new home became a magnet for extended family. He was generous and inclusive. Sally's younger sister, Rebecca, who must have been in her midtwenties, appeared shortly after the house was completed and began attending school with the children.[24] Alec more than likely encouraged her to learn to read and write, but her education was short-lived. According to Daisy, she became pregnant, the father being a local white man Alec knew well. He was not pleased, particularly as the man already had a wife. Besides, after what he had seen during slavery, he did not approve of intermarriage. He made it clear that he wanted his daughters to marry "colored" men. Daisy claimed that Rebecca went to Boston, eventually married, and moved to California.

Alec wanted his children to have all the advantages he had missed. At the top of the list was school. He cut a shortcut through the woods to the one-room schoolhouse, where one teacher taught the first eight grades, after which students would go on to Vermont Academy in Saxtons River. Off the young Turners would go with their lunch pails in the early morning, returning at four o'clock.

One event at school became a major turning point for Daisy. Her narrative is important as it allows an intimate portrait of her father interacting with his daughter, but more than that, portraying his worldview. For Daisy, it was the moment she learned to stand up for herself. She believed she was about eight years old, so this would have taken place in July 1891. There was a special program on the last day of school, and parents from

Grafton District School #11, ca. 1890. Second row: Susie and Daisy; back row: Willie, Susie's twin. Courtesy of the Grafton Historical Society, Grafton, Vermont.

all the outlying district schools would attend the closing exercises at the village school. The teacher, Miss Edison, wanted the children to take dolls of different nationalities and learn verses about the country or region. Miss Edison asked Daisy to take the black doll that would represent Africa. That was to be the only black doll, and Daisy would be the last on the program. Although she liked nothing about this proposal, she said she would discuss it with her parents. Daisy rushed home, eager to talk to her father, but he was busy working. After supper, when the family settled down in the dining room, Alec gave her his undivided attention.

I told him that the teacher wanted me to say a little verse or two and take this black doll in this little dialogue that we was going to have, and what did he think about it. . . . I kind of hesitated, and he asked did I want to do it. I said I didn't mind if it was all right. . . .

Then he begin telling me how Jesus was born. . . . They were very religious, my parents. . . . They always prayed about everything, and we prayed with them and listened. So Father told us how Jesus did everything in seven days, and when he got through, everything that he had done was perfect. It was all right. There wasn't anything to be changed. . . . Everything was just as it should be, always and forever and ever, and so not to worry.

Then he began telling about the houses that were built by different men, and how the colors were put on by painting them, and each one did that, the way they thought they liked it best. . . . No one could say which one was the prettiest or the nicest, but each one was satisfied. Then he told us about the trees, and how some had leaves, and the leaves fell in the fall, and the others were evergreens and never changed, but always were the same. And how lovely each one of them was. And who could say or decide which was the loveliest one or the nicest one of the trees in the forest. Each one decided those kind of things for themselves. So, that was all right.

Our family was very peculiar. They were all colors. That's why I wonder now why they say "black" because there wasn't any of us black, but we were light and tan and cream and some of them so white that you couldn't tell whether they had any Negro blood at all in them. Father was a very peculiar color because his mother was a Cherokee Indian. . . . So, Father talked, and then he prayed a little prayer. . . . He said it was all right for me to take the little verse and to do what the teacher wanted.[25]

Daisy went back to school and diligently learned her verses, but she discovered that the teacher had asked her mother to make sure Daisy wore a particular red ruffled dress for the program. When she learned that the other girls were to wear white dresses, with special sashes and hair ribbons, and the boys were to dress in long sleeves and neckties, Daisy was indignant. Her red dress was an old one she wore frequently; there was nothing special about it. She had a lovely white dress and numerous fancy hair ribbons. She also had a favorite white doll at home, over a foot tall with blue eyes and flaxen hair. She did not like being made to appear different, but her parents told her to do as the teacher wished. Daisy also wanted a chance at the prize, and how could she win a prize if she did not look her prettiest? Even at an early age, Daisy was conscious of style and fashion. Three judges would select the student who presented the best performance. The prizes were to include three gold pieces—a $10, a $5, and a $2.50.[26] She seethed as the teacher made them practice their lines and taught them to curtsey properly. The big day came, and the parents arrived in their best clothes. Benches had been borrowed from the Baptist church for seating and the platform decorated. Her friend Amy Davis was the first to go out on the stage, saying:

My dolly came from sunny France
Her name is Antoinette
She's two years old on Christmas Day
And a very darling pet.

She ended with "*I hope she'll take the prize.*" Daisy remembered Amy gently placing Antoinette in front of her, fluffing out her dress and fixing her hair ribbons. Her anger began to rise.

I began thinking behind the curtain, why in the world had I ever consented to a thing like that? Why had my father and mother allowed me to look like that with that old red dress and ribbons, while everybody else had on new clothes and said something nice. But not me! . . . I was the last one to go out with this black doll, . . . Dinah . . . I made up my mind I wouldn't go . . . I said "I'm not going!" . . . [The teacher] said "Oh, you'll spoil this," and kept talking to me and patting me and trying to urge me to go. But I kept a'saying, "No, I won't go!" And finally, she said she would let me wear her watch and give me some paper money—it would be a dollar—if I would go and say it. . . .

Finally, I grabbed Dinah by one arm, because I was very, very angry. . . . So, instead of going out nicely and . . . saluting like the teacher had taught us to. . . . I went out . . . holding Dinah with one arm. . . . When I got out there, the girls had crowded quite a little bit more than they should by shaking their skirts . . . so that it wasn't leaving me much room to sit. . . . So instead of saying the two verses they had taught me to say, . . . I was very angry and my voice was raised high—mother didn't allow us to raise our voices—but my voice was high. And I said:

You needn't crowd my dolly out,
Although she's black as night
And if she is at the foot of this show
I think she'll stand as good a chance
As the dollies that are white.
My Daddy said that half the world
Is almost black as night
And it does no harm to take a chance
And stay right in the fight.
So sit up, Dinah and look straight
At the judges on the right
And I'll stand by your side
If I do look a fright.
The teacher's face as all can see
Is redder than a beet
And Daddy's come down from the back
And led her to her seat
And gave to me that famous Turner look.
So I'll sit down and shut my mouth up tight
Just like a book.

Instead of setting Dinah down nicely like the other girls had done, I flopped her down pretty hard on the front seat with not much room or space, and set myself down hard behind her. Well, it was such a peculiar moment. I've realized it many times since. It was such a performance. Everybody had always clapped, but nobody clapped or said a word. And Father had come down from the back. And, of course, I had been so long in going out, when I should have gone right out, that my mother had been twisting and sitting like that in her seat. She couldn't keep quiet. . . . And my father's mouth was just as firm—he was wondering why I didn't do like I was supposed to do. And there I was. I hadn't said a word of what the teacher had taught me to say. I had just said what I wanted to say because I was angry. But the judges that were there said it was the best piece of acting that went on, and in the end they gave me the first prize.[27]

Daisy always claimed the first prize was the ten-dollar gold piece.

This story was one that Daisy told over and over—it was her most important touchstone story.[28] She stood tall against what she considered injustice and discrimination. She knew she was different, even though her family never discussed color. Daisy felt that this incident brought the color issue to the fore in her school and made her family, in particular Daisy, acutely conscious of color and with that, a strong sense of difference. This was her awakening to race and racial identity. Over the years, I heard her tell this story many times, word for word the same, indicating its significance to her.

When asked if she had known she was speaking in verse, Daisy answered: "*No! I was angry. I just said what came into my head.*" I realized that when her father recited, sang songs, and told stories after dinner, he was bequeathing Daisy more than a legacy of family heritage, but one of form and style as well. I asked if she could remember the verses the teacher wanted her to say. She thought a moment and then shook her head. I tried again weeks later, and she came up with a single line: "*My dolly comes from Africa, Don't you see*"[29] and then shook her head. That recitation held little consequence for her. Her own embodied her entire being.

Alec continued to improve his farm, gradually increasing his livestock. By this time, he had two or three horses, several cows, three teams of oxen, and numerous sheep. He also began raising dogs. He had gone hunting with his young masters in Virginia and most certainly had watched their dogs being trained. "*Father had these beautiful coon dogs,*" redbone hounds, which he raised and trained to chase foxes and tree raccoons.[30] There were also deer and bear for the taking. Alec trained his dogs, not only to find game, but to find people.

My mother, if she wanted my father in the woods, would put this note on him . . . let the dog loose, [show him] Papu's shirt . . . and say, "Sic him. Get your master. . . ." That dog would . . . start right off into the woods . . . where my father was chopping . . . so as to let him know that something was wrong. And I told you my mother couldn't write, but she would have these notes written that my father had written on big paper bags: "Come home Alec."[31]

Sally also had a cow horn that she could blow, as they had on the Gouldin plantation. One blast on the horn meant there was trouble at home, two blasts indicated something was wrong with one of the children, and three blasts designated fire.

Each fall, men came up from the city to hunt deer, bear, raccoons, foxes, and partridge. According to Daisy, her father had met George Barry and some of the other market men while loading freight at the North Station in Boston. Alec was both sociable and enterprising, and knowing of Barry's interest in hunting, he saw another opportunity to bring in some revenue. Money was always tight, but Alec was ever resourceful. He would guide the hunters, and as his children grew older, Linesy and later his sisters also helped.[32] Once Alec built the new house, he had the hunters stay in the shanty, and later went on to build Birch Dale Camp where men would spend ten days, each paying a dollar a day.[33]

Barry encouraged Alec to send his poultry to him at the Boston Market, to sell before Thanksgiving. Alec always took great care in breeding his livestock, and it was no different with his poultry. To identify his own fowl, he meticulously cut the nail off the third toe. Sending poultry and other goods to the Boston Market grew to be an important stream of income for the Turners, and Sally, with the help of a couple of hired men, the children, and often some neighbors, was in charge of preparing the birds. The children discovered early on, under Willie's instigation, that it was often lucrative to put notes into some of the birds: "*This was my pet gobbler, and I'm having to sell him. I hate to have him go. I wish you could send me back something so I could buy a new vest or a baseball.*" And every so often, they would get something in return. Sally saved paper during the year, the children ironed it, and Sally wrapped the birds neatly and care-

Hunters on Turner Hill, Grafton, Vermont, ca.1930s. Courtesy of the Vermont Folklife Center, Middlebury, Vermont.

fully. The shipment to the market was sent down on the two o'clock Flyer and would arrive in the market by seven o'clock the next morning. The check that came back in the next couple of days was an important source of income for the family.

This particular year, the Turners sent off an exceptional shipment, and their hopes were high that the check would reflect the quality of the poultry. The children rushed to collect the four o'clock mail from the post office and brought the envelope from Mr. Barry back to their parents. Then they waited expectantly, hopping from one foot to the next in eager anticipation as their father opened the envelope. "*When I see our father's face just turn white, and he sunk down and put his hands to his face and burst into tears. My mother run to him with her arms. 'Oh, Alec, what's wrong, what's wrong?' And he just passed her the check with that little bit of money, and she sunk right down by his side and took his hand.*"[34]

A letter from Barry accompanied the check claiming that the poultry Alec had sent was not as good as usual. Some of the birds had spoiled, and he had had to dock Alec for the inferior produce. The check was half of what they expected. "*So Father kind of braced up, and he says, 'How could they do a thing like that? Why, this is terrible!' And he says, 'They know it's wrong, so why would they do it? . . . I thought they were my friends.'*"[35] As Sally comforted her husband, she fumed: "*They never can come up on this hill again.*" But Alec said nothing more and, standing up, said he guessed he would "*go for a little walk. It was time to get the cows.*" But Sally persisted as Alec walked out of earshot. "*This is terrible! This is terrible! I never have trusted him anyway. . . . I've never liked him because he would like to have been a little freer with me . . . and he didn't keep his place always.*"[36]

Meanwhile, Daisy and her siblings were shocked and knew this meant there would be no new coats or shoes in the offing. In the heat of the moment, outraged and indignant at such injustice, Daisy made a snap decision and said to her sisters: "*I'll go to Boston to those men. They're going to give my daddy all of that money. . . . I'll wear my best dress and take Mamu's pocketbook.*" The pocketbook was an alligator bag Sally kept stored away for special occasions. Daisy figured this was just such an occasion. Zebbe went out to grease the buggy wheels, and Violet harnessed Maggie, while Daisy put on her best dress and best shoes. When all was ready, the sisters drove off before their parents realized they were gone.

Daisy thought she was about sixteen at the time, but because she had not matured, she looked more like twelve. They pulled into the Bellows Falls depot where they knew the stationmaster and explained what they were up to. They showed him Barry's letter, which Daisy had carried with her. He agreed it was terrible and asked what she was going to do. She answered: "*I'm going to Boston and I'm not coming back until I have my father's rightful check.*"[37] Her sisters waited until Daisy got on the train, and the stationmaster handed her off to his brother, who was the conductor. Daisy had never been to the market district before, and he explained to her that it was just a little way up Causeway Street and then she must turn right.

Daisy was quickly in the hustle and bustle of the market district with all its distinctive smells of baked bread, fruits and vegetables, and freshly cut meat. Men stooped under quarters of beef, as they hurried from docked vessels up to the market; others pushed wheel barrels in long, white coats; turkeys and chickens hung from hooks outside stalls. She easily found Barry's market stall near 15 Union Street and quickly checked out the poultry, easily identifying her father's with the missing toe. She said she would like to see Mr. Barry, and the men told her that he was expected any minute. She explained:

I want to see him because they have said that my father's turkeys and things had spoiled, and I came down so I could get the rest of our money. . . . I can't have my coat and my sisters' their things . . . if we don't get our true money. . . . There were several raccoons Father had sent in and partridges and . . . gray squirrels, and everything—fancy, extra.

So finally, they set me down in a great big chair, and I sat there . . . so that everybody could be sure to see that alligator pocketbook. . . . When [Mr. Barry] did come, the men was all gathered . . . to see what this little girl was going to do. . . . And, of course, I jumped right up from my seat with the pocketbook out in front to be showed . . . and says, "I've come down to get the rest of my daddy's money. You only sent him so-and-so much, and it ought to have been more."

So his face got just as red as blood, and then it got just as white, like snow. He staggered. And the men all began looking, and one man started laughing: "Hoho, ho ho ho." And he staggered and finally set down . . . the men helped him set down in one of them big chairs. . . . He just looked at me and then I, of course, kept talking. . . .

"You said on this letter that my father's things had spoiled . . . and ours is the best in the market. . . . Those are our turkeys. . . . These is our chickens, and . . . those are the partridges. . . ." And I begin telling what all the stuff was. . . . And his face stayed white. And I says, "My sisters brought me down to Bellows Falls, and I got the train . . . and they told me not to come back, not to show my face, without all of . . . my daddy's money."

They all looked like they were kind of sick. So then, the next thing I knew . . . Mr. Barry stopped like that with his hands up at his face, and the tears were running down his face just like a woman. And two of the men led him out.

The next thing I know, they came in with bags with candy sticking out of the top . . . cookies and things for me to eat . . . a bag of oranges . . . a basket of fruit for my mother . . . a bottle of whiskey for Alec. . . . And then the next thing I know, there's more packages for me . . . a doll and this great long envelope with another envelope and then another envelope.

... That's for Alec, and this one is for Sally. And so they put the envelopes in my pocketbook and gave me all these bags and candies and things to eat. And by that time it got to be around eight or nine o'clock, and so the men said we better get her right back down to the station. So I got this eleven o'clock Flyer from Boston ... to Bellows Falls.[38]

Daisy returned home to high excitement and with her father's money three times over. They all believed justice had been done. Daisy once more recognized the importance of standing up for what was right. Ever the diplomat, Alec, despite Sally's urgings to the contrary, wrote Barry a letter that he was welcome to return to the hill for hunting. Years later, Daisy met Barry's son in Wilmington, Vermont. He was amazed when he heard her name. His father had told the story many times of "this little colored girl that came into the market and made a new man of him and made him a Christian."[39]

In 1888, Rose Turner, one of the eldest twins, began keeping a diary and account book. She was as deliberate and orderly as Alec was, with the same warm personality. She was the first daughter to leave home and one of only three who did not return to Vermont to live. Although Rose never married, her house became a center for visiting sisters and later nieces and nephews. Many lived with her temporarily, and all adored her. She was warm, nurturing, a fine storyteller, successful, and devoted to her church. From working

Rose Turner, Francestown, New Hampshire, 1895. Courtesy of the Vermont Folklife Center, Middlebury, Vermont.

as a domestic, she was able to put aside enough money to establish a sewing business out of her home. Godfrey Hall remembers her as *"a mother with no children of her own, but she certainly did take care of everyone else's. . . . She taught us so much about life . . . being honest and doing the right thing and so forth."*[40] Like her parents, she loved music. She learned all the old slave songs and often sang them, once for a local radio station.[41] She played the piano and, in later life, gave lessons. She steadily sent money home to help out, particularly once her father was no longer able to work, and as did all of the daughters, she visited her family as often as she could.

Rose's accounts were mostly personal, noting the money she earned and spent, but she also indicated the comings and goings of her family and important family events. There appears to be no order to these notes, but, fortunately, she always gave the date for any notation. As a result, it is a treasure trove of family activities and a testament to their closeness. This diary and account book continues until 1902. After that, she kept only account books without much family information.

While raising poultry, eggs, butter, and vegetables was one source of income for the Turners, another was picking berries during the summer season. In 1888, Rose noted they began picking raspberries on July 11; they picked 308 quarts that year. Unfortunately, she neglected to say what they received per quart. At different times, Daisy indicated they used to sell berries at the store or the hotel for ten or twenty-five cents per quart. Both figures are probably right, reflecting an increase in price over the years. Rose noted: *"Mother sold $60 worth of berries in year of 1892."*[42] This was a significant source of income. The girls used this money to buy schoolbooks, and Sally for her sewing and quilting or other household needs. From a portion of these berries, Sally would make pies and jams, canning numerous quarts for winter's use. Berrying excursions were always pleasant outings, and the girls used to go off together, sometimes with their mother, often making an afternoon of it. Because they were in the country and wished to protect themselves from wildcats and bears, they usually took a gun. Their father made sure his sons knew how to handle a gun and trap, and in turn, Linesy had taken it upon himself to teach his younger sisters to shoot.

One summer day Violet, Zebbe, Evelyn, and their mother set out in the morning and climbed up to the second hill, or plateau, above the house.[43] This was one of their favorite berrying spots, as the village spread out below them and to the east extended a vast green landscape, with views all the way to the mountains of New Hampshire. They had almost filled their pails with red raspberries and were thinking it was time to return, when their peace was shattered. Warner Townshend, who kept a number of cows in Saxtons River, had an obstreperous bull that required two men to handle. Such a creature was to be kept fenced with a ring through its nose, but the bull had managed to escape and, smelling the Turner cows, headed over the hill and came up on the hilltop where the girls were picking berries. Sally saw him first and ran screaming through the brush to warn her daughters. Violet had her rifle, loaded with only one shell, on the ground. She looked up as she heard her mother's cries and saw the bull charging down on her. Heart pounding and adrenalin pumping, she grabbed the rifle, took deliberate but hasty aim, and pulled the trigger. To her relief, she saw the bull stumble and fall midstride as her mother crumpled to the ground. All three girls, terrified their mother had been hurt, rushed to her. After several heart-stopping moments, they revived her and began the long trek home, carrying her down the hill. It was a frightening escape and an event well worth memorializing. Zebbe captured it in poetic form and recited it one evening to everyone's delight. Unfortunately, seventy-five years later, Daisy found she only remembered a fragment, but even with those few verses, it catches the essence of the experience.

Men have done brave deeds
And bards have sung them well.
But I, of a young girl's bravery,
Now a tale will tell.

They was up on the Lawrence's hilltop
Close to the Fairbanks wall.
They had been picking wild red raspberries
When she heard her mother's call.

She grabbed her rifle from the ground,
Knowing one shell was all
And at the mad pursuing bull
She sent the only ball.

From her lips there came no murmur,
But from her heart there went a prayer
And when she opened her eyes to the sunshine
She knew that God was there.

Cause just three feet
From her mother's listless form
Lay the mad bull's
Terrible horns![44]

Hunters were not the Turners' only visitors. Alec discovered that other guests from Boston—generally but not always African American—relished the opportunity to come to Vermont during the summer or fall. Alec was happy to make that possible. He enjoyed their company, was a gregarious host, and was proud of the farm he had carved out on that hilltop. They, in turn, liked the change of pace and the sights and sounds of farm living.

Zelma Ida May "Zebbe" Turner, ca. 1908. Courtesy of the Vermont Folklife Center, Middlebury, Vermont.

There was fresh mountain air, the earthy aroma of the barnyard, and the sweet smell of hay as it dried in the sun. They enjoyed berrying, picnicking, playing with the lambs, watching Alec work with his oxen, being woken by the crowing of a rooster, and the singing and dancing so prevalent in Turner family life.

As Alec and Sally's daughters grew older, they discovered it was difficult to find steady work in Vermont. Rose obtained a position as a domestic in Francestown, New Hampshire, in 1890, almost certainly through personal contacts.[45] She remained there, with frequent trips home, until December 1894.[46] All of the older sisters were encouraged by their summer visitors to come to Boston with promises to help them find positions. The city had its allure, not least of which was an African American community. Alec's brother Lindsey Coleman had moved to Everett, just outside of Boston, lured by a job with the Boston Market visitors, and Alec knew he would keep an eye out for his daughters. Rachel, Rose's twin, went to Boston after Christmas of 1891, found work at the Whidden Hospital in Everett, and boarded with her uncle and his family.[47] Nellie followed Rachel in April 1892, working for a hotel in the city proper.[48] Linesy Turner found work in 1892, but he decided to remain in Grafton, logging for George Townshend and adding to his income through hunting, trapping, and guiding.[49]

Ellen "Nellie" Turner, ca. 1910. Courtesy of the Vermont Folklife Center, Middlebury, Vermont.

Rachel Turner, ca. 1910. Courtesy of the Vermont Folklife Center, Middlebury, Vermont.

Linesy Turner, ca. 1900. Courtesy of the Trimble family.

He perfected a scent made from brook trout and skunks oil, used as bait for fox, mink, and "anything on four feet."[50] Reminiscent of his father's medicinal brews, he sold it in Boston for $5 a vial.[51] One year he collected the bounty on seventy-eight hedgehogs.[52]

Once the girls found work, they sent money home when they could afford it. The family bonds were strong, and they kept in close touch, returning to Vermont as frequently as was possible, particularly for Christmas and special celebrations. Since his boyhood, Christmas through New Year's had always been Alec's favorite holiday. Because it was a special time, he and Sally wanted to share it with their children. One year when a number of daughters could not afford to come home, Sally wrote them: *"Alex told me to tell you that another year if you all haven't got money enough to come home on to let him know and he will send it to you because he wants you all home if we live and nothing happens."*[53] Even without much family around that Christmas, the Turners still managed to have twelve for Christmas dinner. Others joined them after dinner; two of their guests brought a banjo and fiddle, knowing the Turners' love of music. They cleared the kitchen and danced until four in the morning.[54]

In 1894, Sally and Alec sent out invitations for their twenty-fifth wedding anniversary. It was to be held, Tuesday, Christmas Day, from three o'clock to ten o'clock.[55] All the family was there along with a large number of guests to help them celebrate.[56] They had a sumptuous meal, including turkey, chicken, wines, and drinks, followed by singing and square dancing in the kitchen to local musicians. As was traditional in the Turner household, Alec would call.

> *Get your little brown heads ready*
> *And watch up on the floor.*
> *Eight hands around and get together.*

And then they would all dance and everybody had a nice time.

> *Balance your partner, double four*
> *Back hands round and then swing again*
> *Meet the other fellow on his own ground.*

And the different ladies would show the gentlemen how well they could dance.[57]

The three oldest Turner sisters were in Boston by 1896 and were joined by Willie the next year.[58] Daisy indicated that the Boston Market men who came to hunt on Turner Hill had lured Willie with a job.[59] Like Rachel, Willie lived in Everett, probably initially with the Colemans.[60] Alec had wanted his son to attend Vermont Academy, but Willie was eager to begin earning money like his sisters,[61] who he knew were doing well and enjoying themselves.

It was only a matter of time before one of the young Turners would succumb to marriage. Nellie was the first, accepting the hand of Silas Hunter Samuels, a man who worked as a chauffeur for a wealthy white family in Lexington, Massachusetts. Her husband, like her father, came from Caroline County in Virginia. The wedding was at the Baptist church in Grafton on March 10, 1898. Rose, Rachel, and Susie were bridesmaids, Linesy served as best man, and Florida (sometimes called Flossie), just five, led the bridal procession with a bouquet of pink roses. The description of the wedding in the local paper floated off the page: "The bride was handsomely gowned in white brocade satin, cut en train, with pearl passementerie garnitures. She wore a bridal veil with orange blossoms. A diamond crescent held the veil in place, while another, equally beautiful, caught together the lace at her throat. Corresponding jewels gemmed the ears."[62] A festive reception followed on Turner Hill, adorned by Sally with a mass of cut flowers and evergreen boughs. The couple headed to Washington, DC, for their honeymoon and then settled in Lexington.

Sometime after this, Rose, now with a steady job in the Boston area as a domestic earning $3.50 per week, bought a house within a block of Nellie's. In 1898, she noted that her sister Susie, after attending Vermont Academy, came to Boston hoping to be a missionary nurse. According to

Chester and Susie Lanier, Melrose, Massachusetts, ca. 1920. Courtesy of the Vermont Folklife Center, Middlebury, Vermont.

Susie's daughter Veronica Lanier, this became impossible when she discovered that she fainted at the sight of blood.[63] For a time Rose and Susie lived together.

Susie was the next daughter to marry, having met Chester Lanier over Thanksgiving dinner at Nellie's.[64] The wedding, held in Grafton in March 1903, was a large festive affair. The *Vermont Phoenix* (Brattleboro) described it enthusiastically as "one of the most attractive Grafton weddings of recent years."[65] Rose, a fine seamstress, made the bride's dress. Susie's unmarried sisters, Rachel, Rose, Daisy, Violet, and Zebbe, attended her, and the two youngest sisters, Evelyn and Florida, served as flower girls. Despite a steady snow, the Grafton Coronet Band serenaded the bride and groom, following their sleigh up the slippery incline to Turner Hill. They continued to play through the night on the piazza, giving the celebrants enough room to dance in the house, stopping every so often to come in and warm themselves with food and a cup of cheer. Sally had cooked for days, and tables were covered with ham, chicken, and turkey, as well as boiled potatoes and cabbage, homemade bread and donuts, and a variety of pies and cakes. As the kitchen rocked with enthusiastic dancers and celebrants, the reception continued until daybreak.[66] Willie, Susie's twin, married Florence Elizabeth Moody from Everett. They were united in Massachusetts on Christmas Eve in 1900.[67]

Alec was pleased with his sons- and daughter-in-law. They were all African American, or colored as he preferred to call them. He had strong feelings about whites having relations with coloreds, and this extended to marriage. He knew that the offspring of such unions frequently suffered, not being fully accepted by either race. He wanted his daughters to have warm family lives and thought that was only possible if they married someone with a similar racial background. My father "*wanted all my sisters to marry colored men . . . cause he thought it the only way and the better way from slavery.*"[68] While he had come to genuinely respect and harbor warm feelings for his neighbors, there was a difference. His younger daughters, particularly those who stayed in Grafton, began to show interest in white men. They were all attractive, and a number of young men buzzed around. Still, Alec set down strict rules and expected them to be followed. If a boy came to take one of his daughters out, he would say: "*Bring her back just as you take her out!*"[69]

Linesy and Zebbe had a double wedding on December 24, 1908, in Grafton, with Linesy marrying Iolanthe Wiley from North Carolina and Zebbe marrying Guy Coleman, Lindsey Coleman's second son. Sadly, Guy drowned in a boating accident shortly after the wedding. Zebbe later married John Grant, whose parents had been slaves in North Carolina. After working in Pittsburgh for several years, they returned to Vermont in 1915. When John Grant first told Zebbe he did not think he could make a living

George Hall and Violet Turner Hall at their marriage in 1909. Courtesy of the Vermont Folklife Center, Middlebury, Vermont.

"in that one-horse town," she retorted: *"My father raised sixteen children there and we lived very well."*[70] They became much beloved citizens of Grafton. John made his living as a carpenter and a house painter, and he was also a longtime member of the Grafton Cornet Band. Zebbe gained a fine reputation for putting on delicious fried chicken dinners.

Violet was the first daughter to marry a white man. She fell in love with George Hall III, whose father had known Alec since his first days in Grafton. Having heard about Alec's blind ditches to drain the land on Bare Hill, Hall hired him to do similar work around the Chester Reservoir. His son George, born in 1869, knew all the Turners, but according to his youngest son, it was not until a Grafton Old Home Day, around 1907, that George noticed Violet. By that time, he was approaching forty, divorced, and a successful farmer, businessman, and legislator. Violet was a young beauty more than fifteen years his junior. Alec respected George Hall, but all the difficulties he feared for his daughter came to pass. George Hall's family never accepted Violet. As her son Godfrey said, *"They taught discrimination!"*[71] A postcard from a Boston friend of Hall's indicated the deep racism they both faced. Godfrey, George and Violet's youngest son, kept the postcard throughout his life as a bitter reminder. The friend told George Hall he was coming up to Chester the next week and hoped to see him. He wrote: "Don't run up to Nigger Hill."[72] Daisy said that during their courtship days, Violet was plagued by a nagging fear that because she was colored, George Hall might leave her for a white girl he considered more attractive.

> *She was very lovely . . . but she had a funny feeling, which . . . some will get and others don't have. I never had any feelings like that . . . I don't think that she felt that she wasn't just as good, cause she felt that she was just as good. But she was very sensitive . . . she didn't mean for anybody to push her aside to make her feel inferior in any way. . . . Because he was white and she was part [Negro] and he would be thinking something. But he was the type of man that would never hurt her feelings or make her feel inferior in any way, shape or form.*[73]

She recited a poem that Violet had written to George, declaring her love, but also making known her worry. It began:

> *I wonder where you are tonight, my love*
> *As all alone I sit and dream.*
> *I wonder if your heart's with me tonight*
> *And if the same stars for you gleam.*
> *I sometimes fear there will be another love*
> *That a fairer face will win your heart.*
> *But oh I hope the day will never come*
> *The day that we two drift apart.*[74]

The marriage was cut short by Hall's death of a heart attack in 1919, leaving Violet and two young sons, George and Godfrey, aged nine and four. Little remained after the estate was settled, and Violet went to Boston to find a job to support her sons.[75] She took in laundry and was able to buy a house, but lost it during the Depression. Later she packed frankfurters for a meat packing company, her hands in brine by the hours, eating away at her skin. She returned home to Vermont in the early sixties.

While Daisy never married, she had a serious affair with a white man, Joseph Boinay (the relationship is discussed later in this chapter), and her two youngest sisters, Evelyn and Florida, married white men. Evelyn wed a Swede, David Karlson, who came to West Rutland to work in the marble quarries. Once he married Evelyn, they moved to Athens, just over the hill from his in-laws. He became road commissioner, while Evelyn, after bringing up three daughters, drove the school bus. He always helped with the haying on Turner Hill. Florida wed an Italian, Angelo Di Benedetto. He was a logger and also helped where he could. Rachel, the oldest daughter and twin to Rose, married Norman Blossom, a white man from Rutland, in 1927 when she was forty-two. They lived in Everett until the late 1940s, when they returned to live on Turner Hill.

(left) Dave and Evelyn Karlson, Athens, Vermont, ca. 1940. Courtesy of the Trimble family.

(above) Dave and Evelyn Karlson with their daughters, Yohanna and Juanita, Athens, Vermont, ca. 1923. Courtesy of the Trimble Family.

The sisters in Boston still visited Vermont frequently, often for a month in the summer. One day when Nellie was waiting for the Boston train in Bellows Falls, a train from New York pulled in. She saw a well-dressed man step down and walk by. She noticed his color change when he saw her, and she wondered about him. Then he came back and spoke to her:

> *"You'll pardon me, madam. I don't mean anything wrong or out of the way. . . . Do you know, or are you acquainted with Alexander Turner?"*
>
> *"Why, yes. My father's name is Alexander Turner."*
>
> *"My God, my God! Pardon me, but that's our slave boy from Virginia. Where is he?"*[76]

They talked, and the stranger explained that he recognized her because she looked so much like her father. Nellie volunteered that she had been up on a visit to her parents and was returning to Lexington. He asked if she could take him to see her father, and Nellie acquiesced, suggesting that they hire a horse at the livery stable to take them up. Daisy told this story several times. It was a significant event for the Turner family. *"You see it is things like that through the years, that keep coming up and coming together."*[77] The man was Jack Gouldin, the boy who had grown up in his grandfather's household and was named for him. Alec had known him well.[78] Jack was also one of the two brothers Alec met on the battlefield.[79] It had been a warm reunion that day, and an even more heartfelt meeting when he walked into Alec's house. *"Weren't they two happy people!"*[80] Like Frederick Douglass, Alec had not run away from his owner; he had run away from slavery.[81]

They spent the afternoon in steady conversation, filling in each other on their lives. Jack told Alec about electricity that was just being marketed, and explained how useful it would be on the hill. He convinced Alec to come visit them in Virginia, but because of an accident shortly after this visit, Alec never did return. Still, they remained in touch, and Daisy recounted how they received *"possum and persimmons and things like that from the south."*[82] Possum had been a special favorite of Alec's when he was a boy on the plantation. Throughout his life, he never lost his early delight for possum and hoecakes.

Sally traveled to Boston about once a year, visiting all her children, and going to the eye doctor.[83] There was always great excitement and preparation for her coming. Occasionally, their father came as well. Bruce Turner recounted when Nellie's husband Silas wanted his father-in-law to see the automobile he drove, so they walked to the garage. *[Silas] coaxed him into the seat of the automobile and said, "We're going for a ride." And my grandfather said, "No we're not!" So Silas said, "Let me push you across the floor." And Grandfather said, "That's all!" So he pushed him back and forth across the floor, and that's all he wanted to do with an automobile because he thought they were infernal.*[84] He was distrustful of any such machine and preferred his horses and oxen for transportation.

Near the end of summer in 1899, Alec had a serious accident. He had taken one of his cows to be bred and was leading her home when he lost his footing.

> *He had the rope around his waist, thinking he could hold her, and she got away from him and dragged him. He couldn't get the rope untied . . . and so she dragged him from the Townshend Road clear back to our gate, where she couldn't get through. When she got there, she had to wait because somebody had to open the gate. By that time, he was just about done. We didn't know how badly he was hurt or what was causing the true trouble. By dragging him like that—down in his hip—it started that bullet he received in the war, and that was what caused his trouble—like arthritis or rheumatism. But it was affecting him quick and fast and he was deteriorating. The doctor kept working on him, thinking it was just a strain when it was something entirely different. And, of course, we didn't know it until too late. My sister Nellie Samuels came from Boston and got him down to the doctors at the Massachusetts General. That was the first of trying X-rays, and they found out what was wrong right away. The bullet affected his hip and spine. So, he didn't walk again for twenty-seven years.*[85]

Daisy is often mistaken when estimating dates and years, but an entry in Rose's diary states, "*Papa was taken sick August 25, 1899.*"[86] Rose had been in Grafton with Rachel, Nellie, and Susie from August 22 to September 14. They had a picnic on Turner Hill just before leaving for Boston.[87] When their father did not recuperate after this injury, all three returned. The *Bellows Falls Times* reported: "Alexander Turner is suffering with rheumatism of the heart."[88] This may have been the mistaken diagnosis to which Daisy referred. Rose listed under expenses for September 1899: "*$.83 Blue film Drs,*" which almost certainly refers to the X-rays Daisy mentioned.[89]

Alec spent the last twenty-three years of his life in deteriorating health and virtually an invalid. Before the accident, his constitution had remained remarkably strong. There are a few references in Rose's diary that Papa was sick, but these appear to have been minor incidents. While his health declined, he continued to be optimistic. His mind was alert, and he remained interested in everything around him. "*We made everything convenient for him: a special wheel chair, a bed, a couch, and a table. We all waited on him. He was happy and got along all right by us taking care of him. He never made one complaint.*"[90] The children helped all they could, but the burden of his care fell to Sally, who also took on more of the farm chores. Florida, the youngest, who was only six or seven when the accident took

Florida Turner and nephew "Little Linesy" (son of Linesy Turner), Turner Hill, Grafton, Vermont, ca. 1903. Courtesy of the Vermont Folklife Center, Middlebury, Vermont. While Linesy was known in the Turner family as "Little Linesy," the date of the photograph suggests that it is probably Bill Rogers, an older son of Linesy Turner's, rather than the boy he had with Iolanthe who died at five.

place, remained at home and, as the years passed, helped more and more with her father's care. Chester Lanier, one of Alec's older grandsons, remembered that she would *"bathe him, feed him, put him to bed, and took general care of him, just like he was a baby. She was a wonderful person."*[91]

Daisy began to entertain the idea of following her older sisters to Boston. Although nearly eighteen, she still resembled a child, and Dr. Shoemaker recommended hormone shots to stimulate growth and maturation. Over the next year and a half, she grew several inches, filled out, and at eighteen years of age had her first menstruation.[92] The draw of the city was strong. Her sisters, as well as the people who came to board with the Turners, encouraged her, and she decided to give it a try. She intended to go to school to learn shorthand. In fact, the *Vermont Phoenix* indicated in November 1900 that she was attending school in Boston.[93]

Her mother composed a poem to say goodbye as she left the homestead. Sally had the ability to do this spontaneously. Without the ability to commit the words to paper, she held them in her head, an ability few of us have today.

> *You're going to leave the old home, dear*
> *Today you're going away*
> *You're going among the city folks to dwell*
> *But if sickness overtake you*
> *Or new friends forsake you*
> *Remember, there's a mother at home, sweet home*
> *There's always a mother at home, sweet home.*[94]

When Daisy went to shorthand school, she experienced her first *"rebuff,"* or discriminatory treatment, other than the black doll incident.[95] This time, she was in unfamiliar territory and acquiesced, although she seethed inside. Over eighty years later, the hurt was still evident in her voice: *"some of the girls welcomed me, but there were two or three snobs, and they didn't want me to be in the class. The teacher was going to lose a trade or start something, if they took me in as one of them."*[96] She left quietly, rejected and forlorn.

She was able to find work in a doctor's office and waited tables for special dinner parties, but became homesick and found herself writing her own account of leaving home. *"I'm longing for my old home, for my old home on the hill."*[97] She remembered her father waiting with the horse to drive her to the Bellows Falls station, quietly weeping as one more daughter left the homestead, and her mother reminding her that home would always be there, if after seeing the sights, she came to feel that the city had no heart.[98] Despite low moments, Daisy remained in Boston on and off for the next thirty years, returning frequently to Vermont.

Rose continued to serve as a domestic for a doctor, but she also took in washing and continued to establish her sewing business. After a number of years working in the hospital as an aid, Rachel became a practical nurse. All the sisters sent money home to their parents. The Turners continued to farm. The younger daughters in Vermont helped with preparing the Thanksgiving turkeys for the Boston Market and sheering the sheep in the spring in order to sell the wool. The family persisted in welcoming paying guests and, until 1910, received money for the hired men working on the roads with the oxen.[99] But even this expense became too burdensome, and, according to Daisy, when Alec discovered one of the men was helping himself to the occasional lamb or hen, he let them go. Sally, now in her fifties, continued looking after the poultry and livestock, sugaring, raising a big garden, and doing light chores. However, competent and hard working as she was, she could not replace Alec, and they were forced to downsize. Alec received a "Soldier's Exemption" from property tax in 1909 and 1910, but thereafter it was disallowed. This may have been in conjunction with Alec's attempt to attain his Civil War pension for which he applied in 1908. He received the final rejection of his application in 1916. By 1912, Alec was receiving $10 per year help from the Campbell Fund.[100] Money was very tight on Turner Hill.

While in Boston, Daisy frequently stayed with Nellie or Susie, but most often boarded with Rose, traveling to and from her various jobs. Rose duly noted it in her account book and charged Daisy $2 per night. Daisy enjoyed city life. She was sociable, vivacious, and a good conversationalist. She loved to dance, enjoyed a good time, and had an eye for fashion. For a period, she worked for Etta Raymond, who had a woman's orchestra in Roxbury.

There was another dimension to Daisy as well: she always claimed to have psychic abilities. She had a particular bond with her father, and when he was cutting wood, she often could tell her brother what kind of wood and how much their father had cut. He would check and she was usually right.[101] Later, when I was visiting her, Daisy said that her father came to her at night to warn or help her, encouraging her with *"Don't give up! Don't give up!"* or *"Be brave! Be brave!"* Sometimes he would sing to her. Occasionally, this would be a song she had not sung to me yet, and once reminded of it, she would do so. One was the particular verse he sang when he closed a concert on a Saturday night: *"Good night, Good night, Good night kind Friends, I bid you all good night."*[102] Her most unusual experience, and one she frequently used to illustrate the strong psychic connection between her father and herself, occurred when she was working for Mrs. Raymond. The intensity of this experience never left her.

> *I had just got to Mrs. Raymond's and taken off my clothing and started to . . . go through the lists of what needed to be done when my father*

appeared to me. And at first it was just a very faint gray light came into the room, and then it grew stronger and stronger, and finally right out of this mist of gray my father's form appeared. . . . He said, "Gal, we need you." . . . and this awful, awful peculiar feeling went from my head right down to my toes, all down my spine. And my father's figure right before me. . . . Well, Mrs. Raymond was very tired and very busy . . . and she had . . . a full schedule for me that day. . . . I just dropped everything and I says, "I've got to go home."

"What do you mean, 'go home'? Are you sick?"

"No, but my father just came to me." . . . She used to come up to Journey's End . . . so she knew my father and the family. So she says, "What's wrong, Daisy?"

"I got to go home. My father wants me. He needs me."

"But not today. You can wait and go tomorrow or this evening after we get through."

"No, I've got to go now." And I says, "Can you give me my fare, some money, five dollars?"

"Why you can have all the money you want, but, Daisy, what is wrong? You're just thinking something is wrong."

"No, I've got to go." I . . . commenced putting on my overshoes and getting my bag and coat out and gloves. . . .

"Daisy, what is wrong?"

"I don't know, but I just know that I've got to go home, up to Grafton, at once."

So it must have been almost ten o'clock then, but I knew there was a Flyer train at eleven that left North Station and got to Bellows Falls around one. . . . So she went right to her purse and passed me some money . . . several bills right in my hand. I just grabbed them in my bag . . . and started on the run. . . . I dashed to the train just in time.

When I got to Bellows Falls, I was able to get from the livery stable a sleigh with bells. But there wasn't anyone that could take me up to Grafton because he said he didn't know if our hill or [any of] the roads [were open.] So, they carried me to a quarry road. . . . I struggled through that snow . . . the shortcut through the woods, which brought me in the back of our house and through the barnyard. . . . Before I got quite there, I could hear the dog a'howling.

As soon as I got into the house my father said, "I thank you, God, for the manifestation of your love and power that you heard my prayer!"

"What's wrong, Dad?"

"It's your mother. She's been gone since morning. . . . It was a cold night and she thought she would go across the field to the barn . . . to pick up the eggs before they froze . . . and to feed the hens. . . ."

She had undertaken to go across [the field] and had got lost in the snow. . . . [She] crossed the brook to the right and got up into the edge of what we call the apple orchard, and couldn't find her way, and had got too cold and was slowly freezing to death. She had called, but no one could hear her. . . . She had kept praying and calling, and that's what kept the dog barking and whining, and my father so uneasy and not knowing what to do.

I just dropped everything and undone the dog. . . . Belle, [a bloodhound] *started right across up to the old shanty . . . and we went up to what we called the Shadberry tree. . . . Then she turned. Well, the minute she turned to the right I could see faint footsteps. . . . Belle kept going and finally crossed the brook. After she had got to the brook, Mother had crawled up beside one of the old black stumps and she had rolled quite a way, the way Father had taught us to do in emergency. After she got to where she couldn't walk, she had rolled over and over in the snow. But she was just about gone. . . .*

She was nothing but ice and snow, and she had been up there since eight that morning in that awful cold. Well, the dog grabbed hold of her skirts and helped me, and together we dragged my mother. . . . My father had taught us always from little children what to do in emergencies, so I was able to get my arms . . . under my mother . . . so as to pull her backward. So, I was bringing my mother like that, and the dog helping me. We worked like that, maybe it took me three quarters of an hour to get her across . . . over the little brook and down the road to the house.

It must have been three o'clock when I got her in on the kitchen floor. I grabbed her clothes, tore everything right off of her. I got a mattress down on the floor and put her on the mattress. Then I started rubbing her all over. My father telling me what to do. I got some brandy down her mouth with a teaspoon, and Father just praying. That is why I know there's such power in prayer. . . . Father and I prayed and worked like sixty. . . . We got my mother rolled in these warm blankets right on the kitchen floor and kept a'giving her warm brandy with a teaspoon . . . and reviving her and gradually she begin kind of unthawing-like. Her feet had been froze and her hands—oh, a terrible sight.

In the meantime, my sister . . . Zebbe made it up the hill through the snow and got there to help me and all. So, that's the way it worked out. We saved our mother's life. And I never could have saved her if it hadn't been for my father speaking to me in West Roxbury, Massachusetts, in Mrs. Sherman Raymond's studio.[103]

Concern for their parents was always upmost in the sisters' minds, and Turner Hill continued to be the focus of family life. Family members would return at every occasion, Willie less so because by this time he was living in Harlem, working for the Armour Meat Company. He had returned from World War I as a top sergeant and had been awarded the Distinguished Service Cross and the Croix de Guerre.[104] With the coming of prohibition,

William "Willie" Turner, ca. 1917. Courtesy of the Vermont Folklife Center, Middlebury, Vermont.

he added to his income by running a still and selling the liquor. He used a dumb waiter in the wee hours to move the liquor from the still on the top floor to a speakeasy in the cellar.[105]

Sally still came to Boston once a year, but all of her daughters returned home as often as they could, and once they began having children, the youngest generation was introduced to Vermont. The first of the grandchildren was Willie Samuels, and he came with his mother, Nellie, for the month of August in 1903.[106] Ronny Lanier, Susie's daughter, was fond of saying, "*We didn't go to the beach in the summer. We went to Vermont.*"[107] Alec was the consummate host, and Turner Hill became a social center. Music was an important part of Turner life, and family members and friends brought their instruments to play and encouraged Alec to sing. The newest generation sat at his feet, absorbing his stories and songs.

On Tuesday, September 2, 1919, Alec and Sally celebrated their golden wedding anniversary. All of their children, except Willie, were present. Ten grandchildren and a crowd of townspeople also joined them. Four

Alec Turner with his grandson Willie Samuels, Turner Hill, Grafton, Vermont, 1903. Courtesy of the Vermont Folklife Center, Middlebury, Vermont.

congratulatory poems were read, undoubtedly some from their daughters, and there was music provided by the Grafton Coronet Band.[108] This was a milestone event for Alec and Sally: a celebration of how far they had come since that day in Washington, DC, armed with only their hopes as they moved into an uncertain new world. They had journeyed a great distance in body, mind, and spirit from the bonds of slavery, through refugee camps, to the embrace of farm, family, and neighbors. Alec and Sally had traveled from slavery to land ownership—something to which they could not have aspired as children. They were far from wealthy, but they were grateful for what they had. They had given their children opportunities they never had, as well as a strong sense of family—a core that permeated family life and remains constant today.

This celebration was a high point during a couple of discouraging years. Violet's husband, George Hall, died of a heart attack while he was in Boston. Nellie's husband, Silas Samuels, also died unexpectedly, followed closely by their son Willie on October 31, 1920. It was thought that over-exertion in a recent one-mile race caused a hemorrhage in his lungs; he developed double pneumonia and died in less than three weeks.[109] Willie was attending Boston University Law School and was to have transferred to Harvard University. He was musical, played both the piano and drums in his school orchestra, and was a fine athlete. His mother could never shake the loss. With no one to care for at home, she found work with Walter and Doris Sands as a housekeeper. She was "Aunt Nellie" to the Sands' children, who remember her as warm and motherly; to this day, they recall her mouth-watering fried corn fritters served with maple syrup—a legacy from her mother.[110]

Meanwhile, Linesy was experiencing the throes of untreated syphilis, which was causing serious mental problems. Possibly, he showed some signs of this back in 1899 when Rose inscribed in her diary: "*Linesy was sick.*"[111] Rose, always the caregiver, took him to Lexington to a doctor and then to the Danvers State Insane Asylum, a residential facility for the mentally ill in Danvers, Massachusetts, where she visited him frequently. He grew worse and eventually ended up in Tewskbury Hospital, a long-term care facility where he died of a brain tumor on January 18, 1921.[112] Alec fervently wanted to bring Linesy's body back so that he could see him one last time, and hold his funeral in the parlor. A wave of sympathy for her father washed over Daisy, and she announced, "*Father, it shall be.*" It

Daisy Turner, ca. 1920. Courtesy of the Vermont Folklife Center, Middlebury, Vermont.

was January, and a big snow was the first deterrent. The logistics of moving a body from Tewksbury, Massachusetts, to Turner's Hill in 1921 were problematic in good weather, but the snow added another dimension. Digging a grave in the frozen ground presented a further challenge. A number of young men volunteered, but it was no easy undertaking. Through his sadness, Alec could not escape the cloak of warmth with which his family embraced him.

During this time, Daisy was in the midst of a torrid affair with Joseph Boinay, a successful white automobile dealer from East Lexington. She met him when she went to his store to buy two harnesses for her father. By 1916, she was in love with him, but there was one problem: he was married. Daisy was in Vermont during the summer and fall of 1916 where he visited every three or four weeks.[113] They rode horseback, fished, and hunted while pursuing a passionate romance.

"My father . . . didn't like this man at all."[114] From what transpired, he was right to distrust Boinay. Daisy confessed sixty years later that Joe Boinay was the one man she had truly loved. *"He broke my heart."*[115] Another time, she said that she was sad that it had not worked out *"because I love families, I love children, I love people, and I had planned a happy wedded life like the others. . . . I carried the torch for him five years. Five years I couldn't give him up. He done me wrong, and I wouldn't go back to him."*[116] For Daisy, this was an affair of the heart, a fatal attraction, which clouded her judgment and reason. Even though she knew the relationship was wrong, she was driven to continue it. She wrote her lover: *"What magic have you used to change me so completely? I would have killed any man if he told me I would do the things I have. I am mad for you. . . . When I think of my home training, my mother. I shake my head in shame."*[117] She wore a gold locket he had given her containing a lock of his hair. Eventually Daisy became a domestic in Boinay's home, and after his wife died in the spring of 1923, they planned to be married that December. Alec delivered an ultimatum to Boinay through his daughter Rose—he was to stay away from Daisy or marry her.[118]

In November, when Boinay asked Daisy to press his jacket, she discovered two letters from Lura Landon, Boinay's bookkeeper.[119] She confronted him, but he dismissed it, saying the woman meant nothing to him. Daisy departed for Vermont to be with her father during his final illness, and when she returned to Massachusetts her worst fears were confirmed. Boinay married Landon the following year. In an attempt to distance himself from Daisy, he fired her and charged her with theft. Devastated, but also outraged by this accusation, Daisy brought three suits in November 1924 against Boinay: $25,000 for breach of promise and two additional damage suits totaling $11,500 for malicious and false accusations of larceny and illegal search of her home.[120] This was a historic case. Never before in a Massachusetts court "had a colored woman filed suit against a white man for breach of promise."[121] Daisy was incensed by Boinay's attempt to malign her, *"a single colored woman in a neighborhood of white folks,"* and was determined to have her due.[122] She believed that he had done this to frighten her from bringing her breach of promise suit. She explained that she had his letters to her, and that he did not want them read in court. Further, Boinay had promised to burn Daisy's letters to him, but instead he had hidden them under a floorboard in a closet, where she discovered them.

It was a sensational trial, thronged with spectators.[123] It began January 21, 1927, in the Middlesex Superior Civil Court of East Cambridge and lasted until January 30, with a jury decision reached on February 2. Boinay tried to counter Daisy's accusations as "blackmail and a rank attempt to get money."[124] It was covered in all the Boston newspapers, in daily accounts with salacious headlines, including "Petting Parties in Woods Figure in Balm Battle," "Ex-Maid Sobs as She Reads Ardent Love Letters in Court," and "Admits She Tried to Kill Boinay."[125] For example, after Daisy found Lura Landon's love letters in Boinay's pocket, she confronted him. The *Boston Post* reported:

> "We had a fight over the kitchen floor," she said. "We tipped over the chairs. . . . His brother Frank came in and said: 'You are a brute to treat Daisy like this. You have always said how much you thought of her, why are you treating her like this. You ought to be ashamed. She ought to have killed you. It would have served you right.'"
>
> "Did you try to kill him?" asked counsel.
>
> "I did." answered Miss Turner in a low voice.
>
> Next morning, she said, Boinay pleaded for forgiveness, put his arms about her and kissed her.
>
> The case will be resumed this morning.[126]

Perhaps it was after this incident that Boinay wrote a poem, "Absolution," to Daisy. It was read into the record to the spellbound courtroom over Boinay's protestations and steadfast denial of authorship.[127] The verse concluded:

> Perchance one day Love's own self again
> May spring from that sweet pity deep within
> Your heart where bitterness so long has lain;
> Then may I seek, and, penitent, may win
> Love's absolution sought through years of pain.[128]

Daisy remembered waiting table in uniform at a dinner party during the trial and hearing *"all these fashionable ladies talking about the case, not knowing this was me, right there, waiting table on them."*[129] In the newspapers, Boinay comes off as both a liar and a cad. He obviously believed that no one would take the word of a "colored maid" over that of her white employer. He testified he never wrote her any letters, and over court laughter, referring to the fact that Daisy had cut a lock of his hair to place in her locket, he blustered: "There is nothing funny about it. . . . She never did it to me, or her head would come off."[130] From the testimony, it is evident that whenever Boinay thought he might not have his way with Daisy, he promised marriage.[131] The letters Daisy read in court were the stuff of soap operas: steamy, provocative, and mortifying to Boinay.

Daisy's nephew Godfrey Hall attended the trial, and when asked what the rest of the family thought about the suit, he said that the sisters believed Daisy was doing the right thing. Two of her sisters testified: Rose to tell of her father's ultimatum to Boinay, and Evelyn to relate Boinay's protestations of love to Daisy as his wife lay dead in the next room.[132] Godfrey remembered Boinay as a *"short, stout man . . . very handsome . . . [and always] very neatly dressed."* He described Boinay's defense attorney, Daniel O'Connell, as huge. He towered above Daisy's attorney Ralph Gloag; nevertheless Gloag prevailed. The jury took eighteen hours to come to the verdict, which came down on Daisy's behalf. It was a landmark decision, the first verdict in Massachusetts in favor of a black woman for breach of contract over a white man. Daisy was awarded $3,750 rather than the $25,000 for which she asked; she did not win on the two additional damage suits.[133] Still, the decision was momentous considering the social climate of 1927. With her victory, Daisy had triumphed over class, gender, and racial barriers with a white, all-male jury.

That day she wore a Parisian hat into court, laughing at the memory, relishing that she portrayed the height of fashion as she posed for the camera. A photograph of Daisy in her hat looks out at the world under the headline "I Am Vindicated."[134] Inwardly, however, she was devastated and profoundly hurt. Passion had made her vulnerable, and she retreated into herself. Never again did she fall in love.

During these events, Daisy was called home to Grafton as her father was failing. It happened to be right after she had discovered the letters from Lura Landon, so her emotions must have been in chaos. All the sisters adored their parents and returned home as soon as the call to come to Vermont went out. Now their father was declining, and just before his favorite holiday of Christmas. He lay quietly in the kitchen surrounded by those closest to him—his wife and nine daughters. He said to them: *"I hate to go and leave you girls, but I feel satisfied because I know that you've got what it takes to hold our little home and the family together."*[135]

"We told him we would never give up fighting for his rights, his human rights, his civil rights, his rights as a human being that Jesus Christ had given him on the cross of Calvary."[136] Sally held his hands, as Alec expressed how good they had been to him all those years he had been an invalid, and if they were just half as good to their mother as they had been to him, everything would be fine. He had just one final wish: *"he wanted us daughters to be the last ones to lay him in his final resting place that was the end of his journey."*[137] He made them feel at peace, leading Daisy to comment, *"how beautifully my father died."*[138]

No matter what the circumstances, Alec Turner was a larger-than-life presence for his family, and he remained so to the very end. His faith still strong, he asked one last time for his daughters to sing one of his favorite hymns:

> Oh, the soul thrilling rapture when I view his blessed face
> And the luster of His kindly beaming eye
> How my full heart will praise Him for mercy, love, and grace
> That prepare for me a mansion in the sky.

And as they sang, Alec, who had cast off the bonds of slavery and forged a new life on a hilltop in Vermont, peacefully drew his last breath. They marked his demise on Thursday, December 20, at 9:30 p.m. He died as he had lived, with reverence for his God, whom he so fervently believed had guided him throughout his life, but particularly to Grafton. In true Turner fashion, Violet captured those last moments in poetry. The verse begins:

> *No tender yet sad farewell*
> *From his quivering lips was heard,*
> *So softly he crossed that quiet stream*
> *That not a ripple was stirred.*
> *He was spared the pain of parting tears*
> *As he left this world of strife,*
> *It was scarcely dying, he only passed*
> *In a moment to endless life.*[139]

The funeral service was held on Turner Hill, Sunday, December 23, and Alec was taken to his final resting place in a horse-drawn sleigh. Eight of his daughters, all in white, served as pallbearers while Rose gently escorted her grieving mother. The sleigh brought his casket to the cemetery, and

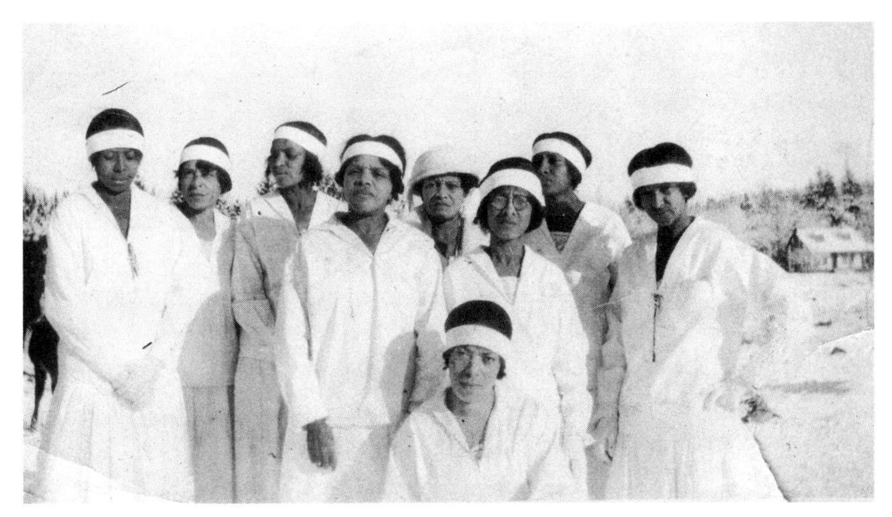

The Turner sisters at their father's funeral, Turner Hill, Grafton, Vermont, December 23, 1923. Back row: Evelyn, Violet, Susie, Rose, Zebbe, Daisy; middle row: Nellie and Rachel; front row: Florida. Courtesy of the Vermont Folklife Center, Middlebury, Vermont.

his daughters carried him to his grave, *"and we lowered his casket in the ground under those white straps so that no other hand would touch him but us daughters."*[140] One last time they sang "My Savior First of All":

> When my life's work is ended and I cross the swelling tide
> And that bright and glorious morning I shall see
> I shall know my redeemer when I pass the other side
> And his smile will be the first to welcome me.[141]

That night it snowed, and they woke to a fresh blanket of white, a peaceful and silent covering embracing their world.

CHAPTER 9

Daisy's Last Years

> I died! I died twice in life: the day my father died and the day that house burned down.
>
> —Daisy Turner, interview with author, December 8, 1983

Alec was deeply mourned by his family, but especially by his wife, Sally. She lived ten more years and *"grieved every day. She mourned my father something terrible."*[1] Alec was a dynamic force, central in family life, but Sally was his lifelong partner, sharing his dreams and his burdens. Together they had left slavery behind them, borne the struggle to shape a homestead out of the wilderness, and built a new life sustained by deep faith and strong family bonds. They had moved a great distance from Virginia, both physically and symbolically, putting to use many skills learned while enslaved

Haying on Turner Hill, Grafton, Vermont, ca. 1925. Courtesy of the Grafton Historical Society, Grafton, Vermont.

and adding a host of new ones. Alec was Sally's rudder, leading her north away from dehumanizing attitudes, and her protector as they ventured forward; she was his comfort and intimate companion. It was an empty world without the one person who had shared all but fourteen years of her life. Without question, Alec was Sally's soul mate.

Her brother, "Uncle Early," moved in with Sally after Alec's death and helped with the chores. He was family and a familiar presence, but by this time he had mental problems and proved to be a burden. Zebbe, Evelyn, and Florida lived nearby and ran errands, worked in the garden, and offered support in any way they could. The other daughters visited as frequently as possible. "*She was surrounded by a great deal of love from her daughters.*"[2] Bruce Turner remembered his grandmother as "*a hardworking person who handled the routine of being a housewife and farmhand all at the same time. And worried about her children, always wanted to see them.*"[3]

Sally continued with the rhythm of farm life, butchering a couple of hogs in November, smoking the hams with corncobs, and sugaring in the spring. Bruce's younger sister Faith recalled helping her grandmother sugar

Sally and Florida Turner, Turner Hill, Grafton, Vermont, ca. 1925. Courtesy of the Vermont Folklife Center, Middlebury, Vermont.

and listening in fascination as Sally related a remarkable occurrence. She collected the sap and was boiling it in a long pan over the archway Alec had built against a stone ledge.

> *She was sitting down by the syrup, and she said something kept saying to her, "Sally, get up and go and look at so and so, and see if the sap has dripped or something." She said to herself, "I just looked at those pails. They're not full." Something said again, "You go and look at them, Sally. Get up and go and look." So, she said she got up, and she went over to look at the pail, and she no more than got very far away when the stones gave way, back to the archway. So, she got up in time!*[4]

She had escaped being crushed and severely burned by the falling rocks and saw this as an example of her Lord protecting her from harm. She still kept a vegetable garden, gathered dandelion blossoms for wine, and canned dandelions and rhubarb in the spring. One year, Faith remembers Daisy sending tulip bulbs for her mother to plant. Sally's eyesight was all but gone, and she mistook the bulbs for onions and fried them for supper. Sally and her brother had eaten them by the time Faith returned from school, so fortunately she did not have any as the effect on the brother and sister was most unpleasant. Sally continued to go berrying, and in the summer and early fall she persisted with her canning, remarking to those who suggested she did not need to do so much: "*When the snow flies, this will taste pretty good!*"[5]

The farm cycle is ever moving, and as Faith pointed out, "*they did the regular work and whatever had to be done.*"[6] But as the years went on, and age slowed energy and strength, it became difficult. While Sally's eyes grew steadily worse and she could no longer sew, she continued to cook, and her granddaughters, as her daughters before them, learned her recipes. One Christmas toward the end of her life, when Sally did not feel well, her granddaughter Sally Turner, Linesy's eldest daughter, made all the pies: mince meat, squash, apple, and blueberry.[7]

The homestead was still the place all the family gathered. Sally always wanted her family around her and encouraged her grandchildren to come. Those from Boston arrived in June and stayed until Labor Day. They helped with the chores: bringing the cows in to be milked, helping Evelyn's husband Dave Karlson with the haying, and pulling weeds in the extensive garden. They also enjoyed fishing, berrying, damming up the brook, walking to the general store, and playing games in the evening such as "Hoist the Green Sail," a two-team version of hide-and-seek. Godfrey Hall remembered with great relish the meals his grandmother turned out over her big wood stove in the kitchen. Chicken dishes were his favorite, with all kinds of fresh vegetables, "*and for dessert we'd have raspberry shortcake. The berries would be cooked on the stove for ten or fifteen minutes and put over the freshly made shortcake.*"[8]

The grandchildren grew up forging strong bonds with their cousins and knowing the warmth of family life. They loved their grandmother, whom they remembered as full of patience and very slight with snowy white hair, and their aunts.[9] "*All the aunts were like our mothers.*"[10] Rose mothered all of Linesy's children and put Bruce through college. Alec's athleticism passed on to many of his grandchildren: George Hall was a fine wrestler, played semipro football and baseball, and was exceptionally strong. Bruce Turner, Godfrey Hall, and Willie Samuels all excelled at track, and Bruce and Godfrey still hold records at Lexington High School.[11] In 1932, at the age of twenty-one, Chester Lanier won both the Golden Gloves boxing trophy, becoming the New England amateur heavyweight boxing champion, and the John L. Sullivan Cup—considered particularly significant as John L. Sullivan would never fight an African American.[12] That same year Chester was elected "Young Man of the Year" in Medford, Massachusetts.[13] His younger sister, Ronny Lanier, always a fine athlete and a track star, was inducted into the Mustang Hall of Fame in October 2010 as one of Medford High School's finest athletes. She received a letter in basketball, field hockey, soccer, softball, volleyball, track, broad jump, and tennis, and served as captain of the softball and tennis teams.

In 1931, Sally sent a letter to Susan Merrill Lewis in Williamsburg, Maine, to catch her up on the Turners' news. According to Daisy, the Turners and Merrills had remained in touch over the years, and Susan Lewis, Adams Merrill's granddaughter, visited them on the hill. This communication also gives voice to Sally's own feeling of accomplishment and satisfaction in her family's achievements. She reported that her grandchildren were "in both high school and college, and that they were prosperous and useful men and women," and that her son William had won both the Distinguished Service Cross and the Croix de Guerre in World War I.[14] Remembering the days in Maine, she confided that she still sang the old songs, particularly to entertain her grandchildren. The Turners never forgot their early years and wanted to keep their history alive for their family.

Christmas remained an important family holiday, and the daughters and grandchildren who could come arrived with great excitement. The holiday continued for a whole week of "*dancing and eating and socializing.*" Rose and Susie played the piano in the front parlor where the dancing took place, and the brothers-in-law played the guitar, fiddle, and harmonica. Grandchildren joined in, with Godfrey Hall on the piano and Bruce Turner on the fiddle, and neighbors came to join in the fun.

By Christmas 1932, Sally's health was beginning to fail. In February she became seventy-eight years old, the same age Alec had been when he died.

Turner Family gathering, Turner Hill, Grafton, Vermont, ca. 1924–25. Left to right, standing: Rose, Rachel, her husband Norman Blossom, Sally (George Hall behind), Nellie, Evelyn, Uncle Early, Daisy; sitting: Dave Karlson, Sally, Bruce, Faith Turner, Godfrey Hall, Florida, Yohanna Karlson. Courtesy of the Vermont Folklife Center, Middlebury, Vermont.

One of her granddaughters remembered singing to her grandmother during her last illness.[15] As did Alec, to the very end, Sally loved hymns, and her daughters continued to pray and sing with her. One of her favorites was "I'm a Child of the King." In the back parlor was the old Mason and Hamlin pump organ. Ronny Lanier used to take her grandmother into the parlor, place her in one of the green upholstered chairs, pump the organ, and play hymns to Sally's great delight.[16]

In late October, word went out that their mother was declining. All the sisters, except Evelyn, who was living over the hill in Athens and was giving birth, were there. As her daughters sang and prayed with her, Sally asked them to keep the faith, hold together as a family, and hang on to the homestead for the love of their parents.[17] It was at that moment that Daisy decided that she would leave Boston and maintain the homestead.

Sally died October 20, 1933. As with her husband and the children who predeceased her, her funeral was held in the back parlor, the most formal room. "*There must have been fifty or sixty people up on the hill when my mother died. Everybody was so nice. They always came from a distance.... The white and the colored came to be there and to pray ... with the family.*"[18] In true Turner fashion, Zebbe memorialized her mother in a poem:

Though years have gone, we can't forget
Those words of love, we hear them yet.
Her dear sweet voice, we hear it yet.
We see her by the old armchair,
My mother dear in humble prayer
Oh praise the name, the humble grace,
We'll meet up yonder face-to-face.
In the Master's kingdom together share
In answer to our mother's prayer.[19]

With Sally's passing, the next generation was faced with a major transition and a new responsibility as caretakers of the homestead and family traditions. After the funeral, Daisy let it be known that she would leave Boston and stay on the hill. She felt the pull of her heritage and wanted to maintain the homestead that her parents had spent the greater part of their lives establishing. She recognized the significance of what her parents had accomplished and wanted to honor it. Through the years, she had internalized their stories and determined they must be passed down to the next generation. To do that, she believed it was critical to maintain the homestead. The family, particularly the grandchildren, must have a place to come. "*She did really do something for us when she decided to stay on the hill by herself like that. And we went up as often as we could. All of us.*"[20]

It was during Sally's final hours that Uncle Early vanished, never to be found. While a massive search was mustered, no sign of William Armstead Early was ever discovered. As with any unresolved disappearance, there were rumors—the most extreme was that Daisy was somehow responsible. This rumor says more about some people's perceptions of Daisy, no doubt fed by the brandishing of her rifle and her contentious nature. Godfrey spoke about this rumor, shaking his head over how some townspeople believed she had burned his body while burning brush. Godfrey had been on the hill at the time of his grandmother's death. "*But that doesn't make any sense. Aunt Daisy made no fires ... before or after [Uncle Early] left the barn.*"[21] The disappearance remained a mystery. Godfrey's brother George spent time hunting and fishing on Turner Hill and was always on the lookout for some sign of his uncle. "*I never found anything. Nobody has ever found any sign of that man. Just disappeared like that! ... His mother prophesied it.*"[22]

As her mother before her, Daisy kept a cow, a few chickens, and a couple of horses. She sold lumber, Christmas trees and wreaths during the season, and took in paying guests, mostly from Boston and New York. Journey's End earned the reputation as a place where one could regain one's health. Daisy also continued to take in hunters. George Hall, Violet's husband, put up the money to build Birch Dale Camp, designed by Alec, on a hillside above the house. Daisy had bought it after her father died, and it was this building she first christened "Journey's End," before extending it to the main house and farm. Bruce Turner remembered family and guests in and out almost every weekend.[23] Grandchildren continued to come up from Boston every summer, and those who lived in Vermont often joined them. Freda Knight, Evelyn's daughter, remembered that Daisy *"always had the lawn mowed and set up the croquet set and then we would eat out on the lawn. She'd make her potato salad, and she was famous for making good cornbreads and gingerbreads in those nice square, black pans. It didn't take her long to whip them up, and they were really good."*[24]

Holidays, particularly Christmas, persisted as a season for family gatherings, and there were many good times. Daisy built a small building that she termed the "dance hall" and put a piano in it. This became the site of the dances, and while relatives took turns playing a variety of instruments, Daisy called and everyone else danced. Bruce Turner became a fine tap dancer and performed to admiring encouragement.

Not much money was coming in, but somehow Daisy hung on. In 1948, Nellie was the first of the sisters to die, followed by Rose, who succumbed to cancer the next year. Susie died in 1952 of a cerebral hemorrhage. Rachel and Norman Blossom built a small camp and moved up on the hill in the early 1950s and both died there, Norman in 1952, and Rachel in 1958. Violet returned home in the early 1960s.

Always protective of their father's land, the sisters, spearheaded by Daisy, brought a lawsuit against the Bragg Lumber Company in 1943. Daisy claimed that Bragg had trespassed and illegally logged her father's land. She finally won a settlement in 1953 from the Vermont Supreme Court.[25] While Daisy took her promise to her dying father to the greatest lengths, all the sisters were activists. They campaigned for women's suffrage and particularly for the election of Consuelo Bailey, the first woman to run for lieutenant governor in 1954. Lucy Daniels of Grafton was active in the women's suffrage movement and took part in demonstrations in Washington, DC. All the Turner sisters joined Daniels in her activist work that paved the way for women to aspire to such offices.[26]

Daisy was the most outspoken of all the sisters and had no trouble in articulating what was on her mind. With her verbal skills, she became the family spokesperson. Perseverance in pursuit of what she believed was right characterized Daisy from her earliest days and frustrated many who had transactions with her. She gained the reputation of being cantankerous and difficult. Some told stories of her sitting by the door with her gun across her knee, threatening to shoot someone. But others, particularly those who spent any time with her, told of her ability with words, her power to evoke the moment through vivid detail, changing cadence, and evocative gestures. Closely associated with her storytelling was her sociability and her pride in her racial identity. "If somebody disrespected her 'blackness' the woman was just fearless," said Paa Beekoe Welbeck, a young Ghanaian student Daisy befriended in the early 1960s.[27]

One afternoon in the summer of 1962, she was playing hymns on the piano in her father's house when Harry Simpson appeared. She had employed him as a handyman and allowed him to stay in Rachel's bungalow for a week while he measured logs. He had been drinking and, as Daisy said, "*commenced this fresh talk.*"[28] Daisy described the incident in her sworn statement:

> *On July 9, 1962, Mr. Harry J. Simpson who had been a worker on my premises came over to my kitchen and said to me, I don't want any of your supper, you've got to die and I am going to kill you tonight. Thinking that he was drunk, I told him that he was drinking, but he denied this, repeating that he had to kill me. He was a man of about 48 years, weighing about 225 pounds, and I at this time was 79 years of age, weighing about 125 pounds. Mr. Simpson kept threatening to kill me and the more I tried to talk him out of it, the more he pressed upon me. I gradually retreated trying frantically to convince him that he was wrong, and I finally retreated from my kitchen into the dining room where I snatched a rifle to hold him off. Gradually I worked my way outside with the rifle pointed at Mr. Simpson who was pressing upon me constantly and when I finally reached the out of doors, I ran for my life to a small cabin nearby where Mr. & Mrs. McIntosh were staying as guests. Mr. Simpson was following close behind. At the McIntosh cabin, I was in a near state of shock asking admittance. They let me in and I sank to the floor. Shortly thereafter I heard Mr. Simpson at the door of the cabin talking to Mr. McIntosh. Mr. Simpson distinctly threatened to break the door down and to kill me and the McIntoshes if they attempted to interfere. I heard him repeat this several times. All this time Mr. McIntosh was at the front door holding Mr. Simpson off with the rifle. Finally Mr. McIntosh was able to talk Simpson off, and at 15 minute intervals he returned twice at the cabin where Mr. McIntosh held him off with the rifle. Finally, Mr. Simpson, went back to the main house and burned it to the ground.*[29]

William McIntosh also gave a statement, corroborating Daisy's story.[30]

Simpson brought a large can of gasoline and used it to soak the house to make sure that the fire would ignite and consume the structure.[31] Still running on adrenalin, Daisy made her way from Birch Dale Camp to Violet's house about a mile away. She could see the house burning as she made her way through the woods, but fearing Simpson would come after her, she traveled slowly and cautiously. She finally reached her sister's house safely and poured out the events of the evening. Violet called the state police and fire department. By the time the firemen arrived, the house was burned to the ground. "*We just lost everything. Everything right in that house went down. I died! I died—twice in life: the day my father died, and the day that house burned down. The beautiful Turner house went down in ashes. That's something never to be forgotten.*"[32]

Simpson was apprehended the following morning. He was prosecuted and sent to jail for eight years, but only served two. According to Daisy's nephews George and Godfrey Hall, Simpson was a drifter and was not stable; he had been in a mental institution before he worked for Daisy.[33]

Nothing could bring back the house into which her father had poured his labor. The fire was a devastating blow for the sisters. All were badly shaken. For Daisy, it was a visceral loss. Gone was the tangible evidence of their family heritage. Not just the house, but Alec's primer, his freedom papers, the silver spurs won by his father, and numerous other mementoes and documents that together told the story of the enslaved boy who traveled north, established himself as a landed farmer, and built a family homestead. He had succeeded on the strength of his ingenuity, labor, desire, and faith, as well as on his engaging personality. All that remained were the memories and her father's stories—stories that gained even more significance for Daisy and that she believed must be told.

I have wondered how much the fire and the loss of family papers played into Daisy's later paranoia and her fear that people were stealing her papers. Some of this was fed by her inability to see and by her habit of putting things in paper bags and then forgetting where they were. But there is no question that the fire seared a deep scar in her psyche. Family and friends, all shaken by the event, came up the next day to sift through the rubble. Not much was recovered, although Daisy did find her father's colt revolver, given to him by Dayton—the one he carried throughout the war. Mary Cummings Archambault, the granddaughter of William and Catherine McIntosh, remembers looking for jewelry that Daisy had lost in the fire. For her it was like a treasure hunt; for Daisy, dismal hopelessness.

Daisy was seventy-nine years old at the time of the fire. She remained on the hill for a year and a half, living in Birch Dale Camp, but when her brother-in-law John Grant died in February 1964, she moved to the village and lived with Zebbe on Hinkley Brook Road. Grant, who had made his living as a carpenter, had built two houses there. Zebbe, using her mother's cooking expertise and recipes, became well known for putting on chicken dinners in her home. People came from miles around; locals frequently came to celebrate special occasions, and visitors from the tavern often found their way to her door. Her nephew, Godfrey Hall, worked for her one summer and found it a lucrative seasonal job. When Daisy moved in with her, Zebbe continued all the cooking and Daisy waited on the table. It was a full meal, starting with a wine cordial and crackers and cheese, followed by soup, and then southern fried chicken, biscuits, baked beans, salads, coleslaw, and concluded with a delicious dessert—a meal one would savor, but after which vow not to eat again for a week.[34]

Grafton had changed since that November day in 1873 when Alec Turner arrived. The middle of the twentieth century ushered in a cultural revolution that exploded throughout Vermont. Better roads and new interstates made Vermont more accessible to urban areas and enabled developing ski resorts to draw weekend visitors from urban centers. Since the last half of the nineteenth century, there had been summer visitors who came to stay on farms, in hotels, and at a variety of residences for the season. But the new highways created a steady influx of newcomers, frequently young skiers who spent the season taking pickup jobs to fund a winter of skiing and then frequently put down roots. Indeed, there was a whole generation of young people, some with considerable wealth behind them, looking for an alternative lifestyle. Many were searching for new ways to engage meaningfully with society, others simply dropped out, eschewing traditional career tracks and experimenting with communal living and mind-altering drugs. With these new inhabitants came different attitudes, values, and lifestyles. Many small farms had disappeared with the added economic pressure to buy tractors, milking machines, and bulk tanks. For many, the gain did not seem to warrant taking on the additional expense, and newcomers were able to purchase land at bargain prices. There was an inevitable clash, which reached its height in the 1980s, between the native Vermonters and the newcomers, or "flatlanders." This was fueled by money and class differences, as well as the feeling that flatlanders were outnumbering natives.[35]

Grafton experienced this change a bit differently. Grafton had always had summer residents, particularly at the Old Tavern, or Phelps Hotel as it was known in Alec's day, but summer people also bought and restored houses and became a permanent part of the community. One of these individuals was Mrs. Rodney Fiske of New York City, who left a large bequest for the benefit of Grafton when she died in 1959. This led to the establishment of the Windham Foundation and to the purchase and restoration of a number of homes and businesses, as well as the support of other organizations devoted to improving life in Vermont. This was an admirable mission, but not everyone approved, particularly some older residents who feared that Grafton would become another Colonial Williamsburg.

Daisy was one of the Windham Foundation's detractors. Part of this was her growing paranoia that increased with age. Her niece Ronny Lanier believed this paranoia had been latent. "*She was always afraid that someone was going to do something to her.*" She pointed out that whenever Daisy put Ronny and her siblings to bed, Daisy insisted on closing the shades so that nobody could see in, "*and of course Mother never pulled the shades . . . Aunt Daisy would pull down every shade so you couldn't see a crack of light. And then she would put out all the lights, and then she would have us looking out the window, and she'd say, 'Now you see that man? He's going to come and get me.' And she would have us scared to death!*"[36] Bruce Turner believed that her paranoia began in the 1920s when she experienced a number of significant losses: her brother Linesy, Violet's husband George Hall, her nephew Willie Samuels, her lover Joseph Boinay, and her father.

She was desperately afraid that the Windham Foundation would take her father's land, and in her diatribes she always referred to it as the "*Windham Foundation,*" with an emphasis on the second syllable. She claimed that they were dealing in drugs as an explanation for their money. I came to understand that she blamed the foundation for what she viewed as the extreme changes in Grafton. This Grafton was very different from the hill farm community in which her father settled and in which she grew up. Bruce Turner also observed a noticeable shift in attitude with the arrival of the newcomers:

> *In the state of Vermont, people are very steady and staid, and they took people for what they were worth, worked with them, and recreated with them. At the present time, there are people from New Jersey, New York, Massachusetts, Connecticut, who have come to the Vermont area with ideas from their community, and they feel that the community should fall in behind them in furthering the ideas that they have about people. And this wasn't true in the old days. Everyone got along very, very well together. And it has gotten to the point now where the people who live in the towns don't have a voice anymore. They have been outnumbered by people who have come from outside and influenced and have taken over, and they're running certain Vermont areas the way they've never been run before.*[37]

This is a familiar attitude expressed by many longtime residents of Vermont, but it fed Daisy's paranoia. She also became fixated on securing her father's Civil War pension. Certainly, it would have been a great monetary help to her in her final days, but more than that, she was convinced that her father was wronged grievously. Alec filed his claim for his Civil War pension on January 2, 1908.[38] It seems to have taken several years for the claim to have been processed. On February 12, 1916, Alec received a letter asking for a sworn statement giving the name under which he enlisted, the date and place of enlistment and discharge, the letter of the company, the number of his regiment, and the names of its officers, as well as the duties he performed.[39] On June 6, 1916, he wrote to answer these questions. He explained that when he first joined the First New Jersey Cavalry as a runaway slave, he was not allowed to enlist. In his application, he noted that he had not been discharged; however, he did not mention that in his letter.[40] These were red flags for any official. His claim was rejected on November 23, 1916,[41] on the grounds that his name could not be found on any rolls of the First or Second New Jersey Cavalry. As an orderly of Ferdinand Dayton, he would have been classified as Dayton's servant and therefore would not have appeared on the army's roster. Daisy rejected this interpretation, believing her father was not a servant, but an active soldier. She felt it was one more injustice heaped on her father, against which she would continue to fight. She knew that he had been in combat, even wounded at Brandy Station, and had been presented with two *"papers for bravery."*

While Alec was aware that he had not enlisted, as the war continued African Americans were allowed to enlist, and black regiments took part in the fighting. Alec had been beside Dayton until that fateful day when the orders came and he was on furlough. It must have been difficult for him to comprehend the red tape that kept him from what he believed was his rightful pension and an acknowledgment of the service he had given so willingly.

In his 1916 letter to the Department of Bureau of Pensions, Alec stated: *"I have been an invalid here with rheumatism and am helpless now. And have been for 18 years. Otherwise I should go to Trenton N.J. where I could find some of the officers that know me."* Alec was not the only escaped slave who experienced this problem. In one of those peculiar twists of history, Humphrey—who had also escaped across the Rappahannock from the Gouldin plantation and had helped guide the raid on Thomas Gouldin's home—faced a similar situation of establishing his claim of service. He acted on Alec's belief that he could find corroboration to substantiate his case. In 1905, Humphrey, who lived in Nutley, New Jersey, traveled to Hamburg in Sussex County to find the postmaster, Henry W. Edsall, who had also taken part in the raid. Although Edsall failed to recognize him "as one of the guides"—suggesting that there had been more than one guide—he was convinced by Humphrey's accurate portrayal of the details of that night.[42] Humphrey hoped to find several men of First New Jersey Cavalry's Company K to establish his claim. Then he would find someone to initiate a special congressional bill to gain his pension—a daunting challenge, to say the least. It does not appear that Humphrey was any more successful than Alec in gaining his Civil War pension.[43]

Daisy fought on. She was visited by Maynard Young, an agent from the White River Junction Veterans Office, who filed a report on July 15, 1968. He was dismissive of the interview, saying that the "Adjutant General of New Jersey has failed to verify any service during this period for anyone by the name of Alexander Turner" and that Daisy was vague as to the letters to and from the Veterans Administration as her attorney had them, but it was not clear who her attorney was. Apparently, "a copy of her mother and father's marriage certificate, a copy of her father's death certificate and her birth certificate were all forwarded to Washington with her claim."[44]

Next she was sent a letter by J. T. Taffe Jr., director of the Compensation, Pension and Education Service, who assured her that he was asking the manager of the Veterans Benefits Office "which has jurisdiction of Civil War Claims, to make certain this matter is given every possible consideration and a report made to you."[45] This was followed by a letter from Martin Brounstein, adjudication officer of the Veterans Benefits Office, on September 16, 1968, stating: "Since there is no record of your father's service your claim must be disallowed."[46] Daisy was eighty-five, and I suspect this flurry of activity may have been the result of work done by Robert Stafford, a former Vermont governor and then a U.S. congressman upon whom John Daniels had prevailed to look into Daisy's claim as a helpless child of a Civil War veteran.[47] However, Daisy's efforts did not reside in one person. Over the years, she had a number of experienced lawyers look into her father's pension, but it always ended in the discovery that, because her father's name did not appear on any official regimental lists, his claim had been rejected in 1916. There was no way of getting around this stumbling block.

In the early 1980s, just before I met her, Daisy turned to Phil Hoff, another former Vermont governor and known for helping the downtrodden. She called him at home.[48] Although he recognized her paranoia, there was just enough credibility in what she said—she gave details as to dates, circumstances, times, and places—that he felt perhaps an injustice had been done. He also mentioned that she had one of the most striking voices he had ever run across. She had two issues she wanted him to investigate: her father's pension and certain land claims. He visited her at home. By this time, she was living by herself, and as I was, he was horrified by her living conditions. He contacted the local fire department, and someone told him that if they went to check on her, she would chase them off with her gun. Hoff called the welfare department, and someone said they would visit her. He also discovered there was a network of local people who looked out for Daisy, including Louise Tanner, Louise Thompson, and her niece Freda Knight, her major caregiver.

Hoff was convinced through Daisy's stories that her father had fought in the cavalry. He contacted Stafford, who told him there was no record of Alexander Turner serving in either the First or Second New Jersey Cavalry. Hoff realized that such an omission could have been deliberate. No one was going to give Alexander Turner any benefit of the doubt, which galled Daisy. Her father had fought bravely and without reservation for the cause of the Union, as well as for his own freedom, and the Union refused to recognize those efforts.

Hoff also looked into Daisy's land issues. He discovered the Bragg Lumber Case and realized there was a problem with the boundary lines because the old brush fences and trees that marked the corners of the property were long gone. Daisy continued to call him frequently, usually early in the morning. As I had come to find, she would start rationally, but then would work herself into a frenzy talking about her father's pension or something about her land. These were flash points with Daisy. Things she believed she owed her father, part of the fulfillment of her promise to him on his deathbed. The fact that she could not accomplish this drove her to distraction.

It took me a while to understand why the land and her father's pension released such rage and frustration. I went to see Daisy to record her life story, but visiting her once a week and focusing on her narrative did not allow much perspective. That came with time and with meeting other people who were part of her world. Dropping in every week for a few hours and a limited purpose did not make me a participant in her everyday life. I thought she listened to the radio when no one was there, as she always seemed to be caught up on the news. And she usually told me when people dropped by. Still, she spent a great deal of time by herself, dwelling on the past.

It took a little over two years to complete both the interview process and the video. I tried to visit her weekly, although less frequently when editing the video began. Once the video was finished, and Daisy had viewed and approved it, I had to turn to other things, though I continued to visit her. My work took me all over the state, so whenever I was in the area I made a point of stopping in.

As her 104th birthday approached, I began to think about a celebration for her. I remembered her interest in Consuelo Bailey, Vermont's first woman lieutenant governor, and asked if she would like me to see if Madeleine Kunin, Vermont's first woman governor, could come help her celebrate. "*You don't mean it!*" I already knew it was a possibility, so I told her I would work on it. The reception took place in early June. Daisy was excited and looked wonderful. Her white hair was coiffed, and she was dressed in a colorful print dress and sparkling earrings; she had both style and presence. Kunin chatted with her respectfully and then asked her to recite something. Daisy was in her element as she began the "Battle of Gettysburg," telling the audience that her father had fought in that battle. It was a long poem I had heard many times, and I realized toward the end she was searching for a line, but she never wavered; instead, she circled around, remembered, and finished perfectly.

I returned a couple of weeks later for Daisy's actual birthday. A group of family and friends sat outside on a lovely June day. Daisy recited, and we sang "Happy Birthday" and had cake. As always with visitors, she rose to the occasion. After seeing her so upbeat—happy, laughing, and engaging with all of us—I fully expected her to live another couple of years. I found myself thinking back to an earlier birthday I had seen memorialized in a photograph taken outside Daisy's house on Hinkley Brook Road. She was with lifelong friend Amy Davis, birthday cake in evidence on a table, and on the back of the photograph was scrawled: "the black doll!" She had outlived everyone in that schoolroom, but Daisy's extemporaneous recita-

Daisy on her 104th birthday, June 21, 1987, Springfield, Vermont. Courtesy of the Vermont Folklife Center, Middlebury, Vermont, photograph by Jane Beck.

tion was as much a part of her very fiber as the quality it exemplified. While she could no longer walk, she was still standing up for who she was. Her voice still held its sway, and we all remained under its spell.

It was six o'clock on a Monday night, February 8, 1988, and I had just come home from work when a reporter called. She said, "Daisy Turner died today. Do you have any comments?" I was not prepared for this and lamely said I had not heard. In my mind's eye, I saw Daisy feeding wood into her stove, stabbing at it with the poker, frying up hamburger and carrots, asking me to find something for her. She was singing, talking, gesturing, and there was her voice, rich, textured, powerful, something that had struck me in our first phone call. "What was she like?" the person on the other end of the line persisted. I took a deep breath. "Well, she was feisty, intelligent, and a real orator." I talked about the importance of her preserving her generational family saga, how unique I believed it was, and how fortunate I felt to have known her.

I called Freda and found that Daisy had died quietly and peacefully, that her heart had given out. There was to be a service at the funeral home in Chester. When I arrived, Freda and her older sister Yohanna McDermott greeted me and led me to Daisy to say good-bye. I was startled at how beautiful she looked in a bright green dress, holding a spray of daisies. Her face was smooth, and she looked years younger than the centenarian she was. Gone was the anger, the lurking paranoia. Here was the woman who loved a good time, who could sing and dance, who called for dances. Here was the woman who had tried to maintain the physical hearth and home of her family and who had given voice to the traditions of four generations. She was the vessel that contained her father's heritage and gave it voice. I looked down at this small woman and marveled at her power and perseverance.

Somehow, the service did not do her justice. So many times as I left her, Daisy would pray over me, the words flowing off her tongue, and when it was my turn, no matter how I tried, I was inept, my prayer halting and hollow. Like my prayers, the service seemed hollow. Daisy, the small woman with so large a presence, who infused her family narrative with power, substance, and humanity, was missing; her vibrant voice, with its cadence, richness, and timbre, was silent. But she had enriched us all. We listened, absorbed, and marveled. As custodian of a multigenerational American family saga, she gave it voice and texture across the ages. She had kept her promise to her father.

AFTERWORD

There's so much inside of me that I don't want lost.
—Daisy Turner, interview with author, September 16, 1985

In 2012, I was on Vermont Public Radio's *Vermont Edition* with Jane Lindholm during Black History Month, talking about the Turners. After the program, I received an email: "I have just looked at the stats on the population at Grafton. The portion that is African American is 0.17%. Since the population is 606, that means there are approximately 2 Black people living there NOW. What happened to the Turners?"

The answer is that over the years the Turners who remained in Vermont have intermarried with the local white population and have blended into the community.[1] Daisy herself commented on this trend: *"I have as many as fifty white relatives."*[2] And Bruce Turner noted: *"I have cousins who have to be pointed out to me as so-and-so's grandson or so-and-so's granddaughter."*[3]

Daisy Turner, Grafton, Vermont, 1984. Courtesy of the Vermont Folklife Center, Middlebury, Vermont, photograph by Jane Beck.

Linda Yarosevich, Alexander Turner's great-granddaughter, had twin sons, Tim and Mike, who told me that when the video *On My Own* was shown in their school, no one realized that Daisy was their aunt. Mike said: *"I'm really proud to have her as my relative."* Linda and her children, the twins and their older sister Sarah, each felt pride in their heritage and in being members of the Turner family.[4]

In 2001, I received a call from Tamara Evanson, who explained that her mother, Janet Severance, had recently discovered that Linesy Turner was her grandfather and wanted to know what the Vermont Folklife Center had on the Turner family. When Janet obtained a copy of her birth certificate, she was astounded to see that her father's race had been recorded as *M* for mulatto. She was stunned and found herself angry at both her parents for never telling her.[5] Her father, Leslie Rogers, had died years earlier, but her mother, Winifred Rogers, confirmed that he was indeed of mixed-race ancestry, and Linesy Turner was his father. Leslie was brought up by his mother, Melvina Wyman Rogers, and her husband, Calvin Rogers. He knew his parentage, as did most of Grafton. Leslie told his son, and his wife

Leslie Rogers, Grafton, Vermont, ca. 1936. Courtesy of Janet Severance.

was to enlighten their daughter, but Winifred overlooked her obligation. Janet realized Winifred's reaction and reticence about the subject suggested distress that resonated from memories of that time in her life. Her family, adamantly opposed to her choice of a husband with a racially mixed heritage, disowned her, leaving deep wounds. A number of townspeople also shunned Leslie and Winifred.[6]

Prejudice was still a part of the social fabric of the community and reinforced the premise that Alec certainly faced it. His stature as a human being, along with his association and support from some of the town fathers, helped buffer him from the onslaught of racial bigotry. His immediate family became part of the community, but intermarriage was another flash point. Alec was upset when his daughters married white men, and George Hall, a longtime white resident of Grafton, experienced considerable hostility from both family and friends when he married Violet Turner. Dave Karlson, the Swede who married Evelyn Turner, and Angelo Di Benedetto, the Italian who married Florida Turner, were immigrants; somehow, that was more acceptable to the Grafton community.

While growing up, Janet sensed discriminatory behavior toward her family but attributed it to her family's poverty. When she saw the *M* on her birth certificate for her father's race, other memories began to fall into place and to take on new significance. Janet remembered her father taking her to visit Daisy once and feeling welcomed into a house where the distinctive smell of wood smoke from the big kitchen stove permeated everything. She remembered a big bear rug on the floor, something Alec had shot many years before, and the head of a favorite horse, Old Tom, mounted on the wall of the back parlor. Years later, when Janet and her husband Don were first married, she was summoned by Daisy to come to Journey's End. She realized in retrospect that Daisy wanted to check out the new addition to the family. Janet had always been fond of Zebbe Grant and had called her Aunt Zeb. She thought everyone called her that, but now she realizes that there was more to it.

As Janet assessed and distilled these new revelations, she shared them with her daughter, Tamara Evanson, who was immediately interested and wanted to know more. She began researching the records, interviewed Janet's mother, gathered photographs, and talked with some of the Turners. Their last stop was to come to the Vermont Folklife Center Archive. When she gave this information to her siblings, they were all excited at the new knowledge. She talked with her cousin, David Rogers, who had no idea about this side of his family, and he also responded positively. The family reactions reminded me of Alec Turner's philosophy of "understanding and contentment": understanding a situation facilitated contentment with the circumstances. The younger generation of the family embraced the knowledge and were not bothered by the stigma of race. When David told his friends about it, he found they had known all along. The Grafton community had not forgotten.

While the Vermont Turners blended into the dominant white society over the generations, the Massachusetts Turners remained African American down to today's great-great-grandchildren. All the grandchildren experienced some form of racial discrimination, and all have married African American spouses. George Hall experienced bigotry when he did not win a deserved high school athletic award. Later, it was announced in the newspaper that a white student had won the prize. George told me, with hurt in his voice, that the recipient was nowhere near the athlete he had been. He dreamed of being on the Boston police force, only to learn that no African Americans would be hired. His brother Godfrey reached a glass ceiling at work and was never promoted, despite skill and seniority. Bruce Turner left Massachusetts because of the discrimination and went to Maryland, where he had a successful career as a high school coach and physical education teacher. Veronica Lanier, the only African American female at Gordon College of Theology and Missions, was told that she would not be welcome

Reverend Veronica Lanier, Melrose, Massachusetts, 1999. Courtesy of the Vermont Folklife Center, Middlebury, Vermont, photograph by Martha Cooper.

at the college banquet—that is, until her classmates rallied round her and said if she didn't attend, they wouldn't either.

Of the Turner grandchildren, Veronica "Ronny" Lanier reminded me the most of Daisy, with one distinct difference: rather than being cantankerous and ornery, Ronny was supportive and accommodating. At ninety-five, she proved a small, white-haired dynamo, supposedly retired but still actively engaged in the Baptist ministry. In 2012, the American Baptist Church awarded her an honorary Doctor of Divinity degree for her lifelong commitment to Christian education. Ronny was the daughter of Susie Turner Lanier, who brought her way of life to her own family and greatly influenced her daughter. Susie had gathered "Indian" medicine with her father and learned many of his cures. This interested her in nursing. Her parents had given her a strong religious foundation; she could quote scripture from Genesis to Revelation.[7] These strains intertwined, and Susie dreamed of becoming a missionary nurse, until it became clear that she could not deal with the sight of blood. Like Daisy, she was dramatic, had a wonderful memory for recitations, and a way with words.

While involved in her missionary work, Ronny's health took a serious turn. After a heart attack, doctors felt there was no hope for her to pull through. It was at this point that she underwent a conversion experience, as had many other Turners. Once recovered, she entered seminary school and was ordained in 1970. Ronny was the first African American Baptist minister in New England, one of only two nationwide, but such a first was not important to Ronny. As far as she was concerned, and reminiscent of her grandfather's attitude, it was the work that counted. I attended both Ronny's ninetieth and ninety-fifth birthday celebrations at the First Baptist Church of Melrose. The church was full, and she received an outpouring of warmth, gratitude, and admiration for her lifetime of accomplishments. I thought about how proud her grandparents would have been to witness these tributes.[8] This was a Turner legacy to which Ronny had added her own twist.

Ronny never lost her love for Vermont, and indeed all the Turner grandchildren held on to their Vermont roots. All felt a pull to return to Turner Hill, even though the homestead was gone and scrub brush was reclaiming the property. On a hot June day in 2002, I walked up the hill with two of Alec's grandchildren, Godfrey Hall and Yohanna McDermott, to commemorate Daisy's birthday. Both laughingly remembered how often they had run up and down that hill to get something at the store, only to find that Daisy had forgotten to tell them about another necessary item, and back they would go again. In those days, it was little more than a track, full of stones and deep crevices caused by hard downpours and runaway

Godfrey Hall, climbing Turner Hill for the last time, Grafton, Vermont, 2002. Courtesy of the Vermont Folklife Center. Middlebury, Vermont, photograph by Jane Beck.

rivulets. By 2002, the road had been widened and graded. Daisy maintained continuous warfare with the town over its condition, and both commented how much she would have liked it.

As we walked, memories flowed. While the distance is only about a mile, the pitch is steady, and I thought of Alec and his barrel of flour. By the time he reached the start of the hill, he had already walked a couple of miles. I could see him, a giant of a man, full of grit and determination, muscles bulging, sweat running down his back, skin glistening, and a firm, even step. It was hot, and I was slapping at mosquitoes, breathing a bit heavier, carrying nothing. The trees made an arching canopy, and the brook tumbled down beside the road. Godfrey waved his hand to indicate some of his favorite fishing pools. We reached a halfway point known as the Middle Gate, although not even the posts remained. This was where Topsy had opened the gate by slipping the rope off the post with her nose, having left Alec behind singing and swapping stories down at the store. This was where George Whitcomb, a neighbor, had been badly stung by a hive of bees. The road is high above the brook here, and Godfrey pointed out the old swimming hole, commenting that some rocks had fallen into it. Every inch had a story.

We continued up the section known as the Steep Pitch, and when reaching the top, we turned and looked out on the hillside to the west. We were well up off the valley floor. Godfrey laughed as he remembered attempting to ski down the Steep Pitch and careening into a snowdrift alongside of the road. Yohanna and Godfrey recalled John Grant driving up during mud season one April. His car came to a stop as one wheel was buried in mud to the rim. John climbed out to survey the damage as Violet walked down the hill. She called out to ask what was wrong, and when John pointed, she bent down and lifted the car out of the mud onto hard ground. Godfrey chuckled about his mother's nonchalance in doing this: "*When Daisy said those girls could work like a man, she meant it.*" Yohanna recalled the story of Godfrey's birth. How her mother, Evelyn, had gone to pick up the doctor, but she did not notice he had had too much to drink until they reached home. The doctor passed out, and her mother had to deliver her sister's baby. Then there was the time that Zebbe and Daisy came up the hill, thinking a dog was following them, only to discover it was a cougar, or catamount as they are known in Vermont. Godfrey stopped for a minute. "*That was the last place my mother saw Uncle Early.*" He had gone out to milk the cow and was never seen again, alive or dead. Godfrey recalled how one time "*when someone called him the N word, Uncle Early butted him with his head and knocked him down. He also butted through a door panel on a bet. But he was a bit mental.*"

The memories were enveloping me. I knew how much Godfrey had been looking forward to this walk. He was eighty-eight, and he knew it would be the last time he would make the climb. He was absorbing it carefully as his eyes captured every detail and his mind roamed the years.

We reached the top and went to find the cellar hole of the Turner homestead. The stone foundation remained. Alec's handiwork was overgrown with brush, but the care was evident, even after all the years. The hole was filled to the brim with the fresh spring water in which Alec had kept his trout, and I thought back to Jack Gouldin's house along the Rappahannock in Virginia, with its kitchen built over a spring, the direct antecedent to this cellar hole. I tried to visualize the Turner structure from the pictures I had seen. The house looked out on a broad flat expanse, with the stream running through the meadow. It was now partially dammed by beavers, flooding the land where Alec had spent so many hours building ditches to drain it, a skill brought with him from his life on the plantation. Across the meadow was "*the 'fur' cornfield.*" Godfrey explained that for a long time he thought it had something to do with fur, rather than being the "far" cornfield. Beyond that had been the original log shanty and a couple of small barns, now lost somewhere among the second growth. Closer to the house and across the brook on a small side hill to the south, beyond where the two large Virginia balm of Gilead poplars had stood, Godfrey pointed to the location of the small camp Rachel had built when she and her husband returned from Everett, Massachusetts, to live on the hill. The family homestead remained a magnet.

To the north, the land rose again. Behind the house there had been a barn and, later, Daisy's dance hall. Beyond that and further to the east was Birch Dale Camp, where Daisy had stayed during the summers when her parents were still alive, as well as after the house had burned. Godfrey was pleasantly surprised: "*I thought it had burned. My father built that for my mother.*" His mother had brought her two children to live there for the first few years after her husband died.

I saw a pile of logs waiting to be trucked off the hill and thought of Alec and his oxen. How many trips with his team would it have taken him to remove that load? As I looked around, I marveled at what he had accomplished. Nature was wresting it back from Alec's orderly, hard-driving determination to carve out his family homestead. Slowly, reluctantly, we turned our backs on the hilltop and quietly found our way down, each with our own thoughts. That day has remained with me, and my mind has returned to it again and again. I have been back a number of times, but that day allowed me to witness the hold Journey's End exerted over family members, the warmth of memories, the respect for their grandparents, the fun of bygone days, the strong feeling of family and kinship.

In 2010, I heard that a species of an endangered northern bulrush had been found on the Turner property, and that the Vermont Fish and Wildlife Department was interested in acquiring the land to conserve it. To do so they could not accept buildings, and therefore Birch Dale Camp, the last remaining structure on the Turner property, was to be torn down. I felt sick. Birch Dale was the last visible vestige of Alexander Turner's extraordinary journey from enslavement to land owner. Fortunately, others had heard Daisy's story through the *Journey's End* radio series and the *On My Own* video. Giovanna Peebles, the state archeologist, and Paul Bruhn, of the Preservation Trust of Vermont, became involved. It was discovered that the architecture of Birch Dale Camp was in the style of a building commonly found in the Virginia Piedmont, not in the hills of Vermont. This was proof that while Alec's body may have been incapacitated, he still was an active participant and obviously had been involved in designing this structure.

The Preservation Trust began work to save the building and designate the surrounding five acres as a historic site that would tell the story of a family who left slavery behind and established a homestead in Vermont. It now appears that Alexander Turner will receive his due recognition. He may not be eligible for a Civil War pension, but his personal courage in fighting for his freedom, his struggle to create a homestead out of the wilderness for his family, and his certainty, described by Daisy, that he "*never wanted to*

Birch Dale Camp (the only remaining building on Turner Hill, Grafton, Vermont), ca. 1917. Courtesy of the Vermont Folklife Center, Middlebury, Vermont.

go no further after he got up on that hilltop" will now be celebrated as a historic site. Without Daisy's voice and her stories, without her ability as a masterful raconteur, the multigenerational family narrative would have been lost.

She may have been cantankerous, but through her feistiness she upheld what she believed was her promise to her father as he lay dying: to never give up fighting for his civil rights as a human being. To honor his memory, she maintained Journey's End for all her family to enjoy, which helped hold them together, and she served as custodian of the family story. In the tradition of the West African griot, her tales leave a cohesive history giving us insight into both events and the emotional meaning carried with them. The Turner saga lives on!

RESEARCH AND ACKNOWLEDGMENTS

The research for this book has taken decades and was a journey in itself. It carried me to England, Africa, Virginia, the Carolinas, Georgia, and Maine. It has been frustrating and exhilarating. There is no way to adequately thank all who have played a role in this project as it has continued across the years.

In the spring of 1985, I began my search for the Jack Gouldin plantation. I wasn't sure if the house remained, but I thought I could locate the land. I met with one of Jack Gouldin's great-grandsons, Worth "Wirt" Gouldin of Bealton, Virginia, who provided directions to the house. His instructions were a bit vague, but he said that behind the house there was a cemetery with his great-grandfather's unmarked gravestone. I was energized by the anticipation of finding the plantation and drove through Fredericksburg,

Jack Gouldin's house, Port Royal, Virginia, 1985. Courtesy of the Vermont Folklife Center, Middlebury, Vermont, photograph by Jane Beck.

out the Tidewater Trail, and toward Skinker's Neck. Somehow, this area had escaped the encroaching sprawl of modern living. I found myself in a morass of back roads and turned on a narrow tree-lined lane, two large fields spread out on either side. I believed I had lost the trail but then saw a house in the distance—not the Tara I had envisioned, but a lonely vestige, sad, in need of repair, painted blue. I was not prepared for the blue color. In my mind, I heard Daisy's voice describing the big white house: *"with four porches, big wide steps leading to a twelve-foot hallway—a mansion!"* There was only a remnant of one porch and no wide steps. Two windows were open on the second floor above the door, and staging stood over the entrance, suggesting that some sort of renovation was taking place. But there was no evidence of anyone on the premises and no other houses in view.

I circled the structure on foot and took photographs. There was no overgrown graveyard; in fact, the ground was clear around the house with woods beyond. Perhaps that was where the graveyard had been, but I did not know where to start a search for it. I learned later that it had been bulldozed. An old barn or shed stood nearby that looked to my untrained eye like an antebellum structure. I fantasized that it might have been the wheat barn where the rafter killed Robert. I was awed by the possibility that this could be where Alec spent his first years. I was uncertain and did not trust that I really had located the plantation. I left wondering how I was going to find answers.

It was two decades later, long after Daisy's death, that I was able to verify that indeed this was Jack Gouldin's house. On my second visit in the spring of 2005, I was with two other people: Gary Stanton (historic preservation professor at the University of Mary Washington in Fredericksburg and a friend and colleague who has helped me at every turn in this project) and Andy Kolovos (loyal friend and archivist at the Vermont Folklife Center). We saw a sign for Hay Mount, which triggered a memory—I recalled reading in the *Fredericksburg Ledger*, when looking through newspapers at the Central Rappahannock Public Library, that Frank Gouldin's young daughter, Mary Alice, had died at Hay's Mount in 1868.[1] Frank Gouldin, Jack Gouldin's youngest son, managed his father's property after his death until the estate was settled in 1872.[2]

As the road curved left, I spotted the house across a vast field. It was painted mustard yellow, and the two large trees standing before it on my previous visit were gone. I was almost certain from their appearance in the photographs I had taken twenty years earlier that these were balm of Gilead trees.[3] After my first attempt to find the Gouldin plantation, Daisy told me that her father had planted two balm of Gilead trees, like those on the plantation, in front of Journey's End. These he had grown from seeds he had obtained from Virginia. I photographed the trees on Turner Hill and was convinced from comparing them to those in the Virginia photograph that they were the same. I wanted to confirm this physical link between Alec and the plantation, if indeed it was the Gouldin plantation.

We came upon a man burning brush, and I was determined to put my questions to rest. The man was George Fisher, the son of the former owner, and he was most congenial. He said the new owner, John Clark, was in the house and would be glad to talk with us. John Clark turned out to be an innovative developer with an evangelist's zeal for his environmentally conscious urban design of four thousand homes, with schools and churches, planned for the land formerly owned by Jack Gouldin. I was still marveling that the landscape had remained relatively unchanged for 150 years, and that Alec would still recognize it. I put all thoughts of the planned development out of my mind and reveled in realizing this was the house; this was the plantation. I was here!

John Clark proved to be very welcoming, was more than willing to show us around, and professed interest in the Turner story. Since that visit, I have been in the house a number of times and have explored the surroundings. With ultimate development of the land in view, Clark had contracted to have an archeological survey done and not only knew the location of a number of the slave cabins, but of the plantation slave cemetery as well.[4] Clark showed us the cemetery site, now with little indication of its former use except for a mass of periwinkles peeking through the leaves. I wondered if I was standing on ground that contained the remains of Robert. If I could peel back the years, what would I see? Were we near where the preacher had raised his arms to the heavens and stopped the coming storm? Only the opaqueness of time stood in my way.

The research and Alec's story had merged. I recognized elements of which Alec had spoken: the great hall and the enclosed staircase leading from it, the room off the hall where Gouldin had kept his trophies, the three staircases that Alec replicated in his own dwelling. I discovered that the Gouldin kitchen had been built over a spring, another detail Alec duplicated. Clark pointed out a section of wall used as a ledger. It was tucked away in a closet on the second floor and preserved with a Plexiglas covering. Under the glass was scrawled the penciled date of 1862 and a listing of items, mostly quilts and blankets. Among them was "Father's blanket," provided by the Gouldins for Confederate soldiers camped on the plantation grounds. I realized this would have dated from the winter of 1862 before Alec took flight. He would have seen the soldiers who must have fueled endless conversation about the war in the slave quarters. Those penciled lines linked me to a reality that had existed 140 years before. I felt I was inhabiting Daisy's stories.

I was fortunate to meet Ken Clark, base historian at Fort A. P. Hill, who showed me an area that had been important to the Gouldins, including the Bethesda Baptist Church, Liberty Baptist Church, and Rappahannock

Academy. Cleo Coleman, a native of Caroline County, shared her wealth of knowledge and personal family stories and has proved to be a tremendous resource. I have Marie Morton to thank for making available her work on the histories of the different parcels of land that make up Fort A. P. Hill and for her explanations as to how different farms amalgamated into the Gouldin property related to one another.

I was not so fortunate in locating the vessel that carried Daisy's great-grandmother from London to Africa. I began with Daisy's grandfather's name, Berkeley, and looked for its antecedents in England. There was an Earl of Berkeley, but no one in the Earl's line had a daughter who could fit the specifics of the story. Nina Staehle did some initial research for me and introduced me to the workings of the National Archives. I had no ship's name, no owner, no captain, and no date. Daunting, but I thought if I could find ships wrecked on the West African coast between 1790 and 1815, I might be able to identify the vessel. I went through *Lloyds List* and the *Times* (London) to find possibilities. One of the first I came up with was the brig *Jane*, lost in 1810 on the coast of Africa. My heart skipped a beat when I saw it was owned by Alexander Anderson; of course, a daughter would name her son after her father. Alexander Anderson and his brother John, nephews of successful merchant and diplomat Richard Oswald, inherited his thriving merchant house at Philpot Lane in London. Alexander Anderson had a daughter who proved to be a little young; however, he had a niece, Elizabeth Anderson, living with him. Her mother had died shortly after her birth in South Carolina, and she and her brother were sent back to England. I was thrilled to learn that she had been married to Robert Brown right before the *Jane* left port. It took a long time to discover anything about Robert Brown, but I learned that Anderson had gone bankrupt by 1814. With the slave trade over, a highly leveraged Anderson could not keep his head above water. I have Duncan Harrington to thank for finding a rich treasure trove of documents from which I learned a great deal about Anderson's merchant trade.

In the end, this research, which took over a year and included three trips to the National Archives in Kew, was all for naught as I discovered that Robert Brown did not die in 1810, but almost two decades later. I did pursue two other ships—the *Resolution,* which was owned by Thomas Wilson and lost in 1810 on the coast of Africa, and a vessel called the *Eloisa*, which was lost on the coast of Africa in 1802. Neither search was conclusive. Perhaps no record of the shipwreck exists, but I am convinced that somewhere between Ouidah, Benin, and Lagos, Nigeria, a ship went down, and a white English woman and a black African man came together to birth a man who not only would take part in the slave trade, but would become entwined in its shackles. This man, Alexander or Alessi, had a heritage that was both African and British. As he had grown up in West

Africa, he was culturally more African than British. He had the athletic prowess of his father as well as his mother's DNA, symbolized by the gold locket and wedding ring she gave him. In the Turner narrative, this legacy and identity spanned time and distance.

I had to learn my way through a maze of records at numerous archives and research institutions, and many individuals helped me along the way. Please see the full list of archives and research institutions consulted for this project in the bibliography.

In Virginia, I spent rewarding time at the Virginia Historical Society, the Library of Virginia, and the Virginia Baptist Historical Society, all in Richmond. In Fredericksburg, at the Central Rappahannock Heritage Center, Tony Kent and Diane Ballman led me to key material on Jack Gouldin. Barbara Willis of the Central Rappahannock Public Library helped me navigate the Virginia Room, showed me helpful background material, gave me access to her files, and kept me nourished on marvelous meals and great conversation. Barry McGhee at the Fredericksburg Circuit Court Archive encouraged me through a mound of court cases he had spent years cataloging, pointing me in useful directions and finding plats that aided my understanding of the area around Skinker's Neck. In Tappahannock, the local records of Essex County enabled me to chart the history of the Gouldin family. In all these repositories, there were wills, court cases, plats, deeds, tax records, diaries, and newspaper clippings.

In Washington, DC, I spent days at the Library of Congress and at the National Archives, looking through Civil War pension records, military service records, Freedmen's Bureau documents, legal documents in the case of *US Government v. the Schooner Phoenix*, to name a few. Florida historian Gail Swansen helped me in my search for information on the *Fenix*. There were the official records of the First New Jersey Cavalry as well as regimental accounts, letters, and diaries. Sonya Hulburt and Jesse R. Phillips shared their great-grandfather's Civil War memoir. During our correspondence, Sonya also shared a clipping written by Jennie Sweetman on "Gillman the Spy," who turned out to be Humphrey, an enslaved man who also had escaped from the Gouldin plantation and reputedly guided the raid on the Tom Gouldin plantation.[5]

In Maine, I found the records of the Merrill Slate Quarry at the Maine Historical Society Library in Portland. I had seen a piece on the "Negro Colony" written by Susan Merrill Lewis, granddaughter of A. H. Merrill, and hoped her notes might be in the quarry papers. They were, although there was nothing new about Alec. What proved to be a gold mine of information were the quarry pay records, a complete set for the years Alec was there. They included how many hours each man had worked, how much he was paid, and when he was absent. This showed Alec's tremendous capacity for work; he consistently earned the most pay. His recorded comings and goings meshed with Daisy's narrative, although he was in Maine a couple of years longer than she had indicated. Bill Sawtell sent me to Earle Shettleworth of the Maine Historic Preservation Commission in Augusta, Maine, who provided photographs of the freedmen at work in the quarry.

Vermont held its own treasures of town records, diaries, court cases, personal papers, the 1880 agricultural census, and newspaper articles. Eli Prouty and Maureen Fletcher were particularly helpful and opened doors to the rich treasure trove at the Grafton Historical Society. Likewise, Cynthia Gibb at the Grafton town clerk's office guided me through the various records. In the Vermont Folklife Center's Daisy Turner collection, which I had gathered through the years, I came across Rose Turner's diary and account book for the years 1888 to 1902. It provided a great deal of information about family activities and dates. This proved extremely helpful in understanding when and where the younger Turners went to work in the Boston area.[6] Mary Archamhault shared her own family's rich archive of affidavits and letters around the period of the burning of the Turner homestead, another unexpected but very welcome source.

In North Carolina, I was fortunate to have a number of conversations with Barbara Duncan, education director at the Museum of the Cherokee in Cherokee. I spent several days in the museum's archive, guided by assistant archivist Mike Littlejohn.

In England, I was overwhelmed by the treasure trove at the National Archives and spent several weeks in Kew researching lost ships, as well as the British-African trade. I also visited the Church Missionary Society in Birmingham at the University of Birmingham, reading some of the early missionary accounts particularly regarding Nigeria and the ongoing slave trade. Because the Turners were Yoruba (both according to family tradition and to genetic testing), I was convinced that the shipwreck had occurred somewhere between Ouidah, Benin, and Lagos, Nigeria, and I felt it was important to read some accounts of that region.

Equally imperative was visiting coastal West Africa from Cape Coast Castle, Ghana, to Lagos, Nigeria, as well as Yoruba villages, to learn about cultural and spiritual traditions. I have Noah Katcha to thank for this opportunity. Noah and Martine de Souza took me to meet greatly respected Fa priest Odeyemi Egnile, who expanded my understanding of the spiritual world through stories of his own life experience, strongly held beliefs, and ritual traditions.

It has been a long, comprehensive journey with a host of people to thank for all their help along the way. At the top of my list are all the members of the Turner family. They were so warm, welcoming, and forthcoming. I interviewed most of the grandchildren of Alec and Sally, along with Janet Severence, Tamara Evanson, and David Rogers, who shared their new discoveries and relationships with me as they unfolded. It is with great sadness that I have watched the ranks of the older generation thin until only Ronny Lanier remained. Now she too is gone. The march of time is relentless, but the Turner oral narrative remains a unique treasure, a monument to the family history over two centuries.

There are a few more that I must recognize: Ellen McCulloch-Lovell, executive director of the Vermont Arts Council in 1983, for understanding the importance of interviewing Daisy Turner, the hours it would take to gain Daisy's trust and to do her story justice; Caroline Alexander for her enthusiasm and steadfast support, for excellent suggestions regarding searching for elusive sources, for generosity with source material, and for her attention to vividness and style; Meg Ostrum for always being an excellent sounding board and source of ideas; Rex Ellis for his thoughts on shaping this work and for helping me think through different ideas.

I have to thank Dick Goodyear, for his able translation of materials involving the Spanish schooner *Fenix*, Paul Lovejoy for his suggestions of avenues to explore, and T. J. Desch-Obi for his help with West African martial arts. Amy Merrill Taylor proved a resource in pointing me toward different records on the Freedman's Bureau and Reconstruction. Daisy Broudy read every word of my earliest draft, providing much needed feedback, suggesting sections to cut or expand, serving as a general sounding board, and assuring me that the bones of a book were there.

Then there were the scholarly historians from Middlebury College: Bill Catton (retired), Amy Morsman, and Bill Hart, who took time away from busy schedules to meet with me and critique various chapters. Amy plowed through the whole manuscript and provided both helpful and astute suggestions.

For reading different versions of the manuscript, I must thank Hope Matthiessen, Debora Kodish, Wilsonia Cherry, Sally Taylor, Rae Harrell, John Roberts, Patricia Turner, Mara Williams, Sylvia Grider, and Jessica Hoffman Davis. All were both encouraging and constructive in their comments. Thanks also go to those who brought their expertise on specific chapters, particularly Ann Ferrell, Andy Kolovos, Jerrilyn McGregor, and Susanne Rappaport. For tightening my loquacious prose and for being someone I could count on to keep me on point, I am indebted to editor Carol Terry and to Jane Curran for her skills at copyediting. I also need to express warm thanks to Laurie Matheson, editor-in-chief, and Jennifer Comeau, editorial, design, and production manager, and the rest of the team at the University of Illinois Press. Without them there would be no *Daisy Turner's Kin*.

All this help was invaluable and is reflected in the book. However, I take full responsibility for any shortcomings. I remain eternally grateful to those who so willingly gave of themselves and of their time.

APPENDIX

Turner Family Genealogical Chart

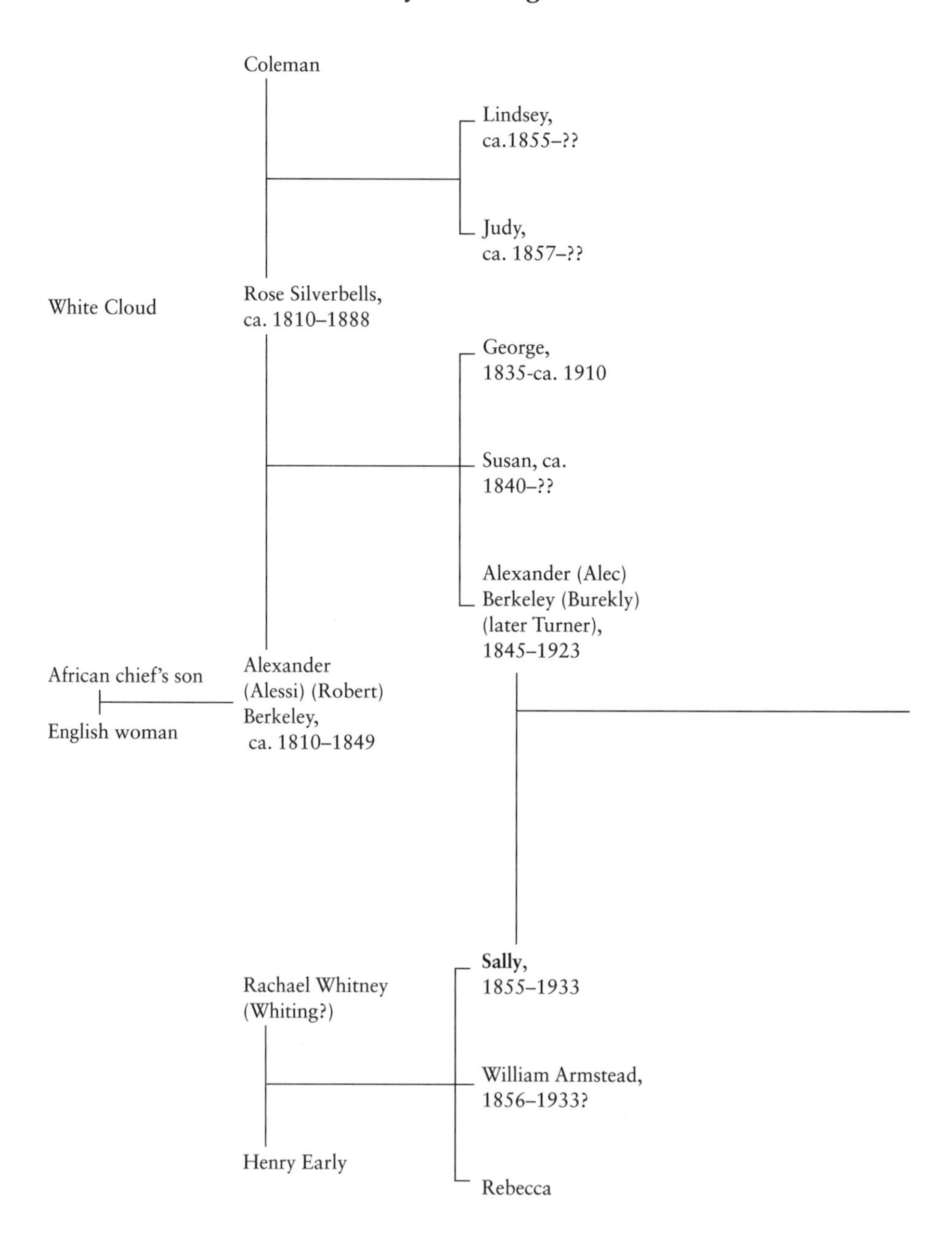

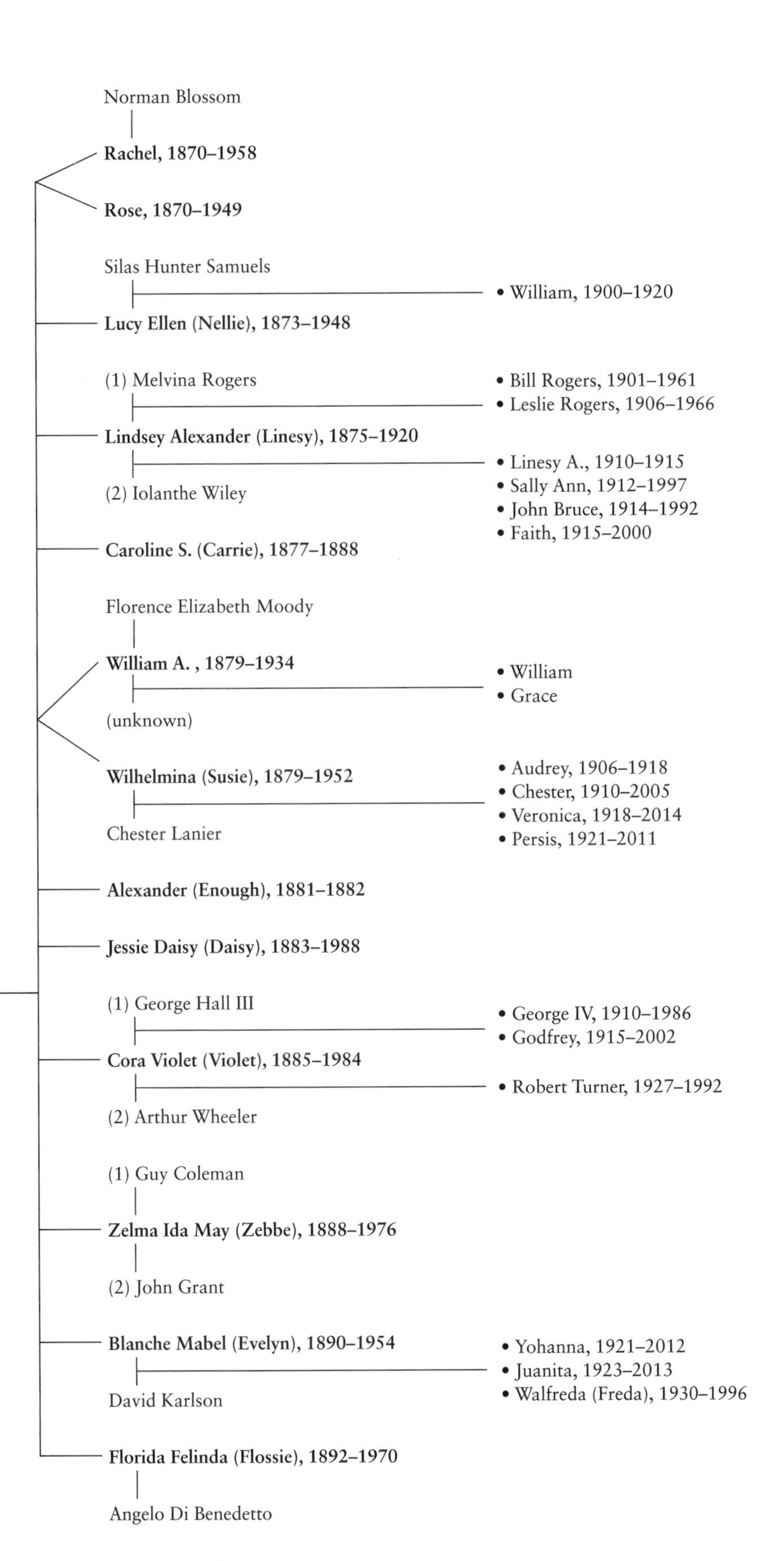
Norman Blossom
Rachel, 1870–1958
Rose, 1870–1949
Silas Hunter Samuels
• William, 1900–1920
Lucy Ellen (Nellie), 1873–1948
(1) Melvina Rogers
• Bill Rogers, 1901–1961
• Leslie Rogers, 1906–1966
Lindsey Alexander (Linesy), 1875–1920
• Linesy A., 1910–1915
• Sally Ann, 1912–1997
• John Bruce, 1914–1992
• Faith, 1915–2000
(2) Iolanthe Wiley
Caroline S. (Carrie), 1877–1888
Florence Elizabeth Moody
William A. , 1879–1934
• William
• Grace
(unknown)
Wilhelmina (Susie), 1879–1952
• Audrey, 1906–1918
• Chester, 1910–2005
• Veronica, 1918–2014
• Persis, 1921–2011
Chester Lanier
Alexander (Enough), 1881–1882
Jessie Daisy (Daisy), 1883–1988
(1) George Hall III
• George IV, 1910–1986
• Godfrey, 1915–2002
Cora Violet (Violet), 1885–1984
• Robert Turner, 1927–1992
(2) Arthur Wheeler
(1) Guy Coleman
Zelma Ida May (Zebbe), 1888–1976
(2) John Grant
Blanche Mabel (Evelyn), 1890–1954
• Yohanna, 1921–2012
• Juanita, 1923–2013
• Walfreda (Freda), 1930–1996
David Karlson
Florida Felinda (Flossie), 1892–1970
Angelo Di Benedetto

NOTES

Introduction. The Turner Narrative and Memory

1. See Spindel, "Assessing Memory," 247–61; see also Portelli, *Death of Luigi Trastulli*. Portelli points out that oral history tells us less about events than about meaning.
2. Thelen, *Memory and American History*, ix, vii–xiii; see also Schrager, "What Is Social," 76–97; and Tonkin, *Narrating Our Past*, 105: "nobody's ability to recall is independent of social milieu," and 112: "Memory is part of cognitive empowering and a means to being; it is developed through social interaction; it is medium as well as message."
3. An example of such a technique is the stylized opening of a folktale: "once upon a time, a long long time ago. . . ." Many cultures have stylized endings, as in the Lesser Antilles, "The wire bend, my story end."
4. Miller, *African Past Speaks*, 10.
5. Coser, *Maurice Halbwachs*, 83.
6. DNA test kit results, ID # 1004149, June 22, 2006, from African Ancestry, Washington, DC, in private collection. David Rogers's great-grandfather was Linesy Turner—Alec's oldest son, who had two sons by Melvina Rogers.
7. An example of changed cultural elements would be their different spiritual upbringings.
8. George Hall, interview with author, January 7, 1986.
9. John Leavitt, interview with author, September 15, 2007. Leavitt never did cut the lumber because he discovered that what Daisy wanted cut was not on her land.
10. Ibid.
11. John Bruce Turner, interview with author, January 29, 1989.
12. Sally Turner Neale, interview with author, February 22, 1989.
13. Sarah Alden Derby Gannett, granddaughter of Theodore Roosevelt, in discussion with the author, September 27, 1984.
14. Daisy Turner, interview with author, December 8, 1983.
15. "Grafton Girl Nearly Murdered," *Vermont Phoenix* (Brattleboro), December 30, 1910.
16. Alexander Turner, Declaration for Pension, dated January 27, 1916, Record Group 15, National Archives and Records Administration, Washington, DC.
17. See Pyne, *Ride to War*, 15–21, for a description of escaping contrabands and the raid on the Gouldin plantation; see also National Archives and Records Administration, M346, "John Gouldin No. 228," for a listing of the slaves who

escaped from John Gouldin. Both Alec and Humphrey are among the slaves "abducted and harbored by the enemy."

18. Merrill Quarry payroll records, Collection 131, Greenleaf-Merrill Family Papers, 1819–1917, MS 215, Maine Historical Society, Portland, ME.

19. "Local Intelligence: Grafton," *Vermont Phoenix*, November 21, 1873.

20. Thompson, "Life of a Vermont Farmer," entry for November 12, 1873.

21. Douglass, *Narrative of the Life*.

22. The trickster, a hero in African lore, overcomes a more powerful opponent through cleverness, wit, and deception. Likewise, the strong man is greatly admired.

23. Preston, *Young Frederick Douglass*, xv.

24. Portelli, *Death of Luigi Trastulli*, 50. An example of a hidden aspect of an event is the raid on the Gouldin plantation undertaken by Broderick. Alec emphasizes stealing food from the plantation and the killing of the overseer.

25. For information on the raid, see Pyne, *Ride to War*, 11–22; Kester, *Cavalryman in Blue*, 13; "Stealing a March," *Harper's Weekly* 4 (1863): 250; National Archives and Records Administration M346, Confederate Citizens File, Receiver General 109, Roll 0366, Doc. 77: John Gouldin, and Doc. 87: Thomas W. Gouldin. Gouldin reported the loss of a horse and some wine from this raid.

26. John [Jack] Gouldin, will dated February 1, 1863, Caroline County Will Book 31: 48, Central Rappahannock Heritage Center, Fredericksburg, VA. Describing a line on his property, Gouldin writes: "in a straight line in a SE direction to the fork of a ditch north of Rose's house one prong of which goes to Skinker's Pines and the other to the Old Quarter Spring." Rose was the plantation seamstress and Alec's mother.

27. John Leavitt, interview with author, September 15, 2007.

28. Daisy Turner, interview with author, untaped conversation. When I questioned her about this, Daisy said Alec had them sent from Virginia, as he never returned after coming north.

Chapter 1. Meeting Daisy

1. Dot Nadeau, "She Has a Story to Tell," *Brattleboro (VT) Reformer*, July 2, 1983, 1, 9.

2. The Windham foundation was established in 1959 by a bequest of Mrs. Rodney Fiske of New York City. The foundation's mission is "to promote the vitality of Grafton and Vermont's rural communities through its philanthropic and educational programs and its subsidiaries whose operations contribute to these endeavors."

3. Tanner, *Homestead*.

4. As a folklorist, I use the ethnographic interview—a methodology employed to understand historical, cultural, and personal experiences. See Conklin, "Ethnography," 172–78. See also Mintz, "Anthropological Interview," 18–26.

5. Daisy Turner, interview with author, May 10, 1984.

6. See Blight, "If You Don't Tell It," 27.

7. Cleo Coleman, interview with author, March 22, 2005.

8. Daisy Turner, interview with author, November 9, 1983.

9. Ibid., March 15, 1984.

10. Ibid., September 23, 1983.

11. Walker, *Quarry*; Tanner, *Homestead*.

12. Richard Andrews, "Young Springfield Man Denies Charges of Murder," *Rutland (VT) Herald*, June 9, 1984, 1, 14; Monica Allen, "Death of Grafton Man Ended Five-Year-Old Relationship," *Rutland Herald*, June 9, 1984, 1, 14; Dorothy Nadeau, "21-Year-Old Denies Murder in Grafton," *Brattleboro Reformer*, June 9, 1984, 1, 14.

13. "Journey's End" was the name Daisy gave to the homestead on Turner Hill.

14. See "Journey's End" chapter for Daisy's black doll story.

15. Daisy Turner, interview with author, September 16, 1985.

16. Burns, "Universe of Battle."

17. In 1984, I became the executive director of the Vermont Folklife Center, a private, nonprofit organization overseen by a board of directors.

Chapter 2. African Roots

1. According to Daisy, this event took place in the early 1800s. This reconstruction is based on several sources: Daisy Turner's narrative; Leonard, *Western Coast of Africa*, 112, which includes a description of a tornedo; Whitford, *Trading Life*, 117; Falconbridge, *Narrative of Two Voyages*, 42; J. Adams, *Remarks on the Country*, 57–61, 164; and, Crow, *Memoirs*, 100, 233.

2. See Hancock, *Citizens of the World*, 111–12.

3. Daisy Turner, interview with author, December 14, 1983, and February 1, 1984. Daisy indicated this was the case with her great-grandmother and her husband. She always claimed that they were wealthy and of high social status, usually a "*Lord and Lady.*" This was a common trait Daisy had throughout her narrative. This does not mean it was not the case, only that it is not reliable. She tantalizingly told me: "*It came to me about a month ago what their names were, Lord and Lady, and when it comes again I'll dash and write it down.*"

4. See Corry, *Observations*, 8.

5. Daisy Turner, interview with author, June 28, 1984, and February 15, 1984; Allon Schoener, unpublished video of Daisy Turner and Zebbe Grant, recorded July 18, 1974, in Allon Schoener's private collection.

6. See the introduction for more on DNA testing in the Turner family.

7. See Cape Town reference, dated February 21, 1817, T70/150, Manuscript Collection, National Archives, Kew, London, England.

8. Pedler, *Lion and the Unicorn*, 12.

9. Law, *Ouidah*, 125; Newbury, *Western Slave Coast*.

10. Strickrodt, "Afro-European Trade Relations," 175–80.

11. Bold, *Merchants' and Mariners' African Guide*, 61.

12. Strickrodt, "Afro-European Trade Relations," 212; see also Sorensen-Gilmour, "Slave Trading along the Lagoons," 84.

13. Law, "Trade and Politics," 321.

14. Daisy Turner, interview with author, November 9, 1983.

15. Morton-Williams, "Yoruba Kingdom of Oyo," 37–41. During the eighteenth century, the Yoruba kingdom of Oyo, under King Abiodun, "extended their empire to the south-west to secure access to the Atlantic along a trade route of more than two hundred miles." See also Law, "Lagoonside Port," 32–34.

16. Newbury, *Western Slave Coast*, 8; Morton-Williams, "Yoruba Kingdom of Oyo," 36.

17. Daisy Turner, interview with author, June 28, 1984.

18. Law, *Ouidah*, 29; see also Rev. Charles Andrew Gollimer, journal entries dated January 17, 1845, and September 20, 1845, CA2/043, Church Missionary Society Archives, University of Birmingham, Birmingham, England.

19. Adams, *Remarks on the Country*, 6.

20. Daisy Turner, interview with author, February 15, 1984.

21. See Curtin, *Image of Africa*.

22. Falconbridge, *Narrative of Two Voyages*, 43.

23. Daisy Turner, interview with author, October 25, 1983.

24. Akintoye, *History of the Yoruba People*, 36.

25. I suspect Daisy's great-great-grandfather was a chief. Every town or village had a chief. With Daisy's propensity to inflate the title of an individual, if she had done so, she would have indicated the son was a chief. But she always spoke of him as "*the son of a chief.*"

26. Johnson, *History of the Yorubas*, 116.

27. Ibid., 90; see also Ojo, *Yoruba Culture*, 131.

28. See Hinderer, *Seventeen Years in Yoruba Country*, 31, 57.

29. Falconbridge, *Narrative of Two Voyages*, 88–89.

30. Curtin, *Image of Africa*, 87; Law, *Ouidah*, 80.

31. Rediker, *Slave Ship*, 244.

32. Mouser, "Trade, Coasters and Conflicts," 53.

33. Adams, *Remarks on the Country*, 201–2.

34. John Field to Rev. H. Wright, letter dated January 1878, CA2/038, 24:31, Church Missionary Society Archives, University of Birmingham, Birmingham, England.

35. Osborne, "Yoruba Village," 191.

36. Daisy Turner, interview with author, June 28, 1984. While Daisy could not remember the pronunciation of the boy's name in this interview, she referred to it in her interview with Steve Goodman on May 8, 1976. When I asked Yoruba speakers what such a nickname would be, I was told that his name would be pronounced "Alesande" and his nickname would have been "Alessi."

37. Akintoye, *History of the Yoruba People*, 37; Curtin, *Africa Remembered*, 255.

38. Johnson, *History of the Yorubas*, 79.

39. Morton-Williams, "Yoruba Kingdom of Oyo," 40.

40. Law, *Oyo Empire*, 269.

41. Morton-Williams, "Yoruba Kingdom of Oyo," 41.

42. Akintoye, *History of the Yoruba People*, 38.

43. Ibid., 37.

44. Morton-Williams, "Outline of the Cosmology," 246.

45. Odeyemi Egnile, interview with author, Egnile Hocon, Ouidah, Benin, December 1, 2011, notes in author's private collection.

46. This was known as *Agbagbbeisse* or *Akinsse*. Ogunlede Onashilou, interview by the author, November 28, 2011.

47. Such a locket and ring would not have survived Alessi's capture.

48. Sorensen-Gilmour, "Slave Trading along the Lagoons," 5.

49. Law, "Trade and Politics," 338, 346.

50. Strickrodt, "Afro-European Trade Relations," 192; see also Priestly, *West African Trade*, 127.

51. Daisy Turner, interview with author, March 1, 1984.

52. Ibid.

53. Ibid., February 15, 1984, and March 1, 1984.

54. Ibid., February 15, 1984.

55. See chapter 3, "Jack Gouldin and Robert Berkeley," for more on Daisy's father's attitude toward his father.

56. Law, "Atlantic Slave Trade," , 124.

57. Law, "Trade and Politics," 348; Eltis, *Economic Growth*, 126.

58. Although Alessi may have dealt with illicit American slavers, I believe the ship that captured him as a slave was a Spanish ship, the *Fenix*.

59. Daisy Turner, interview with author, June 28, 1984.

60. Eltis, *Economic Growth*, 168.

61. Sorensen-Gilmour, "Slave Trading along the Lagoons," 90.

62. Law and Strickrodt, *Ports of the Slave Trade*, 90.

63. Ibid., 168.

64. Daisy Turner, interview with author, March 1, 1984.

65. Eltis et al., *Trans-Atlantic Slave Trade*.

66. Daisy Turner, interview with author, June 28, 1984.

67. Corwin, *Spain and the Abolition of Slavery*, 53.

68. Murray, *Odious Commerce*, 89–91: Spain condemned the slave trade but refused to prosecute it; see also Klein, *Atlantic Slave Trade*, 191.

69. Isaac Mayo to Martin Van Buren, letter dated June 5, 1830, Supreme Court Case Papers, United States v. Schooner Feniz, in 230/1/33/2, Box 4, National Archives and Records Administration, Washington, DC.

70. See Swanson, *Slave Ship Guerrero*, 2, 7.

71. Kennedy, *African Colonization*, 976.

72. Crew list, Supreme Court Case Papers: United States v. Schooner Feniz, 230/1/33/2, Box 4, National Archives.

73. Isaac Mayo, "Private Journal at Sea from 1826 to 1830," Naval History and Heritage Command, Washington DC.

74. Joaquin Roig to Francisco de la Torre, Havana, letter dated May 21, 1829, Supreme Court Case Papers, United States v. Schooner Fenix, September 1831, 230/1/33/2, Box 4, National Archives and Records Administration, Washington, DC.

75. See Dike, *Trade and Politics*, 52.

76. Ortega, "From Obscurity to Notoriety."

77. Eltis, *Economic Growth*, 168.

78. Jones, "Little Popo and Agoue," 122.

79. Ortega, "From Obscurity to Notoriety," 297.

80. Daisy Turner, interview with author, September 28, 1983.

81. Eltis et al., *Trans-Atlantic Slave Trade*; Commodore Jesse D. Elliott, commanding U.S. Naval Forces in the West Indies, to John Branch, Secretary of the Navy, letter dated July 11, 1830, Supreme Court Case Papers, United States v.

Schooner Feniz, 230/1/33/2, Box 4, National Archives and Records Administration, Washington, DC. Elliott states that the captain of the *Fenix* claimed that the *Manzaneras* had been on the coast "at the period of his departure," "had depredated on the American ship *Candau* last fall," was captured by the British in April of that year, and had left Galinhas on the Windward Coast in March of that year. The captain of the *Fenix* probably meant that both the *Fenix* and the *Manzaneras* had been gathering slaves at the same time, somewhere between the Windward Coast and Calabar.

82. MacKenzie, *Last Years*, 128.

83. Ortega, "From Obscurity to Notoriety," 297.

84. Mayo, "Private Journal at Sea." An entry regarding provisions found aboard the schooner *Fenix*, dated July 17, 1830, states: "rice in these vessels, is the only food given to the slaves."

85. James T. Wilson, first lieutenant of the *Grampus*, testimony dated November 29, 1830, Supreme Court Case Papers, United States v. Schooner Feniz, in 230/1/33/2, Box 4, National Archives and Records Administration, Washington, DC. Wilson's testimony stated that on June 4 the *Fenix* was "twenty-four days from the coast of Africa bound for Cuba."

86. J. D. Elliott to the House of Representatives, letter dated July 11, 1830, Supreme Court Case Papers, United States v. Schooner Feniz, in 230/1/33/2, Box 4, National Archives and Records Administration, Washington, DC.

87. C. J. Hall, statement dated June 4, 1830, Supreme Court Case Papers, United States v. Schooner Feniz, in 230/1/33/2, Box 4, National Archives and Records Administration, Washington, DC.

88. It is not customary for one vessel to approach another without showing its colors.

89. Mayo to Van Buren, letter dated June 5, 1830.

90. Ibid.

91. Ibid.

92. Log of USS *Grampus*, dated 1830, entry 118, #4 of 12, Record Group 24, Records of Navy Bureau of Navigation, National Archives and Records Administration, Washington, DC.

93. Elliott to Branch, letter dated July 11, 1830.

94. See Austen, "Slave Trade," 238.

95. Daisy Turner, interview with author, June 28, 1984.

96. Ibid., February 15, 1984.

97. Deputy Marshal O. H. Burlingame, statement dated September 21, 1830, Supreme Court Case Papers, United States v. Schooner Feniz, 230/1/33/2, Box 4, National Archives and Records Administration, Washington, DC.

98. John Branch to Waters Smith, letter dated September 13, 1830, M205, Roll 1: 162, National Archives and Records Administration, Washington, DC.

99. Leon Woodbury to the Navy Department, letter dated February 9, 1832, M205, Roll.1: 170, National Archives and Records Administration, Washington, DC.

100. "On the capture, by a United States vessel, of the Spanish ship Fenix, with African slaves on board, and under suspicion of piratical intent, with a recommendation for the maintenance, etc., of the slaves: communicated to the House

of Representatives, January 18, 1831," ibiblio: The Public's Library and Digital Archive website, http://www.ibiblio.org/pha/USN/1831/18310118Fenix (accessed September 27, 2012).

101. John Nicholson, US marshal, statement dated July 17, 1835, United States v. 62 Africans in Schooner Fenix, file # 2933, no. 23, National Archives and Records Administration Southwest Region, Fort Worth, Texas.

102. Daisy Turner, interview with author, March 1, 1984.

103. With the extensive cultivation of cotton in the Deep South, slave traders generally traveled south to sell their merchandise. Thus, Gouldin's purchase ran counter to the general flow of the trade.

104. Daisy Turner, interview with author, February 15, 1984.

105. Ibid.

106. Ibid.

107. Steward, *Twenty-Two Years a Slave*, 16.

108. Ibid.

109. Daisy Turner, interview with author, February 1, 1984.

110. John Gouldin, will dated February 1, 1863, Caroline County Will Book 31: 48, Central Rappahannock Heritage Center, Fredericksburg, VA; see also Gutman, *Black Family*, 244. Gutman points out that by 1783, enslaved African Americans had both Anglo-American given names and surnames. Surnames were usually different from their owners' surnames. He believed that this indicated the rapid acculturation of the enslaved in terms of naming practice and the desire to define immediate slave families, and that this was to differentiate them from their owners.

Chapter 3. Jack Gouldin and Robert Berkeley

1. Wirt Gouldin, interview with author, March 14, 1985.

2. The combine harvester was just coming into use in the 1860s. Gouldin also used a wheat fan, two corn shellers, and a seed sower.

3. Broaddus, *History of the Broaddus Family*, 43.

4. The Gouldin name is spelled numerous ways. In Essex County, it is most frequently written as Goulding or Golding, although it is also found in Caroline County as Goulden, Goulding, and Golden, as well as Gouldin. See Essex County, Virginia, Patent Book, 4: 99, Essex's Clerk's Office, Tappahannock, VA.

5. Essex County, Virginia, Patent Book, 6: 532, Essex's Clerk's Office, Tappahannock, VA.

6. Garnett, *Historical Address*, 18.

7. Slaughter, *Settlers, Southerners, Americans*, 29.

8. Garnett, *Historical Address*, 18.

9. Will of William Goulding, Essex County Will Book, 14:164, Essex's Clerk's Office, Essex County Circuit Court, Tappahannock, VA.

10. Will of Simon Goulding Jr., Essex County Will Book, 15:178, Essex's Clerk's Office, Essex County Circuit Court, Tappahannock, VA.

11. Garnett, *Historical Address*, 33; see also appendix 6.

12. Slaughter, *Settlers, Southerners, Americans*, 30.

13. Garnett, *Historical Address*, 14.

14. Slaughter, *Settlers, Southerners, Americans*, 43.

15. Ibid., 44.

16. Caroline County, Virginia, Property Tax Records, 1783–1799, Reel 71. Library of Virginia, Richmond, VA.

17. Fort A. P. Hill was established as an army training facility in 1941. It continues to be a training and maneuver center and encompasses seventy-six thousand acres.

18. See John Gouldin, Estate inventory, Caroline County Will Book 19: 272–73, December 20, 1816, Central Rappahannock Heritage Center, Fredericksburg, VA.

19. Ibid.; Jesse Gouldin, Estate, Accounting of Expenses, Caroline County Will Book, 19: 306–9, March 10, 1817, Central Rappahannock Heritage Center, Fredericksburg, VA.

20. Jesse Gouldin, Estate, Accounting of Expenses.

21. June [Jane?] Goulden et al. v. John Goulden's Infants, January 12, 1818, Caroline County, Virginia Court Records, 1742–1833, 1787–1810, Central Rappahannock Heritage Center, Fredericksburg, VA.

22. John [Jack] Gouldin, Estate sale, Caroline County, Virginia, Will Book, 32: 265–36, September 12, 1864, Central Rappahannock Heritage Center, Fredericksburg, VA.

23. For example, see Taliaferro v. Gray etc., CR-SC-H, 274–11 (1826), and Guy v. Riddle, CR-SC-H, 120–24, (1821), Fredericksburg Historical Court Records, Circuit Superior Court of Law and Chancery of Spotsylvania County, Fredericksburg, VA.

24. Wiggins, "Sport and Popular Pastimes," 70, 157.

25. Ibid., 155.

26. Gorn, *Manly Art*, 34; Rhoden, *$40 Million Slaves*, 34.

27. See Fleischer, *Black Dynamite*, 19: Zachery Molineaux was accused of assault, but because of his good record during the war, he was admonished, he made an apology, and his case was dismissed. Others suggested that Tom's grandfather, also enslaved, was famous for his boxing prowess; see also Grombach, *Saga of the Sock*. Grombach was himself a boxer and competed in the 1924 Olympics.

28. Fleischer, *Black Dynamite*, 19. Fleischer based this information on "a Philadelphia clipping of 1788." Because this clipping is no longer extant, and Fleischer's source cannot be verified, this information has been called into question by scholars such as Elliott Gorn. See Gorn, *Manly Art*, 34.

29. Gorn, *Manly Art*, 34.

30. Ibid., 35.

31. The slave narratives were collected in the 1930s by the Federal Writers Project, under the Works Progress Administration. In 2007, Bilal Abdulhakim Muhammad, a skilled trainer of young boxers in Newport News, Virginia, told me about the strong boxing tradition in his family that went back to the days of slavery. He related that the old-timers used to train for bare-knuckle fighting by digging potatoes with their hands, hitting the green stump of a felled tree with their fists, and gaining strength through backbreaking labor and lifting watermelons. To improve their footwork, they practiced dance steps including the shuffle and something akin to modern-day breakdancing.

32. Lussana, "To See Who Was Best," 901–22.

33. Grombach, *Saga of the Sock*, 40.

34. Jackson and Teeples, *Virginia 1820 Census Index*.
35. Advertisement, *Virginia Herald*, December 29, 1830, 3.
36. Daisy Turner, interview with author, April 12, 1984.
37. See Genovese and Fox-Genovese, *Fatal Self-Deception*.
38. Daisy Turner, interview with author, December 12, 1984.
39. John [Jack] Gouldin to Robert Holloway, note, August 9, 1860, 2004-040-246-028, Central Rappahannock Heritage Center, Fredericksburg, VA.
40. Daisy claimed her grandfather fought against Chicken George, who is featured in Alex Haley's *Roots*, and that Haley sent someone to interview her; I could not confirm this.
41. Daisy Turner, interview with author, March 1, 1984.
42. See Lussana, "To See Who Was Best," 901–22. Lussana points out that through boxing and wrestling activities "enslaved men took part in African-derived community-forming rituals that underscored rank, status, and leadership roles in the slave community and fostered male solidarity. . . . These fighting activities were potentially important avenues of male bodily resistance to the symbolic and economic imperatives of slavery" (904). See also Rhoden, *$40 Million Slaves*, 49: "Sports, for many of the enslaved men in particular, became a ritual of reclaiming one's manhood."
43. Berlin, *Making of African America*, 69.
44. Rhoden, *$40 Million Slaves*, 55: "The plantation athlete assumed a prestigious though ambiguous status, within the plantation hierarchy." Here he is speaking of two worlds, one defined by the white owners, the other by the black slaves. Those blacks who were seen as working closely with whites were often regarded with suspicion by the rest of the black community, but the most talented enslaved athletes had the respect of both their community and the white owners.
45. Daisy Turner, interview with author, January 11, 1985.
46. Wiggins, "Sport and Popular Pastimes," 239.
47. The deed has not survived, as Caroline County deed books prior to 1836 were destroyed during the Civil War. The Caroline County Land Tax Book indicates that Benjamin Taliaferro and Theodore Garnett received 1,390 acres from the estate of Charles C. Taliaferro in 1833. This land was valued at $34,018. Theodore Garnett's share was 720.5 acres at Hayes Mount. This was sold to John Gouldin for $17,009. Tax records indicate that the land was valued at $17,009. Caroline County Land Tax Books, 1833, 1834, 1835, Central Rappahannock Heritage Center, Fredericksburg, VA.
48. Daisy Turner, interview with author, January 11, 1985.
49. Ibid., March 1, 1984.
50. Lussana, "To See Who Was Best on the Plantation," 909.
51. Ibid.
52. Bibb, *Narrative of the Life*, 23.
53. Lussana, "To See Who Was Best on the Plantation," 910; see also Desch-Obi, *Fighting for Honor*.
54. Henson, *Life of Josiah Henson*, 14.
55. Daisy Turner, interview with author, March 1, 1984.
56. Ibid., March 15, 1984, and September 23, 1983.
57. Daisy Turner, interview with author, August 28, 1985.

58. Ibid., March 15, 1984.

59. Ibid., March 1, 1984.

60. Warden, *Statistical, Political, and Historical Account*, 393.

61. Finger, *Eastern Band of Cherokees*, 14.

62. Ibid., 13–14.

63. Daisy Turner, interview with author, March 15, 1984.

64. Daisy said White Cloud might have been her grandmother's uncle (interview with author, June 21, 1985). This may well have been true, as the Cherokee were a matrilineal tribe, and the brother of Silverbells' mother would have been a special relation to her.

65. Daisy Turner, interview with author, June 7, 1985.

66. For fastening bells on their clothing or moccasins, see Payne Mss 87-04, Box 2, Folder 1, 60, and Mss 87-04, Box 2, Folder 2, 18, 235, Museum of the Cherokee Indian, Museum Archives, Cherokee, NC.

67. Daisy Turner, interview with author, November 1, 1983.

68. Ibid., March 29, 1984.

69. Miles, *Ties That Bind*, 141–42: "Native people in the Southeast viewed kinship, not freedom, as the antithesis of slavery."

70. Micou v. Gouldin, 2004-040-208-052 (1849), Central Rappahannock Heritage Center, Fredericksburg, VA. The Caroline County Census of 1870 indicates that Rose was born in 1810, making her twenty-five in 1835. Caroline County, Virginia, Census Record, 1870, Ninth Census of the United States, National Archives and Records Administration, Washington, DC.

71. Daisy Turner, interview with author, June 28, 1984.

72. Ibid., March 15, 1984.

73. Deaths, *Fredericksburg (VA) Ledger*, February 10, 1868. The name "Hays Mount" most likely came from Ann Robinson Hay, great-grandmother of Charles Champe Taliaferro and former owner of at least a portion of his property. This name apparently morphed into the current name of Haymount. After Jack Gouldin died and his son Frank was living there, Frank's young daughter died, and the newspaper article referred to the location of her death as "Hay's Mount." See Cultural Resources, "Cultural Resource Reconnaisance [*sic*] Survey."

74. Essex County, VA, Property Tax Records, 1827–1835, Reel 74, Library of Virginia, Richmond, VA.

75. Caroline County, VA, Property Tax Records, 1835, Reel 74, Library of Virginia, Richmond, VA.

76. Daisy Turner, interview with author, March 15, 1984.

77. Daisy Turner, interview with author, September 28, 1983.

78. Miles, *Ties That Bind*, 52–55.

79. Caroline County, VA, Census Record, 1870, CRHC 2004-040-208-052, Central Rappahannock Heritage Center, Fredericksburg, VA.

80. Alec and George both spelled Berkeley with a "u" although in a number of variations: Burekly, Burkly, and Burkley.

81. Daisy Turner, interview with author, January 11, 1985.

82. Ibid.

83. Ibid.

84. William R. Bernard, "Commonplace Book 1847–50," Msss 5:5/B4567:1, Virginia Historical Society, Richmond, VA.

85. Robb, *Welcum Hinges*, 22.
86. See Scarborough, *Masters of the Big House*, esp. 1–17 for overview.
87. Kate Buckner diary, entry dated July 29, 1857, Jim Patton's Papers in the Virginia Room at Central Rappahannock Regional Library, Fredericksburg, VA.
88. Advertisement of Corbin land tracts, August 26, 1860, Fredericksburg Historical Court Records, CR-CI-H Corbin v. Corbin 1866, 74-01, Circuit Superior Court of Law and Chancery of Spotsylvania County, Fredericksburg, VA; and advertisement of Merryman tract, March 1861, Merryman v. Merryman, Fredericksburg Historic Court Records, CRHC 2004-040-220-029, Circuit Superior Court of Law and Chancery of Spotsylvania County, Fredericksburg, VA.
89. Commonwealth v. Holloway, CRHC 2004-040-224-083 (1866), Fredericksburg Historic Court Records, Circuit Superior Court of Law and Chancery of Spotsylvania County, Fredericksburg, VA.
90. Gorn, "Social Significance of Fighting," 23.
91. Faulkner, *Absalom, Absalom!*, 20–21.
92. Daisy Turner, interview with author, February 15, 1984.
93. Ibid., June 7, 1985.
94. Ibid., December 12, 1983.
95. Bibb, *Narrative of the Life*, 23.
96. Daisy Turner, interview with author, September 28, 1983.
97. Liberty Baptist Church, Minutes, 1830–1851, Virginia Baptist Historical Society, University of Richmond, Richmond, VA.
98. Slaughter, *Settlers, Southerners, Americans*, 77–78.
99. Sobel, *Trabelin' On*, 87.
100. Wingfield, *History of Caroline County*, 323; Liberty Baptist Church, Minutes, 1830–1851. When Jack Gouldin joined the Liberty Baptist Church, he reported that he came from Zion Church, although I did not find him listed there. Liberty would have been closer to his new property on the Rappahannock.
101. Ryland, *Baptists of Virginia*, 286.
102. Bethesda Baptist Church, Minutes, July 1847, Virginia Baptist Historical Society, University of Richmond, Richmond, VA.
103. Ibid., Minutes, May 1849.
104. Fredericksburg Deed Book, 1850–1853, 152, Fredericksburg Circuit Court, Fredericksburg, VA.
105. See Cultural Resources, "Cultural Resource Reconnaisance Survey," 44; see also John [Jack] Gouldin Estate inventory, Caroline County Will Book, 31:101, April 14, 1863, Central Rappahannock Heritage Center, Fredericksburg, VA.
106. Daisy Turner, interview with author, September 28, 1983.
107. Ibid., February 15, 1984, and March 1, 1984.
108. Ibid., January 11, 1985.
109. Ibid., December 14, 1983.
110. Ibid., March 29, 1984.
111. Ibid., February 15, 1984.
112. Slaughter, *Settlers, Southerners, Americans*, 137.
113. Ibid.
114. Daisy Turner, interview with author, October 12, 1983.
115. Ibid., June 28, 1984.
116. Ibid., October 12, 1983.

117. Ibid., June 28, 1984. Alec's years may be a little off, and he may have been around five or six.

118. Ibid., June 28, 1984.

119. Ibid., October 12, 1984.

120. Ibid., June 28, 1984.

121. See Sobel, *Trabelin' On*, 198; this was most likely the "second burial," which would be a more elaborate commemoration service.

122. Daisy Turner, interview with author, October 12, 1983.

123. Ibid.

124. Odeyemi Egnile and Martine de Souza (in Egile Hocon, Ouidah, Benin), interview with author, November 28, 2011 (notes in author's private collection).

125. Daisy Turner, interview with author, December 14, 1983.

126. Suit against Wesley Wright for the unlawful assembly of slaves in August 1863, Central Rappahannock Heritage Center, 2004-040-224-089. This case was brought more because of a personal slight than for the fact that holding a funeral gathering was contrary to the law. Fitzgerald, *Different Story*, 9.

127. Slaughter, *Settlers, Southerners, Americans*, 137: "Slaves held festive funerals to dispel the grief of a mourning family, an African tradition that remained strong in the antebellum period."

128. Daisy Turner, interview with author, June 28, 1984.

129. Raboteau, *Slave Religion*, 231: usually these slave preachers were illiterate.

130. Ibid., 231.

131. Daisy Turner, interview with author, October 25, 1983.

132. Raboteau, *Slave Religion*, 233.

133. Bethesda Baptist Church, Minutes, September 1866, Virginia Baptist Historical Society, University of Richmond, Richmond, VA.

134. Daisy Turner, interview with author, June 28, 1984.

Chapter 4. Plantation Life

1. Alec always referred to him as "old Gouldin" to his children.

2. See John [Jack] Gouldin, will dated February 1, 1863, Caroline County Will Book 31:48, Central Rappahannock Heritage Center, Fredericksburg, VA.

3. Fitzgerald, *Different Story*, 22.

4. See Morgan, *Emancipation in Virginia's Tobacco Belt*.

5. Caroline County, Virginia, Slave Census, 1860, John Gouldin, National Archives, Washington, DC.

6. John Gouldin, will dated February 1, 1863.

7. Alec Turner's grandson, Godfrey Hall, remembered his grandfather's love of hoecakes. Godfrey Hall, interview with author, February 3, 2003.

8. In the 1860 census, although no names are given, it is possible to find that household on the slave list because we know Rose was born in 1810, her oldest son in 1835, Susan probably a couple of years later, and Alec in 1845. I never had a satisfactory answer from Daisy as to who their father was. Rose, as head of her household, had all her children living with her until the eldest, George, set up his own household, cohabiting with his wife, Eliza, around 1861. See "Register of Colored Persons of Caroline County, State of Virginia, Cohabiting Together and

husband and wife on 27th February, 1866," Central Rappahannock Heritage Center, Fredericksburg, VA. See also Gutman, *Black Family*; Stevenson, *Life in Black and White*, 222. Stevenson states: "matrifocality was a fundamental characteristic of most slave families, even when fathers lived locally." This would have held true for Rose as a Cherokee. There was remarkable stability within these families, and it served as an important transmitter of culture.

9. Gutman, *Black Family*, 14.

10. Daisy Turner, interview with author, March 29, 1984. Daisy remembered Alec talking about his father and mother, particularly his mother: "*He was very interested in his mother. His mother had great power with him and she was a smart woman.*"

11. Ibid., March 15, 1984. When I asked Daisy about this, she was very definite that Rose had such a machine. She explained that Rose was a great favorite with Gouldin and that he had bought this for her, sometimes from New England, sometimes from Washington. This certainly could have been the case as the sewing machine was first invented in 1845, although it was not in general use until around 1856. At this time it would have been a novelty. See Fox-Genovese, *Within the Plantation Household*, 124; Genovese, *Roll, Jordan, Roll*, 551. These homespun slave garments were known as *osnaburgs*, and while the cotton cloth was both durable and sturdy, it was extremely rough.

12. Daisy Turner, interview with author, March 15, 1984.

13. White, *Ar'n't I a Woman?*, 128. Not only did the job of seamstress carry prestige, but it allowed for self-expression and creativity.

14. Schwartz, *Born in Bondage*, 64; Daisy Turner, interview with author, February 1, 1984; see also White, *Ar'n't I a Woman?*, 115.

15. Wiggins, "Sport and Popular Pastimes," 48.

16. Ibid., 56, notes the similarity of slave games to African games.

17. John Bruce Turner, interview with author, January 29, 1989. Alec told his grandson about these various games.

18. George Hall, interview with author, January 15, 1986; see Wiggins, "Sport and Popular Pastimes," 70–71.

19. Caroline County, Virginia, Property Tax Records, 1838, Central Rappahannock Heritage Center, Fredericksburg, VA.

20. Cultural Resources, "Cultural Resource Reconnaisance [*sic*] Survey."

21. Fannie Lewis Gwathamey Adams, "Reminiscences of a childhood spent at 'Hayfield' Plantation near Fredericksburg, VA during the Civil War," Mss1/F5785b53, p. 5, Virginia Historical Society, Richmond, VA.

22. Alec described many of these outbuildings to Daisy. See John Gouldin, will dated February 1863; John Gouldin, estate inventory, Caroline County Will Book 31:101, April 14, 1863; John Gouldin, estate sale, Caroline County Will Book 32:265–69, September 12, 1864, Central Rappahannock Heritage Center, Fredericksburg, VA.

23. Caroline County, Virginia, Agricultural Census, 1860, John Gouldin, National Archives, Washington, DC; Daisy Turner interviews.

24. See advertisement of Corbin land tracts, August 26, 1860, Fredericksburg Historical Court Records, CR-CI-H Corbin v. Corbin 1866, 74-01, Circuit Superior Court of Law and Chancery of Spotsylvania County, Fredericksburg, VA; see also

advertisement of Merryman tract, 1831, Merryman v. Merryman, Fredericksburg Historic Court Records, CR-SC-H 200-3, Circuit Superior Court of Law and Chancery of Spotsylvania County, Fredericksburg, VA.

25. Caroline County, Virginia, Slave Census, 1860, John Gouldin; Caroline County, Virginia; Property Tax Records, 1850–1862, Central Rappahannock Heritage Center, Fredericksburg, VA; Fitzgerald, *Different Story*, 10, indicates most slaves are referred to as servants.

26. Wheat was mowed with a scythe fixed with a wooden cradle, which had five long wooden fingers to gather in the stalks. Usually the best mower would be placed at the end, to keep everyone moving. He would also be the lead singer, singing to keep up a steady rhythm and speed.

27. Caroline County, Virginia, Agricultural Census, 1850 and 1860, John Gouldin. Gouldin extracted 300 pounds of honey in 1850, and 150 pounds in 1860.

28. Daisy Turner, interview with author, October 12, 1983.

29. See Fry, *Night Riders*, 6: "Chicanery and cunning were employed on a day-to-day basis to get choice food, easier work, uninhibited movement from one place to another, and uninterrupted secret assembly. Pranks were also executed simply to strike at the establishment, such as urinating in food served to the masters."

30. See Bethesda Baptist Church Records, 1847–1878, Virginia Baptist Historical Society, University of Richmond, Richmond, VA.

31. Robb, *Welcum Hinges*, 25.

32. See White, *Ar'n't I a Woman?*, 123; Robb, *Welcum Hinges*, 25. When allowed to relax, slaves would often gather in a cabin to listen to the older women tell stories.

33. This story is in the "John and Old Master" tradition—a cycle of trickster tales frequently told by slaves. See Dickerson, "'John and Old Master' Stories," 418–29. Dickerson points out that "by describing the relationship between slaves and masters as one of continuing conflict, the stories expressed rebellion against the system which went far deeper than the vicarious identification with a successful trickster."

34. See White, *Ar'n't I A Woman?*, 46–61. White delineates the idealized "Black Mammy" commonly found in memoirs written after the Civil War: "Mammy was the woman who could do anything, and do it better than anyone else . . . Mammy was selected 'for her worth and reliability.'" She is also remembered for her love and warmth.

35. Caroline County, Virginia, Federal Census, 1850, transcribed by Mark Anderson Sprouse, Iberian Publishing Company, Athens, GA, 1997.

36. *Fredericksburg (VA) News*, January 28, 1859, 3:1. He apparently died suddenly. What "interesting" refers to is tantalizing.

37. It is doubtful that Alec as a youth understood the subtle class distinctions of new wealth as opposed to old aristocratic wealth, and it is more probable that he lumped wealth and social standing together.

38. See Rawick, *From Sundown to Sunup*, 62.

39. See Escott, *Slavery Remembered*, 120.

40. Zephie's full name was Josephine A. Broaddus. We know her nickname because Alec named one of his daughters Zebbe in honor of *"the little missus."* Alec's pronunciation of "b" for the "ph" sound accounts for the difference.

41. Jacobs, *Incidents in the Life*, 5: "I was born a slave; but I never knew it till six years of happy childhood had passed away."

42. Daisy Turner, interview with author, June 28, 1984.

43. See Blassingame, *Slave Community*, 209.

44. Broaddus, *History of the Broaddus Family*, 38.

45. Blassingame, *Slave Community*, 140.

46. Daisy Turner, interview with author, February 1, 1984.

47. Ibid., June 28, 1984.

48. Ibid.

49. See Schwartz, *Born in Bondage*, 99.

50. See Gutman, *Black Family*, 319; Schwartz, *Born in Bondage*, 156; Henson, *Life of Josiah Henson*, 21–22; Wiggins, "Sport and Popular Pastimes," 75.

51. Fitzgerald, *Different Story*, 27.

52. Guardian Bond, December 12, 1853, Caroline County, Virginia, Library of Virginia, Reel 28, Guardian Bonds, 1844–1858, 136, Richmond, VA. Zephie was the daughter of Gouldin's daughter Maria Ann, who was married to Joseph Broaddus in 1841. Maria Ann died either in childbirth or shortly thereafter, and her parents took in Zephie to raise. When Joseph Broaddus died several years later, Jack Gouldin became her legal guardian.

53. John Gouldin, will dated February 1, 1863.

54. Daisy Turner, interview with author, November 30, 1983.

55. Ibid., June 28, 1984.

56. When working with the records at the Bowling Green Court House, in Bowling Green, Virginia, I asked what kind of name "Pusley" was, and was told that it was "Presley," but was frequently pronounced "Pusley" by local African Americans.

57. Daisy always referred to Pusley as an overseer, but he was probably one of a number of "drivers," who acted as foremen. Pusley most likely was in charge of the younger slaves. See Genovese, *Roll, Jordan, Roll*, 365–88.

58. Contract between Thomas Robinson (overseer for Samuel Skinker) and Samuel Skinker, Robinson v. Skinker, 1824, CR-WC-H, 230-6, Circuit Superior Court of Law and Chancery of Spotsylvania County, Fredericksburg, VA.

59. Daisy Turner, interview with author, June 28, 1984.

60. Most frequently Daisy referred to Pusley as mulatto, but occasionally she would describe him as white, explaining that there were mulatto overseers as well.

61. John Gouldin, Estate inventory, February 10, 1817, Caroline County Will Book 19: 272–73, Central Rappahannock Heritage Center, Fredericksburg, VA.

62. Schwartz, *Born in Bondage*, 108.

63. Daisy Turner, interview with author, February 1, 1984.

64. Caroline County, Virginia, Agricultural Census, 1860, John Gouldin.

65. Painter, *Creating Black Americans*, 102–4.

66. Daisy Turner, interview with author, August 14, 1984.

67. Fitzgerald, *Different Story*, 76

68. Cleo Coleman, interview with author, March 22, 2005.

69. Kate Buckner, diary, entry dated July 4, 1858, Jim Patton's papers, Virginia Room, Central Rappahannock Regional Library, Fredericksburg, VA.

70. John Bruce Turner, interview with author, January 29, 1989, and March 22, 2005.

71. Sobel, *Trabelin' On*, 82–83: "The churches became moral courts and considered social relations between wives, husbands, children, and slaves, business dealings, gambling, stealing, tale-bearing, lying, intoxication, and sexual immorality. No area of concern was proscribed." Indeed, the Bethesda Baptist Church records numerous inquiries into possible misconduct and punishments for white members.

72. Bethesda Baptist Church Records, March and May 1856, Virginia Baptist Historical Society, University of Richmond, Richmond, VA.

73. Ibid. A typical entry reads: "Feb. 1856: to attend to matters of discipline among the colored members Churchill Grimes a freeman of color excommunicated from this church for the sin of falsehood and contempt of the church. Bro L. P. Todd and John W. Holloway apt a committee to notify Grimes a free man of color to attend church mtg on the next 3rd Lord's day at this place to atone for misconduct. The case of Matilda a servant of T.W. Gouldin postponed. The case of Susan and Jim servants of John Gouldin continued. Nelson a servant of Bro J. Gouldin dealt with for theft and upon professing repentance was retained in the fellowship of the church."

74. Ibid., August and November 1859.

75. Dixon, "Singing Swords," 301.

76. See chapter 5, "Civil War," for more on Alec's religious conversions.

77. Guild, *Black Laws of Virginia*, 175–76.

78. Daisy Turner, interview with author, June 28, 1984.

79. Zelma Ida May "Zebbe" Turner, born August 18, 1888.

80. Daisy Turner, interview with author, June 28, 1984.

81. Dixon, "Singing Swords," 308.

82. John Bruce Turner, interview with author, January 29, 1989.

83. Douglass, *Narrative of the Life*, 25–26.

84. Fitzgerald, *Different Story*, 19.

85. John Bruce Turner, interview with author, January 29, 1989.

86. The practice of breeding slaves was reported by a number of travelers to the South and was well known by the slave community. See Schwartz, *Born in Bondage*, 188; Fitzgerald, *Different Story*, 25. Another former Virginia slave, Elige Davison, "indicated that his master had intentionally bred him to a number of women." See Rawick, *From Sundown to Sunup*, 88.

87. When Gouldin submitted a list of his slaves "abducted and harbored by the enemy" on October 15, 1862, he valued sixteen-year-old Alec at $1,500. His most valuable slaves, three men and one woman, were valued at $1,600–$1,700. See John Gouldin, statement, Confederate Citizens File, M346, Record Group 109, Roll 0366, Document 77, National Archives and Records Administration, Washington, DC.

88. A vegetable material was derived from the bark of hemlocks that was an important ingredient for tanning leather.

89. For a cure for mange, see Tayloe Mss T28d27673–27683, Virginia Historical Society, Richmond, VA.

90. Slaughter, *Settlers, Southerners, Americans*, 95.

91. Bethesda Baptist Church Records, April, 1858, Virginia Baptist Historical Society, University of Richmond, Richmond, VA.

92. Daisy Turner, interview with author, July 23, 1985, and August 28, 1985.

93. George Hall, interview with author, January 7, 1986.

94. See Roberts, *From Trickster to Badman*; see also Dorson, *American Negro Folktales*, 132–35; Brewer, *Worser Days and Better Times*, 108–10; Levine, *Black Culture and Black Consciousness*, 105; Desch-Obi, *Fighting for Honor*, 109.

95. John Bruce Turner, interview with author, January 29, 1989.

96. See Jacobs, *Incidents in the Life*.

97. Daisy Turner, interview with author, June 28, 1984.

98. Dorsey, *Caroline County, Virginia*, 5.

99. Daisy Turner, interview with author, June 28, 1984.

100. Alexander Turner to Mr. E. C. Turnan, Department of Bureau of Pensions, letter of application for Civil War pension dated June 6, 1916. This was a follow-up letter to his initial pension request.

101. Adams, "Reminiscences." Buttermilk was something soldiers considered a luxury. Fannie Lewis Gwathmey Adams, who grew up near Fredericksburg, recalls soldiers who "would always come to our big brick dairy where Bessie and I would fill their canteens with butter milk."

102. *Works Progress Administration of Virginia Historical Inventory*, 2:210–15, March 24, 1937, Library of Virginia, Richmond, VA.

103. John Gouldin, statement, Confederate Citizens File.

104. Although difficult to read, the inscription is dated 1862 and lists such items as "4 pair blankets," "2 bed quilts," "2 white spreads," "Father's blanket," and "1 wagon," among a number of other unreadable items.

105. See advertisement of Corbin land tracts, August 26, 1860. It seems that Gouldin never finished paying for this land, and at his death his executors requested that the land be sold to pay off the note and interest as they no longer had the slaves necessary to work the land. Corbin's fishery had been esteemed "the most valuable herring fishery on the river." See also Dickenson v. Poindexter CR-LC-H, 1838, 56-2, Fredericksburg Historic Court Records, Circuit Superior Court of Law and Chancery of Spotsylvania County, Fredericksburg, VA.

106. See advertisement of Merryman tract, 1831.

107. John Gouldin, estate inventory, Caroline County Will Book 31:101–2, April 14, 1863, Central Rappahannock Heritage Center, Fredericksburg, VA.

108. Berlin, *Generations of Captivity*, 250.

109. Daisy Turner, interview with author, November 18, 1983.

110. Thomas W. Gouldin, statement, dated October 27, 1862, Confederate Citizens files, Record Group 109, Roll 0366, Document 87, M346, National Archives and Records Administration, Washington, DC.

111. Silas B. Gouldin, statement, October 27, 1862, Confederate Citizens Files, Record Group 109, Roll 0366, Document 87, M346, National Archives and Records Administration, Washington, DC.

112. Henry Pyne, First New Jersey Cavalry chaplain, wrote a history that is considered the most complete account of their Civil War service. Pyne, *Ride to War*, 16.

113. Ibid.

114. John Bruce Turner, interview with author, January 29, 1989.

115. See Alec Turner, to Bureau of Pensions, letter with pension form dated January 27, 1906, Record Group 15, National Archives and Records Administration, Washington, DC. Apparently, Alec used the name Alexander Walker briefly, so that Jack Gouldin could not identify him as one of his slaves and thus return him to the plantation.

Chapter 5. Civil War

1. Alec Turner, to Bureau of Pensions, letter dated June 16, 1916, Record Group 15, National Archives and Records Administration, Washington, DC.; see also Hepworth, *Whip, Hoe, and Sword*, 259–60: "We could trust [freedmen] implicitly on all common points. They knew whether there were any rebels in that parish; and, if there were, where they were stationed. But we never could trust their estimate of distance between one mile and six, and are as likely to say five hundred as fifty." Time and space had different meanings for the enslaved than those with the luxury of free passage. Alec's distance of five miles is more likely to be ten.

2. Pyne, *Ride to War*, 16; "Stealing a March," *Harper's Weekly* 4 (1863): 250.

3. "Gillman the Spy," *Sussex (NJ) Independent*, August 11, 1905.

4. Pyne, *Ride to War*, 16.

5. Virgil (Vergie) Broderick (Brodrick) to his father John S. Broderick, letter dated April 30, 1862, https://www.flickr.com/photos/8379107@NO3/sets/72157624120966988/ (accessed 2013).

6. Kester, *Cavalry Men in Blue*, 13.

7. Pyne, *Ride to War*, 17: Pyne indicates two Negro guides; Longacre, *Jersey Cavaliers*, 40: Longacre indicates three guides; "Stealing a March," 250: indicates three guides.

8. John Gouldin, statement, October 15, 1862, Confederate Citizens File, M346, Record Group 109, Roll 0366, Document 77, National Archives and Records Administration, Washington, DC. This is part of the Confederates Citizens File where plantation owners had the opportunity to make a claim of lost property. Jack Gouldin claimed he lost twenty-nine slaves. The document provides the name, sex, age, and value of each slave. Humphrey's age was given as twenty-six, and his value as $1,200. Alec's age was sixteen, and his value $1,500. Only two men were valued higher than Alec: one, age twenty-four, at $1,600, and one, age twenty-two, at $1,700.

9. Eugene Broaddus was a member of the Ninth Virginia Cavalry. See "Ninth Virginia Cavalry"; "Stealing a March," 250.

10. Pyne, *Ride to War*, 19.

11. "Ninth Virginia Cavalry."

12. Pyne, *Ride to War*.

13. Marie Morton, e-mail with the author, April 2, 2013; see Marie Morton, *Revised Integrated Cultural Resources*, 44, 47, 92–95.

14. Daisy claimed her father begged the soldiers not to burn the plantation. It is doubtful this was ever part of their plan. The looting was not the focus of the raid, but certain goods could not be overlooked.

15. Daisy Turner, interviews with author, December 14, 1983, and June 28, 1984.

16. Ibid., June 28, 1984.

17. Again, there is a discrepancy as to number of captors, with reports ranging from five to fourteen: Alec Turner's story via Daisy; Pyne, *Ride to War*; "Stealing a March," 250; Longacre, *Jersey Cavaliers*, 41; Kester, *Cavalryman in Blue*, 13; Joseph Layton, "Layton Memoirs," 4. The memoirs are courtesy of the private collection of Sonya Hulbert and Jesse R. Phillips, Branchville, NJ. Joseph E. Layton, Corp. Co. H, First New Jersey Cavalry, was promoted to sergeant June 1, 1862, and discharged with a disability March 15, 1863. Dorsey, *Caroline County, Virginia*, 13.

18. Thomas W. Gouldin, statement, dated October 27, 1862, Confederate Citizens File, M346, Record Group 109, Roll 0366, Document 87, National Archives and Records Administration, Washington, DC. Because he was a deacon and major figure in the Bethesda Baptist Church, I wondered about his wine, but apparently these were not considered "spirituous liquors." Local winemaking was practiced by most farmers in Caroline County, with dandelion, grape, blackberry, and peach being the most common.

19. McPherson, *Battle Cry of Freedom*, 355; see also Masur, "'Rare Phenomenon,'" 1050–83, esp. 1051: Masur points out the significance of the term *contrabands* as the transition of status of a people; they were neither property nor free people.

20. Masur, "'Rare Phenomenon,'" 355.

21. Berlin et al., *Slaves No More*, 30.

22. J. F. Gouldin, statement on Gouldin's behalf by Samuel Berlin, October 31, 1862, Confederate Citizens File, M346, Record Group 109, Roll 0366, Document 80, National Archives and Records Administration, Washington, DC. Apparently some slaves did return. Both Ned Sales and Armstead are listed in Jack Gouldin's affidavit of October 1862, and both were named in his will written in February 1863.

23. John Gouldin, statement, October 15, 1862, Confederate Citizens File.

24. Ibid.

25. Longacre, *Jersey Cavaliers*, 41. In Broderick's April 30 letter to his father, he stated: "We are in front of Fredericksburg. We see the pickets every day on the opposite side of the river. Yesterday we returned from our scout to King George Co."

26. Morgan, *Emancipation in Virginia's Tobacco Belt*, 117.

27. J. F. Gouldin, statement on Gouldin's behalf by Samuel Berlin, October 31, 1862.

28. See White, *Ar'n't I a Woman?*, 167.

29. Ibid., for her discussion of the slave owners' distress with the departure of their "black mammies."

30. Daisy Turner, interview with author, September 28, 1983.

31. "Stealing a March," 250; see also Jennie Sweetman, "N.J. Cavalry's Gillman the Spy Re-examined," *New Jersey Sunday Herald* (Sussex County), July 3, 2011; see also "Gilman the Spy," *Sussex (NJ) Independent*, August 11, 1905.

32. Wheaton, *Surgeon on Horseback*, 11.

33. See Berlin, *Generations of Captivity*, 252: "By the summer of 1862, tens of thousands of black men and women, almost all of them former slaves, constructed fortifications, drove wagons, chopped wood, cooked food, prepared camps, and nursed the sick and wounded for the federal army and navy."

34. Bureau of Pensions, to Alexander Turner, letter of pension rejection dated February 29, 1908, Record Group 15, National Archives and Records Administration, Washington, DC.

35. Quarles, *Negro in the Civil War*, 94: "there were more than 200,000 Negro civilians in the service of the Northern armies as laborers, cooks, teamsters and servants."

36. Wheaton, *Surgeon on Horseback*, 163.

37. Ibid.

38. Obituary for Ferdinand Dayton, *Trenton (NJ) Daily State Gazette*, November 3, 1866. Dayton died November 1, 1866, in Natchez, Mississippi. He had leased a cotton plantation and was "engaged in cultivation at the time of his death," which was described as resulting from "congestion of the brain." This suggests encephalitis caused by a virus or bacteria, perhaps entering the body from a mosquito bite.

39. Daisy Turner, interview with author, June 28, 1984.

40. Manning, *What This Cruel War*, 13.

41. Ferdinand V. Dayton, to his mother Margaret Dayton, letter dated June 1, 1864, William L. Dayton Papers, 1791–1897, Manuscripts Division, Department of Rare Books and Special Collections, Princeton University Library, Princeton, NJ.

42. Daisy Turner, interview with author, March 29, 1984.

43. Ferris, "Dayton, William Lewis."

44. G. W. Adams, *Doctors in Blue*, 50.

45. Ibid., 66: "The assistant surgeon, accompanied by an orderly carrying hospital knapsack filled with emergency supplies, went with the stretcher bearers to establish a 'primary station,' just outside musketry range. There first aid was given and the regimental ambulances loaded. Another of his duties was supervision of the stretchermen so far as his location and circumstances permitted. The stretchermen were supposed to cover the field and give no excuse for a soldier to leave the line in order to escort the wounded to the rear. When they found a wounded man incapable of walking . . . the stretchermen would carry him to the primary station, using a practiced pace to hold the patient's suffering to a minimum. There the assistant surgeon, with the help of his orderly and usually of a hospital steward, would give him liquor to counteract shock, and administer first aid with an equipment consisting of pails, basins, sponges, lint, and bandages. The treatment was usually limited to a tourniquet and bandages. The patient would then be put in one of the regimental ambulances and taken to the field hospital."

46. Wheaton, *Surgeon on Horseback*, 11.

47. William W. L. Phillips, to William L. Dayton, letter dated May 16, 1862, William L. Dayton Papers, 1791–1897, Manuscripts Division, Department of Rare Books and Special Collections, Princeton University Library, Princeton, NJ.

48. Col. M. H. Beaumont, "Reminiscences of the First New Jersey Cavalry," manuscript written in the field, SDEA4002, Department of Defense, Adjutant General's Office (Civil War) Memorials of Officers, New Jersey State Archives, Trenton, NJ.

49. Ibid.

50. "Report of Surg. Ferdinand V. Dayton, Second New Jersey Cavalry, November 1864," in *The War of the Rebellion: A Compilation of the Official Records of the Union and Confederate Armies*, series 1, vol. 41, part 1, *Reports* (Washington, DC: Government Printing Office, 1893), 343 (Google Books search).

51. Ferdinand V. Dayton, to his mother Margaret Dayton, letter dated December 9, 1862, William L. Dayton Papers, 1791–1897, Manuscripts Division, Department of Rare Books and Special Collections, Princeton University Library, Princeton, NJ.

52. Dayton, to his mother, letter dated June 1, 1864.

53. Layton, "Layton Memoirs," 5; Longacre, *Jersey Cavaliers*, 41.

54. A regiment has roughly 600–750 men commanded by a colonel; a brigade has 2,000–2,500 men commanded by a brigadier general or senior colonel.

55. Phillips to Dayton, letter dated May 16, 1862.

56. Layton, "Layton Memoirs," 5.

57. Beaumont, "Reminiscences."

58. See John Gouldin, statement, October 15, 1862, Confederate Citizens File; Thomas W. Gouldin, statement on Gouldin's behalf by Samuel Berlin, October 27, 1862, Confederate Citizens File; J. F. Gouldin, statement on Gouldin's behalf by Samuel Berlin, October 31, 1862, Confederate Citizens File.

59. See the *Richmond (VA) Daily Dispatch*, March 30, 1863, for an example of the kind of ad Dr. Thomas Gouldin would have been running: "Ran away:—$100 reward.—Ran away from the Danville and Greensboro' Railroad, about the 7th of this month, (March,) two negroes, named Emanuel and Dennis. Emanuel is about thirty-five years of age, five feet ten inches in height, of a dark gingerbread color. Dennis is about fifteen years of age, of a rather brighter color than Emanuel, with quite a pleasing countenance when spoken to, it is thought they are aiming to get back to Caroline county, but may [try] to pass themselves off as free and attach themselves to the army, or remain lurking in the neighborhood of Richmond. The above reward will be given for their delivery to either of the under signed, near Rappahannock Academy, or secured so that we get them."

60. Jennie Sweetman, "N.J. Cavalry's Gillman the Spy Re-examined," *New Jersey Sunday Herald*, July 3, 2011; "Gilman the Spy," *Sussex (NJ) Independent*, August 11, 1905.

61. Beaumont, "Reminiscences."

62. Layton, "Layton Memoirs," 5.

63. John Bruce Turner, interview with author, January 29, 1989.

64. John H. Lucas, to his brother, letter dated May 29, 1862, Lucas Family Papers, Wilson Library, University of North Carolina. John Lucas, Captain Co. F, First New Jersey Cavalry, was killed in action at Sulphur Springs, October 12, 1863.

65. Daisy Turner, interview with author, December 14, 1983.

66. These were probably meritorious certificates made out by a ranking officer, possibly Wyndham; see Quarles, *Negro in the Civil War*, 84.

67. Daisy Turner, interview with author, August 14, 1984.

68. It is not my purpose to give a minute account of the First New Jersey Cavalry's movements, but rather to underscore those battles Alec mentions and the insights we gain through Dayton's actions.

69. Layton, "Layton Memoirs," 6.

70. Ibid.

71. Pyne, *Ride to War*, 32.

72. Ibid.

73. Ibid., 37.

74. Col. Kane was the leader of the Bucktails, a Pennsylvania regiment; see Glover, *Bucktailed Wildcats*.

75. Ferdinand V. Dayton, to his mother Margaret Dayton, letter dated June 6, 1862, William L. Dayton Papers, 1791–1897, Manuscripts Division, Department of Rare Books and Special Collections, Princeton University Library, Princeton, NJ.

76. Wayland, "Fremont's Pursuit of Jackson," 339.

77. Beaumont, "Reminiscences."

78. Daisy Turner, interview with author, November 30, 1983.

79. Surgeons carried instrument cases at all times, allowing them to treat minor injuries, such as lancing boils, suturing wounds, or even amputating fingers or toes. Beaumont, "Reminiscences."

80. Foster, *New Jersey and the Rebellion*, 426; Beaumont, "Reminiscences."

81. Beaumont, "Reminiscences."

82. Foster, *New Jersey and the Rebellion*; Beaumont, "Reminiscences."

83. Beaumont, "Reminiscences"; Pyne, *Ride to War*, 64.

84. Pyne, *Ride to War*, 65.

85. Ibid.

86. Ibid., 66.

87. G. W. Adams, *Doctors in Blue*, 127.

88. Pyne, *Ride to War*, 67.

89. Ibid.

90. Beaumont, "Reminiscences."

91. The First New Jersey Cavalry and the Ninth Virginia Cavalry were engaged in a number of the same battles: the second Battle of Bull Run, Brandy Station, and Gettysburg.

92. Daisy Turner, interview with author, October 12, 1983; see also Daisy Turner and Zebbe Grant, interviews with Allon Schoener, October 26 and 29, 1973, Daisy Turner Collection, Rose Turner Box, Vermont Folklife Center, Middlebury, VT.

93. Daisy Turner, interview with author, September 28, 1983.

94. Pyne, *Ride to War*, 85; G. W. Adams, *Doctors in Blue*, 73.

95. Daisy Turner, interview with author, June 28, 1984.

96. Dayton, to his mother, letter dated December 9, 1862.

97. Ibid.

98. Longacre, *Jersey Cavaliers*, 122.

99. Ibid.

100. Ibid.

101. Greiner, Coryell, and Smither, *Surgeon's Civil War*, 60.

102. Daisy Turner, interview with author, December 14, 1983.

103. Lucas, to his brother, letter dated July 8, 1862.

104. The condition known as "grease heel" appears on the lower leg as scruffy patches below the hair; untreated the skin becomes deeply cracked and infected.

105. Pyne, *Ride to War*, 107.

106. Longacre, *Jersey Cavaliers*, 131.

107. Daisy uses "general" for ranking officers. Both Lieutenant Colonel Broderick and Major Shelmire were in the thick of fighting and lost their lives during the battle.

108. Daisy Turner, interview with author, November 30, 1983.

109. Ibid., December 21, 1983.

110. Pyne, *Ride to War*, 281, citing Marcus L. W. Kitchen.

111. Daisy Turner, interview with author, November 30, 1983.

112. Toombs, *New Jersey Troops*; Thomas, *Some Personal Reminiscences*, 10.

113. Daisy Turner, interview with author, October 12, 1983; November 30, 1983; February 1, 1984; August 14, 1984. Daisy told this story a number of times, but never with any more detail. The Confederate officer's rank varied from colonel to general, but she could not remember his name. It was for this feat that Alec was awarded his second "paper for bravery."

114. Pyne, *Ride to War*, 123.

115. Daisy Turner, interview with author, June 28, 1984. In 1899, Alec was dragged by a cow and injured. Daisy related that he was taken to Boston, where a doctor discovered the shell and removed it.

116. See LaFantasie, *Twilight at Little Round Top*.

117. Daisy Turner, interview with author, July 23, 1985.

118. This is confusing because those serving in the First New Jersey Cavalry were mustered out July 25, 1865. Dayton was promoted to surgeon in the Second New Jersey Cavalry on July 3, 1863. He was not mustered out until November 1, 1865, at Vicksburg. Although Alec tells us in his pension letter dated June 16, 1916, that he went with Dayton again, in another application to the Pension Office, he states in a scribbled note with his January 27, 1906, application that he was on furlough when the orders came for the Second New Jersey Cavalry to travel west and thus was left behind. See Alec Turner, letter with pension form to Bureau of Pensions, dated January 27, 1916, Record Group 15, National Archives and Records Administration, Washington, DC.

119. Alec Turner, letter with pension form, January 27, 1906.

120. Foster, *New Jersey and the Rebellion*, 591.

121. This was the case at City Point between November 1862 and May 1864. James Blakenship, historian at City Point Unit, Petersburg National Battlefield, National Park Service, to author, email dated November 15, 2010, in the author's collection.

122. Rufus Ingalls, to General M. C. Meigs, letter dated June 24, 1865, Record Group 92, E. 238, Box 317, City Point, National Archives and Records Administration, Washington, DC.

123. Trudeau, *Last Citadel*, 132.

124. Ibid., 134.

125. Daisy Turner, interview with author, October 12. 1983.

126. Brager, *Petersburg*, 79; Trudeau, *Last Citadel*, 131–41.

127. "General Grant's Campaign—The Charge on Cemetery Ridge, After the Explosion, July 30, 1864: Sketched by A. R. Waud," *Harper's Weekly*, August 27, 1864, 550.

128. Trudeau, *Last Citadel*, 140.

129. Daisy Turner, interview with author, October 25, 1983.

130. Manning, *What This Cruel War Was*, 215.

131. Daisy Turner, interview with author, October 25, 1983.

132. John Bruce Turner, interview with author, January 29, 1989.

133. Virginia Writers' Project, *Negro in Virginia*, 236.

134. Ferdinand Dayton, Military Service Records, 519, Record Group 94, National Archives and Records Administration, Washington, DC.

135. Alexander Turner, Pension Form, January 18, 1906, Record Group 15, National Archives and Records Administration, Washington, DC.

136. Daisy Turner, interview with author, November 18, 1983.

137. Ibid., February 15, 1984.

138. Ibid., July 23, 1985.

139. "President Lincoln Visits Fredericksburg," *Christian Banner Newspaper* (Fredericksburg, VA), May 27, 1862.

140. Beck and Graff, *On My Own*.

Chapter 6. Postwar

1. Berlin et al., *Slaves No More*, 180n195.
2. Ibid., 159–60.
3. Kilburn Knox, to James A. Hardie, Inspector General, letter dated October 13, 1864, K11 Record Group 159, National Archives and Records Administration, Washington, DC.
4. C. E. Compton, to James A. Hardie, Inspector General, letter dated July 30, 1864, K11 Record Group 159, National Archives and Records Administration, Washington, DC.
5. Caroline County, Virginia, Register of Children of Colored Persons, 1866, CRHC 2004-040-008, Central Rappahannock Heritage Center, Fredericksburg, VA.
6. Thomas Gouldin, testimony in Dickinson Adm v. Gouldin, October 5, 1877, CRHC 2004-040-246-028, Central Rappahannock Heritage Center, Fredericksburg, VA.
7. John Gouldin, estate sale, Will Book 32, 265–269, September 12, 1864, Central Rappahannock Heritage Center, Fredericksburg, Virginia.
8. On February 9, 1870, Josephine (Zephie) Broaddus married Major John H. Peebles and moved to Pitt County, North Carolina. She died there on July 27, 1876. See Pitt County Marriage register 1868–1948, C.079.63002, Pitt County Court House, Greenville, NC; Kittrell, *Cemetery Survey of Pitt County*.
9. Thomas Gouldin, testimony in Dickinson Adm v. Gouldin, October 5, 1877, CRHC 2004-040-246-028, Central Rappahannock Heritage Center, Fredericksburg, VA.
10. See John Gouldin, will dated February 1, 1863, Caroline County Will Book 31: 48, Central Rappahannock Heritage Center, Fredericksburg, VA. Two-thirds of the land had been divided between Gouldin's living sons, Thomas and Frank. See also McConkey, Parr and Co. v. Corbin, etc., CR-CI-H, 199-1, Folder 3 of 11, Fredericksburg Circuit Court, Fredericksburg, VA. The land Jack had bought from Corbin had been sold. As executors of his will, Tom and Frank petitioned to sell the land as they discovered further payments and interest were due, and that without slaves they had no means of working it.
11. John Gouldin, estate sale, Will Book 32, 265–69, September 12, 1864, Central Rappahannock Heritage Center, Fredericksburg, VA.
12. Thomas W. Gouldin, Confederate Amnesty Papers, dated May 29, 1865, M1003, Record Group 94, Roll 0061, National Archives and Records Administration, Washington, DC.
13. Daisy Turner, interview with Steve Goodman, May 8, 1976, Vermont Folklife Center, Middlebury, VT.
14. Daisy Turner, interview with author, February 1, 1984.
15. Ibid.
16. John Bruce Turner, interview with author, January 29, 1989.
17. Daisy Turner, interview with author, February 1, 1984.
18. Ibid., December 21, 1983.
19. Ibid., June 28, 1984. The school Alec attended would have been rudimentary and almost certainly not a college.

20. Daisy Turner, interview with author, August 31, 1984. I could not locate the Cameron and Osborne grocery store in any of the directories of Trenton or its environs, Camden, or Jersey City (which was mentioned on Alec's pension application), but because of the black community and the school, I suspect it must have been in or near Camden. Daisy had never been to New Jersey and often referred to Trenton and Camden interchangeably. As Dayton lived in Trenton, the confusion was compounded. At one point, Daisy said that Alec went to night school in Camden and worked at Osborn and Cameron's grocery store there.

21. Wright, *Education of Negroes*, 142–48.

22. Reiss, *Public Education in Camden, N.J.*, 65.

23. Ibid., 66.

24. Wright, *Education of Negroes*, 146–47.

25. This probably occurred in Camden.

26. John Bruce Turner, interview with author, January 29, 1989.

27. Daisy Turner, interview with author, April 20, 1984.

28. *Trenton (NJ) Daily State Gazette*, November 3, 1866.

29. He gave Mason's Island as his residence on documents filed with the Freedman's Bureau for his transportation to Maine. Transportation Order 746, M1055, Roll 18, July 29, 1868, National Archives and Records Administration, Washington, DC.

30. George Hall, interview with author, January 7, 1986.

31. John Bruce Turner, interview with, January 29, 1989. This was a common image, as when one moved quickly in a Prince Albert coat, the fashionable dress of the day, the tails would fly back. See Robb, *Welcum Hinges*, in which Uncle Woodson, a former slave on Gay Mont plantation, near Jack Gouldin's, exclaims: "My coat tail was sailing out and flat enough to play marbles on."

32. McFeely, *Yankee Stepfather*, 26.

33. Susan Merrill Lewis, unpublished MS about Brownville and Williamsburg, Ms 215, 100–101, Collection 131, Greenleaf-Merrill Family Papers, Maine Historical Society, Portland, ME.

34. Ibid.

35. Ibid.

36. Macdougall and Roberts, "Brownville Slate and Slaters," 61.

37. Susan Merrill Lewis, notes on "The Negro Colony," MS 215, Collection 131, Greenleaf-Merrill Family Papers, 1819–1917, Maine Historical Society, Portland, ME.

38. Macdougall and Roberts, "Brownville Slate and Slaters," 61.

39. Sawtell, *Merrill Slate Quarry*.

40. A. H. Merrill, to the Freedman's Bureau, letter dated July 12, 1868, M1902, no. 18, vol. 88:93, 96, National Archives and Records Administration, Washington, DC.

41. Lewis, "Negro Colony." Merrill lived in Williamsburg; his quarry was in Brownville, a distance of only a couple of miles.

42. Daisy Turner, interview with author, September 23, 1983.

43. Merrill Quarry payroll records, 1868–1873, MS 215, Collection 131, Greenleaf-Merrill Family Papers, Maine Historical Society, Portland, ME.

44. Douglass, *Narrative of the Life*, 98.

45. Mcdougall and Roberts, "Brownville Slate and Slaters," 58.
46. Ibid., 61. This actually occurred long after Alec had left the quarry on June 20, 1904.
47. Lewis, notes on "Negro Colony."
48. Bethesda Baptist Church, Records, Letters of Dismissal granted, September, 1869, Baptist Historical Society, University of Richmond, Richmond, VA.
49. Daisy refers to the freedmen coming off the same plantation as her mother as "the Early slaves." I was not able to locate the Early plantation.
50. Daisy Turner, interview with author, June 28, 1984.
51. Faith Turner Hawkins, interview with author, February 22, 1989.
52. Merrill Quarry payroll records, 1868–1873.
53. See Sally Early, death certificate, 1933, Grafton Town Records, Grafton, VT. Sally was actually the daughter of Henry Early.
54. Daisy Turner, interview with author, June 28, 1984. Daisy was referring to the fact that slaves were not allowed to marry.
55. According to Daisy, Liza was one of the "Early slaves." She may have been Dick King's wife, or became Dick King's wife, for in the 1870 Maine Census, Richard King is listed with his wife Elizabeth, the only Elizabeth in the group of freedmen. Dick King came in the first group of freedmen. Piscataquis County, Maine census, 1870, National Archives and Records Administration, Washington, DC.
56. Daisy Turner, interview with author, June 28, 1984. Piscataquis County, Maine census, 1870, National Archives and Records Administration, Washington, DC.
57. "The Great Gale," *Boston Daily Advertiser*, September 9, 1869, 1.
58. Ibid.
59. Ibid.
60. "The Great Gale," *Boston Daily Advertiser*, September 11, 1869, 1. I wondered if perhaps the *Cambridge* had been their vessel, but it was towed into Rockland on September 10 and taken to Bangor the next day. Alec was at work by September 10.
61. John Bruce Turner, interview with author, January 29, 1989.
62. Lewis, "Negro Colony" and notes; see also Merrill Quarry payroll records, 1868–1873; Barry, "Negro Folk-Songs from Maine," 13–16, 21–24.
63. Daisy Turner, interview with author, April 20, 1984.
64. Ibid., June 28, 1984.
65. A photograph of Alec at the quarry at the beginning of this chapter suggests that he did hold that position. Note how he is dressed; he even wears his pocket watch.
66. From the quarry records, Lindsey was calling himself "Linzey" at this period.
67. Sawtell, *Early Brownville*, 55: "About one-third of the black workers died, leading the others to decide to return to warmer climes."
68. Sawtell, *Merrill Slate Quarry*. On August 1, 1871, Merrill wrote in his diary: "Contracted with 15 men for a year at $290 per month and boarded. And 2 men at $1.50 per day—they board themselves. One man Mr. Burgeson at $300 a year and board him. He is Interpreter. And boy at $80 per year and board 2 women at $50 per year and board. They are to cook for the men and take care of house (boardinghouse) for me. And one woman for my house at $100 per year."
69. Daisy Turner, interview with author, November 30, 1983.

70. See chapter 7, "Vermont," for more on Alec's philosophy of "contentment and understanding."

71. The family name has been spelled numerous ways over the years. Robert took the name originally as Berkeley, as described earlier. Burekly is how George spelled his name in Maine. Most of the freeedmen were illiterate and therefore would not know how to spell their names. As a result, on the quarry payrolls there is inconsistency in the spelling of names. Lindsey is one example. Burekly is another. Based on the original Berkeley, there are several different spellings.

72. Merrill Quarry Payroll Records, September and October 1873. George's son Robert appeared on the quarry payroll later when he was thirteen years old.

73. Daisy Turner, interview with author, June 28, 1984.

74. Phillips Street may have been their first residence in Boston. Apparently they moved with the help of the doctor to Cambridge Street, which is closer to the hospital. Daisy gives several different street numbers, but this suggests that Alec was very specific as to where they lived. Daisy, who was not born at the time, probably did not remember the address accurately but retained the fact that her father was always careful to be specific.

75. Daisy Turner, interview with author, June 28, 1984.

76. Lewis, unpublished MS about Brownville and Williamsburg, Ms 215, 102.

77. Ibid.

78. Ibid.

79. Ibid.

80. Want ads, *Boston Herald*, June 9 and 16, 1873.

81. Ibid., July 8 and 9, 1873.

82. John Bruce Turner, interview with author, January 29, 1989; Cawley and Cawley, *Tales of Old Grafton,* 98.

83. Daisy Turner, interview with author, January 18, 1984.

84. Ibid., June 28, 1984.

85. In 1881, White's employee Vestus A. Wilbur joined him as a partner. White and Wilbur manufactured lumber and shingles and produced cider.

86. Daisy Turner, interview with author, December 12, 1984.

87. Ibid.

88. According to Daisy, Grafton was about to lose its town charter. This is a constant in her story; however, I have found no evidence of this happening; more likely it was to borrow money to keep the sawmill afloat. She claimed that the documents saving the town were filed in Newfane Court, but I have not been able to locate them either. Around this time, a number of towns did lose their charters.

89. Daisy Turner, interview with author, June 28, 1984. Daisy is referring to those instances when Alec felt the power of prayer, including when Liza prayed during the hurricane on the boat to Bangor, when the preacher lifted his arms to the heavens and stopped the storm at his father's funeral, and before he went into his first battle during the Civil War.

90. *Bellows Falls (VT) Times*, "Grafton," August 18, 1881.

91. Daisy Turner, interview with author, May 10, 1984.

92. Ibid., January 18, 1984. Daisy describes White and Wilbur staying with her father: "They didn't have any money to go to a hotel so Papu took Charles White and Vestus Wilbur to their house down on 81 Cambridge Street in Boston, and the

two grandmothers gave them meals, and Papu said they set up with their heads on the table and in their clothes till the next morning."

93. Ibid.

94. Ibid., May 10, 1984.

95. John Bruce Turner, interview with author, January 29, 1989.

96. Ibid.

97. Cawley and Cawley, *Tales of Old Grafton*, 98–99.

98. John Bruce Turner, interview with author, January 29, 1989.

99. Skunk's oil was an old remedy for lung disease.

100. Daisy Turner, interview with author, June 28, 1984.

Chapter 7. Vermont

1. During the 1850s, Grafton had a population of 1,300. See Thompson, "Life of a Vermont Farmer."

2. Frank V. Wilbur, "Memories of Old Grafton," *Bellows Falls (VT) Times*, July 6, 1961, B: 8.

3. "Local Matters, Grafton," *Bellows Falls Times*, November 14, 1873.

4. John Bruce Turner, interview with author, January 29, 1989.

5. Daisy Turner, interview with author, August 14, 1984.

6. Chester Lanier, interview with author, July 9, 2001.

7. Cawley and Cawley, *Tales of Old Grafton*, 113.

8. This was typical of the barter (and neighborly) economy practiced in the small towns of Vermont. Credit was often extended to locals. Eggs and butter might be used to pay a store bill, or perhaps the store owner would put off payment until harvest time, when the customer would have cash on hand.

9. Bernie Record, with Iva Fisher, interview with author, April 3, 2002.

10. John Bruce Turner, interview with author, January 29, 1989.

11. Ibid.

12. Guyette, *Discovering Black Vermont*, 5.

13. Gerzina, *Mr. and Mrs. Prince*, 145–61.

14. See Lovejoy, "Racism in Antebellum Vermont," 58–59; see also Brown, "'Not Only Extreme Poverty,'" 71–82.

15. Lovejoy, "Racism in Antebellum Vermont," 59; see Blassingame, *Autobiographical Writings*, 45.

16. Mary X. Barrett, "Charles Barrett Biographical Sketch," box VII, folder 40, University of Vermont Library, Burlington, VT.

17. Daisy Turner, interview with author, March 29, 1984.

18. Walker, *Quarry*.

19. Ibid., 306.

20. Hugo, *Writing for Her Life*, 18.

21. Daisy Turner, interview with author, April 20, 1984.

22. Walker, *Quarry*, 279.

23. Thompson, "Life of a Vermont Farmer."

24. Daisy Turner, interview with author, June 7, 1985.

25. Daisy Turner, in Beck and Graff, *On My Own*.

26. Daisy Turner, interview with author, July 23, 1985.

27. Barrett, "Charles Barrett Biographical Sketch."

28. See Berlin, *Making of African America*, 27: those who had been enslaved were denied both citizenship and land ownership, both important to an individual's personal and social identity.

29. Grafton Tax Records, 1879, Town Clerk's Office, Grafton, VT.

30. Sherman, Sessions, and Potash, *Freedom and Unity*, 376; see also Albers, *Hands on the Land*, 155.

31. Daisy Turner, interview with author, December 14, 1983.

32. "Local Matters, Grafton," *Bellows Falls Times*, June 6, 1882.

33. Daisy Turner, interview by the author, November 30, 1983.

34. See Thompson, "Life of a Vermont Farmer," 1873 entry.

35. Daisy Turner, interview with author, November 18, 1983.

36. Ibid.

37. Ibid., November 30, 1983.

38. "Local Intelligence, Grafton," *Vermont Phoenix* (Brattleboro), December 25, 1874.

39. "Local Matters, Grafton," *Bellows Falls Times*, February 5, 1875.

40. Grafton, Vermont, Birth and Death Records, Book 2: 101–102, January 29, 1879, Town Clerk's Office, Grafton, VT.

41. John Barrett (November 28, 1866–October 17, 1938) became a well-known diplomat and war correspondent. See Mary X. Barrett, "Charles Barrett Biographical Sketch," folder 32. Caroline Sanford Barrett grew up in Orwell, Vermont, and taught school in Orion, Alabama, before she was called home by her father in 1857 when tensions began to rise.

42. The land was owned by Charles White and Vestus Wilbur, the men for whom Alec was working.

43. Thompson, "Life of a Vermont Farmer."

44. Ibid.

45. Ibid.

46. Daisy Turner, interview by the author, October 5, 1983.

47. Grafton, Vermont, Birth and Death Records, Book 2: 179.

48. Daisy Turner, interview with author, September 28, 1983, and August 18, 1984.

49. "Local Matters, Grafton," *Bellows Falls Times*, September 20, 1883.

50. Daisy Turner, interview with author, June 28, 1984; see also Pettengill, *History of Grafton*, 79–81.

51. John Bruce Turner, interview with author, January 29, 1989.

52. This technique may well have been learned from his father and is most likely African in origin. See Desch-Obi, *Fighting for Honor* 2, 173–74.

53. Daisy Turner, interview with author, November 30, 1983.

54. Thompson, "Life of a Vermont Farmer," introduction.

55. Ibid.

56. Ibid.

57. Ibid., 1871 entry; Daisy Turner, interview with author, December 8, 1983, and November 30, 1983.

58. Thompson, "Life of a Vermont Farmer," March 1877 and December 1878 entries.

59. Daisy Turner, interviews with author, November 1 and 30, 1983.
60. Ibid., October 19, 1983.
61. Ibid., April 11, 1985.
62. Ibid., August 8, 1984.
63. Grafton, Vermont, Land Records, Book 15: 531, Town Clerk's Office, Grafton, VT; Athens, Vermont, Land Records, Book 6: 330, Town Office, Athens, VT; Thompson, "Life of a Vermont Farmer," 1872 entry.
64. Grafton, Vermont, Land Records, Book 15: 531–32; Athens Land Records, Book 6: 330–331.
65. Beck, "Alec Turner," 77.
66. "Local Matters, Grafton," *Bellows Falls Times*, April 20, 1881.
67. Ibid., August 4, 1881.
68. "Local Matters, Grafton," *Bellows Falls Times*, August 28, 1884.
69. Daisy Turner, interview with author, April 12, 1984.
70. Ibid., May 24, 1984.
71. Ibid., December 14, 1983.
72. Ibid.
73. Ibid. Daisy tended to exaggerate sums of money. It is more likely that he received $25, which would have been substantial.
74. The Morgan horse, first brought to notice by Vermont breeder Justin Morgan, had been a favorite in the cavalry. Alec had admired the Morgan horse during the Civil War and had been impressed with how well the breed survived Sherman's strenuous March to the Sea.
75. Daisy Turner, interview with author, October 24, 1984.
76. Ibid.
77. Ibid.
78. "Local Matters, Grafton," *Bellows Falls Times*, January 3, 1884.
79. "Local Intelligence, Grafton," *Vermont Phoenix*, January 4, 1886.
80. Daisy always claimed he owned it, but I never could locate a deed. I suspect he rented it from Charles Sherwin, a carriage painter for the Frenches. There is no evidence that he lived there, although he may well have during cider season.
81. Beck and Graff, *On My Own*.
82. Daisy Turner, interview with author, January 4, 1984.
83. Ibid., April 20, 1984.
84. Ibid., July 23, 1985.
85. Ibid., December 14, 1983.
86. Ibid., March 29, 1984.
87. Ibid., December 8, 1983.
88. Probably a holdover from his boyhood when he never had enough to eat.
89. Daisy Turner, interview with author, December 8, 1983.
90. Ibid., November 30, 1983.
91. Ibid., November 11, 1983.
92. John Bruce Turner, interview with author, January 29, 1989.
93. Daisy Turner, interview with author, November 30, 1983.
94. Ibid., December 8, 1983.
95. Ibid.
96. John Bruce Turner, interview with author, January 29, 1989.

97. Ibid.
98. Daisy Turner, interview with author, April 12, 1984.
99. John Bruce Turner, interview with author, January 29, 1989.
100. Daisy Turner, interview with author, April 12, 1984.
101. At minimum, Alec had two hired men, although when seasonal work was heavier, as during haying, there would have been more. These hired men were local white men.
102. Daisy Turner, interview with author, January 18, 1984.
103. Dorothy Schumann, "Turner Sisters Urge Vote for Mrs. Bailey on Nov 2, 1954," *Bellows Falls Times*, October 25, 1952, A: 5.
104. Daisy Turner, interview with author, September 25, 1985.
105. Ibid.
106. Ibid., July 24, 1985.
107. Ibid., December 8, 1983.
108. Mrs. Belle Rice was Oscar Rice's wife. Oscar was Alec's great friend.
109. Daisy Turner, interview with author, December 14, 1983.
110. Ibid.
111. Ibid., August 14, 1984.
112. Ibid., July 24, 1985.
113. Ibid., June 28, 1984.
114. Ibid., August 28, 1985.
115. Ibid., September 28, 1983.
116. Ibid., August 28, 1985.
117. Ibid., May 10, 1984.
118. Ibid., November 21, 1984.
119. Athens, Vermont, Land Records, Book 6: 361.
120. Daisy Turner, interview with author, November 18, 1883. See Grafton, Vermont, Land Book 16:248.
121. Henry Thompson, diary, entry dated August 25, 1886, Grafton Historical Society, Grafton, VT.
122. John Bruce Turner, interview with author, January 29, 1989.
123. See Beck, *Gulley*, 36.
124. John Bruce Turner, interview with author, January 29, 1989.
125. Daisy Turner, interview with author, October 25, 1983.
126. Ibid.
127. Ibid., September 23, 1983.
128. "Local Intelligence, Grafton," *Vermont Phoenix*, November 5, 1886.
129. See Berlin, *Making of African America*, 25–28, for a discussion of the importance of home, place, and rootedness for former slaves after the Civil War.

Chapter 8. Journey's End

1. Daisy Turner and Zebbe Grant, interview with Allon Schoener, October 26, 1973, Vermont Folklife Center, Middlebury, VT. Usually rickets is noticeable in a child at six months to two years of age. Daisy apparently had a serious case. The family doctor, Dr. Foss, had the local cobbler make braces for her to wear on her legs.

2. Daisy Turner, interview with author, April 12, 1984.

3. Ibid., October 12, 1983.

4. Daisy Turner and Zebbe Grant, interview with Allon Schoener, October 26, 1973.

5. Daisy Turner, interview with author, December 8, 1983.

6. "Snowed Under," *Vermont Phoenix* (Brattleboro), March 16, 1888.

7. Jan Albers, "Recent Snowstorm Recalls the Biggest Blizzard of Them All: The Storm of 1888," *Addison County Independent* (Middlebury, VT), March 15, 2007.

8. See "Snowed Under," *Vermont Phoenix*; see also: "Blizzard," *Bellows Falls (VT) Times*, March 15, 1888, A: 1; "Great Snow Storm and Greater Gale," in "Local Matters," *Bellows Falls Times*, March 15, 1888; "Mountain of Snow, the Worst Snow Storm Ever," *Rutland (VT) Herald*, March 15, 1888; Thompson, "Life of a Vermont Farmer," 1888 entry.

9. Daisy Turner, interview with author, January 18, 1984.

10. Thompson, "Life of a Vermont Farmer," 1888 entry.

11. Caroline Barrett to John Barrett, letter dated August 16, 1888, Barrett Family Collection, box 2, folder 31, University of Vermont Library, Burlington, VT. Because John Barrett had named Carrie after his mother, I looked through the Barrett Family Collection for any mention of Carrie Turner in Caroline Barrett's letters. I was rewarded by a brief reference in a letter she wrote to her son John, which was started on Thursday, August 15, and finished on Sunday, August 19, 1888: "I had hoped that Rachel Turner [one of the twins] would be able to come back but a younger sister's illness and death has kept her at home. I hope though she will return tomorrow." Caroline Barrett was expecting company and needed help with her domestic chores. There is no recognition that this was the daughter who was named for her. Her focus is elsewhere. She is obviously distant from the Turner situation, although she was very much aware of it, and I suspect this is more reflective of a subtle class difference, which in those days was always present but never mentioned. It was farm families whose young girls needed extra income to whom Caroline Barrett turned for domestic help. That summer she had had great difficulty in finding steady help, and she mentioned that to John. Rose's records supply specifics about Carrie's illness and death. See Rose Turner, account book and diary, 1888–1902, Vermont Folklife Center, Middlebury, VT.

12. Daisy Turner, interview with author, October 25, 1983.

13. Ibid.

14. See note 40 in chapter 4, "Plantation Life," for the origin of Zebbe's nickname.

15. "Local Matters, Grafton," *Bellows Falls Times*, August 23, 1888.

16. Godfrey Hall, interview by the author, June 7, 2001.

17. Ibid., May 25, 2001.

18. Veronica Lanier, interview with author, May 8, 2001, quoting her mother, Susan Turner Lanier.

19. George Hall, interview with author, January 7, 1986.

20. Daisy Turner, interview with author, December 14, 1983.

21. Ibid., November 30, 1983.

22. Ibid.

23. Grafton, Vermont, Town Report, 1889, Town Clerk's Office, Grafton, VT. Previously Rachel had been living somewhere in the village, perhaps at the Poor

Farm, as it appears that she had some support from the town. The Campbell Fund was a $5,000 legacy left to the town of Grafton in 1880 by David Campbell for the benefit of the inhabitants and their successors. This fund was to be used for the poor and destitute. Alec also contributed $10 to his mother-in-law's care. On November 1, 1889, the overseer of the Poor House charged $1 for "moving Mrs. Early" to Turner Hill.

24. Grafton, Vermont, Town School Records for Number 11 school district, 1888, Grafton Town Clerk's Office, Grafton, VT.

25. Daisy Turner, interview with the author, June 11, 1984.

26. Ibid., August 14, 1984. A $10 gold piece sounds a bit extravagant. Daisy claimed that the summer visitors to the hotel used to donate the prizes. A $1 gold piece sounds more reasonable. Even that is excessive when one considers a cord of wood cost $2. Daisy always claimed she won a $10 gold piece, but the amount is not important to her story; winning the prize is.

27. Daisy Turner, interview with the author, June 11, 1984.

28. See the discussion of touchstone stories in the introduction.

29. Daisy Turner, interview with author, April 11, 1985.

30. Ibid., July 24, 1985.

31. Ibid., August 14, 1984.

32. "Local Matters, Grafton," *Vermont Phoenix*, November 2, 1906. Daisy recounted how she shot a deer while guiding Wesley Ives. The local newspaper reported that it was a 250-pound buck. In a separate item, the *Phoenix* announced that Wesley Ives of Meriden, Connecticut, was boarding at Alexander Turner's during hunting season.

33. Daisy Turner, interview with author, November 30, 1983. Birch Dale Camp is the one building that remains on Turner Hill.

34. Ibid., November 18, 1983.

35. Ibid., August 14, 1984.

36. Ibid., June 11, 1984.

37. Ibid., August 14, 1984.

38. Ibid., August 8, 1984.

39. Ibid., November 18, 1983.

40. Godfrey Hall, interview with author, May 25, 2001.

41. Ibid.

42. Rose Turner, account book and diary, 1888–1902.

43. Although Evelyn's birth name is listed as Blanch[e] Mable Turner, she seems to have been known alternately as Evelyn and Mabel. See Grafton, Vermont, Records, Births and Deaths, Book 4: 15–16, 1883–1896, Grafton Town Clerk's Office, Grafton, VT.

44. Daisy Turner, interview with author, July 23, 1985.

45. Rose Turner, account book and diary, Address Book 1.

46. Rose Turner, account book and diary, 1888–1902.

47. Rose Turner, account book and diary, Address Book 1.

48. Ibid. Although Rose's spelling and handwriting are sometimes difficult to decipher, it appears that Nellie worked for the Hotel Edinburgh at 261 Columbus Avenue, Boston.

49. Rose Turner, account book and diary, 1888–1902.

50. *Five Dollars and a Jug of Rum*, 46.

51. "Bruce Turner Visits His Birthplace," *Grafton (VT) News*, November 1991.
52. "Local Matters, Grafton," *Bellows Falls Times*, May 7, 1903.
53. "Alex" is an example of different spellings recorded of Alec's name. Sally Turner, to Rose, Daisy, and Nellie, letter dated New Year's, 1912, written by Linesy's wife, Iolanthe, Daisy Turner Collection, Rose Turner Box, Vermont Folklife Center, Middlebury, VT.
54. Ibid.
55. Alec and Sally Turner, anniversary invitation, 1894, Daisy Turner Collection, Rose Turner Box, Vermont Folklife Center, Middlebury, VT.
56. "Bellows Falls News, Grafton," *Vermont Phoenix*, Friday, December 21, 1894.
57. Beck and Graff, *On My Own*.
58. Rose Turner, account book and diary, 1888–1902.
59. Daisy Turner, interview with author, September 28, 1983.
60. Rose Turner, account book and diary, Address Book 1.
61. Thompson, "Life of a Vermont Farmer," 1883 entry. Vermont Academy in Saxtons River was established by the State Baptist Convention in 1876 as a coeducational boarding school.
62. "Bellows Falls News, Grafton," *Vermont Phoenix*, March 18, 1898.
63. Veronica Lanier, in discussion with the author, May 18, 2011.
64. Veronica Lanier, interview with author, June 25, 1992.
65. "Bellows Falls News, Grafton," *Vermont Phoenix*, March 20, 1903.
66. Veronica Lanier, interview with author, June 25, 1992.
67. Mr. And Mrs. Zachariah Moody, Wedding Invitation, December 24, 1900, Rose Turner Collection, Vermont Folklife Center, Middlebury, VT. The marriage was of short duration, and although Willie eventually had two children, these were by other partners. These other relationships are not represented in the family tree in the appendix.
68. Daisy Turner, interview with author, December 21, 1983.
69. Ibid., October 25, 1983.
70. Cawley and Cawley, *Tales of Old Grafton*, 108. Several of the sisters claimed that Alec and Sally had sixteen children. These must have included stillbirths; I can only account for thirteen children.
71. Godfrey Hall, interview with author, February 22, 2002.
72. Ibid., February 3, 2003.
73. Daisy Turner, interview with author, November 30, 1983.
74. Ibid., September 25, 1985.
75. Godfrey Hall, interview with author, February 3, 2003.
76. Daisy Turner, interview with author, September 28, 1983.
77. Ibid.
78. This meeting had to have taken place after Nellie's marriage in 1898, possibly in May 1899. According to Rose Turner's diary, Nellie returned to Boston on May 11. I suspect the meeting took place before Alec's accident.
79. Daisy Turner and Zebbe Grant, interview with Allon Schoener, October 26 and 29, 1973. Alec's discovery of the two Gouldin brothers on the battlefield is discussed in chapter 5, "Civil War."
80. Daisy Turner, interview with author, September 28, 1983.

81. Preston, *Young Frederick Douglass*, xv; Douglass told a former master: "I ran away, not from you, but from slavery."
82. Daisy Turner and Zebbe Grant, interview with Allon Schoener, October 26 and 29, 1973.
83. Veronica Lanier, in conversation with the author, 2013. In later life, Sally became blind. I initially assumed this might be from cataracts, as Daisy was all but blind from cataracts when I met her. However, Veronica Lanier told me Sally's eyesight had been affected when she was butted by a ram.
84. John Bruce Turner, interview with author, January 29, 1989.
85. Daisy Turner, interview with author, October 12, 1983.
86. Rose Turner, account book and diary, 1888–1902.
87. "State News, Grafton," *Bellows Falls Times*, August 30, 1899.
88. "In the State, Grafton," *Bellows Falls Times*, September 30, 1899.
89. Rose Turner, account book and diary, 1888–1902.
90. Daisy Turner, interview with author, October 12, 1983.
91. Chester Lanier, interview with author, July 9, 2001. Other grandchildren were not so charitable to Florida. Godfrey and George Hall both referred to her as "the black sheep" as she earned a prison sentence for extortion.
92. Daisy Turner, interview with author, April 12, 1984.
93. "Bellows Falls News, Grafton," *Vermont Phoenix*, November 23, 1900.
94. Daisy Turner, interview with author, July 9, 1985.
95. Ibid.
96. Ibid., November 18, 1983.
97. Ibid., July 9, 1985.
98. Ibid.
99. Grafton, Vermont, Town Reports, 1900–1911.
100. See the description of the Campbell Fund in note 23 above.
101. Daisy Turner, interview with author, April 12, 1984.
102. Ibid., July 23, 1985.
103. Ibid., August 14, 1984, and October 12, 1983.
104. George Hall, interview with author, January 7, 1986. Hall said admiringly: "*Any time a black man can come back a top sergeant, back in those days, you had to be good.*" Willie Turner fought in World War I with the 39th Regiment of the New York National Guard. African American fighting troops fought under the French flag with the Moroccans and thus were awarded French medals.
105. Ibid.
106. "Bellows Falls News, Grafton," *Vermont Phoenix*, August 7, 1903.
107. Veronica Lanier, interview with author, May 8, 2001.
108. "Neighboring Towns, Grafton," *Vermont Phoenix*, September 5, 1919; see also "Grafton, Married 50 Years," *Bellows Falls Times*, September 4, 1919.
109. "Promising Career Ends," *Lexington (MA) Minute-Man*, November 5, 1920.
110. Frank Sands, in telephone conversation with the author, June 20, 2012.
111. Rose Turner, account book and diary, 1888–1902.
112. Godfrey Hall, interview with author, February 22, 2002; Linesy Turner, death certificate, 1921, Grafton Town Clerks' Office, Grafton, VT.
113. "Testifies Boinay Spoke of Divorce," *Boston Daily Globe*, January 26, 1927.

114. Daisy Turner, interview with author, October 25, 1983.
115. Ibid.
116. Ibid., November 18, 1983.
117. "Says He Planned to Wed Maid," *Boston Post*, January 26, 1927.
118. "Boinay Makes Sweeping Denial," *Boston Daily Globe*, January 22, 1927.
119. "Admits She Tried to Kill Boinay," *Boston Daily Globe*, January 27, 1927.
120. "Negress in Suits Names White Man," *Boston Herald*, January 21, 1927; "Boinay Makes Sweeping Denial," *Boston Daily Globe*, January 22, 1927.
121. "Boinay Makes Sweeping Denial," *Boston Daily Globe*, January 22, 1927.
122. Ibid.
123. "Arguments Monday in Boinay Suits," *Boston Daily Globe*, January 29, 1927.
124. Ibid.
125. "Petting Parties in Woods Figure in Balm Battle," *Boston Advertiser*, January 26, 1927; "Ex-Maid Sobs as She Reads Ardent Love Letters in Court," *Boston Daily Globe*, January 27, 1927; "Admits She Tried to Kill Boinay," *Boston Herald*, January 27, 1927.
126. "Admits She Tried to Kill Boinay," *Boston Daily Globe*, January 27, 1927.
127. "Never Let Maid Cut Lock of Hair," *Boston Post*, January 22, 1927.
128. "Rival's Letters Found in Pocket," *Boston Post*, January 27, 1927.
129. Daisy Turner, interview with author, October 25, 1983.
130. "Denies He Wrote Letters," *Boston Herald*, January 22, 1927; "Boinay Makes Sweeping Denial," *Boston Daily Globe*, January 22, 1927; "Never Let Maid Cut Lock of Hair," *Boston Post*, January 22, 1927.
131. "Never Let Maid Cut Lock of Hair," *Boston Post*, January 22, 1927.
132. "Courting Girl Year Wife Died," *Boston Post*, January 29, 1927.
133. "Daisy J. Turner Gets Verdict of $3750," *Boston Daily Globe*, February 2, 1927.
134. "'I Am Vindicated,' Cries Maid After $3750 Love Award," *Boston Advertiser*, February 2, 1927.
135. Daisy Turner, interview with author, November 9, 1983.
136. Ibid., August 14, 1984.
137. Allon Schoener, unpublished video of Daisy Turner and Zebbe Grant, recorded July 18, 1974, in the photographer's private collection.
138. Daisy Turner, interview with author, December 14, 1983.
139. Verse courtesy of Godfrey Hall.
140. Daisy Turner, interview with author, August 14, 1984.
141. Ibid., April 20, 1984,

Chapter 9. Daisy's Last Years

1. Daisy Turner, interview with author, November 1, 1983.
2. Veronica Lanier, interview with author, September 22, 1999.
3. John Bruce Turner, interview with author, January 29, 1989.
4. Faith Hawkins, interview with author, February 22, 1989.
5. Veronica Lanier, interview with author, June 25, 1992.
6. Faith Hawkins, interview with author, February 2, 1989.

7. Sally Turner Neale, interview with author, February 2, 1989.
8. Godfrey Hall, interview with author, February 3, 2003.
9. Yohanna McDermott, interview with author, January 19, 1989.
10. Veronica Lanier, interview with author, September 7, 1999.
11. Veronica Lanier, in discussion with the author, June 22, 2011.
12. Chester Lanier, interview with author, July 9, 2001.
13. "A Celebration of the Life of Chester Arthur Lanier, Jr. at Riley Funeral Home, May 13, 2005," order of service and obituary for the funeral of Chester Arthur Lanier Jr. (November 5, 1910–May 9, 2005), Roxbury, MA.
14. Susan Merrill Lewis, "The Negro Colony," MS 215, Collection 131, Greenleaf-Merrill Family Papers, 1819–1917, Maine Historical Society, Portland, ME.
15. Freda Karlson Knight, interview with author, January 18, 1989.
16. Veronica Lanier, interview with author, September 22, 1999.
17. Allon Schoener, unpublished video of Daisy Turner and Zebbe Grant, recorded July 18, 1974, in the photographer's private collection.
18. Daisy Turner, interview with author, October 24, 1984.
19. Ibid., July 23, 1985.
20. Godfrey Hall, interview with author, February 22, 2002.
21. Ibid., May 25, 2001.
22. George Hall, interview with author, January 7, 1986.
23. John Bruce Turner, interview with author, January 29, 1989.
24. Freda Karlson Knight, interview with author, January 19, 1989.
25. Daisy Turner et al. v. Alba M. Bragg et al., court opinion filed October 6, 1953, Vermont Supreme Court Judgement, 118 VT, 43–49, Montpelier, VT.
26. Dorothy Schumann, "Turner Sisters Urge Vote for Mrs. Bailey on Nov 2, 1954," *Bellows Falls (VT) Times*, October 25, 1952, A: 5.
27. Paa Bekoe Welbeck, fieldnotes, conversation with author, dated October 10, 2007, in the author's collection.
28. Daisy Turner, interview with author, December 8, 1983.
29. Daisy J. Turner, *Affidavit by Commonwealth of Massachusetts, County of Middlesex, Town of Chelmsford, September 17, 1964*. Affidavit courtesy of Mary Archamhault and in her personal collection. Daisy was trying to prevent Simpson from being released from prison after serving only two years of a four- to eight-year sentence. William McIntosh helped her get a lawyer.
30. William H. McIntosh, *Affidavit by, Commonwealth of Massachusetts, County of Middlesex, Town of Chelmsford, September 17, 1964*. Affidavit courtesy of Mary Archamhault and in her personal collection.
31. George and Godfrey Hall, interview with author, January 7, 1986.
32. Daisy Turner, interview with author, December 8, 1983.
33. Godfrey Hall, interview with author, February 3, 2003; George and Godfrey Hall, interview with author, January 7, 1986.
34. Beatrice Fisher, interview with author, September 27, 2001.
35. Sherman, *Imagining Vermont*, 44: "In 1960 approximately 75% of Vermont residents were born here, but by 2005 that number was around 53% of the population."
36. Veronica Lanier, interview with author, May 8, 2001.
37. John Bruce Turner, interview with author, January 29, 1989.

38. Alexander Turner, Declaration for Pension, dated August 8, 1907, Record Group 15, National Archives and Records Administration, Washington, DC.

39. E. C. Tieman, Acting Commissioner, to Alexander Turner, Co. I, First New Jersey Cavalry, letter dated February 12, 1916, Section D, Civil War Division, Orig. No. 1369.715, Record Group 15, National Archives and Records Administration, Washington, DC.

40. Alexander Turner, Pension form, Department of the Interior, Bureau of Pensions, dated January 27, 1916, Record Group 15, National Archives and Records Administration, Washington, DC.

41. Bureau of Pensions, letter of pension rejection to Alexander Turner, dated November 23, 1916, Record Group 15, National Archives and Records Administration, Washington, DC.

42. Jennie Sweetman, "N.J. Cavalry's Gillman the Spy Re-examined," *New Jersey Sunday Herald* (Newton), July 3, 2011; "Gillman the Spy," *Sussex (NJ) Independent*, August 11, 1905.

43. Unfortunately, we do not know the name under which Humphrey applied for his pension. There is no record of Humphrey Gillman.

44. Report of Contact, Maynard Young, White River Junction, VT, July 15, 1968, Record Group 15, National Archives and Records Administration, Washington, DC.

45. J. T. Taaffe Jr. to Daisy Turner, letter dated July 22, 1968, Record Group 15, National Archives and Records Administration, Washington, DC.

46. Martin Brounstein, Veterans Benefits Office, to Daisy Turner, letter dated September 16, 1968, Record Group 15, National Archives and Records Administration, Washington, DC.

47. Here Daisy was referring to her rickets as a child.

48. All of the material concerning Daisy Turner and Phil Hoff is from an interview of Philip Hoff with the author, May 15, 1991.

Afterword

1. All fifth-generation Vermont Turners appear to be racially white.

2. Daisy Turner, interview with author, August 14, 1984.

3. John Bruce Turner, interview with author, January 29, 1989.

4. Tim, Mike, Sarah, and Linda Yarosevich, interview with author, January 19, 1989.

5. Janet Severance, interview with author, July 15, 2011.

6. Ibid.

7. *One in Several Million.*

8. Sadly, Ronny Lanier succumbed to colon cancer on May 28, 2014. With her death, all of Alec and Sally Turner's grandchildren have gone.

Research and Acknowledgments

1. *Fredericksburg Ledger*, February 10, 1868, Central Rappahannock Public Library, Fredericksburg, VA.

2. John Gouldin, will dated February 1, 1863, Caroline County Will Book 31:48, Central Rappahannock Heritage Center, Fredericksburg, VA.

3. Sievers, *Herb Hunters Guide. Populus candicans*, a large tree reaching one hundred feet in height with a maximum trunk of about six and a half feet.

4. The property remains undeveloped at this writing. With the downturn of the economy, John Clark lost the funding he had in place for his dream development.

5. Jennie Sweetman, "N.J. Cavalry's Gillman the Spy Re-examined," *New Jersey Sunday Herald*, July 3, 2011.

6. Rose Turner, account book and diary, 1888–1902, Daisy Turner Collection, Rose Turner Box, Vermont Folklife Center, Middlebury, VT.

BIBLIOGRAPHY

Archives

Athens Town Office, Athens, VT
Central Rappahannock Heritage Center, Fredericksburg, VA
Central Rappahannock Regional Library, Fredericksburg, VA
Church Missionary Society Archives, University of Birmingham, Birmingham, England
Essex's Clerk's Office, Essex County Circuit Court, Tappahannock, VA
Fredericksburg Historical Court Records, Circuit Superior Court of Law and Chancery of Spotsylvania County, Fredericksburg, VA
Grafton Historical Society, Grafton, VT
Grafton Town Records, Grafton Town Office, Grafton, VT
ibiblio: The Public's Library and Digital Archive website
Library of Congress Manuscript Division, Washington, DC
Library of Virginia, Richmond, VA
Maine Historical Society, Portland, ME
Maine Historic Preservation Commission, Augusta, ME
Museum of the Cherokee Indian, Museum Archives, Cherokee, NC
National Archives and Records Administration, Southwest Region, Fort Worth, TX
National Archives and Records Administration, Washington, DC
Naval History and Heritage Command, Washington, DC
Princeton University Library, Princeton, NJ
[U.K.] National Archives, Kew, Richmond, Surrey, United Kingdom
University of North Carolina Library, Durham, NC
University of Vermont Library, Burlington, VT
University of Wyoming, American Heritage Center, Laramie, WY
Vermont Folklife Center, Middlebury, VT
Vermont Historical Society, Barre, VT
Vermont State Library, Montpelier, VT
Virginia Baptist Historical Society, University of Richmond, Richmond, VA
Virginia Historical Society, Richmond, VA

Printed and Online Material

Adams, George Worthington. *Doctors in Blue: The Medical History of the Union Army in the Civil War*. Baton Rouge: Louisiana State University Press, 1996.

Adams, John. *Remarks on the Country Extended from Cape Palmas to The River Congo. . . .* London: Cass, 1966.

Akintoye, S. Adebanji. *A History of the Yoruba People*. Dakar, Senegal: Amalion, 2010.

Albers, Jan. *Hands on the Land: A History of the Vermont Landscape*. Rutland, VT: Orton Family Foundation, 2000.

Austen, Ralph A. "The Slave Trade as History and Memory: Confrontations of Slaving Voyage Documents and Communal Traditions." *William and Mary Quarterly*, 3rd series, 58 (2001): 229–244.

Barry, Phillips, ed. "Negro Folk-Songs from Maine." *Bulletin of the Folk-Song Society of the Northeast*, no. 8 (July 1934): 13–16; no. 10 (1935): 21–24.

Beck, Jane. "Alec Turner: The Measure of a Man." *Visit'n* 10 (2004): 62–85.

———. *The Gulley: A Place Apart*. Barre, VT: Norman and Frances Lear, 1984.

Berlin, Ira. *Generations of Captivity: A History of African-American Slaves*. Cambridge, MA: Belknap Press of Harvard University Press, 2003.

———. *The Making of African America: The Four Great Migrations*. New York: Viking, 2010.

Berlin, Ira, Barbara J. Fields, Steven F. Miller, Joseph P. Reidy, and Leslie Rowland. *Slaves No More: Three Essays on Emancipation and the Civil War*. Cambridge: Cambridge University Press, 1992.

Bibb, Henry. *Narrative of the Life and Adventures of Henry Bibb, An American Slave, Written by Himself*. New York: Henry Bibb, 1849.

Blassingame, John W., ed. *Autobiographical Writings*, New Haven: Yale University Press, 1999.

———. *The Slave Community: Plantation Life in the Ante-Bellum South*. New York: Oxford University Press, 1972.

Blight, David. "If You Don't Tell It Like It Was, It Can Never Be As It Ought to Be." In *Slavery and Public History: The Tough Stuff of American Memory*, edited by James O. Horton and Lois E. Horton, 19–33. Chapel Hill: University of North Carolina Press, 2006.

Bold, Edward. *The Merchants' and Mariners' African Guide: Containing an accurate description of the Coast, Bays, Harbours, and Adjacent Islands of West Africa*. London: Norie, 1822.

Brager, Bruce. *Petersburg*. Philadelphia: Chelsea House, 2003.

Brewer, James M. *Worser Days and Better Times*. Chicago: Quadrangle Books, 1965.

Broaddus, A. *History of the Broaddus Family, From the Time of the Settlement of the Progenitor of the Family in the United States down to the Year 1888*. St. Louis: Central Baptist Print, 1888.

Brown, Richard D. "'Not Only Extreme Poverty, but the Worst Kind of Orphanage': Lemuel Haynes and the Boundaries of Racial Tolerance on the Yankee Frontier, 1770–1820." In *Making a Living*, edited by Robert L. Hall and Michael M. Harvey, 71–82. Boston: New England Foundation for the Humanities, 1995.

Cawley, James, and Margaret Cawley. *Tales of Old Grafton*. South Brunswick, NJ: A.S. Barnes, 1974.

Conklin, Harold. "Ethnography." In *International Encyclopedia of Sciences*, edited by David L. Sills, 5:172–78. New York: Macmillan, 1968.

Corry, Joseph. *Observations Upon the Windward Coast of Africa . . . made in the years 1805 and 1806*. London: Nicol, 1807. Reprint, Charleston, SC: BiblioBazaar, 2006.

Corwin, Arthur F. *Spain and the Abolition of Slavery in Cuba, 1807–1886*. Austin: University of Texas Press, 1967.
Coser, Lewis A. *Maurice Halbwachs on Collective Memory*. Chicago: University of Chicago Press, 1992.
Crow, Hugh. *Memoirs of the Late Captain Hugh Crow. . . .* London: Cass, 1970.
Cultural Resources, Inc. "A Cultural Resource Reconnaisance [*sic*] Survey of Twenty Five Archaeological Sites within the 1605-Acre Haymount Property for the Purposes of Site Re-identification and Evaluation, Caroline County, Virginia." Prepared for the John A. Clark Company. Rockport, ME: Cultural Resources, Inc., June 18, 2004.
Curtin, Philip D. *Africa Remembered: Narratives by West Africans from the Era of the Slave Trade*. Madison: University of Wisconsin Press, 1967.
———. *The Image of Africa: British Ideas and Action, 1780–1850*. Madison: University of Wisconsin Press, 1964.
Desch-Obi, M. Thomas J. *Fighting for Honor: The History of African Martial Art Traditions in the Atlantic World*. Columbia: University of South Carolina Press, 2008.
Dickerson, Bruce D., Jr. "The 'John and Old Master' Stories and the World of Slavery: A Study in Folktales and History," *Phylon* 35, no. 4: 418–29, 1974.
Dike, K. Onwuka. *Trade and Politics in the Niger Delta, 1830–1885*. Oxford: Clarendon Press, 1956.
Dixon, Melvin. "Singing Swords: The Literary Legacy of Slavery." In *The Slave's Narrative*, edited by Charles T. Davis and Henry Louis Gates Jr., 298–317. New York: Oxford University Press, 1985.
Dorsey, R. Corbin. *Caroline County, Virginia in the Civil War, 1861–1865*. [Virginia]: R. C. Dorsey, [1990?].
Dorson, Richard M., ed. *American Negro Folktales*. Greenwich, CT: Fawcett, 1967.
Douglass, Frederick. *Narrative of the Life of Frederick Douglass, an American Slave*. 1849. Reprint, New York: Barnes and Noble, 2003.
Eltis, David. *Economic Growth and the Ending of the Transatlantic Slave Trade*. New York: Oxford University Press, 1987.
Eltis, David, Stephen D. Behrendt, David Richardson, and Herbert S. Klein. *The Trans-Atlantic Slave Trade: A Database on CD-Rom*. Cambridge: Cambridge University Press, 1999.
Escott, Paul. *Slavery Remembered: A Record of Twentieth-Century Slave Narratives*. Chapel Hill: University of North Carolina Press, 1979.
Falconbridge, Anna Maria. *Narrative of Two Voyages to the River Sierra Leone During the Years 1791, 1792, 1793. . . .* 1794. Reprint, Liverpool: Liverpool University Press, 2000.
Faulkner, William. *Absalom, Absalom!* New York: Vintage Books, 1935.
Ferris, Norman B. "Dayton, William Lewis." American National Biography Online. http://www.anb.org/articles/04/04-00305.html (accessed February 2000).
Finger, John R. *The Eastern Band of Cherokees, 1819–1900*. Knoxville: University of Tennessee Press, 1984.
Fitzgerald, Ruth Coder. *A Different Story: A Black History of Fredericksburg, Stafford and Spotsylvania, Virginia*. Greensboro, NC: Unicorn, 1979.
Five Dollars and a Jug of Rum: The History of Grafton, Vermont, 1754–2000. Grafton, VT: Grafton Historical Society, [2000?].

Fleischer, Nat. *Black Dynamite: Story of the Negro in Boxing*. New York: C. J. O'Brien, 1938.

Foster, John Y. *New Jersey and the Rebellion: A History of the Services of the Troops and People of New Jersey in Aid of the Union Cause*. Newark, NJ: Martin R. Dennis, 1868.

Fox-Genovese, Elizabeth. *Within the Plantation Household*. Chapel Hill: University of North Carolina Press, 1988.

Fry, Gladys-Marie. *Night Riders in Black Folk History*. Knoxville: University of Tennessee Press, 1975.

Garnett, Henry Wise. *Historical Address on the History of Essex County, Virginia . . . July 4,1876*. Washington, DC: Judd and Detweiler, 1876.

Genovese, Eugene D. *Roll, Jordan, Roll: The World the Slaves Made*. New York: Vantage Books, 1976.

Genovese, Eugene D., and Elizabeth Fox-Genovese. *Fatal Self-Deception: Slaveholding Paternalism in the Old South*. Cambridge: Cambridge University Press, 2011.

Gerzina, Gretchen Holbrook. *Mr. and Mrs. Prince*. New York: Harper Collins, 2008.

Glover, Edwin A. *Bucktailed Wildcats: A Regiment of Civil War Volunteers*. New York: Thomas Yoseloff, 1960.

Gorn, Elliott J. *The Manly Art: Bare-Knuckle Prize Fighting in America*. Ithaca, NY: Cornell University Press, 1986.

———. "The Social Significance of Fighting in the Southern Backcountry." *American Historical Review* 90, no. 1 (1985): 23.

Greiner, James M., Janet L. Coryell, and James R. Smither, eds. *A Surgeon's Civil War: The Letters and Diary of Daniel M. Holt*. Kent, Ohio: Kent University Press, 1994.

Grombach, John V. *The Saga of the Sock: A Complete Story of Boxing*. New York: A. S. Barnes, 1949.

Guild, June Purcell. *Black Laws of Virginia*. Lovettsville, VA: Afro-American Historical Association of Fauquier County, Virginia, 1995.

Gutman, Herbert G. *The Black Family in Slavery and Freedom, 1750–1925*. New York: Vintage Books, 1976.

Guyette, Elise A. *Discovering Black Vermont: African American Farmers in Hinesburgh, 1790–1890*. Lebanon, NH: University Press of New England, 2010.

Hancock, David. *Citizens of the World: London Merchants and the Integration of the British Atlantic Community, 1735–1785*. Cambridge: Cambridge University Press, 1995.

Henson, Josiah. *The Life of Josiah Henson: Formerly a Slave*. 1849. Reprint, Bedford, MA: Applewood Books, 2002.

Hepworth, George H. *The Whip, Hoe, and Sword; or, The Gulf-Department in '63*. Boston: Walker, Wise, 1864.

Hinderer, Anna. *Seventeen Years in Yoruba Country*. London: The Religious Tract Society, 1872.

Hugo, Ripley. *Writing for Her Life: The Novelist Mildred Walker*. Lincoln: University of Nebraska Press, 2003.

Jackson, Ronald Vern, and Gary Ronald Teeples, eds. *Virginia 1820 Census Index*. Bountiful, UT: Accelerated Indexing Systems, 1976.

Jacobs, Harriet A. *Incidents in the Life of a Slave Girl: Written by Herself.* 1861. Reprint, Cambridge, MA: Harvard University Press, 1987.

Johnson, Samuel. *The History of the Yorubas from the Earliest Times to the Beginning of the British Protectorate.* London: Routledge and Kegan Paul, 1966.

Jones, Adam. "Little Popo and Agoue at the End of the Atlantic Slave Trade: Glimpses from the Lawson Correspondence and Other Sources." In *Ports of the Slave Trade (Bights of Benin and Biafra): Papers from a Conference of the Centre of Commonwealth Studies, University of Stirling,* edited by Robin Law and Silke Strickrodt, 122–34. Stirling: University of Stirling, 1999.

Kennedy, John P. *African Colonization—Slave Trade—Commerce. . . .* Washington, DC: Gales and Seaton, 1843.

Kester, Donald E. *Cavalryman in Blue: Colonel John Wood Kester of the First New Jersey Cavalry in the Civil War.* Hightown, NJ: Longstreet House, 1997.

Kittrell, William B. *Cemetery Survey of Pitt County, North Carolina.* Greenville, NC: Pitt County Historical Society, 2007.

Klein, Herbert S. *The Atlantic Slave Trade.* Cambridge: Cambridge University Press, 1999.

LaFantasie, Glenn W. *Twilight at Little Round Top: July 2, 1863, the Tide Turns at Gettysburg.* New York: Vintage Books, 2005.

Law, Robin. "The Atlantic Slave Trade." In *Yoruba Historiography*, edited by Toyin Falola, 124–36. Madison: University of Wisconsin, 1991.

———. "A Lagoonside Port on the Eighteenth-Century Slave Coast: The Early History of Badagri." *Canadian Journal of African Studies* 28, no. 1 (1994): 32–59.

———. *Ouidah: The Social History of West African Slaving "Port," 1727–1892.* Athens, OH: Ohio University Press,, 2004.

———. *The Oyo Empire c. 1600–1836: A West African Imperialism in the Era of the Atlantic Slave Trade.* Oxford: Clarendon Press, 1977.

———. "Trade and Politics behind the Slave Coast: The Lagoon Traffic and the Rise of Lagos, 1500–1800." *Journal of African History* 24, no. 3 (1983): 321–48.

Law, Robin, and Silke Strickrodt, eds. *Ports of the Slave Trade (Bights of Benin and Biafra.* Centre of Commonwealth Studies Occasional Paper 6. Stirling, Scotland: Centre of Commonwealth Studies, University of Stirling, October 1999.

Leonard, Peter. *The Western Coast of Africa: Journal of an Officer . . . in 1830, 1831, and 1832.* Philadelphia: E. C. Mielke, 1833.

Levine, Lawrence. *Black Culture and Black Consciousness.* New York: Oxford University Press, 1977.

Longacre, Edward G. *Jersey Cavaliers: A History of the First New Jersey Volunteer Cavalry, 1861–1865.* Hightstown, NJ: Longstreet, 1992.

Lovejoy, John M. "Racism in Antebellum Vermont." *Vermont History* 69 (2001): 48–65.

Lussana, Sergio. "To See Who Was Best on the Plantation: Enslaved Fighting Contests and Masculinity in the Antebellum Plantation South." *Journal of Southern History* 76, no. 4 (2010): 901–22.

Macdougall, Walter M., and Gwilym R. Roberts. "Brownville Slate and Slaters." *Down East*, September 1968, 61.

MacKenzie, Averill. *The Last Years of the English Slave Trade: Liverpool, 1750–1807.* London: Putnam, 1941.

Manning, Chandra. *What This Cruel War Was Over: Soldiers, Slavery, and the Civil War*. New York: Alfred A. Knopf, 2007.

Masur, Kate. "'A Rare Phenomenon of Philological Vegetation': The Word 'Contraband' and the Meanings of Emancipation in the United States." *Journal of American History*: 93, no. 4 (2007): 1050–83.

McFeely, William S. *Yankee Stepfather: General O. O. Howard and the Freedmen*. New York: Norton, 1994.

McPherson, James. *Battle Cry of Freedom: The Civil War Era*. New York: Oxford University Press, 1988.

Miles, Tiya. *Ties That Bind: The Story of an Afro-Cherokee Family in Slavery and Freedom*. Berkeley: University of California Press, 2005.

Miller, Joseph C. *The African Past Speaks: Essays on Oral Tradition and History*. Folkestone, England: Dawson, 1980.

Mintz, Sidney W. "The Anthropological Interview and the Life History." *Oral History* 7 (1979): 18–26.

Morgan, Lynda J. *Emancipation in Virginia's Tobacco Belt, 1850–1870*. Athens: University of Georgia Press, 1992.

Morton, Marie. *Revised Integrated Cultural Resources Management Plan: Historic Context Development, Fort A.P. Hill, Virginia, February 18, 2013*. Report Prepared for U.S. Army Garrison, Environmental & Natural Resources Division, Directorate of Public Works, Fort A.P. Hill, Virginia, February 8, 2013.

Morton-Williams, Peter. "An Outline of the Cosmology and Cult Organization of the Oyo Yoruba." *Africa* 34, no. 3 (1964): 243–61.

———. "The Yoruba Kingdom of Oyo." In *West African Kingdoms in the Nineteenth Century*, edited by Cyril Daryll Forde and P. M. Kaberry, 36–69. London: Oxford University Press, 1967.

Mouser, Bruce L. "Trade, Coasters and Conflicts in the Rio Pongo from 1790 to 1808." *Journal of African History* 14, no. 1 (1973): 45–64.

Murray, David R. *Odious Commerce: Britain, Spain, and the Abolition of the Cuban Slave Trade*. Cambridge: Cambridge University Press, 1980.

Newbury, C. W. *The Western Slave Coast and Its Rulers: European Trade and Administration among the Yoruba and Adja-Speaking Peoples of South-Western Nigeria, Southern Dahomey and Togo*. Oxford: Clarendon Press, 1961.

"The Ninth Virginia Cavalry—Company B: Caroline Light Dragoons—Caroline County." Enlisted May 6, 1861 (Organized in 1859). Roster. http://www.9thvirginia.com/cob.html (accessed 2012).

Ojo, G. J. Afolabi. *Yoruba Culture: A Geographical Analysis*. London: University of London Press, 1966.

One in Several Million. Melrose, MA: Friends of the Rev. Veronica H. Lanier, 2009.

Ortega, Jose Guadalupe. "From Obscurity to Notoriety: Cuban Slave Merchants, and the Atlantic World." In *The Changing Worlds of Atlantic Africa: Essays in Honor of Robin Law*, edited by Toyin Falola and Matt D. Childs, 287–304. Durham, NC: Carolina Academic Press, 2009.

Osborne, Oliver H. "The Yoruba Village as a Therapeutic Community." *Journal of Health and Social Behavior* 10, no. 3 (1969): 187–200.

Painter, Nell Irwin. *Creating Black Americans: African-American History and Its Meanings, 1619 to the Present*. New York: Oxford University Press, 2007.

Pedler, Frederick. *The Lion and the Unicorn in Africa: A History of the Origins of the United Africa Company, 1787–1931*. London: Heinemann, 1974.

Pettengill, Helen M. *History of Grafton, Vermont: 1754–1975*. Grafton, VT: Grafton Historical Society, 1975.

Portelli, Alessandro. *The Death of Luigi Trastulli and Other Stories: Form and Meaning in Oral History*. Albany: State University of New York Press, 1991.

Preston, Dickson J. *Young Frederick Douglass: The Maryland Years*. Baltimore: Johns Hopkins University Press, 1985.

Priestly, Margaret. *West African Trade and Coast Society: A Family Study*. London: Oxford University Press, 1969.

Pyne, Henry R. *Ride to War: The History of the First New Jersey Cavalry*. New Brunswick, NJ: Rutgers University Press, 1961.

Quarles, Benjamin. *The Negro in the Civil War*. Boston: Little, Brown, 1953.

Raboteau, Albert J. *Slave Religion: The "Invisible Institution" in the Antebellum South*. New York: Oxford University Press, 1978.

Rawick, George P. *From Sundown to Sunup: The Making of the Black Community*. Westport, CT: Greenwood, 1972.

Rediker, Marcus. *The Slave Ship: A Human History*. London: Viking, 2007.

Reiss, Fred. *Public Education in Camden, N.J.: From Inception to Integration*. New York: iUniverse, 2005.

Rhoden, William C. *$40 Million Slaves: The Rise, Fall, and Redemption of the Black Athlete*. New York: Crown, 2006.

Robb, Bernard. *Welcum Hinges*. New York: E. P. Dutton, 1942.

Roberts, John W. *From Trickster to Badman: The Black Folk Hero in Slavery and Freedom*. Philadelphia: University of Pennsylvania Press, 1989.

Ryland, Garnett. *The Baptists of Virginia, 1699–1926*. Richmond: Virginia Baptist Board of Missions and Education, 1955.

Sawtell, William R. *Early Brownville and Her Slate Quarry*. Portland: Maine Historical Society, 1987.

———. *The Merrill Slate Quarry of Brownville*. Milo, ME: Penquis, 2008.

Scarborough, William Kauffman. *Masters of the Big House: Elite Slaveholders of the Mid-Nineteenth-Century South*. Baton Rouge: Louisiana State University Press, 2003.

Schrager, Samuel. "What Is Social in Oral History." *International Journal of Oral History* 4, no. 2 (1984): 76–97.

Schwartz, Marie Jenkins. *Born in Bondage: Growing Up Enslaved in the Antebellum South*. Cambridge, MA: Harvard University Press, 2000.

Sherman, Michael. *Imagining Vermont: Values and Vision of the Future, Final Report of the Council on the Future of Vermont*. Montpelier: Vermont Council on Rural Development, 2009.

Sherman, Michael, Gene Sessions, and P. Jeffrey Potash. *Freedom and Unity: A History of Vermont*. Barre: Vermont Historical Society, 2004.

Sievers, A. F. *The Herb Hunters Guide*. Misc. publ. no. 77. Washington, DC: U.S. Department of Agriculture, 1930.

Slaughter, James B. *Settlers, Southerners, Americans: The History of Essex County, Virginia, 1608–1984*. [Tappahanook, VA]: Essex County Board of Supervisors,, 1985.

Sobel, Mechal. *Trabelin' On: The Slave Journey to an Afro-Baptist Faith*. Princeton, NJ: Princeton University Press, 1988.

Sorensen-Gilmour, Caroline. "Slave Trading along the Lagoons of South-West Nigeria: The Case of Badagry." In Law and Strickrodt, *Ports of the Slave Trade*, 84–95.

Spindel, Donna J. "Assessing Memory: Twentieth-Century Slave Narratives Reconsidered." *Journal of Interdisciplinary History* 27, no. 2 (1996): 247–61.

Stevenson, Brenda E. *Life in Black and White: Family and Community in the Slave South*. New York: Oxford University Press, 1996.

Steward, Austin. *Twenty-Two Years a Slave and Forty Years a Freeman*. Reading, MA: Addison-Wesley, 1969.

Strickrodt, Silke. "Afro-European Trade Relations on the Western Slave Coast." PhD diss., University of Stirling, 2002.

Swanson, Gail. *Slave Ship Guerrero: The Wrecking of a Spanish Slaver off the Coast of Key Largo, Florida with 561 Africans Imprisoned in the Hold While Being Pursued by the British Warship HBM Nimble in 1827*. West Conshohocken, PA: Infinity, 2005.

Thelen, David P., ed. *Memory and American History*. Bloomington: Indiana University Press, 1990.

Thomas, Hampton S. *Some Personal Reminiscences of Service in the Cavalry of the Army of the Potomac*. Philadelphia: L. R. Hamersley, 1889.

Thompson, Henry. "The Life of a Vermont Farmer and Lumberman: The Diaries of Henry A. Thompson of Grafton and Saxtons River," edited by Stuart F. Heinritz. Proceedings of the Vermont Historical Society 42, no. 2 (1974): 89–139.

Tonkin, Elizabeth. *Narrating Our Past: The Social Construction of Oral History*. Cambridge: Cambridge University Press, 1992.

Toombs, Samuel. *New Jersey Troops in the Gettysburg Campaign: From June 5 to July 31, 1863*. Orange, N.J.: Evening Mail Publishing House, 1888.

Trudeau, Noah Andre. *The Last Citadel: Petersburg, Virginia, June 1864–April 1865*. Baton Rouge: Louisiana State University Press, 1991.

Virginia Writers' Project. *Negro in Virginia*. Winston-Salem, NC: John F. Blair, 1994.

Walker, Mildred. *The Quarry*. New York: Harcourt, Brace, 1947.

Warden, David B. *A Statistical, Political, and Historical Account of the United States of North America: From the Period of Their First Colonization to the Present Day*. Vol. 2. Edinburgh: 1819.

Wayland, Francis F. "Fremont's Pursuit of Jackson in the Shenandoah Valley.: The Journal of Colonel Albert Tracy, March–July 1862." *Virginia Magazine of History and Biography* 70, no. 3 (July 1962): 332–54.

Wheaton, James W. *Surgeon on Horseback: The Missouri and Arkansas Journal and Letters of Dr. Charles Brackett of Rochester, Indiana, 1861–1863*. Carmel, Indiana: Guild Press of Indiana, 1998.

White, Deborah Gray. *Ar'n't I a Woman? Female Slaves in the Plantation South*. New York: Norton, 1985.

Whitford, John. *Trading Life in Western and Central Africa*. Liverpool: Porcupine Office, 1877.

Wiggins, David K. "Sport and Popular Pastimes in the Plantation Community: The Slave Experience." PhD diss., University of Maryland, 1979.

Wingfield, Marshall. *History of Caroline County, Virginia: From Its Formation in 1727 to 1924*. Richmond, VA: Trevvet Christian, 1924.

Wright, Marion M. Thompson. *The Education of Negroes in New Jersey*. New York: Teachers College, Columbia University, 1941.

Audiovisual Materials

Beck, Jane, and Ev Grimes. *Journey's End: Memories and Traditions of Daisy Turner and Her Family.* Narrated by Barbara Jordan. Originally a Vermont Public Radio series aired February 1990. Middlebury, VT: Vermont Folklife Center, 2004. DVD.

Beck, Jane, and Wes Graff. *On My Own: The Traditions of Daisy Turner.* Recorded 1986. Middlebury, VT: Vermont Folklife Center and the University of Vermont, 1986. DVD.

Burns, Ken. "The Universe of Battle." In *The Civil War*, aired September 1990. Burbank, CA: 2004. DVD.

Tanner, Louise, prod. and dir. *Homestead: The Puzzle of Daisy Turner and Turner Hill.* New York: Lancelot Junior, Ltd., 1979. Videocassette (VHS).

INDEX

Note: Common names and nicknames of individuals are placed within parentheses. Married women's names are either double-posted at maiden and married names or cross-referenced from maiden name to last known married name. Page numbers in italics indicate illustrations or maps.

JANE C. BECK is Executive Director Emeritus and Founder of the Vermont Folklife Center. She received the Lifetime Achievement Award from the Center for Vermont Research at the University of Vermont in 2011.